Rediscovering Jesus in Our Places

Rediscovering Jesus in Our Places

Contextual Theology
and Its Relevance to Contemporary Africa

ELIA SHABANI MLIGO
foreword by Halvor Moxnes

RESOURCE *Publications* · Eugene, Oregon

REDISCOVERING JESUS IN OUR PLACES
Contextual Theology and Its Relevance to Contemporary Africa

Copyright © 2020 Elia Shabani Mligo. All rights reserved. Except for brief quotations in critical publications or reviews, no part of this book may be reproduced in any manner without prior written permission from the publisher. Write: Permissions, Wipf and Stock Publishers, 199 W. 8th Ave., Suite 3, Eugene, OR 97401.

Resource Publications
An Imprint of Wipf and Stock Publishers
199 W. 8th Ave., Suite 3
Eugene, OR 97401

www.wipfandstock.com

PAPERBACK ISBN: 978-1-7252-6352-9
HARDCOVER ISBN: 978-1-7252-6353-6
EBOOK ISBN: 978-1-7252-6354-3

Manufactured in the U.S.A.   05/26/20

*To Upendo, Grace and Faraja, our beloved daughters,
for the academic excellence you have shown so far;
best wishes to you as you strive to climb
the academic ladder in your own specialties!*

"If our theology [. . .] restricts itself to an academic exercise taking place exclusively in the lecture halls of universities and highly specialized institutes and seminaries, or mainly at overseas conferences, we must necessarily conclude that it can be **of no relevance whatsoever for our African society.**"

—Bujo, *African Christian Morality*, 124–125.

Contents

Foreword by Halvor Moxnes		ix
Aknowledgements		xv
List of Acronyms		xvii
1	Contextual Theology and the Concept of Place	1
2	Meaning and Practice of Contextual Theology	51
3	Contextual Theology in Africa	100
4	Practical Theology as Contextual Theology	142
5	Contemporary Practical and Contextual Issues in Africa	151
6	Trends of Contextual Theology in Africa: From Liberation to Reconstruction	238
References		263

Foreword

Contextual Theology in the Time of the Coronavirus Disease 2019 (Covid-19) Pandemic

As I write this foreword, the *Coronavirus disease 2019 (COVID-19)* is spreading all over the world, challenging structures, making our individual and communal lives uncertain. I am confident that Elia Shabani Mligo's book on contextual theology will have a longer life than the *Coronavirus disease 2019 (COVID-19)* pandemic. However, being in the midst of it, it is impossible not to think about and reflect upon how the pandemic will affect our lives. Moreover, since people on all continents have experienced the pandemic, the memories will be with us for a long time. And, I think, the experience of this pandemic may affect the way we do contextual theology in various places of the world.

"There is no such thing as 'theology,' There is only contextual theology." This is a statement by Stephen B. Bevans, one of the pioneers of contextual theology. In one sense it is correct, since all theology is undertaken in a context of culture, politics, social relations, economy, *etc*. However, there is a difference between saying that a theology can only be understood from its context, and saying that theologies must be self-consciously contextual. Contextual theology in the latter sense arose in situations where there was a hegemonic theology that claimed to be universal. This hegemonic theology was based on political, economic and ecclesiastical power in Europe and North America. Bevans' statement does not consider the enormous differences between those who do theology from a position of power and those who do it from a marginal position. Thus, even if the name «context» is the same, there are great differences between contexts.

I think there is good reason to reserve the name «contextual theology» for theologies that have arisen outside of the hegemonies of power, among marginalized groups or indigenous societies, or in previously colonized regions. It is therefore Mligo's emphasis that contextual theology represents something new: First, it is a new agenda in that the issues and questions arise from the local context. Second, there is a new method in terms of a dialogue between local experiences and the Bible. Third, there are new voices coming into the theological discussions; people who have previously been excluded or who have been silenced, may now enter into the discussion. Finally, there is also a new form of dialogue between the local context and the global one, as well as between the Bible and local cultures.

I think that the experiences of the *coronavirus disease 2019 (COVID-19)* pandemic will impact the way we do contextual theology. First, there is a new agenda compared to traditional theology; at issue now is the very survival of our communities and societies. The pandemic has broken down differences between people, between rich and poor; everybody is at risk. This is a new situation for the rich, the young and the healthy; everybody is now vulnerable. Strong measures are introduced to stop the spread of the virus: closing of schools and all forms of sport events, cultural activities, religious meetings, imposed quarantine for individuals and even large cities and countries. In this situation, we all experience it as an extreme state of emergency. It is a matter of protecting our bodies and our communal body. It comes at a personal and communal cost, not only in personal discipline, but also at enormous economic loss, for the individual and for society.

All governments now promote a policy of inclusion and solidarity. The old and people living with chronic illnesses are most at risk; so all are asked to show solidarity by following the rules to avoid the spread of infection. In the midst of individualistic cultures, where individual freedom, choice and personal preferences are the ideal, governments appeal to solidarity, to putting individual preferences to the side for the good of the community. Government spokespersons speak like pastors, emphasizing that we all depend upon one another; we must seek, not our own good, but the good of others.

In this way the pandemic has created new agendas for politics, for how people live together as societies and communities, and for our values and identities. Reflecting upon this "new" situation, I realize that this has been the situation out of which many forms of contextual theologies have emerged over the last decades. Crises, life threatening epidemics, extreme lack of resources, exposure to danger, isolation—all of these experiences are common to marginalized groups, societies and countries. I realize—and apologize—that as long as these crises and epidemics happened outside Europe and North America, they did not fully enter into our consciousness. Maybe the present crisis that has hit also the centers of power equally hard, will create an awareness of being in the same boat. It is to be hoped that all of us will realize that theological questions are not dealing with abstract issues or dogmatic details; they come directly out from experiences of life and death. Faith in God and Jesus is not something in addition to these experiences; it is a response to the questions which arise from them.

The pandemic has created a new agenda for doing theology. Theology can no longer be done from top down; rather, it must be a result of people crying to God for help, for ways of understanding what it really means to believe in God as creator and Jesus Christ as savior in this situation. Moreover, the pandemic teaches us that a theology can not only be for normal times, it must help us survive when our contexts change.

The author of this book, Elia Shabani Mligo, some years ago wrote an important book that illustrates how issues from a life-threatening crisis present new agendas for theology. He did his PhD in Contextual Theology at a Western institution, the University of Oslo in Norway, which, however, encouraged students to explore theological issues in their own contexts. His work was published as *Jesus and the Stigmatized: Reading the Gospel of John in a context of HIV/AIDS-Related Stigmatization in Tanzania* (Wipf & Stock 2011). Mligo's PhD thesis is an excellent example of how contextual theology represents a renewal of ways of doing theology. First, the issues arise out from a situation in the local context; second, it engages the Bible in a dialogue with contextual experiences, and third, it brings in new voices, which have not participated in theological conversations earlier.

Mligo's starting point was the experiences of people in Tanzania living with HIV/AIDS. He was concerned with their situation; they suffered stigmatization not only from society at large, but even from their own churches. Traditional church teachings of moral judgement in the name of God did not give much support. Mligo wanted to contribute to changes in the theology and policy of churches towards people living with HIV/AID. Therefore, he included people who suffered from HIV/AIDS in this process, so that they were also recognized as contributors to a renewal of the theology of the church.

Mligo developed a dialogue between a group of people who did Bible reading and his own academic study of John's gospel. The texts were chosen to correspond to the situation of the group and their experiences of being stigmatized. Mligo chose narratives from the Gospel of John where Jesus included people who had been stigmatized, *e.g.*, the Samaritan woman, (John 4), and the woman caught in adultery (John 8). Reading the stories of Jesus and the stigmatized, the study group found many similarities with their own situation. As a result, they developed their own images and names for Jesus that responded to their experiences of being stigmatized. There were already names for Jesus drawn from African traditions, *e.g.*, Chief, Ancestor,

African Healer. However, the group of people with HIV/AIDS did not find that these names reflected their experience of Jesus as a relational human being. Instead, they found consolation in speaking of him as their "compassionate companion," a co-traveller in their stigmatizing situation.

This example of contextual theology by a Bible study group in Tanzania represented a renewal of theology. In this case, ordinary believers combined Bible reading and their own experiences into a theology of support and trust. Christians without theological training found a way to speak of Jesus that challenged traditional theology that had focused on dogmatic issues and moral rules. A situation of a life-threatening crisis led to a new focus, on Jesus as the compassionate companion. And Mligo refers to a colleague theologian who says that "Compassion is the concept in Christian ethics which is most important to focus on today."

It was no coincidence that the new perspective was based on stories of Jesus relating to people in crises. In many cases, practitioners of contextual theology look for parallels to present crises in narratives from the Bible. Mark's gospel is a case in point. Different from the other gospels, Mark renders few of Jesus' sayings; he focuses on what Jesus did when he travelled around Galilee, accompanied by large crowds. Mark's storyline in the first part of the gospel gives the impression that he describes a Galilee which is suffering a crisis. Mark's narrative of Jesus' exorcisms, healings of the sick and miraculous feedings of the hungry presents him as responding with compassion to crises that many people experienced. Mark tells of Jesus healing deeds which the other gospels also tell us what Jesus said, his parables and sermons. In either case, the gospels presented a contextual theology for their time; they found ways of speaking of Jesus, telling stories about him that were helpful in relation to their own experiences.

The experience of doing theology in times of crisis makes Mligo's book an expert guide for students and others interested in contextual theology. The first chapter provides an overview of different forms of contextual theology, *e.g.*, liberation, feminist and Black theologies. However, its main focus, and what makes this book special, is his focus on contextual theology in Africa. There has been much discussion on the relations to African religion(s) and the growth of indigenous churches, and Mligo argues for a positive attitude to African Traditional Religion. This is not an uncontroversial standpoint; however, I suggest that it should be considered a parallel to the encounter with Hellenism in Early Christianity. The writings that became New Testament were written in Greek, and that was also the language of the first Christian writers. Language is part of a culture, so Christians had to express their beliefs with the concepts and understandings of Hellenistic culture. That became the dominant form of Western Christianity and theology. However, this encounter between the message of Jesus Christ and Hellenistic culture should not be the only possible version of Christianity; an encounter with African society and culture should be equally legitimate.

Mligo's last chapter about theological movements from liberation theology to African reconstrution theology opens up for a discussion that will engage students as well as professors. If liberation was the main paradigm for theology under apartheid and colonial domination, is there now a need for a new paradigm in the post-apartheid and post-colonial context? Mligo introduces the position of scholars who argue for a "reconstruction theology"; they see the present situation as one of reconstructing and rebuilding African nations from the scars of colonialism. They take their biblical model from the Book of Nehemiah and the reconstruction of the temple after the return from Babylonian exile. This is a proposal that is bound to create discussions in the classrooms. Not all will agree that liberation is a past stage because most African states hardly fulfill the expectations of liberty they had when the colonial rule ended. Moreover, the role of churches under authoritarian regimes in many countries is becoming an increasingly critical issue. Many will see the main task of contextual theology not so much to confront traditional, Western theology, as to struggle for freedom of faith and human rights in many countries where they are under threat.

Obviously, Mligo does not provide all answers in this book; however, he introduces readers to the most important questions for all who will reflect theologically on many of the important contextual issues in Africa and the world today.

HALVOR MOXNES,
Professor Emeritus,
Faculty of Theology, University of Oslo, Norway

Acknowledgments

This book is produced under the cooperate efforts of many people. I am grateful to anyone who contributed towards the production of this book in one way or another. Specifically, I would like to mention the following: First, my colleagues at the Faculty of Theology—Teofilo Kisanji University (TEKU) (Dr. Ronald Mbao, Dr. Tuntufye Mwenisongole, Ezekia Majani, Revocatus Meza, Mary Kategile, and Ekisa Shibanda) for their moral and material support during the various discussions with them.

Second, I honor the contribution of Prof. Halvor Moxnes, Professor Emeritus at the Faculty of Theology-University of Oslo TF-UiO in Norway. His reading and commenting on the first draft of the manuscript helped to sharpen the argument of the book. I also appreciate for his willingness to write the foreword. I do not forget the editors and typesetters at W&S for their excellent work. More specifically, I owe a word of thanks to Dr. Savanah N. Landerholm for the excellent working cooperation we had during the typesetting stage.

Third, I appreciate the contribution of my students at TEKU in various undergraduate and postgraduate courses. They have always been my best teachers. I benefited intensely from the encounters during the various teaching sessions. Indeed, they taught me greatly during the various enriching class discussions.

Last, but not least, my family members—my wife Ester and our three daughters Upendo, Grace and Faraja—for their constant prayers towards my academic success. I dedicate this book to them to honor their intellectual progress as they advance with education in various levels in the disciplines and areas of specialty.

In honoring the various contributions made, this book uses an inclusive plural pronoun "we" to refer to the author (instead of an individualistic singular "I") to appreciated the cooperate work done between the various contributors and the author. May the Almighty God, creator of heaven and earth, grant peace of mind and blessed life to all academicians and non-academicians involved in the production of this book in one way or another!

List of Acronyms

AACC	All Africa Conference of Churches
AIC	African Indigenous/Independent/Initiated Churches
AIDS	Acquired Immune Deficiency Syndrome
ANC	African National Congress
ATR	African Traditional Religion
BCE	Before Comon Era
CATI	Conference of African Theological Institutions
CCAWT	The Circle of Concerned African Women Theologians
CEB	*Communidades Eclesiales de Base*
CELM	*Consenjo Episcopal Latinoamericano*
EATWOT	Ecumenical Association of Third World Theologians
ELCT	The Evangelical Lutheran Church in Tanzania
HIV	Human Immunodeficiency Virus
INATE	The International Network in Advanced Theological Education
LEGATRA	Lesbians, Gays, Bisexual and Transgender persons Association
LGBT	Lesbian, Gays, Bisexual and Transgender relationships
NCC	National Council of Churches
NGO	Non-Governmental Organization
OAIC	Organization of African Instituted Churches

PCC	Pentecostal Charismatic Churches	
TEC	Tanzania Episcopal Conference	
TEF	Theological Education Fund	
TEKU	Teofilo Kisanji University	
TF	*Det Teologiske Fakultet* (The Faculty of Theology)	
UCM	University Christian Movement	
UiO	*Universitet i Oslo* (The University of Oslo)	
US	United States	
USA	United States of America	
WCC	World Council of Churches	
W&S	Wipf and Stock Publishers	
WSCF	World Student Christian Federation	

1

Contextual Theology and the Concept of Place

INTRODUCTION

In one of the working days of the week, after my friend and I had taken lunch at the University cafeteria, we relaxed on our seats. One among fellow members of staff joined us and initiated conversations. He asked us: "Do you believe that Jesus turned water into wine as stipulated in John's gospel?" We kept silent, just looking at him in a perplexed stance because the question was too abrupt for us to respond. He continued, "I, myself, don't believe in Jesus who changes water into alcoholic wine so that people may drink it and become drunkard. I don't believe in Jesus who drinks alcohol which is forbidden in the Bible. I believe in Jesus who drinks non-alcoholic wine." My friend with whom I sat joined the conversation; he asked, "Where would Jesus get wine without alcohol?" The member of staff replied with righteous indignation saying, "I do not know, but what I know is that my Jesus could not drink alcoholic wine." The following conversations were greatly heated and ended with disagreements.

In the above conversations we find two representations of Jesus: Jesus who changes water into alcoholic wine and drinks it; and Jesus who changes water into non–alcoholic wine and drinks it. The two representations of Jesus are enshrined in the mindsets of the two conversing friends, each representing the way he has come to discover Jesus in his Christian life. The question of who Jesus is to me or any of the conversing friends has been answered well, each one of them according to his discovery. This is what entails the rediscovery of Jesus of the Bible according to one's own place, according to one's own location. The above conversation indicates that not all people in the world perceive Jesus in the same way. Jesus is perceived differently in various locations and abodes; yet each perception is closer to the real Jesus! Hence, Jesus who is relevant to time and place depends greatly on the way people interpret him according to their cultural or religious lenses. The task of this chapter is to lay a foundation in regard to contextual theology and its relation to people's places of abode. It discusses the way it emerged, the challenges it faces, the way people came to be interested in it despite the various challenges, and the various forms of this kind of theology.

THE CONCEPT OF PLACE

Before venturing the main tenets of the chapter, we first introduce the concept of place and its relation to contextual theology. In his book *Putting Jesus in His Place*, Moxnes has primarily argued for the Jesus of history located in the Jewish context. Moxnes portrays Jesus who can be understood basing on his Jewish context while recognizing the various places occupied by minority groups in the 21st century. As Moxnes sees, place has been forgotten in scholarship despite its importance. We always speak of place in various references of our communication: things being 'in place,' being 'out of place,' things having 'their specific places,' *etc.*[1] All these references indicate the importance of place as an abode.

In the introduction to his Thesis, Inge writes: "Our very existence as embodied beings means that at any given moment we will be in one particular place. We must have a place in which to stand—place is as necessary as food and air to us. The events that shape our lives happen in particular places, nothing we do or are, nothing that happens to us is unplaced."[2] How then should we conceptualize the meaning of the concept of place? As Inge, taking ideas from Harvey, has just pointed out: "the term 'place' has an extraordinary range of metaphorical meanings: 'We talk about the place of art in social life, the place of women in society, our place in the cosmos, and we internalise such notions psychologically in terms of knowing our place, or feeling that we have a place in the affections or esteem of others.' He goes on to remind us that by 'putting people, events and things in their proper place' we express

---

1. Moxnes, *Putting Jesus in His Place*, 6.
2. Inge, "A Christian Theology of Place," 4.

norms."[3] These words cement on the importance of place, not only for physical human experiences, but also emotional and spiritual experiences.

In addition, Cresswell provides the following definition of the concept of place:

> Place is a meaningful site that combines location, locale, and sense of place. Location refers to an absolute point in space with a specific set of coordinates and measurable distances from other locations. Location refers to the 'where' of place. Locale refers to the material setting for social relations—the way a place looks. Locale includes the buildings, streets, parks, and other visible and tangible aspects of a place. Sense of place refers to the more nebulous meanings associated with a place: the feelings and emotions a place evokes.[4]

In order to illustrate this definition, Cresswell provides an example of Baghdad in Iraq:

> Consider the location 33.3251 44.4221 [degrees]. This location in abstract space marks the city of Baghdad in Iraq. While its location tells us where Baghdad is and enables us to locate it on a map or program it into a Global Positioning System, it does not really tell us much else. Baghdad is also a locale. It has mosques, homes, markets, barricades, and the Green Zone. It has a material structure that, in part, makes it a place. And finally Baghdad has senses of place. Some of the meanings associated with Baghdad are personal and vary according to whether you are an occupying soldier, a Sunni or Shi-ite Muslim, someone who is trying to make a living, or a tourist who visited in the 1970s. [. . .]. Baghdad, like all places, has a location, a locale, and senses of place.[5]

Therefore, it is in this illustration that Cresswell makes the conceptualization of concepts of location, locale and sense of place understood clearly.

Moreover, the value and importance of place was first discovered by the Greeks. The Greeks, particularly Plato, used the term *chora* to mean 'space or place'. Plato did not distinguish between *chora* and *topos*. Cresswell presents the Platonic concept of *chora* to be

> in the context of an account of the origins of existence and the process of 'becoming'. Becoming, in Plato's terms, is a process that involves three elements—that which becomes, that which is

---

3. Inge, "A Christian Theology," 9.
4. Cresswell, "Place," 1.
5. Cresswell, "Place," 1.

the model for becoming, and the place or setting for becoming. This final element is '*chora*', a term which implies both extent in space and the thing in that space that is in the process of 'becoming'. It is often translated as a receptacle and differs from the void of '*kenon*' (abstract space) in that it always refers to a thing within it—it is not empty. Topos is often used interchangeably with *chora* in Plato but is usually more specific. While *chora* most often referred to a place in the process of becoming, *topos* would refer to an achieved place. Later Aristotle would use chora to describe a country while topos would describe a particular region or place within it. Both chora and topos would become part of geographical language through the notion of chorology (study of regions) and topography (the shape of the land surface). Both chora and topos are different from the notion of kenon (the void) in that they refer to something more particular—more like place than space. While *kenon* is limitless space chora and topos are finite and contain things.[6]

However, Louw further asserts that "In the Platonic understanding, *chōra* is a nourishing and maternal receptacle, and is related to *topos*, a particular, definable place of human encounter."[7] Hence, the concept of place, whether referring to geographical location, a locale or a sense of place, has to do with the question of identity. It expresses who one is at that particular place.

Identity in a place is not permanent but temporal. It is not inborn but built. Qazimi provides an example of travelers to foreign countries in order to illustrate the temporal and constructed nature of identities in particular places. He writes that the awareness of the significance of places is clearly recognized

> when people travel from one country to another, or from their homeland to another country. Often people become aware of their own sense of place and identity and begin to realize that atmosphere is different and do not feel 'at home'. There are several different elements such as; landscape, weather, the type of houses, culture even things as sounds and smells are not those that we are used to. On the other hand, if somebody decides to move to a new country or place all of these things will gradually become familiar; a new sense of place will be developing and then it becomes part of our identity.[8]

---

6. *Ibid.*, 2 (italics added).
7. Louw, "Space and Place in the Healing of Life," 435.
8. Qazami, "Sense of Place," 307.

The temporal nature of identity depicted by Qazimi above originates from the temporal nature of places themselves. Low confirms that "places are socially constructed by the people who live in them and know them; they are politicized, culturally relative, and historically specific multiple constructions [. . .]."[9] Hence, it is in these temporal and socially constructed places where people gain a sense of identity.

Since the question of place has to do with the question of identity, Cresswell relates that

> In any given place we encounter a combination of materiality, meaning, and practice. Most obviously, perhaps, places have a material structure. [. . .]. The idea of meaning has been central to notions of place since the 1970s in Human Geography. Location became place when it became meaningful. [. . .]. Meanings can be very personal and connected to individuals and their personal biographies—places where we fell in love, or where loved ones are buried, or where we went to school. But meanings are also shared and, in some important ways, social. [. . .]. While meanings are shared they are never fixed once and for all, and always open to counter meanings produced through other representations. Finally, places are practiced. People do things in place. What they do, in part, is responsible for the meanings that a place might have. [. . .]. Places are continuously enacted as people go about their everyday lives—going to work, doing the shopping, spending leisure time, and hanging out on street corners. The sense we get of a place is heavily dependent on practice and, particularly, the reiteration of practice on a regular basis.[10]

The above statement indicates that since places and identities are socially constructed and temporal, so does the meanings of those places. Meanings are constructed by individuals, and can be shared to social groups and become meanings of society.

Cresswell concludes that "Materiality, meaning, and practice are all linked. The material topography of place is made by people doing things according to the meanings they might wish a place to evoke. Meanings gain a measure of persistence when they are inscribed into the material landscape but are open to contestation by practices that do not conform to the expectations that come with place. Practices often do conform to some sense of what is appropriate in a particular place and are limited by the affordances

---

9. Low, "Towards an Anthropological Theory," 21–22.
10. Cresswell, "Place," 2.

particular material structures offer."[11] According to Cresswell, the meaning constructed cannot escape the materiality of the particular place and the inscribed various practices, though can be contested due to lack of conformity to what is expected.

Being linked to identity through its materiality, meaning and practice, place becomes acute in the era of globalization where the globalizing forces long for homogenizing the various cultural identities into one Super-culture which hardly recognizes the various meanings and practices of particular places. Within this context, Staalsett writes: "we are simultaneously faced with homogenisation, fragmentation, social polarisation and ethnic strife."[12] It is in this context where the search for a more just human community is being done.

Moreover, since it has to do with the question of identity, place is not just a piece of land. It entails relationships in human lives. It is a ground of shared experiences and socialization among those who belong to the particular place. In the presence of God in a place, inhabitants of that place construct who they are and what their thought forms are. Therefore, in Christian understanding, a place begins with God and ends with God because place cannot be place without God being a co-inhabitant.

Since theology becomes relevant in particular places if God becomes a co-inhabitant with people in their places, there is an intimate relationship between theology and people's places. The concept of place is the major concern in contextual theology. Theology is theology in a place. It is the understanding of God's dealing with people in a particular place, in a particular context. Recognizing the importance of place in theological reflections, Staalsett also writes: "in accordance with 'the contextual turn' in Christian theology, we have seen a flourishing of contextual christologies lately. In contextual theology, the 'place' or 'location', (*locus*) bears particular significance."[13] Therefore, one of the weaknesses of this book is that it hardly focused on what the reader would expect from the promises heavily put in the title of the book. The reader would probably expect to see the book focusing on Jesus, his life, his ministry and its relevance to contemporary Africa. This focus is hardly the case with this book and its content.

Following the relationship between place and context stated by Staalsett in the previous paragraph, the title of this book suggests for Jesus (God) that inhabits in a place.[14] It suggests for the rediscovery of Jesus (God) who

11. *Ibid.*
12. Staalsett, "Introduction," vii.
13. *Ibid.*, viii.
14. The title of this book is a reformulation of the theme discussed by the INATE participants in their second consultation that took place at Sao Leopoldo in Brazil in June 1999 to suit the purpose and focus of this book (see Staalsett, "Introduction," x).

is active in particular places where people have various life experiences. This book does not focus on Jesus as a historical figure in the way presented by scholars of historical Jesus in all their quests;[15] rather, it focus on God (Jesus as one person of the godhead included) and the way Africans can experience God's dealings with them in their own places. It envisages discerning once again the way God relates to people of a particular place, a relation that was taken for granted before. Therefore, the book is all about contextual theology and its relevance to particular contexts in the ever-changing contexts in Africa. The main assumption throughout this book is that theology becomes relevant when it presents God to people, not as a foreign Savior but as the one that emanates from people's own places, in their own contexts. The African theologian Benezet Bujo has put this assumption more clearly: "If our theology [. . .] restricts itself to an academic exercise taking place exclusively in the lecture halls of universities and highly specialized institutes and seminaries, or mainly at overseas conferences, we must necessarily conclude that it can be *of no relevance whatsoever for our African society*."[16] The following section discusses when and how people became interested in contextual theology in Africa.

EMERGENCE OF CONTEXTUAL THEOLOGY

The interest in contextual theology began between 1950s and 1970s. It is in this period when the paradigm shift in theological thinking began from Latin America spreading to other parts of the world including Africa. This paradigm shift led to the rise in new questions without readymade answers, the challenge of old answers as not taking seriously the emerging new realities, and the emergency of new Christian identities as a result of the challenges posed by new questions to old answers.[17] It is in this context of interaction between new and old answers where the concept of contextualization emerged. A theologian Ray Wheeler asserts that the word "contextualization" was first used by Shoki Coe, a Taiwanese, who is believed to be one of the founders of contextual theology. Coe was born in Taiwan in the year 1914, studied in Tokyo imperial University in Tokyo Japan and graduated his Degree in Philosophy (1934—1937). Coe returned home in Taiwan after his graduation. He then joined theological studies in Britain: Overdale College in Birmingham (1937—1938) and thereafter Westiminster College (1938—1941).[18]

15. See for example Crossan, *The Historical Jesus*.
16.. Bujo, *African Christian Morality*, 124–125.
17. Schreiter, *Constructing Local Theologies*, 2–4.
18. Wheeler, "The Legacy of Shoki Coe," 78.

The whole study context, which Coe passed through, provided him an important life experience, especially in his life in Britain where he taught Japanese at London University of Oriental Studies after graduating his studies in 1941. In the year 1947, Coe returned home in Taiwan and was appointed Principal of Tainan Theological College serving for 18 years. Within this period of service as Principal, Coe witnessed tremendous economic, political, social and religious changes which forced him to see the possibility of having another way of doing theology. Wheeler reports about the experience of Coe during his service as Principal of Tainan Theological College in Taiwan: "During his eighteen years of service in Taiwan, Coe found himself in a region caught in the throes of radical social change. He would later describe the situation of postwar Asia as 'a world where one of the key words is change, not only ordinary change but radical change, not merely radical change but sometimes revolutionary change.'"[19] Wheeler's words above indicate that Coe, in the eighteen years of service in Taiwan as Principal of a theological college, began to sense that the ways of doing theology which prevailed in that time were not sufficient to satisfy the needs of the ongoing changes. It is in this context whereby Coe introduced the notion of '*Contextualization*' of theology as a response to the '*universalizing theology*' that was being done in his time that hardly took into account the contexts and questions asked in those contexts.[20] Wheeler further notes about Coes experience: "The methods of the traditional three-self movement were inadequate to address the reality of the context in which Coe found himself and the church in Taiwan. A new method of assessment, which he labeled 'contextualization,' was needed to effect truly incarnational ministry. Coe described contextualization as a continual interplay between the transcendent text of Scripture and the ever changing context in which it must be interpreted. He recognized that effective incarnational ministry depends on a continual willingness to face Scripture's summons to transformation in the midst of changing social, political and economic circumstances."[21]

In the year 1965, Coe was appointed a leader of The World Council of Churches' Theological Education Fund (TEF). He presented a Paper proposing the notion of 'Contextualization' in the WCC's meeting of 1971. The title of his paper was "Dogmatic or Contextual Theology." The concept of

---

19. *Ibid*.

20. Though the term 'contextualization' is new, yet its practice is old. The practice of contextualization was practiced even during the biblical times. For more elaboration, please read Johnson, "Contextualization," 9, and Engle, "Contextualization in Missions," 86.

21. Wheeler, "The Legacy of Shoki Coe," 78.

'contextualization' was born from this meeting; and hence, a great impact and interest in this new kind of theology began and spread all over the world.[22]

In Africa, in particular, Diane B. Stinton reports that "In 1977, the Pan-African Conference of Third World Theologians, held in Accra, Ghana, gave a clear call for how theology was to be done: "The African situation requires a new theological methodology that is different from the approaches of the dominant theologies of the West. [. . .]. Our task as theologians is to create a theology that arises from and accountable to African people."[23] Stinton further adds: "This new approach was called '*contextual*' theology, for it was to be 'accountable to the context people live in.'"[24] Hence, it is in this background that the Pan-African Conference mentioned in this paragraph above recommended the sources for contextual theology in Africa to be the following: "(1) *The Bible and Christian heritage*; (2) *African anthropology and cosmology* [. . .] (3) *African traditional religions* [. . .] (4) *African Independent churches*; and (5) *Other African realities* [. . .].[25] Each of the mentioned sources contribute to the articulation of contextual theology in Africa in one way or another depending on the place and experiences of people in that place.

CONTEXUAL THEOLOGY AND ITS CHALLENGES

Why did the interest in the contextualization of theology in Africa come up? In other words we can ask: why did an interest in place or context begun to occupy the minds of scholars in Africa after Coe's address at the WCC's meeting in 1971? The interest in context stems from the denotation of the word 'context' in relation to the changes in social, political, economic, cultural and religious domains which existed in the 1970s. Burtness, as quoted in Pobee, states:

> the word 'context' is a key to a very modern awareness of the interpenetration of subject and object. It is a word which points to the demise of absolutes and the embracing of relativities, whether in physics or theology or politics. It is a reminder that the inductive method, whether in the chemistry laboratory or in a Bible study group, yields probabilities rather than necessities. It signals an eagerness to live with specifics rather than generalities, with particulars rather than universals. 'Context' is a word

22. Cf. Engle, "Contextualization in Mission," 86–88.
23. Stinton, "Africa's Contribution to Christology," 18.
24. *Ibid*. (Italics for emphasis is in original).
25. *Ibid*., 19. (Italics for emphasis is in original).

which fits naturally with such phrases as theory of relativity, scientific method, situational ethics, and statistical probabilities. It is a very modern word and a very modern emphasis.[26]

Reasons for the Great Interest in Context-Based Theology

Basing on the pressure of context indicated in the above quotation, some of the reasons for this interest in context-oriented theology in Africa were the following: first, the coming to voice of so many Christian communities, for example the women and the poor. Women movements for equality in various sectors, domestic, leadership positions, *etc* signal the emergence of the urge to read scriptures and do theology in the frameworks of the movements. The poor and their rejection to be subjugated by the rich in various aspects of human life signal the need to read scriptures and do theology in this context.

What language did these voices speak to the existing dogmatic theological reflections of the West? Oduyoye reports that "Like the Samaritans at the well, African theologians are now saying to their tutors [the Western missionaries]: 'It is no longer because of your words that we believe, for we have heard for ourselves, and we know that this is indeed the Savior of the world' (Jn 4: 42)."[27] Therefore, according to Oduyoye, the various voices of scholars in their contributions of publications and conferences were a clear movement towards an African relevant theology.

The second is the dissatisfaction with inherited ways of doing Christian theology and mission work. The missionaries considered Africans as animals without religion, human rights and civilization. Masondo echoes: "According to this Eurocentric worldview, the degeneration was so bad that Africans had reached the same level as animals and were thus referred to as beasts or brute. The absence or lack of religion went along with the lack of 'other defining human features, such as institution of marriage, system of law, or any formal political organisation' [. . .]. The assertion that Africans lacked religion and they were on the same level with animals meant that they had no human rights."[28] Quoting from Chidester, Masondo adds: "As animals by comparison to Europeans, therefore, indigenous people who lacked a religion also lacked any recognizable human right or entitlement to the land in which they lived."[29]

---

26. Pobee, "Good News," 20.
27. Oduyoye, *Hearing and Knowing*, 5.
28. Masondo, "The History of African Indegenous Churches," 91.
29. *Ibid*.; *cf.* Mwihia, "A Theological Analysis of African Proverbs," 18–20.

On the above bases, the task of missionaries was to tame the beast; and in order to tame the beast they had to use the gospel as the main weapon of civilizing the uncivilized beast. Wafawanaka states: "When the missionaries came to Africa, they came to convert, preaching a gospel of 'repentance for the forgiveness of sins.' While this message was in line with Jesus' teaching, it was woefully inadequate in light of African realities. The kingdom of God was presented as something transcendental, something to be enjoyed in the hereafter [. . .]. Very little preaching was done on the realities of economic poverty, oppression, exploitation, let alone the impact of colonialism."[30] This is a type of missionary activity which the missiologist Samuel Escobar calls "the Constantinian pattern" which African propagators of the gospel should not embrace. Escobar states: "The urgency of the question is also determined by the need for a radical departure from the Constantinian pattern of a missionary enterprise that relied on military power, economic conquest, and technological prowess."[31] Escobar, quoting Vinay and Chris, further emphasizes: "The images of Jesus Christ imported from the West have on the whole been found wanting—too conditioned by Constantinian Christianity with all its ideological distortions and cultural accretions, and terribly inadequate as a basis for the life and mission of the church in situations of dire poverty and injustice. This has led to the search for a Christology which will have as its focus the historical Jesus and provide a basis for Christian action in contemporary society."[32] However, Imasogie contends that "Christianity is the universal religion which only becomes an authentic religion for a particular people when their world view and self-understanding within that world view are taken seriously as they are confronted with the claims of Christ. Failure to do this, invariably, leads to ambivalence in their Christian commitments, especially in times of crisis."[33]

Muneja, quoting Fredericks, further emphasizes on the attitude which missionaries had when they came to Africa as he reports: "Western Missionaries marginalised virtually everything that had to do with traditional world view [. . .] they succeeded in convincing Africans to dress, talk, walk and even eat like themselves. But they failed to make Africans realise that

---

30. Wafawanaka, "African Perspectives on Poverty," 492; *cf.* Mokhoathi, "From Contextual Theology," 1–2; Duncan, "A Place in the Sun?" 333–334; *cf.* Tutu, "African Theology," 57–58.

31. Escobar, "The Search for a Missiological Christology," 200.

32. *Ibid.*, 217. The 'historical Jesus' portrayed here is not the one conceived by the Liberal theologians, the one associated with the 'historical-critical methods' in order to construct him. Rather, it refers to Jesus recorded in Scriptures, the one who related with the lowly people in their living situations.

33. Imasogie, *Guidelines for Christian Theology*, 24.

Christianity is comprehensive and that it seeks to address. Indeed African religious experiences were driven to the periphery, because everything of African origin was considered pagan."[34] However, it is true that in doing that, missionaries were "too much involved with their own culture (colonialism included), did not understand much of the African culture, and worked hard to destroy what they did not understand [. . .]. This error [. . .] resulted in the perception of the Christian identity as equivalent to the western cultural and religious heritage."[35]

The above quotation highlights that there was no mutuality between African world view and the Christian religion brought by the missionaries due to injustices of colonialism. Colonialism and the activities of missionaries focused on a similar objective—to exploit the African material and human resources for the betterment of their home countries. Nasimiyu-Wasike notes:

> The injustices of colonialism in Africa are well documented. Colonial powers found cheap labour, raw materials and rich natural minerals for their industries back home [. . .] Africa was divided among the European powers without any consideration of the indigenous peoples [. . .]. The ethnic differences were highlighted by the colonial powers, and this has resulted in bitter strife in several countries [. . .]. It is unfortunate that during the colonizing period, the Christian Churches went along with and even sometimes participated in the process [. . .]. Missionaries in their colonial context misinterpreted and misrepresented African cultures and traditional religions [. . .]. The missionaries were unable to penetrate the African world view and therefore they limited themselves to the misinterpretation of the African worldview [. . .]. They concentrated on the details of traditions that they could not join in one unity [. . .].[36]

In sticking to the misinterpreted African cultures, missionaries did not manage to enhance the required mutuality between Christianity and African worldview. Mutuality was not attained because "Mutuality is an interplay, a two-way or reciprocation. This can happen only in a healthy, open relationship [. . .]. Mutuality cannot take place unless the past cultural misconceptions are uprooted [. . .]. As long as the West continues to view its culture as superior and cannot allow itself to 'bend low', authentic genuine mutuality

---

34. Muneja, *HIV/AIDS and the Bible*, 44; cf. Cox, "Why Rang Christians," 3.
35. Mokhoathi, "From Contextual Theology," 1–2.
36. Nasimiyu-Wasike, "Is Mutuality Possible?" 45, 46, and 48

cannot be embarked on."[37] Therefore all missionary activities highlighted by scholars above intensified theologians' and normal people's dissatisfaction with the inherited ways of doing theology wishing for change.

At the universal level, "Theologians throughout the world who felt a call to speak more relevantly to their age and generation freed themselves from traditional dogmatic and systematic theology and focused on life issues. Instead of telling people what questions to ask and then furnishing them with answers, theologians began to listen to the questions people were asking and then seek the answers."[38]

At the local level, this dissatisfaction was noticed when Christians practiced ATR together with Christianity. Among the Rangi people of Kondoa Dodoma in Tanzania, for example, Christianity was not received for theological reasons; rather, it was only for material gains. The Rangi priests, who were mostly trained in Europe, marginalized the Rangi traditional beliefs as being superstitious while emphasizing the western tradition. Cox states this point more clearly: "One of the biggest reasons for Rangi believers to still engage in ATR is because Christianity was not adopted for theological reasons. Rangi people did not hear the Gospel as preached by the Catholic priests and intellectually agree that such beliefs were 'better' or more 'true' than their ATR beliefs. Many, if not most, accepted Christianity because of the material benefits that it brought."[39] It means that its acceptance was not because of its relevance to the context of the Rangi people and their cultural worldview.

In fact, most of the Rangi converts to Christianity were caught on what Musimbi R. A. Kanyoro says as the African proverb of "the dilemma of the hyena." Kanyoro states this dilemma: "The hyena was following the general direction of the aroma of barbecuing meat. He wanted a share of this enticing and mouth-watering meat. Suddenly his path forked into two. He was not sure which one would lead him to the meat. In his uncertainty, he put his legs astride the two paths and tried to walk along both and oops! The poor hyena split in the middle. Alas!"[40] Relating to the dilemma of African Christians, Kanyoro further adds, "The African Christian walks with one foot in African Religion and culture and another in the church and western culture."[41] Kanyoro's proverb above indicates the firm root of African religion and culture which makes it difficult for Africans to jettison it in favor of

37. Ibid., 46, 48.
38. Oduyoye, *Hearing and Knowing*, 3.
39. Cox, "Why Rangi Christians continue to Practice African Traditional Religion?" 3
40. Kanyoro, *Introducing Feminist Cultural Hermeneutics*.
41. Ibid., 13.

a foreign religion. This is what made Christianity lack relevance among the Rangi who were deeply rooted in their African religion and culture.

Due to lack of relevance of Christianity, Rangi Christians live a double life, that is life in church and life outside the church. Cox states it:

> In many ways, another contributing factor to ATR still being practiced among the Rangi is the lack of relevance to their everyday lives. [. . .]. Rangi life is replete with rituals. There are rituals for purifying a woman after childbirth, for smelting iron, for welcoming in the New Year, for beginning the harvest, for purifying a man after sexual activity, for announcing a marriage and many more. These activities take place everyday among the Rangi. It is granted that the Catholic Church in Haubi does have rituals, but these are almost exclusively limited to the sacraments, church holidays and the order of the church service itself. For the Rangi, Christianity does not offer help in these other areas. There are no rituals to help with the harvest or to welcome in the New Year. The Italian priests only taught what they learned themselves in Italy. They were not aware that in Rangi culture there was the felt need for a ritual to cover these other items mentioned. As a result of a Christian alternative to these rituals, Rangi Christians, in effect, operate on two different planes. In the church building, they follow the rituals (sacraments and holidays) that the priests first taught them. For the traditional rituals that the Church did not address, they continued with their traditional practices.[42]

Hence, the double life of the Rangi Christians indicates the task of Christians in Africa. As Oduyoye rightly puts it, "Christians in Africa must deal with the gap between 'Christianity preached' and 'Christianity lived.'" They must deal with racism among children of One God and disciples of the One Christ, with the exploitation and dehumanization of the sister and brother for whom Christ died. [. . .]. We have to face [this question]: What does Christianity offer that the natural religion of our peoples does not offer?[43]

Moreover, the dissatisfaction with the kind of theology brought to Africa was not only noticeable among Africans. Some missionaries also noted such a gap between the theology brought by missionaries and the realities of the African people. A missionary John V. Taylor is quoted by Stinton saying that in Africa "Christ has been presented as the answer to the questions a white man would ask, the solution to the needs that Western man would feel,

---

42. Cox, "Why Rangi Christians continue to Practice African Traditional Religion?"7; cf. Sarpong, "Christianity and Traditional African Religion," 26–27.

43. Oduyoye, *Hearing and Knowing*, 9.

the Saviour of the world of the European world-view, the object of adoration and prayer of historic Christendom."[44] Taylor further asks: "But if Christ were to appear as the answer to the questions that Africans are asking, what would he look like? If he came into the world of African cosmology to redeem Man as Africans understand him, would he be recognizable to the rest of the Church Universal? And if Africa offered him the praises and petitions of her total, uninhibited humanity, would they be acceptable?"[45]

As depicted by Wafawanaka and Taylor above, in the old way of doing Christian theology, "Christian theology has often been seen as inspired and so, in effect, as true and as beyond the critical questioning. More than this it has been seen as universally true, as objective and valid regardless of the particular location, time or circumstances out of which it emerged. This kind of status was accorded to Christian theology because of the sources from which it was understood to have emerged, those of scripture and tradition. Both of these were seen as unchanging and non-specific in cultural and experiential terms."[46] New questions were being asked and the existing traditional theology inherited from the missionaries was not able to provide answers. Questions like how to celebrate the Eucharist in places whereby wheat and grapes are not predominantly grown, baptism to some tribes like the Maasai to whom pouring water on the head of a woman implies a curse to her with infertility, the policy of baptizing polygynists,[47] *etc*. Such questions needed new ways of understanding reality that captures the experiences of people. Under the above-described situation, theologians started to see the deficiency in the theology brought by missionaries.

In Africa, for example, theologians started to ask questions such as the following: "what do we make of this new thing [Christianity] in Africa which the missionaries brought? Is there such a thing as African Christianity, and if there is what form should it take? Most importantly, what relation does it have to the indigenous traditions of the continent?"[48] Furthermore, Bediako, quoting the missionary John V. Taylor, writes: "Christ has been presented as the answer to questions a white man would ask, the solution to the needs that western man would feel, the Saviour of the world of the European worldview, the object of the adoration and prayer of historic Christendom.

---

44. Stinton, "Africa's Contribution to Christology," 16; *cf.* Kunhiyop, "Challenges and Prospects," 66–67.

45. *Ibid*.

46. Pears, *Doing Contextual Theology*, 8.

47. In regard to the question of baptizing polygynists and the way it is controversial to the church in Africa, see Kiwovele, "Polygyny as a Problem" & Currens, "A Policy of Baptizing Polygynists."

48. Dyrness, *Emerging Voices*, 42.

But if Christ were to appear as the answer to the questions that Africans are asking, what would he look like?"[49] These questions pointed to the strangeness of the Christianity and Jesus brought by the missionaries in relation to the indigenous traditions of African people; which made them fail to answer African people's questions.

The third is the need to find theological expressions more attuned to changing realities in particular places. Tutu has clearly reiterated: "Christianity, to be truly African, must [. . .] speak in tones that strike a responsive chord in the African breast and must convict the African of his peculiar African sinfulness. It must not provide him with answers to questions he has never asked. It must speak out of and to his own context."[50] The traditional ways of reading the Bible, used in the west for a long time, and inherited by Africans from western missionaries provided old answers to new questions. Muneja, taking ideas from Kathide is convinced that "European theology is 'irrelevant' in certain aspects; since it has made students studying theology to concentrate on the past problems and debates of the European Church, while not being sensitive to current pressing social-economic needs."[51] The old answers that were provided to new questions did not capture the real situation of the people in their particular contexts. Colonialism and imperialism continued with the use of the Bible and theology to justify such unjust structures. This led to people's search for the new identity of Christianity in the midst of their life questions.

The fourth is the traditional reading of the Bible inherited from the western missionaries' search for meaning in texts which was considered to be universal and the one intended by the author of the text. Contextual theology has a different emphasis. It emphasizes that a contextual reading of the biblical text should take into account the particular contexts of people and the questions of life they face in those contexts. De la Torre clearly states: "To read the Bible [contextually] is to grasp God in the midst of struggle and oppression. Hence, such a reading attempts to understand why God's people find themselves struggling for survival within a society that appears to be designed to privilege one group of people at the expense of others."[52] These words indicate that despite lack of adequate answers to contextual African questions, traditional western reading of the Bible makes Africans slaves in their minds and thinking. It inculcates in African minds a western thinking contrary to questions of their daily lives. Jione Havea writes thus in regard

---

49. Bediako, "Jesus in African Culture," 93.
50. Tutu, "African Theology," 59.
51. Muneja, *HIV/AIDS and the Bible*, 43–44.
52. De la Torre, *Reading the Bible*, 4.

to the notion of colonization of African minds through the reading of the Bible: "It does not really matter that the Bible is in the hands of Africans, and of Asians and Icelanders, and so forth, if they are to interpret it according to the teachings of white men. The South has the Bible and the numbers, but the North determines how we read the Bible and how we contextualize. Our minds are still conned and colonized."[53] Havea's words indicate that colonialism in terms of African minds will be eradicated only if the Bible will fully be entrusted to the hands of Africans themselves to interpret it according to their context and problems. A reading which is western oriented provides answers to questions in the west, irrelevant to questions in African contexts.

The fifth was the bad mentality (*kasumba mbaya*) among most Africans that anything Western is good. A theologian Chepkwony puts it: "[. . .] Africans believe that everything western is good and a sign of civilization, whereas that which is African is regarded as bad, primitive and of little value. This perception is common, which explains why we prefer to buy imported goods other than our own, made in Africa. In the same way imported religion is perceived as better and superior to African Religion."[54] Another theologian Ezeugu emphasizes:

> Through centuries of European enslavement and colonization, Africans have been programmed to be their own worst enemies. They have been conditioned, through language and the visual arts, to see whatever is African as inferior, if not all together negative. [. . .]. Africans now share with their erstwhile colonial masters the conviction that white is good and black is evil. We freely use the radically exclusive and condemning language of Eurocentric origin, such as, black Tuesday, black market, black magic, black lie, black mail, blacklist, black book, and even black Mass, with the understanding that black is negative or evil, where as their white counterparts, white magic, white lie, white list etc. are regarded as positive.[55]

---

53. Havea, "The Cons of Contextuality," 41. The words "*the South*" and "*the North*" are used in this book as representatives of particular countries. The South represents the so called Third World or developing countries. The North represents the countries of the First and Second worlds such as North America, Great Britain, Germany, France, Japan and other countries of the European Union. These countries are located north of the equator; hence, bearing the name *Northlandia* (see Wyngaard, "In Search of Root causes of Poverty," 32n7; *Cf.* Girolamo, "Liberation Theology," 3n12.

54. Chepkwony, "African Religion," 47.

55. Ezeugu, "The African Origin of Jesus," 281; *cf.* Knighton, "Issues of African Theology," 147–148.

The bad mentality among Africans stated by theologians above has caused most African theologians trained in the west to continue teaching western oriented theologies in African universities after they graduate and come back to their own countries. A theologian Tuesday Adamo clearly reiterates: "Most African biblical scholars are trained in the West. Those who are even trained in African higher institutions are trained and still being trained in the western tradition. After going back to Africa, those of us who are trained in western tradition soon discovered that the very western methodological tradition to which [sic!] we are well schooled do not satisfy the situation in Africa."[56] Therefore, the above reasons for the interest in context-related theology indicated the challenge which the emerging contextual theology posed to the existing traditional theology. Furthermore, the above reasons indicate the urgent need for the "biblically based, missiologically oriented, educationally shaped, pastorally advocated and spiritually empowered,"[57] way of doing theology that takes into account the lived experiences of African people.

However, despite the weaknesses of the missionary approach to African cultural worldview that caused the above dissatisfaction of Africans, yet it is better to recognize its contribution without over-exaggerating its weaknesses. The Ghanaian theologian Kwame Bediako warns us about romanticizing the missionaries' weaknesses and leaving aside their contributions when he states: "And yet the negative side of the missionary history in Africa must not be exaggerated, for several reasons. Firstly, the vitality of our Christian communities bear witness to the fact that the gospel really was communicated, however inadequate we may now consider that communication to have been."[58] Bediako's statement indicates that as the coin has two sides, the missionaries' endeavor to propagate the gospel also had two coins. Hence, as we now consider the weaknesses of their work, we should also focus on the reality and success of their work. As the missionaries' universal theology faced challenges and dissatisfaction, so is contextual theology. In the following subsection we consider some of the challenges which contextual theology faced in the course of its development.

Challenges facing Contextual Theology

Since the time it began, contextual theology has been developing. In its development, contextual theology has faced a lot of challenges. Some of such

---

56. Adamo, *Explorations in African Biblical Studies*, 3.
57. Pobee, "Good News," 20.
58. Bediako, "Jesus in African Culture," 93; *cf.* Kunhiyop, "Challenges and Prospects," 64.

challenges, according to Nichols and Harsfjord, are the following:[59] First, critics assert that there is no theology without a context. So, to speak of contextual theology is a vague terminology. It is to speak about the whole theology because there is no theology developed out of context.

Second, critics assert that Contextual theology is emotional. It is a result of people's emotional thinking about life and its perils.

Third, critics assert that since contextual theology starts with people's life experiences, there is a problem of romanticizing experience more than the authority of the Bible. This is dangerous because experiences of people are not the same everywhere, and the Bible is forced to adhere to experiences instead of being the guide on people's experiences.

Fourth, critics challenge the locus of theology. The notion that the ordinary reader of the Bible (untrained reader) is the great interlocutor in the process of doing theology more than the trained theologian cannot be clearly conceived. Their criticism is based on the notion that most of the theological writings are produced by trained not untrained theologians. For them, a non-trained Christian can hardly provide a theological articulation at the level which the trained theologian is expected to do.

Fifth, critics challenge that the emphasis of contextual theology that the poor and marginalized groups are the main focus in doing theology does not do justice to the doctrine of salvation. Contextual theology is charged of being exclusive against the inclusive doctrine of salvation. The doctrine of salvation is inclusive not exclusive as contextual theology is. Jesus died on the cross for all people, not just the poor and marginalized people romanticized in contextual theology.

Despite the above-listed challenges, contextual theologians are aware of the current globalized context and the efficacy of the universal theology. Morekwa rightly states: "We live in a globalised world. There is a need for a theology which is directed to universality. Theology is the instrument which brings the world together into common understanding on issues of religion, economics, politics etc. This means that there is no way the world can avoid globalisation. People are moving from one country to another and from one continent to the other. Theology should be able to create a conducive atmosphere for people to practise their faith freely and universally and for people to tolerate other faiths. Theology therefore, should be contextual in a universal world."[60] Within this globalized context, contextual theology continues to grow very fast. Now we talk of 'contextual theologies,' not only

---

59. Nichols, "The Danger of Including Contextualization in Theological Method," 59–62; and Harsfjord, "Challenging Context," 142–143.

60. Morekwa, "Doing Theology in the Post-liberation Era," 57.

one contextual theology. The following section discusses some of the forms of contextual theology, their emergence and their practices.

FORMS OF CONTEXUAL THEOLOGY

There are several branches of contextual theology currently known. Some of these branches are named according to where they originate and practiced. Such branches include Liberation Theology, Black Theology, Minjung Theology, Third- Eye Theology, Dalit Theology, People's Power Theology, Feminist Theology, and the theology of Inculturation. We examine each of these theologies below.

Liberation Theology

Liberation theology in Latin America emerged due to the concern of Latin American theologians for the poor and marginalized people.[61] It is a theology that emerged within the Catholic Church in the 1950s and 1960s reacting against poverty and social injustice in Latin America. The conference of the Latin American catholic bishops that met in Medellin in Colombia in 1968 (CELM—*Consenjo Episcopal Latinoamericano*) was the turning point of Liberation Theology in Latin America despite the movement that went on before. In this conference, bishops insisted on 'the preferential option for the poor' and considered the Catholic Church of Latin America as the 'the Church of the poor'.[62] In the midst of Capitalism and the production of victims, a situation where there was a deepening of poverty, the globalization of market economy, resurgence of issues relating to sexism and racism, it was considered that the church should side with the poor and defend their lives. In this case, Liberation Theology was considered as the theology of life (*teologia de la vida*) and its reflection focused mainly on the God of life (*el Dios de la vida*) against the idols of death that prevailed in the Latin American society under Capitalism.

Some of the pioneer theologians of Latin American Liberation Theology were Juan Luis Segundo, Gustavo Gutiérrez, Leonardo Boff, Pablo Richard, and Jon Sobrino in the Catholic Church side. In the Protestant

---

61. The descriptions provided in this part are based on Gutiérrez, "Notes for a Theology of Liberation"; Berryman, "Latin American Liberation Theology"; Muneja, *HIV/AIDS and the Bible*, 42–44.

62. Some scholars are hesitant to use this concept charging it to present God as God of favoritism contrary to the way Jesus presented God in his earthly ministry (see Steyn & Masango, "The Theology and Praxis," 7).

church side there were theologians Jose Miguez Bonino, Elsa Tamez and Rubem Alves. These theologians were first committed to the struggles of the wretched and exploited masses of Latin America. Out of their life and reflection on that commitment, the theology of liberation emerged. In this case, the production of theology was the second act; the first act was commitment to the lived reality of the marginalized. The theology they produced was rooted greatly on *praxis* (*action* on the lived reality, *i.e.*, involvement in the liberation process, and *reflection* on what has been acted upon, *i.e.*, critical evaluation of the involvement in the liberation struggle), a concept found in the Marxist philosophy. In that case, the Vatican accused Liberation theology as being a 'camouflaged Marxism'.

The main activity of liberation theology was done at the grassroots level by priests, nuns, pastors and lay people. They started operating small Christian communities in the grassroots (CEB—*Communidades Eclesiales de Base*) through which they learned to interpret the Bible in their context and realities of life. In the activities of Small Christian Communities, Liberation theology became a theology of the Latin American people, based on their lived experiences. Robert McAfee Brown says clearly in his Preface to Gutierrez's book *The Power of the Poor in History*, that "liberation theology is a theology of the people, a by-product of the ongoing struggle of the poor to overcome oppression, rather than a theology of the experts crafted in quiet libraries and then offered to 'the masses.'"[63] This statement means that the pioneer professional theologians mentioned above were not owners of theology in the real sense; rather, they were just communicators of theology articulated by communities in the grassroots. Robert McAfee Brown puts it clear: "This is not theology created by the intelligentsia, the affluent, the powerful, those on top; it is theology from the bottom, from 'the underside,' created by the victims, the poor, the oppressed. It is not theology spun out in a series of principles or axioms of timeless truth that are then 'applied' to the contemporary scene, but a theology springing up out of the poverty, the oppression, the heartrending conditions under which the great majority of Latin Americans live."[64]

The difference between the dominant theology of the northern hemisphere (which Gutierrez calls 'progressive theology') and that of Latin American masses is that the former struggles to answer the question of increasing unbelief in the midst of secularization, Enlightenment and globalization; the question here is how to believe in God in a world of science and technology. The question of Latin American Liberation theology was

63. Gutierrez, *The Power of the Poor*, vi.
64. *Ibid.*, vii.

different: how can one believe in a personal God in a world where society makes people nonpersons.[65] The first question asks the rationale of believing in God in a situation where science, technology, science and globalization provide all what they need. The second question asks for the rationale of believing in God in a situation where society considers some groups of people, created by God, as nonpersons. Therefore, the two theologies are different in trajectory and method.[66]

Despite its eminence, like any other hermeneutical method, liberation theology has been criticized in various ways. Muneja, quoting from Bray and Ochegbue, summarizes the criticisms: "1) it reduces faith to politics; 2) it gives a one-sided interpretation of the Bible by stressing only its political element; 3) it uses the Bible to support its political ends by encouraging chauvinism; 5) it has supported other forms of human sexuality against traditional Christianity; 6) it has sometimes resorted to violence."[67] These are the dark sides of liberation theology in Latin America. Despite its dark sides, it has other forms. One such forms is black theology in the African context which we now turn and consider in detail below.

Black Theology

What is Black theology? As the name 'Black Theology' suggests, this is a form of liberation theology among black people and their experiences. Baffel, taking ideas from Maimela, defines it: "Black Theology as a conscious, systematic, theological reflection on black experience, characterised by oppression, humiliation and suffering in white racist societies in North America and South Africa."[68] Black Theology in the USA and South Africa emerged due to struggles for civil rights of black people. Tshaka and Makofane, using some ideas from Maimela, assert that the concept of 'black' can be understood ontologically and symbolically. "When used ontologically, black refers literally to certain people and is specific and therefore particular. As such it is confined to black people and their concerns. When used symbolically the word refers to 'every human situation of enslavement, domination and oppression and therefore to the situation of deprivation, powerlessness and of being the underdog who suffer injustice at the hands of the powerful and the ruling elite.'"[69] Molobi further notes: "The symbolic

---

65. *Ibid.*, viii.
66. *Ibid.*, viii, 92–94.
67. Muneja, *HIV/AIDS and the Bible*, 43.
68. Baffel, "Black Theology and Black Experience," 3.
69. Tshaka & Makofane, "The Continued Relevance of Black Liberation Theology," 533.

value of the word "black" captures the broken existence of Black people; it also summons them collectively to burst the chains of oppression and engage themselves creatively in the construction of a new society."[70]

However, scholars find that Black theology done in the USA and that done in South Africa had a common focus which occasioned them. Both focused on *the liberation of black people from the scourge of racism.*[71] Chimhanda aver:

> The Black Theology of South Africa and the Black Theology of North America have one common foundational focus, that is, the liberation from racism. [. . .]. In the book, *Black Theology in the USA and South Africa*, Hopkins (1989: x–xii) affirms this connectivity of purpose. Where Black Theology in the USA addressed racial oppression of blacks that has its roots in slavery, the Black Theology in South Africa focused on liberation from apartheid rule. Black Theology's agenda is to explore black consciousness and power to liberate the black poor fully culturally, politically and spiritually.[72]

Here, we concentrate much on the South African Black Liberation theology and its context of emergence. Black theology in South Africa had its context of emergence. Its context was the Black Consciousness movement that existed in the 1960s and early 1970s. The black consciousness movement was propagated by young black South Africans who had a great influence from the philosophy of black consciousness that existed in that time due to racial categorizations in the South African society. Tshaka and Mafokane write: "In South Africa, Black liberation theology was expressed under the banner of the Black Consciousness Movement which owes its being to students such as Steve Biko, Barney Pityana, Harry Nengwenkulu and others who were galvanized by the then political situation into organising themselves into being a vanguard for the black peoples' total emancipation from the political pangs into which they were plunged by white racism in South Africa."[73] The major issue in the black consciousness movement was opposing the oppression and exploitation of the majority black South Africans by the minority whites. In this case, the Black consciousness Movement could not exist in "a homogeneous, non-exploitative egalitarian society."[74]

---

70. Molobi, "The Past and Future of Black Theology," 11.

71. Chimhanda, "Black Theology of South Africa," 435.

72. Ibid.

73. Tshaka & Mafokane, "The Continued Relevance of Black Liberation Theology," 534.

74. Ibid.

In regard to the emergence of Black Theology in South Africa, Tshaka and Mafokane write:

> "Black liberation theology emerged in South Africa during the late 1960s. As a project, it was inspired by the liberation theologies of Latin America, the civil rights movement in the USA, the prophetic voice of Martin Luther King Jr. as well as the pioneering work of James Cone. It was transported from the shores of the United States of America to South Africa as an intellectual project which was made possible by the University Christian Movement (UCM) in 1971. All this occurred under the directorship of Basil Moore and was first spearheaded in South Africa by Sabelo Ntwasa."[75]

Some other theologians of Black theology in South Africa include: Desmond Tutu, Manas Buthelezi, Simon Maimela, Takatso Mofokeng, Itumeleng Mosala, Allan Boesak, Buti Tlhagale, etc.

In this context, "Black theologians argued, with justification, that not only was the church relatively silent on the question of oppression, but that the thoroughly western and white outlook of its theology helped to reproduce the basic inequalities of an apartheid society."[76] Jordaan also writes about the situation in South Africa: "For more than 300 years now, Black people in South Africa have been brutally forced to live as aliens in their own land. Their land was stolen from them, and they were subjugated to become slaves under a master on their own land. This "master" class of whites also brought along with them a religion, named Christianity, for what they taught and lived was not the Christianity of a Christ who had come to set the captives free, but rather of one who said to Black people to be submissive to their bosses and indoctrinating them to believe that they are inferior beings, reducing them to nothingness."[77]

It is in this situation where black theology emerged as a "weapon of struggle" against the dehumanizing culture and theology of the minority whites. The main endeavor was to bridge the emerging theology and the culture of the oppressed and marginalized black South Africans as opposed to the existing theology which based on the culture of the white people and racial categorization in the South African society.[78] This means that Black

---

75. Ibid., 533–534; Cone, "Black Theology."; Molobi, "The Past and Future of Black Theology," 2–3; Solomons, "Liberation or Reconstruction," 16–20.

76. Mosala, "Biblical Hermeneutics," vii; Muneja, *HIV/AIDS and the Bible*, 44.

77. Jordaan, "The Emergence of Black Feminist Theology," 43.

78. Ibid., x.

Theology could not emerge and could not be relevant in "a homogeneous, non-exploitative egalitarian society."[79]

The emerging Black Theology, as was liberation theology before it, used Karl Marx's method of social analysis as a starting point. By the use of Marx's historical materialism as a method for social analysis, black theology emphasized on the following teachings: Jesus Christ, is God of the oppressed and exploited masses of South Africa, liberation from domination and exploitation by the few whites is the main message, and the trained theologian in white theological institutions are swimming in the era of confusion in the emerging paradigm of black theology. According to Black Theology, "images of God as a just, loving and merciful Father did not correspond with the harsh reality of racism, landlessness, economic exploitation and political powerlessness."[80]

Despite its various criticisms from what calls itself as universal theology, contextual theologians still find black theology to be as relevant even in the post-independence South Africa as it was in the time of its inception. This relevance is mainly because despite the flag independence that South Africa obtained the aspects that occasioned the emergence of black theology still persist. Chimhanda, quoting Hopkins, calls what persists in the post-independence South Africa as "the 'multilayered reality of black oppression' through subtle and overt racism. There are many black people living below the poverty line. The level of illiteracy among blacks is still very high. There are thousands of poor landless blacks clamouring to be resettled [. . .]. In a patriarchal society and the high prevalence of HIV/AIDS (where poverty and disease are mutually influencing), black women in particular bear the brunt of racial, gender, and class marginalizations."[81]

A similar sentiment is echoed by Buffel: "The truth is that twenty-two years after liberation, South Africa is still a divided country [. . .]. The black experience is still different from the white experience. Blacks still live in parts that are predominantly black and whites live in parts that are predominantly white. Blacks still live in poverty and whites in wealth. The new South Africa, like the end of colonialism, did not bring about economic transformation in Africa as it did in Asia; if anything, it entrenched the economic inequalities inherited from colonialism."[82] Baffel adds: "We still have the dual economy, the first and the second economy which consists of a mixture of extreme wealth and power on the one hand and extreme poverty on the other. Extreme wealth is in the hands of whites and extreme poverty affects mainly

---

79. Tshaka & Makofane, "The Continued Relevance of Black Liberation Theology," 534.
80. Ibid., 535.
81. Chimhanda, "Black Theology of South Africa," 437.
82. Buffel, "Black Theology and the Black Experience," 2.

blacks."[83] Therefore, according to Baffel, "Black Theology is a theology of the people that must be liberated from academic books, from comfortable conference centres, seminaries and universities but unleashed into the streets where there is pain and suffering as a result of poverty and oppression."[84] Moreover, Punt maintains: "A number of recent events in South Africa have driven the materiality of human existence and the nature of our bodily to some of the furthest limits since the end of Apartheid in April 1994. Our contemporary South African is, not unlike many other African and Two-Thirds World countries, marked by deep-set problems of hunger and poverty and disease, homelessness and marginalisation, violent crimes and rape, widespread corruption and political instability—to name a few."[85]

Black theology is now not done and used ontologically to refer to a particular group of people, but still used symbolically. As Tshaka and Makofane write, "When used ontologically, black refers literally to certain people and is specific and therefore particular. As such it is confined to black people and their concerns. When used symbolically the word refers to 'every human situation of enslavement, domination and oppression and therefore to the situation of deprivation, powerlessness and of being the underdog who suffer injustice at the hands of the powerful and the ruling elite.'"[86]

Feminist Theology

After considering Black Theology, we now turn to Feminist Theology as another form of Liberation Theology in the context of women emancipation struggles. Feminist Theology emerged due to women awareness of themselves in relation to God's freedom. The main concern of feminist theology is to critically evaluate the way women relate to the Divine (God) and the society as equals with their counterparts men. In Christianity, feminist theologians evaluate the way in which the Divine relates to them and the way this relationship suggests for the equal encounter of the Divine between men and women. However, feminist theology is not only practiced in Christianity, but also in most other world religions. Feminist theology looks at the various aspects of religions, scriptures, worship, and personal experiences. In these aspects their concern is who is included and who is excluded leading them to conversations with men in regard to equality as

83. Ibid.
84. Ibid., 5.
85. Punt, "Pauline Bodies," 466.
86. Tshaka & Makofane, "The Continued Relevance of Black Liberation Theology," 333.

created beings. Some prominent earlier feminist theologians in the western world include Mary Daly, Rosemary Radford Ruether, Elizabeth Schussler Fiorenza, Phyllis Trible and Salie McFague.

The Cause of Its Emergency

The major cause for the emergence of feminist movement in the world is normativity in terms of the relationship between men and women stated in the above paragraph. The normative consideration of men as being above women in various aspects, which creates power relationship between them, is one of the main causes of the emergence of women protest. As Matsoso asserts: "Feminist theologies have emerged as an alternative approach to the traditional model. Feminist theologians argue that maleness can no longer represent the normative human behaviour."[87] In fact, feminist theology is a theology of protest that seeks emancipation of women from androcentric conception of life as being normative.

Normativity has made androcentrism an acceptable aspect, even among women themselves, especially in patriarchal societies. Yoranda Dreyer clearly notes: "In male-dominated societies women are socialised to accept negative images attributed to them by others (weak, passive, submissive or evil and wild—virgin or slut) and internalise this in the form of a negative self-perception which detracts from the possibility of having a meaningful life."[88] Hence, whatever that can be said about feminism in all its movements—liberal, socialist Marxist, romantic, liberation hermeneutic, or radical feminism—is centred on the struggle of women towards gender equality between their counterpart men.[89]

What is accepted without questioning are the socially constructed roles of women. Some of such roles have been highlighted by Elisabeth Schusller Fiorenza:

> In a sexist society woman's predominant role in life is to be man's helpmate, to cook and work for him without being paid, to bear and rear his children, and to guarantee him psychological and sexual satisfaction. Woman's place is in the home, whereas man's place is in the world earning money, running the state, schools, and churches. If woman ventures into the man's world, then her task is subsidiary, as in the home; she holds the lowest-paid jobs, because she supposedly works for pocket

---

87. Matsoso, "Luke and the Marginalized," ix.
88. Dreyer, "Women's Spirituality," 2.
89. *Ibid.*

money; she remains confined to women's professions and is kept out of high-ranking positions.[90]

It is in these women roles where the androcentric normativity is emphasized and power relation between men and women is experienced.

Its Brief Historical Background

Historically, the concept of "feminism" is credited to the French Hebertine Auclert who is considered to be the first to use the term in 1882. It means that in Western Europe and United States, feminism started since the nineteenth century due to the rise in industrial sector, which prompted for the division of labor between men and women. This industrial revolution emerged as a consequence of the French and American revolutions. However, emancipatory ideas in Western Europe and the United States were there even before the 19th century. Due to attitudes towards women, women were considered subordinate to men and underwent various discriminatory actions against their rights to education and participation in issues of their normal lives, considering them as being weak and incapable. It was in this context that feminist movements such as the abolition movement of Sarah and Angeline Grimke and other American women of the time emerged in the United States. It is during this time when the *Women's Bible* was composed by Elizabeth Cady Stanton.[91]

Types of Feminist Theology

Anne M. Clifford has divided feminist theology into three categories: Revolutionary, reformist and reconstructionist feminist theologies.[92] Revolutionist feminist theology is more radical in the sense that it advocates the break away from the Christian religion because, according to Revolutionist feminists, it embraces teachings that are oppressive to women. Some proponents of this category of feminist theology include Matilda Joslyn Cage, Susan B. Anthony, Elizabeth Cady Stanton and Mary Daly. Mary Daly, for example, considers the break away from Christianity as the only way for women to free themselves from the Christian androcentric teachings and a male God. She sees Christianity as being a prison from which women have

---

90. Fiorenza, "Feminist Theology," 606.

91. See Maseno & Mligo, *Women within Religions*, 17, 22 & 69–74.

92. Clifford, *Introducing Feminist Theology*, 32–38; *cf.* Nunes & Deventer, "Feminist Interpretation," 740–741.

to walk out of it if they are to be free. Daly states: "We have been locked in this Eden of his [*i.e.*, God the Father] far too long. If we stay much longer, life *will* depart from this planet. The freedom to fall out of Eden will cost a mirror-shattering experience. The freedom—becoming—survival of our species will require a continual, communal striving in be-ing. This means forging the great chain of be-ing in sisterhood that can surround non-being, forcing it to shrink back into itself."[93] What Daly communicates in the above statement is that women have been ruled by the male God of the Bible as a result of being members of the Christian religion; and that they need to free themselves from the shackles of the Christian God before life departs from this planet. However, this category of feminist theology is not embraced by all feminist theologians, especially most African Christian women who consider the Christian faith and the Bible as emancipatory tools if used properly. Hence, according to Clifford, Revolutionary feminist theology has led most women in the Western world, who were once Christians, to turn to worshipping the ancient goddesses because they find them to be more empowering to them than the Christian male God.[94]

Reformist feminist theology is more accommodating category than the other two. Proponents of this category advocate remaining in Christianity with the focus on reforming it. They do not advocate worshiping the goddesses as an alternative to the Christian male God, but find that there are enough and adequate resources in Christianity to enable them effect the necessary changes from within it. These theologians argue that if women are provided opportunities do church ministries and hold church offices that are predominantly held by men, it can help reduce the existing chasm between men and women within the church. A good example of adherents to this category of feminist theology are some African women who have decided to remain in Christianity but enhancing change from within.[95]

Reconstructionist feminist theology stands in between the two previously discussed categories. This is a feminist theological movement that combines the reformist and revolutionary theological movements. Adherents to this category are not satisfied with the reformist feminist theology, but would like to see a deep reformation accompanied by liberation and reconstruction taking place within the church and in society at large.[96] One proponent of such a category of feminist theology is Letty Russell. Russell states: "This is the survival skill for anyone who wishes to participate in

---

93. Daly, "The Looking Glass Society," 192 (italics is in original).
94. Clifford, *Feminist Theology*, 32–33.
95. Ibid., 33.
96. Ibid., 33–38.

God's housekeeping chares. By knowing the social structures and psychological dynamics of the old house of bondage, we can work to subvert those structures and to limit their power in our lives and institution."[97] Here Russell advocates for the subversion of oppressive elements in cultures and traditions within Christianity to bring about liberation of women without breaking away from Christianity and its biblical teachings.

Feminist Theology in Africa

The African context had no exception in regard to the asymmetrical power relations between men and women in terms of feminist theological categories discussed in the above paragraphs. In the South African context of apartheid, both white and black women faced asymmetrical power relations with their counterpart men. Jordaan reports it: "They form 70% of the unemployed community. They have to cook, wash, clean in their own homes after a hard day's work. (Those who are lucky to have Jobs) They form 60% of the church members, but are labeled as weaker, subordinate, and non-thinking people by their own men. They can raise the funds, but are not allowed to determine how the funds will be spent."[98] According to Jordaan, women in South Africa experienced a double suffering—from apartheid and from the oppression of men exerted against them in the homes and in the public sphere.

In the Tanzanian context, Kategile avers: "During the colonial era African women suffered what we can call 'double oppression': as Africans, they were oppressed by colonizers, and as women oppressed by men."[99] Kategile is of the view that despite being the majority in churches, they are misrepresented in various spheres of church life such as Church leadership and ordained ministry. According to her, this misrepresentation calls for women empowerment for them to realize their potentials.[100] Therefore, as Jordaan points it out in the above paragraph, Kategile also seems to hold a similar view that oppression of women was experienced from both the colonialists and African men in the homes, churches and other public spheres of life.

The double oppression of women in the Tanzanian contexts highlighted by Kategile in the above paragraph is also experienced by widows. In most African contexts widows suffer 'double tragedy'—they lose their

---

97. Russell, "God Housekeeping," 232. Other major proponents include Phyllis Trible, Elisabeth Schüssler-Fiorenza, and Rosemary Radford Ruether.

98. Jordaan, "The Emergence of Black Feminist Theology," 44.

99. Kategile, "I Long for Women to be Empowered," 119.

100. Ibid., 119–127.

CONTEXTUAL THEOLOGY AND THE CONCEPT OF PLACE 31

beloved husbands and are grabbed of the possessions by the relatives of their diseased husbands. An example of this kind tragedy is reported by Chirongoma in the Zimbabwean context. Chirongoma, after interviewing Tambudzai who lived in Kambuzuma Harare—a widow who experienced such a double tragedy, reports her story at length:

> My problems started when my husband Zvenyika became very ill and stopped working. We were living in Kambuzuma, Harare in the house that we acquired together whilst he was still working and I also worked at the market selling fruit and vegetables. However, when his parents and brothers came and found him in such a critical state, they insisted that we must take him to the village so that they may establish the cause of his sickness. We therefore hired a car to take him to the village and upon arrival; they invited a n'nga (traditional practitioner) who diagonized that Zvenyika had been bewitched by someone who wanted to inherit his possessions. My in-laws then started accusing me of witchcraft and they insisted that I should confess having bewitched him. I tried to explain that he had his medical records that indicated that he was suffering from HIV and IDS related ailments, but they even went further accusing me of having passed on the infection to him. All hell broke loose after my husband's death and burial. Whilst I was still morning Zvenyika, his eldest brother went to Harare and carried all the movable possessions to the village. He even rented the house to some tenants and I was left with nothing. They all told me that everything belonged to their diseased relative and since I'd bewitched him, I should therefore leave and go to my parents. They even wanted me to leave my children behind which I resisted. When I went back to Harare to visit my friends and collect some of my credits, all my friends at the market encouraged me to report this to the police. At first I was reluctant because I didn't want to fight against my children's relatives, fearing that it could offend their ancestors. However, after realizing that I could not cope financially, struggling with my medical bills and all my children being sent away from school due to failure to pay school fees, I finally reported the case to the police. It was a long and strenuous process since our marriage was under customary law, we attended several court sessions with my brother in-law insisting that he was entitled to inheriting Zvenyika's property including myself and the kids. I finally won the case and repossessed our house but we suffered terribly in the process. My main worry

right now is that if I die before my children are mature enough, they might again have everything grabbed away from them.[101]

Chirongoma concludes that a situation such as the one experienced by Tambudzai "encircles women in a vicious circle of grinding poverty, forcing them to adopt risky survival skills, exposing them to more vulnerability of HIV infection."[102] The deaths of their husbands cause them to enter into harsh legal battles with relatives who fiercely long to grab the possession which widows earned with their husbands in their husbands' life times.

In fact, similar situations appear in other parts of Africa apart from South Africa, Tanzania and Zimbabwe where the power relation between men and women is mainly based on cultural norms and values. Hence, while South African feminist theology emerged from the political oppression, the cause of power relation in most other parts of Africa is cultural orientation of societies.

African feminist theologians started to theologize by using feminist approaches in the late 1980s. Mercy Amba Oduyoye is credited of being the first woman to introduce this kind of theology in her ground breaking book *Hearing and Knowing* originally published by Orbis books in 1986. In this book Oduyoye calls the attention of the society about the role of women in relation to that of men. She states: "Feminism [. . .] highlights the woman's world and her worldview as she struggles side by side with the man to realize her full potential as a human being. [. . .]. Feminism then emphasizes the wholeness of the community as made up of male and female beings."[103] Oduyoye emphasized that the concept of feminism should not be taken as a word just for women; rather, it is the word for both men and women who see the need for human wholeness—that society is whole when both males and females realize their potentials without bias.[104]

Oduyoye's book raised the enthusiasm of women scholars throughout Africa. However, as stated above, in Africa feminism has a unique emphasis. African feminists claim to have unique experiences based more on their historical and cultural backgrounds. Instead of being a confrontational encounter between males and females in search for rights, most of them emphasize on coexistence. It is on this ground that African feminists reject calling themselves as "feminists" opting for the term "womanist" instead. These African women call their theology as "womanist theology" or

---

101. Chirongoma, "Women's and Children's Rights," 53.
102. Ibid, 53–54.
103. Oduyoye, *Hearing and Knowing*, 121.
104. Ibid., 121–122.

"African women theology." Mercy Amba Oduyoye inaugurated this kind of theology at a conference in Accra Ghana. Gathogo puts this point clearly:

> In the Accra Conference of 1989, where Oduyoye delivered her inaugural address, she urged African Christianity to do a "two-winged" theology through which both women and men could communicate with God [. . .]. In emphasising that a bird cannot fly by one wing, she was attempting a reconstruction of the traditional approach to theologising in Africa where one gender did theology almost to the exclusion of the other. By her two-winged theology, Mercy Oduyoye [. . .] was urging for inclusivity as opposed to exclusivity, unity as opposed to division and respect in gender relations.[105]

In this case, Oduyoye was working under the reconstruction theology which will be discussed in chapter six within this book.

Why did African women theologians reject the concept of feminism? The theologian Chisale provides the answer to this question: "Globally, feminism is associated with women who have issues, or difficulty relating to men or women, or women who have failed in their marriages."[106] Most African women engaged with womenist theology have their marriages and do not encounter problems in their marital relationships with their husbands. Therefore, calling themselves feminists equates them with women who have bad marital reputations, or those who have failed in maintaining their marriages, a thing they would not prefer to hear.

Within the above context of womanist theology, African women theologians reflect on various themes such as community, Christology, ecclesiology, eschatology, empowerment and liberation, and are organized into various organizations. Such organizations include the Ecumenical Association of Third World Theologians (EATWOT) and the Circle of Concerned African Women Theologians (CCAWT) which act as forums for meeting and articulating theology on the stated themes.[107]

Feminist Theology in Asia

In the Asian continent, feminist theology found roots on the experience of the wider Asian people. Despite that Asia is a wider continent, rich in both

---

105. Gathogo, "Mercy Oduyoye," 5; *cf.* Landman, "Mercy Amba Ewudziwa Oduyoye."

106. Chisale, "Patriarchy and Resistance," 30.

107. For more about African feminist theology see Maseno & Mligo, *Women within Religions*, 28–39.

human and natural resources, yet it is submerged in an abject poverty. The history of colonialism among Asian countries makes them pray to imperialism furthered by few elites who exploit the majority in the name of caste system.[108] This situation makes women suffer greatly. Mananzan reports that "In this situation Asian women suffer double and triple oppression. Aside from discrimination and subordination, women suffer various forms of violence, both domestic and social. They are also victims of trafficking in different forms: as prostituted women, mail-order brides, overseas contract workers, domestic helpers and entertainers."[109] Therefore, it is within this context where feminist theology is practiced by different activists (community organizers, students in theological institutions, socially oriented activists, and leaders of churches), in various forms (grassroots people's movements, organized theological networks, ecumenically designed conferences, and publications in journals and books).[110]

As noted in the discussion of African feminist theologians above, Asian feminists also protest against the use of the word "feminist" to identify with their theology. They also do not prefer to call themselves "feminists." Rather they would prefer to call their theology as Asian Women's Theology. Pui-lan reports: "Not all women theologians in Asia want to be identified as feminist theologians. The term 'feminism' is controversial in some parts of Asia because it sometimes connotes a radicalism and separatism advocated by middle-class European and American women [. . .]. Many prefer to call their work Asian women's theology instead of feminist theology, to avoid the negative connotation of a militant, separatist and man-hating stance."[111] In this case, Asian women, as were their counterpart Africans, find the demand for their rights from men is not a confrontational encounter between the two genders; rather, it is a coexistence and negotiation. Asian women, as African women are, practice a theology of relationship instead of that of confrontation and strife.

The Mujerista Theology among Hispanic/Latina Women

In the United States, Hispanic/Latina women have called their liberation theology as *mujerista* Theology. The word *mujerista*, coined by Ada Maria Isasi-Diaz, is a Spanish word for "womanist." Geer utters clearly that

---

108. Pui-lan, *Introducing Asian Feminist Theology*, 12–13.
109. Mananzan, "Feminist Theology," 21.
110. Pui-lan, *Introducing Asian Feminist Theology*.
111. Ibid., 9.

> *Mujerista* theology is a constructed, contextualized liberation theology by Latinas. *Mujeristas* assert that 'theology is a praxis— that is, reflection-action that in a spiraling motion integrates the faith of Latina women with the struggle for liberation-fullness of life.' *Mujeristas* contend that their social location as both women and Latinas in the United States places them among the most marginalized. Latinas of all economic classes in the United States lag behind in education, health access and economic wellbeing, relative to other women, with the exception of African American and Native American women who share these lower echelons of societal status, putting them at a higher risk for sexual exploitation.[112]

Therefore, as a reflection-action (praxis) theology, *mujerista* is a theology of relationship. It is a theology that understands salvation as "having a relationship with God, a relationship that does not exist without love of neighbor [. . .]. Sin is viewed as that which hurts relationship."[113] Its goal is "to provide a platform for the voices of Latina grassroots women, to develop a theological method that takes seriously the religious understandings and practices of Latinas as a source for theology; to challenge theological understandings, church teachings, and religious practices that oppress Latina women [. . .]."[114] It is a theology that provides to Latina women their due respect and dignity as human beings in their relationship with men in the various spheres of life, including their relation with nature.

Ecofeminism

Ecofeminism is feminist theology linked to ecological crisis. The term "ecofeminism was coined by a Frechwoman called Francoise d'Eaubonne in 1974 in her book *Le Feminisme ou la Mort* (*Feminism or Death*).[115] While feminism is a movement towards women emancipation from oppression by their counterpart men, "Ecology examines how natural communities function to sustain a healthy web of life and how they become disrupted causing the death of animal and plant life."[116] The fact that we live on earth and obtain our life nourishment from what the earth has to provide to us is equated with our birth and nourishment from our human mothers. Salman

---

112. Geer, "Truth Be Told," 24.
113. Ibid.
114. Isasi-Diaz, *Mujerista Theology*, 1.
115. Maseno & Mligo, *Women within Religions*, 113.
116. Ibid.

states succinctly the role of our human mothers: "Women world wide [sic], are often the first ones to notice environmental degradation. Women are the first ones to notice when the water they cook with and bathe the children in, smells peculiar: they are the first to know when the supply of water starts to dry up. Women are the first to know when the children come home with stories of mysterious barrels dumped in the creek: they are the first to know when children develop mysterious ailments."[117] Following this profound role of our human mothers, it is considered that there is a link between the oppression of women and the oppression and destruction of nature, both needing emancipation. Therefore, the term ecofeminism links the struggle to towards ending the oppression of women and the oppression and destruction of nature in the earth we reside.

Minjung Theology

Minjung Theology in Korea is another form of contextual theology. It emerged in the 1970s due to concerned Korean struggle for social and political justice. This is a South Korean version of liberation theology which takes into account the cries and groans of the suffering people. Chung clearly captures: "Korean Minjung Theology is a Korean contextual theology emerging from the struggle for social and political justice in Korea. It began in the 1970s against the backdrop of the political oppression and developed during the political dictatorship of the 1980s. This Korean contextual theology defines minjung as the social, political, and economic suffering people, or simply, "the underdogs" as opposed to the rich and powerful [. . .]."[118] Therefore, following this definition, *minjung* theology is not a theology of the elites, rather a theology of the downtrodden people at the margins.

Historically, *minjung* theology emerged from governmental dictatorship and the masses decision to resist, which eventually resulted into oppressions. Kim, quoting Lee, reiterates:

> In 1972 President Park Chung-[H]ee declared Martial Law across the country in order to maintain power. The ideology of his regime was based on the concept of "national security" and the promotion of economic growth. Opposition forces were systematically described as "communists" and put down with brutal force. Many church groups stood up against the dictatorship and growing infringement of human rights, such as the Urban Industrial Mission, the Korean Student Christian Federation,

117. Salman, "Ecofeminist Movements," 183.
118. Chung, "Munster and Minjung," 36.

the Christian Ecumenical Youth Council, the Catholic Farmers' Union and the Catholic Commission for Justice and Peace, and similar organisations. Christian 'koinonias'–mission groups– were organised to care for the people who were oppressed and marginalised, the *minjung*.[119]

Hence, minjung theology is a kind of Korean liberation theology emerging from people's social political situation enforced to people in Korea by the brutal government.

On the one hand, the suffering and marginalized people are referred to as "*han*." The meaning of *han*, according to Lee, as quoted in Chung, is "a deep resentment against unjustifiable suffering."[120] Lee's words, as quoted in Kim, define *han*: "Han is a Korean word which may be defined as 'deep agony and sorrow,' 'accumulated bitterness,' and 'resentment.' It can also be translated as a collective feeling of unresolved resentment against unjustifiable suffering."[121] Moreover, quoting the words of Nam-Dong Suh, Kim defines it: "'han' is an underlying feeling of the oppressed Korean people. [. . .] it is a dominant feeling of defeat, resignation, and nothingness."[122] Hence, the *han* of the minjung is the major concern of minjung theology even more than the minjung's *sin*; and the role of the church is to remove the minjungs' *han* because it is the one that leads the minjung to committing *sin*.[123]

On the other hand, the word "Minjung" is also a Korean word. It is composed of two Chinese characters "*min*" which means "people" and "*jung*" which means "the mass or crowd." Hence, the word Minjung can be translated as "the majority of people" or "the mass of people"; however, it does not capture the full reality of the living reality of the Korean society.[124] The term *minjung* encompasses the oppression of the *minjung* in various

119. Kim, "Reillumination of Minjung Theology," 38; *cf.* Kim, "Minjung Theology," 53. According to Yoon Ki Kim, "Nam-Dong Suh and Byung-Mu Ahn are the ones who first used the term "minjung theology" in the mid-1970s. Suh is one of the founders of minjung theology, who introduced the notion of *han*, a unique Korean word, which is one of the core concepts of minjung theology. Ahn is a New Testament scholar who is known as the other founder of minjung theology. In Ahn's book, *Jesus of Galilee*, he concentrates on the word *ochlos* in the Gospel of Mark to match it with the word "minjung" in developing minjung theology." (See Kim, "Reilluminating Minjung Theology," 38) These two theologians are among the "liberal theologians" who pioneered Minjung Theology in Korea.

120. *Ibid.*

121. Kim, "Minjung Theology," 58.

122. *Ibid.*

123. *Ibid.*, 58–59.

124. Hwang, "The God of all the Earth," 110; Kim, "Reillumination of Minjung," 37; *cf.* Van Leest, "The Impacts of Concepts," 7–8; Kim, "Minjung Theology," 53–54.

spheres of their lives: culturally, socially and economically. According to Kim Yong-bok, as quoted in Philpott, these are types of minjung, "Woman belongs to minjung when she is politically dominated by man. An ethnic group is a minjung group when when it is politically dominated by another group. A race is minjung when it is dominated by another powerful ruling race. When intellectuals are suppressed by the millitary power elite, they belong to minjung. Of course, the same applies to the workers and farmers."[125] These aspects of the Korean situation are what distinguish *minjung* theology in Korea from liberation theology in Latin America mainly concerned with poverty and the relationship between the rich and the poor.[126]

The question is this: Why did *minjung* theology develop in the Korean society? In most cases, *minjung* theology emerged due to the cry of *minjung* for a better and just society. This cry was hardly satisfied by the existing traditions and religions, especially Confucianism and Buddhism, the dominant religious traditions of the Koreans. Golijanin describes this situation more openly:

> Throughout the history of this particular Christianity, one can notice the constant cry of people not just for a better society, but also for a better spiritual basis for the society or, to put it more simply, for a better God. The most humane of all humanist philosophies in the history, Confucianism, proved to be useless in the society that wants to advance further from the strictly juridical way of thinking. Surely, the teachings of Confucius were the best original East Asian ideology, but these teachings could not improve the bad social conditions of the lower classes, because Confucius himself never resolved this problem to the end. There was not some loving figure in Confucianism, such as personal God or saviors from the worldly evils, which means that people had to turn to other systems, such as primitive native religious systems or Buddhism, to find a condolence in the promises of afterlife. Naturally, this produced the feeling of confusion regarding the validity of old Korean religions. None of their philosophies and ideologies offered a definitive answer to the issues of an ordinary man.[127]

Koreans encountered a difference in the new religion (Christianity) since its inception.[128] The figure of Jesus and his suffering captured the reality of the

125. Philpott, *Jesus is Tricky*, 113.
126. Kim, "Minjung Theology," 60.
127. Golijan, "Jesus Christ and the Minjung," 52.
128. Eunsoo Kim reports that the first Church was built in Korea in 1887 (see Kim, "Minjung Theology," 53).

suffering masses in Korea. The words of Golijan testify this factual power of Jesus and Christianity among the minjung of Korea:

> The very figure of Jesus Christ corresponded to the life conditions of most of the Koreans in the time when Christianity was first introduced to their land. Jesus suffered as they suffered, He was poor as they were poor, and He became one with the oppressed masses in order to save them. Buddha was not such figure, nor was Laozi. These two sages were primarily concerned with the individual, placing less emphasis on the society as a living organism that has more of a purpose then just to offer physical security. Buddha saw all worldly affairs as *dukha* (suffering), while Laozi was mostly skeptical regarding struggle for better social circumstances; both sages recommended an individual meditation, leading to the end of troubled existence, or to the physical immortality. Confucius was the only one who went further than that, but he was not able to find better role models for people than old Chinese (mythological) sage-emperors.[129]

In this case, minjung theology found a way among Koreans to regain identity while Jesus and his ministry being their primary paradigm.

Biblically, the New Testament bases of *minjung* theology, according to its proponents, is Jesus' ministry to the *ochlos* (the *minjung*), the crowd around him. These groups that surrounded Jesus were mostly "those who were religiously forsaken, economically alienated, and politically oppressed."[130] *Minjung* theology rests on the strong reciprocal relationship between the *ochlos* (the *Minjung*) and Jesus, such that the *ochlos* (the *minjung*) is identified as Jesus and Jesus is identified as the *ochlos* (the *minjung*). Chung clearly states about this reciprocal relationship between Jesus and the *ochlos* (the *minjung*): "Such a reciprocal relation is too strong even to the extent of identifying Jesus with the *ochlos*-minjung [. . .]. In Minjung Theology, Jesus' incarnation is, therefore, caught up in the *ochlos*-minjung's deification so that Jesus is minjung and vice versa [. . .]."[131]

Another New Testament base for Minjung Theology is the crucifixion of Jesus. For Minjung theologians, the arrest and death of Jesus is conceived as being a politically oriented event. Jesus' attack on the existing conventions and unjust political leadership of his time led to his oppression and death as its consequence. For minjung theologians, Jesus entered the world of minjung, protesting the Jerusalem rulers and oppressive actions to the

---

129. Golijan, "Jesus Christ and the Minjung," 52.
130. Chung, "Munster and Minjung," 37n15.
131. *Ibid.*

minjung, which eventually led him to persecution and death. In this case, Jesus' suffering and death stands as a symbol of the minjung, as Kim quoting Byung-mo Ahn, states: "It was not Jesus of Nazareth but rather minjung who was unjustly tried and crucified [. . .]. Jesus as the Son of Man is just a collective symbol. The death of minjung on the cross represents the breaking of a vicious circle of avenging violence by means of violence. That Jesus was raised means that the minjung of Galilee were raised [. . .]."[132]

The Old Testament base for *minjung* theology is the Exodus event. The Exodus of the Hebrews from Egypt to Canaan is read as an historical event that correlates to the need for the *minjung* of Korea to depart from their oppressive structures. Therefore, according to Eunsoo Kim, being influenced by liberal theologians such as Moltman, Loffler, Pannenberg, and Bonhoefer, "minjung theologians insist that the point of departure for a proper Christian theology must be the presupposition that God is the God of the minjung and that his salvation history is a history of his liberation or salvation of the minjung from the hands of their oppressors."[133]

Third-Eye Theology

Another form of contextual theology is the Third-eye theology in Taiwan. This form of contextual theology is clearly articulated by the well-known theologian Choan-Seng Song in his various theological writings including the book *Third-Eye Theology: Theology in Formation in Asian Setting*. In his theological thinking, Song draws from Buddhism and Confucianism as his source of wisdom and material to inform his theological thinking. It is from Buddhism where the concept of "Third-Eye Theology is drawn.[134] Quoting Song, Moe states: "Zen wants us to open a third-eye, as Buddhists call it, to the hitherto unheard-of region shut away from us through our ignorance. When the cloud of ignorance disappears, the infinity of heavens is manifested where we see for the first time into the nature of own being."[135] Therefore, the Buddhist concept of Enlightenment which Song uses proposes for the new awareness for Assians to see the situation they are in with a "Third-Eye," an inner eye of the Asian people themselves that triggers enlightenment within them to produce a theology coming from the womb of Asian people.

---

132. Kim, "Minjung Theology," 56–57.
133. Kim, "Minjung Theology," 54.
134. Moe, "A Critical Reading," 195; *cf.* Keung, "A Critical Assessment," 16.
135. *Ibid.*

In his theological thinking, Song conceives of three kinds of theologies operating in the Asian context. The first and second theologies are inadequate while the third is adequate because it emanates from the womb of the Asian people themselves. Moe puts it: "For Song, the "first-eye" represents doing theology with Hebrew and Greek eyes, whereas the "second-eye" represents doing theology with Western eyes, German ones in particular. [. . .]. Song argues that first and second-eye theologies are incapable of the third-dimensional insight of Asian stories. He, therefore, proposes a Third-eye Theology as a re-thinking about the contextual relationship between the stories of Jesus and the stories of Asian people."[136]

The concern of Song in his writings is on two main themes: the *liberation of theology* and the *theology of liberation*. In the theme of the liberation of theology, Song argued that the Asian theology should be liberated from the shackles of Western thought; while in the theme of the liberation theology he argues that the Asian people should be liberated from the shackles of poverty, marginalization and other various forms of suffering.[137] Therefore, according to Song, the proper theology for Asian people must take seriously their culture and their real life of suffering (*dukkha*) caused by social-political and economic circumstances.

Song proposes that for Asian theology to respond to the dominating Western theology and be beneficial to Asian people's lived experiences, it should be an '*angry theology*' and '*weeping theology*.' In his words, Song says: "Asian third world theology has appeared on the world theological scene as an angry theology. It is angry at the domination of Western enlightenment patterns of thought. Our contextual theology has also to be a weeping theology. It is weeping at suffering around us—endless wars, bottomless poverty, and cruel suppression of human rights. We hear God weep and lament"[138] In this case, the Third-Eye theology of Song is a form of the theology of liberation which is constantly opposed to the dominant Western theology "more interested in the metaphysics of God than in the concrete acts of God in society and history."[139]

In his book, Song emphasizes that theology should listen to the existing spirituality of the Asian people and learn from it. In this book, Song challenges western theology that blossomed in the western world as being

136. *Ibid.*

137. *Ibid.*, 194.

138. Song. *Tell Us Our Names*, 10. Song's two themes of 'Liberation of Theology' and 'Theology of Liberation' are articulated in his other writings, such as Song, *The Compassionate God*; Song, *Theology from the Womb of Asia*; Song, *Jesus, the Crucified People*; Song, *Jesus & the Reign of God*; and Song, *In the Beginning was Stories*.

139. Keung, "A Critical Assessment."

irrelevant to the spirituality outside "the framework of Constantinian Christianity." Song asserts:

> In recent years, however, it has become increasingly obvious to many thinking people, both in the East and in the West, that the theology constructed on the marriage between Christianity and western civilization cannot serve the spirituality that grows, develops and creates outside the framework of Constantinian Christianity. This does not deny the contributions of traditional academic theologians in the West to their churches and societies. [. . .]. They have helped shape the spirituality that has blossomed into western culture. But it cannot be denied that they are limited in their ability to interpret the spirituality that lies beyond their knowledge and experience.[140]

In this kind of theology, Song makes a considerable contribution to the interaction between Christian faith and contemporary political, social and religious life of the Asian people.

Despite the nuanced articulation, Song's theology has not gone without criticisms. One among the criticisms of Song's theology is whether there is a possibility to have true liberation of theology from Western thought forms and regain the true Asianness. In his criticism to Song's theology, Keung argues:

> What troubles us is Song's suggestion of the reclamation of the Asianness and the abandonment of Western tradition. It is true that we can turn our heads away from the literature of Western theology and concentrate on the resources of Asia. Nonetheless, as ones which have gone through the Western education, we cannot escape the influence of Western tradition. Actually Western tradition is already a, smaller or larger, part of our prejudices. At least part of our spectacles are irreversibly Western made. Song is no exception. As a man who was educated in the West and is now living and teaching in North America, he can claim no pure Asianness. His prejudices are to a large extent different from that of native Asians. He can only understand Asian cultures from a foreign point of view.

Keung's criticism means that it is hard to jettison Western prejudices to those educated in the Western tradition despite being angry with them and aspiring to free from them. According to Keung "it is often through the encountering of other cultures that the weaknesses and incompleteness of our

---

140. Song, *Third-Eye Theology*, 5.

prejudices are exposed."[141] Song's awareness of the wickedness of the Western culture over the Asian culture was because of his encounter with the Western culture which he now denounces. In fact, this challenge remains genuine to all Western trained scholars striving towards context-oriented theology in their own places of origin.

Dalit Theology

Dalit Theology is another form of contextual theology within Asia. It is a theological perspective practiced in India. It is a theology of Dalit communities in relation to the caste system practiced in India for many years. Dalit communities are not only found in India; they are also found in countries like Burma, Sri Lanka, and Nepal.[142] In defining the concept of Dalit, Azariah avers: "in the Old Testament language of Hebrews also, a root word 'Dal' is used to mean 'crushed' or 'downtrodden' and this term is increasingly being used in India today [. . .]. Etymologically Dalit is he who is broken or oppressed [. . .]. [Hence,] It describes the predicaments of those who are alienated from social equality, economic justice and human freedom."[143]

Moreover, Rajkumar, as quoted in Johnson Petta, writes: "Understanding Dalits inevitably entails understanding the Indian caste system."[144] The word Caste originates from the Latin word *castus*, which means *pure* or *chaste*. Its first use was in the form of the Spanish word *Casta* which meant "tribes, species or races, and was used in reference to the mixed breed between Europeans, Indians and Africans."[145] In the real sense, when speaking of the caste system, it refers to four main groups of people in the following order: at the top are the Brahmins (priests and teachers), followed by Kshatriyas (rulers and warriors), Vaishyas (merchants and farmers), and Shudras (workers and craftspeople). Apart from the above caste social groups, there exists another group of people which is not worth being placed into any of the above castes. This group consists of the "outcasts" of the Indian society despite that they constitute the majority of the existing Indian society.[146] Petta further notes: "While the outcastes are not part of the caste system, their lives are inextricably tied to caste system. For many of the outcaste communities in India today, life continues to be ordered and

141. Ibid. 38.
142. Petta, "In Search of Contextual Pastoral Theology," 9.
143. Azariah, "Doing Theology in India," 40.
144. Petta, "In Search of Contextual Pastoral Theology," 16.
145. Ibid., 17.
146. Ibid., 16–19.

governed by the principles of the caste system. Who they are (cultural identity), where they live (designated areas of habitation), what they can do or not do (occupational restrictions), how they related to other social groups (social, commensal and matrimonial relations) continue to be shaped by the cultural rules of caste system."[147] These outcaste people have been named with various derogatory names. Petta writes about the derogatory names of the outcastes and the emergence of the name Dalit:

> Throughout the known history of the caste system, the outcastes of the Indian society have been called by a variety of pejorative terms such as Chandalas (dirty), Panchamas (the fifth caste) Avarnas (without caste). Untouchables, Depressed classes (under British rule) and Harijans (God's children, Gandhi) are terms used before the word 'Dalit' gained widespread appeal among the caste oppressed communities to assert their selfhood and identity. Etymologically, the term Dalit is derived from a Sanskrit word dal meaning crack, split and open. In its adjective form it means burst, split, broken or torn asunder, crushed and destroyed. The term was first used in the nineteenth century by a Marathi social reformer and revolutionary Mahatma Jyotirao Phule to 'describe the outcastes and untouchables as the oppressed and broken victims of [the] caste-ridden society.'[148]

The beginning, continuation, and language used by Dalit Theology reflects the experiences of the Dalits themselves. As Petta elaborates: "Dalit theology emerges from below and does not use the Sanskrit language, the language of the brahamanic culture, but uses the language of Dalit people. Dalit theology uses Dalit stories, songs, values, sufferings to 'interpret their history and culture, and to articulate a faith to live by and to act on.'"[149] The main goal of this theology also focuses on the needs of the Dalits as Petta, quoting Balasundaram, writes: "[t]he goal of Dalit theology is the liberation of the Dalits and their empowerment, *i.e.*, strengthening Dalits, providing comfort to them, the good news that God is with them in their struggle, that they are God's children and that they have their own God-given identity and that they are people with worth and dignity. That is, human dignity is more important than the question of economic emancipation."[150] Therefore, having this goal and articulation, Dalit theology stands as a counter theology, a different theology from the traditional Indian Christian theology based

---

147. Ibid., 19.
148. Ibid., 24.
149. Petta, "In Search of Dalit Contextual Pastoral Theology," 90.
150. Ibid.

on the brahminic tradition and the western theology which both did not address the needs, sufferings and aspirations of the Dalits.[151]

Theology of Struggle

Theology of Struggle (or People's Power Theology) is mostly done in Philippines. The Philippines is a country with the majority people being Roman Catholic Christians and few of them are Protestants and people who belong to non-Christian faiths. However, as the theologian Crecencio puts it: "Today, poverty is one of the most malign social problems in the Philippines. According to a National Statistics Office 2015 report, 'More than 26 million Filipino remain poor with almost half, or a little more than 12 million, living in extreme poverty and lacking the means to feed themselves.'"[152]

Despite the large number of Christians within the country, the statistics provided by Crecencio indicate that Christianity in Philippines seems to have hardly addressed pressing issues of injustice, poverty and corruption prevailing in society. Instead of being a weapon to fight against the colonial Christianity, Christianity has been a tool to perpetuate it. It has been a tool to enhance the existence of neo-colonial Christianity. Crecencio further states: "In consequence, conditions of poverty and inequitable distribution of wealth in Philippine society remains a major concern of contemporary Filipino theologians. In response, liberation theology has become a popular theological approach for dealing with poverty and wealth distribution."[153]

Another problem with the Philipino Christianity is its lack of proper roots to people's cultural backgrounds. The theologian Michaael M. Ramos states succinctly:

> From the foregoing, the question that arise here are the following: how much of the Filipino cultural system has influenced the faith they have received so that Christianity becomes the faith of the Filipino people? Has the Filipino culture really been inculturated? Has the gospel sufficiently taken root in our culture? Or perhaps, it is more like a question whether Filipinos had been truly Christianized or Christianity had simply been Filipinized. Hence, the problem of faith and culture abound for Filipino theologians and scholars lies in how to be authentically Filipino and authentically Christian in the culture that they find themselves in.[154]

---

151. Chako, "The One and the Many," 54.
152. Crecencio, "Grassroots Theology," 2.
153. *Ibid.*
154. Ramos, "Inculturating Theology," 695; *cf.* Fernandez, "Towards a Theology of

Indeed, with these pressing questions, such kind of Christianity is worthy being criticized and transformed to suit people's real cultural and political and economic situations.

Theology of Inculturation

In African context, the prominent form of contextual theology is inculturation theology. How did this form of theology emerge and what are its main tenets? Since the coming of Christianity in the African soil, there was a yearning for maintaining the African identity in the midst of foreign imposed values. Inculturation was one of the responses of African Christians at the encounter between two cultures—African and European cultures. Ukpong lists four responses when Christianity was brought to Africa by European Christian missionaries. The first one was the rejection of Christianity by the indigenous Africans in favor of their culture and religion. Indigenous Africans saw Christianity a being foreign and a threat to their indigenous cultural values. The second was the rejection of a western form of Christianity (not Christianity itself) in favor of an African oriented Christianity. In this rejection, African Christians developed African Instituted Churches as alternatives to European oriented churches brought by the missionaries.[155] The third response was the practice of syncretism.[156] African Christians played double standard religious lives. During joys, they adhered to Christianity in its missionary tune; but during problems, they resorted to their traditional culture and religion in order to satisfy themselves to what they thought was not found in Christianity. Mugambi states this concern more clearly when he states: "On the one hand, they accepted the norms introduced by the missionaries who saw nothing valuable in African culture. On the other hand, the converts could not deny their own cultural identity. They could not substitute their denominational belonging for their cultural and religious heritage. Yet they could not become Europeans or Americans merely by adopting some aspects of the missionaries' outward norms of Struggle."

155. Mveng, "Christianity and the Religious Culture of Africa," 7–9; cf. Hastings, *A History of African Christianity*, 67–85.

156. In this book, the concept of 'syncretism' is used to mean "The process by which elements of one religion are assimilated into another religion resulting in a change in the fundamental tenets or nature of those religions. It is the union of two or more opposite beliefs, so that the synthesized form is a new thing. It is not always a total fusion, but may be a combination of separate segments that remain identifiable compartments." (Imbach, "Syncretism," 1062, cf. Schmidt, "The Creation of Afro-Caribbean Religions," 236; Riddle, "Syncretism and New Testament," 17).

conduct."¹⁵⁷ Mugambi's statement means that Africans longed to be in the midst of a foreign religion without jettisoning any of them.

A good example of African syncretistic life among Africans is provided by Richard Cox when writing about the Rangi ethnic group of Kondoa District, Dodoma Region in Tanzania. Cox explains about Rangi Christians:

> Many Rangi do not see a problem with holding on to both ATR and Christian beliefs. For many in the West this is a logical inconsistency, but for the Rangi this is a practical outworking of their lives and cultures. This syncretistic mixture is what has been modeled for them in the past and it seems to work for them practically. Indeed, it could be said about most believers in a particular religious tradition that the belief espoused and the practices adhered to are not logically consistent. Therefore this syncretistic amalgamation is acceptable among the Rangi. It is simply a matter of fact that Rangi Christians do not understand the majority of the implications that Biblical teaching has for their daily lives; thus the reason for the continued syncretism.¹⁵⁸

Moreover, Schineller adds that for most African Christians the "key moments of human life—birth, marriage, healing, death, burial—are celebrated in two different ways and places in Africa, namely in the traditional religious manner, and then in the Christian manner. There is little interaction or integration between the two. Marriage is celebrated in the home in the traditional manner, and then the couple comes to church for the church wedding."¹⁵⁹ This syncretistic way of life embraced by most Africans makes the process of inculturation difficult, challenging and delicate.

The fourth response was the practice of inculturation. What is inculturation? Amore helpful definition of this concept is that of Pedro Errupe as quoted in Schineller. Errupe defines it: "Inculturation is the incarnation of Christian life and of the Christian message in a particular cultural context, in such a way that this experience not only finds expression through elements proper to the culture in question, but becomes a principle that animates, directs and unifies the culture, transforming and remaking it so as to bring about 'a new creation.'"¹⁶⁰ In this practice, African Christians transform the western oriented values which the missionaries came with them as they brought Christianity making them fit in the African way of

---

157. Mugambi, "Christianity and the African Cultural Heritage," 519–520.

158. Cox, "Why Rangi Christians continue to Practice African Traditional Religion?" 8

159. Schineller, "Inculturation: A Difficult and Delicate Task," 109.

160. *Ibid.*

living.¹⁶¹ The process of inculturation is the transformation of the incompatible values within the missionary Christianity making them compatible with the African ways of living and practice in order to make Christianity at home (permanent) to Africans. Hence, inculturation theology, with its origin in the Roman Catholic circle, practiced in the West, Central and East Africa, "is a way of doing Christian theology, a method of reflecting on the Christian faith in relation to the African context using the mediation of African cultural resources."¹⁶²

Ngong has these words about inculturation theology: "This form of theology rejects what is seen as Western imposed forms of theologies [. . .] while calling for the construction of theologies that take the cultures of indigenous peoples seriously. The theology of inculturation can be seen as a form of contextual theology that has characterized Christian theology for almost as long as the faith itself."¹⁶³ It involves the process of rooting the church in a particular culture. Other names which were used in inferring to the development of African theological thinking towards inculturation were African Theology (*Theologia Africana*),¹⁶⁴ African Christian Theology, translation, interculturation, christanization, adaptation, and indigenization/Africanization, Situation theology, Incarnation, *etc*.¹⁶⁵ Therefore, the background for the beginning of inculturation theology is the yearning of Christians for total freedom from the colonial powers—a freedom from both political and cultural domination.¹⁶⁶

The terms listed above, though refer to the same reality of inculturation, have slight differences: *adaptation* refers to selecting some particular aspects (rites, customs or cultural values) from a particular culture purifying them and inserting them to Christian aspects where they seem to be similar. In this process, most of the aspects which seem not to match with Christianity are left unattended. *Indigenization* referred to the promotion of indigenous ministers in the ministry in various levels of the church as a means of making the church owned by the natives themselves. *Reformulation* or *translation* referred to the use of the native languages as a means of

---

161. Ukpong, "Inculturation Theology," 530; *cf.* Balcomb, "Theological Education," 576–577.

162. Ibid., 531; *cf.* Stinton, "Africa's Contribution to Christology," 21–24; Kurgat, "The Theology of Inculturation."

163. Ngong, "Theology as the Construction of Piety," 355.

164. Sawyerr, "What is African Theology?" 17–23; *cf.* Kurgat, "The Theology of Inculturation." There is certainly an existence of African traditional and Islamic theologies. Strictly speaking, the use of the concept of African Theology in this book connotes African Christian Theology.

165. *Cf.* Akao, "The Task of African Theology," 342.

166. Han & Bayers, "A Critical Evaluation," 7.

making natives hear the gospel in their own languages. Incarnation refers to the act of Jesus and his divine presence on earth as a paradigm for the gospel to be present to African cultures. As Jesus Christ became a human being and dwelt among human beings, the gospel needs to incarnate itself into the various cultures where it is communicated. *Interculturation* referred to the interdependence and enrichment between the encountering cultures. Christianity with its cultural background and the African cultures should enrich between themselves as they encounter each other. However, none of these concepts seemed to reflect adequately what is required to be done in order to really make Christianity at home.[167]

The theology of inculturation can be properly explained through considering its importance and necessity to making the life of the church and Christian faith in Africa lasting. Waliggo, quoting Wijngaards, states:

> The durability of Christian faith in Africa will not depend on its network of schools and parishes, hospitals and other institutions. Economic strength and even political support will not guarantee its future. The permanence of Christianity will stand or fall on the question whether it has become truly African: whether Africans have made christian ideas part of their own thinking, whether Africans feel that the Christian world view has become part of truly African aspirations."[168] Basing on this statement, Waliggo defines inculturation to be a "movement which aims at making Christianity permanent in Africa by making it a people's religion and a way of life [for Africans] which no enemy or hostility can ever succeed in supplanting or weakening.[169]

Methodologically, the theology of inculturation has followed two main approaches basing on its starting point. Some theologians have started their theologizing from the biblical text moving to the reality of African people (from text to real lived experience). Examples of such theologians include: Jesse Mugambi, Peter Kanyandago, and Douglas Waruta. These theologians start by drawing themes from the biblical texts and applying it to the current reality of African experiences. Other theologians start from the real lived reality of African people to the text (from real lived experience to biblical text). Some among such theologians include: Judith Bahemuka, Charles Nyamiti, Kwesi Dickson, John Pobee, Harry Sawyerr, Anselm Sanon and Benezet Bujo. In this methodological approach, as Stinton quotes Nyamiti, "the author examines the mystery of Christ from either the perspective of

---

167. Waliggo, "Making a Church that is truly African," 11–12.
168. Waliggo, "Making a Church that is Truly African," 12.
169. *Ibid.*, 13.

the African worldview, or from the angle of some particular theme taken from the African worldview or culture."[170] In using these methodological approaches, inculturation contributes to the Christological quest in the various African contexts.

CONCLUSION

Generally, this chapter has argued that "modern African theology emerged as a response to missionaries' derogatory attitude towards the African cultural-religious traditions and the imposition of Western ecclesial-cultural values on the church in Africa."[171] The forms of contextual theology discussed above are just some of the numerous branches of contextual theology. The emergence of contextual theologies, most of them under the umbrella term of inculturation theology and under the names of the contexts where they originate, indicate the fast growing nature of contextual theology.

One of the propositions argued within this chapter was about the relationship between the concept of place and the articulation of theology. The chapter discussed the concept of place in its various dimensions and the need for theology to be place-oriented. This chapter also discussed what prompted the emergence of a theology that took into account people's places and some of the forms of this place-based theology. Some of the forms discussed are Liberation Theology in Latin America, Black Theology in South Africa and USA, Munjung Theology in Korea, theology of struggle in the Phillipines, Dalit Theology in the context of the Indian caste system, feminist theology and Inculturation theology in Africa north of the Limpopo river.

However, the theology of inculturation, as any other method, has been criticized of being syncretistic as it tends to absorb from African Traditional Religion some values that are contrary to the teachings of the mainstream Christianity; and that it should be treated with care when used in local theologizing to differentiate idea that do not belong to the mainstream Christianity. Critics see that equating the God worshiped in ATR and that of Christianity as being against the teachings of mainstream Christianity.[172] Despite the criticisms mentioned, inculturation stands at the heart of the lives of African Christians at the encounter with Christianity as a foreign religion imposed to African people with their strongly held ATR.

---

170. Stinton, "Africa's Contribution to Christology," 22–23.
171. Han & Bayers, "A Critical Evaluation," 8.
172. Muneja, *HIV/AIDS and the Bible*, 45.

2

Meaning and Practice of Contextual Theology

INTRODUCTION

In the previous chapter, we discussed the concept of place and its relation to contextual theology. We also discussed the reasons for the emergency of contextual theology in the 1970s and the legacy of Shoki Coe in the contextualization of theology. We asked the question as to why contextual theology emerged and stated that the major reason for its emergency was the failure of traditional theology to take seriously the context of people in Africa. Traditional theology failed to provide adequate answers to people's problems, for example, those relating to poverty, suffering due to HIV/AIDS, *etc*. This failure of traditional theology led people into searching for a theology that was relevant to their context.

The first chapter of this book ended by discussing some of the forms of contextual theology in Africa and other parts of of the world. Having discussed some of the forms of contextual theology, we should ask: what then is contextual theology? How urgent is it in the twenty-first century Africa? How should this theology be done in this century in order to cater people's needs? This chapter is concerned about these questions. It concentrates on three aspects: the proposed meaning of contextual theology as theologians understand it, the urgent need for it in the ever-changing African context, and the way it should be done in order to address people's needs in this context.

DEFINING CONTEXTUAL THEOLOGY

There is hardly a satisfactory definition of any concept or terminology that leaves all readers without doubt. Neither can any one of the definitions we attempt in this section be of that nature. This section surveys various attempts towards the meaning of contextual theology and how they illuminate us in our continuous thinking about it. We begin by deducing the meaning of contextual theology from the background of the word "context." According to Rilloma, "The word 'context' originated from the Latin '*contexere*' which means 'to weave or join together.' The noun form '*contextus*' refers to what is woven together, what is held together as connected whole."[1] Rilloma further notes that the word context relates to texts and historical situations. "In relation to a text," Rilloma asserts, "the context may be a unit of words or sentences in which the text is set and to which it is connected (literary context). It may also refer to the historical situation in which the text was set and out of which it arose (historical context)."[2] In his part, Geheman moves from texts to the lives of people. He maintains: "By 'context' we refer to the whole environment in which the people of God live, including the social economic, educational, religious, philosophical and political; in brief, man's culture."[3] In this case, the contextualization of biblical texts and of theology should refer to the cry for the recognition of the relevance of the current place and its questions.

Following the above background of the word context, the definition of contextual theology is best placed within the wide definition of theology, and Christian theology in particular. A theologian Peter O. Okafor defines theology at length:

> Theology is commonly defined as "faith seeking understanding" (*fides quaerens intellectum*). Since what we mean is Christian theology, we can also define it as Christian faith trying to understand the things of God as revealed in Jesus Christ. As Jesus is the Word made flesh, he is God in context [God in place], sharing our condition in the human culturally conditioned world. He was a male, a first century Jew, and shared the culture of his own people. In this mystery of the incarnation, he made use of all that is familiar to us, in order to communicate his divine life and grace. This is the way for theology to follow if it is to remain relevant in today's world. Theology must be contextual. It must speak to man where he is. It must address human questions

1. Rilloma, "Contextualizing Theological Education," 114–115.
2. Ibid., 115.
3. Geheman, *Doing African Christian Theology*, 80.

and concerns in the light of the faith. In this way, theology is no longer simply a study of God but a study of what God says and does in a context. This is because we Christians believe in God who is present and active in each local context—in the face of neighbour and stranger, in the depths of human culture and experience, or in the life we seek to build together. That is why theology ought to be contextual. It is not just a matter of academic analysis, it rather emerges from a life of prayer and practice—in a community that meets God in Word and Sacrament, that listens to the wisdom of Tradition, and that seeks to discern and respond to his presence and action in the world. [. . .] the challenge of contextual theology is the challenge of relevance. Every genuine theological reflection must show its relevance by engaging consciously the context of its theologizing.[4]

In another vein, Gathogo, taking ideas from Mugambi, puts forth this definition of theology: Theology is "a systematic discourse about God, a discourse which can be expressed contextually in Europe, Africa or elsewhere."[5] According to Okafor's and Gathogo's statements above, a theology that tries to express the things of God should take the nature of God as its paradigm. By nature, God is contextual. God revealed the contextual nature through the incarnation of Jesus for the whole world. God became a human being through Jesus and dwelt among people with a particular cultural orientation. Jesus shared with the people of his context the life and experiences of that life. Jesus observed and participated in what was going on in the context of his time. It is therefore in the contextual nature of God where the need for theological relevance is found. In this case, contextual theology poses the challenge of relevance in whatever theological reflection done.

In his book *Models of Contextual theology*, Bevans expounds the above notion further when he says: "There is no such thing as 'theology'; there is only contextual theology [. . .]."[6] Knighton further clarifies, "There is no universal, immutable model of theology, but there are situations in space [including Africa and its diverse cultures] and time, there are cultures and histories, which throw up new questions that demand theological answers [. . .]."[7] Bevans and Knighton speak of theology as being contextually based theology. For them, we cannot speak of theology as being without context.

---

4. Okafor, "The Challenge of Contextual Theology," 1; *cf.* Schreiter, *Constructing Local Theologies*, 75.

5. Gathogo, "Liberation and the Reconstruction," 81.

6. Bevans, *Models of Contextual Theology*, 3.

7. Knighton, "Issues of African Theology," 147.

Every theology has a context, and thus every theology is contextual theology. As a reader of this book, do you agree with them? Why?

One important reason for asserting that every theology is contextual theology is that every theology arises out of particular place, situation, and cultural setting which profoundly shapes its agenda, methodology, and themes of discussion. In the material used for the Study Week of the Southwest Liturgical Conference in 2010, being aware of the importance of culture, Bevans stressed this point:

> All theology is contextual. One can even say that there is no such thing as 'theology,' because there is only contextual theology: African American, Latino/a, Asian, Liberal Protestant, Neo-orthodox, Congolese, feminist or womanist, Thomist, White U.S. American or European. Theology has always been contextual, whether Elohist or Priestly in the Old Testament, or Matthean, Johannine or Pauline in the New Testament. Ephrem the Syrian in the fourth century did theology in a distinctly West Asian way; Augustine theologized in the context of controversies that raised key questions for Christianity: the validity of Baptism, the necessity of grace, the instability of the present world. Aquinas's context was the new culture of thirteenth century Europe and the recent re-discovery of Aristotle; Luther's context was widespread corruption in the church and emerging individuality in Western thought; Teresa of Ávila's was the Catholic Reformation. De las Casas did theology as he argued for the rights of indigenous Americans; Schleiermacher theologized in dialogue with the Enlightenment's "turn to the subjective;" Karl Rahner tried to make sense of a world torn apart by war, and Rosemary Radford Ruether theologizes with the conviction that Christianity must include women's flourishing.[8]

Therefore, Bevans' emphasis is in line with Tutu who also insisted: "There must of necessity" [. . .] "be a diversity of theologies, and our unity arises because ultimately we all are reflecting on the one divine activity to set man free from all that enslaves him."[9] Another theologian, Polkinghorne, emphasizes Bevan's point above by writing: "The accounts that the theologians give us are not utterances delivered from some point of lofty detachment, in-dependent of culture—views from nowhere, as it were—but they are all views from somewhere, offering finite and particular human perspectives

---

8. Bevans, "Contextual Theology," 1; cf. Bevans, *Essays in Contextual Theology* 30–46; Okofor, "The Challenge of Contextual Theology," 7.

9. Knighton, "Issues in African Theology," 147.

onto the infinite reality of God."[10] In this case, the contextualization of theology should refer to people's meaningful responses to their respective situations at the encounter with the gospel message.

Another possible reason for asserting that theology is contextual is the significant shift in the understanding of the nature of truth and knowledge influenced by post-structuralism and postmodernism as being fluid, unstable and tentative. Pears has elaborated the influence of this shift in the understanding of knowledge and its influence to theology:

> In the last half of the twentieth century and into the twenty-first century Christianity has been influenced by a number of cultural shifts. One of these is the [significant] shift from a perspective which views truths and human knowledge as universal to a perspective which views them as shaped, determined and even validated by specific cultural, social and political contexts. This shift is informed by the insights and criticisms of poststructuralism and postmodernism and whilst it is not always played out or followed through to its full conclusions it is nevertheless having a profound impact on the place of Christian theology and the Christian Church in the world today.[11]

According to Pears, the shift in the view of truth and knowledge is one of the sources of theology being done more dialogically than as a theology with claims valid in all places. Theology is no longer inspired, objective, true, beyond questioning and universal regardless of the location it emanates (*theologia perennis*); rather, it is a theology which is shaped and relevant to particular places and their pertinent questions.

According to Bevans, "Doing theology contextually is to do theology in dialogue with two realities: the experience of the past recorded in Scripture and the church's tradition(s) and the experience of the present or the context in which Christian theologians live."[12] The concept of context itself encompasses several aspects. Bevans lists four aspects that constitute the concept of context: "Contexts consist of at least four aspects: present human experience (a personal health crisis, a presidential election), social location (being a woman, being young), one's cultural identity (sometimes closely connected with a particular religion, like Buddhism in Thailand), and change within a context (globalization, democratization)."[13] Therefore, as Muneja quotes Mashau and Fredericks, "our theological reflections

---

10. Pilkinghorne, *Theology in the Context of Science*, 1.
11. Pears, *Doing Contextual Theology*, 7.
12. Bevans, "Contextual Theology," 1, *cf.* Okafor, "Editorial: Pope Francis," viii.
13. Ibid.

about God can only find true meaning when issues raised by the Bible find relevancy in the specific contexts."[14] Through taking seriously the present experience in particular places, contextual theology is something different from traditional theology in both method and perspective—it is something new perspective formed from the old, and is a paradigm shift.

Contextual Theology as a Theology formed from the Traditional

Traditional theology is reflected on faith basing on the two locations (*loci theologici*) which are the *Scripture* and the *tradition*.[15] In most cases, traditional theology bases on these two locations to theologize and is considered as *theologia perennis*, a universal and unchanging theology. Scripture is the Word of God. It is unchanging. The tradition is where Scriptures emanated; it is also unchanging.[16] Okafor rightly states: "traditional/classical theology which was considered as changeless in content and is above culture and historically conditioned expression."[17] Therefore, to theologize, according to traditional theology is to take the unchanging Scriptures and Tradition seriously to produce a universal and unchanging theology. This is the theology which the Church has passed on from the first century throughout until now.

Here it can be noted clearly that both Scripture and Tradition are very far from people's current situations. The Scripture was not intended to current people and their problems. It was intended to people of the first century. The tradition into which Scriptures emerged is not our current twenty-first century tradition. It is the tradition of people of the first century. Now the question is this: What has Scripture and Tradition of the first century to do with people of the current 21st century and their problems? It is in response to this question that a new theological thinking emerges when theologians use the ancient scriptures and traditions to make them relevant to the twenty-first century situation.

We can learn an example from Jesus himself, as God incarnate. His birth, his ministry and his death and resurrection have important things to us. Jesus came to a context where theology was done; there was an understanding of reality according to the contemporary situation. Jesus came with his own perspective to the existing reality. Jesus took the perspective of the

---

14. Muneja, *HIV/AIDS and the Bible*, 42.

15. By "tradition" here we mean the context from which Scriptures emanated, the context from which the authors of scriptures wrote scriptural texts and communicated their messages.

16. Bevans, *Models of Contextual Theology*, 3–5.

17. Okafor, "The Challenge of Contextual Theology," 3.

poor and marginalized: He was born in a poor situation, raised by a poor family, sided with the poor and marginalized people throughout his ministry. Therefore, in its method and perspective, contextual theology follows the footsteps of Jesus and his perspective. In both method and perspective, it presents a paradigm shift from the old way of theologizing to the new way.

Contextual Theology as a Paradigm Shift

The above mentioned perspective of Jesus makes contextual theology important. We can still emphasize that contextual theology is nothing but a *shift in methods of theologizing and perspectives through which theology is done in particular contexts*. It is a shift in point of view through which we articulate theology in the various places. The emergency of various branches of contextual theology in various places, as we noted above, demonstrate that perspectives and methods of theologizing are important for this kind of theology. The question is: What happens when a new theological paradigm emerges? What is expected to happen when contextual theology emerges as a theological paradigm? The social scientist Thomas Kuhn, in his book *The Structure of Scientific Revolutions* provides an illuminating response to what happens when paradigm shift happens. Mligo quotes from Kuhn:

> When the new paradigm emerges, it challenges the existing one forcing it to change the way it dictates scientific practice. At the same time the existing paradigm also resists to the challenge by trying to maintain the existing way of generating knowledge and interpreting it. The revolution emerges when the new paradigm supersedes the existing paradigm by proving that its ideas are worthwhile and people should take their attention towards them. The revolution forces contemporary researchers to adhere to the existing paradigm in whatever they think and act about science.[18]

Moreover, Kee quoting Kuhn, further writes: "Paradigm 'defines for a scientific community the types of questions that may be legitimately be asked, the types of explanation that are to be sought, and the steps of solutions that are acceptable."[19] As Kuhn points out, the emphasis on contextual theology is a paradigm shift that challenges traditional theology forcing researchers to adhere to the patterns and thought forms of particular contexts. Therefore, the theologian Chris Budden clarifies this point: "Contextual theology

---

18. Mligo, *Doing effective Fieldwork*, 90.
19. Kee, *Christian Origins*, 176.

challenges the view that theology is simply reflection on Scripture and tradition seen as two unchanging and culturally neutral sources, and insists that present human experience [in a particular place] is a crucial part of the theological task."[20]

The theological challenge posed by contextual theology is necessary in order to cope with the current context of globalization. Bevans says: "The contextualization of theology—the attempt to understand Christian faith in terms of particular context [perspective]—is really a theological imperative."[21] What does Bevans mean by the above statement? Bevans most likely means that there is something new that needs to be added to traditional theology today in order to make it as contextual as it was in the time when Scriptures were produced.

What is that important thing? That important thing, according to Bevans, is "present human experience" which is the *"locus theologicus"* (another source in doing theology).[22] This present human experience is what we call 'present context' or 'present perspective' vividly experienced in particular places where people live. In the real sense, it is here where we see the difference between contextual and traditional theologies. Taking ideas from Yuzon, Okafor lists two major differences between contextual and traditional theologies:

> In the first place, [contextual theology] recognizes the critical importance of human experience as a source for reflection on Christian faith and moral. Second, due to its rootedness in concrete human experience in a particular culture and society, it speaks primarily to that context. As such, it does not pretend to be unchanging, above culture and universally applicable in a normative way to all other particular contexts at all times and places. Since it is a theology that arises out of a particular context, contextual theology is something that is relevant in relation to a certain place and time. It can therefore be definite, at best, but not definitive.[23]

According to the above statement, contextual theology is traditional because it uses Scriptures and tradition of the first century to understand Christian faith in the current people's experiences of reality in a particular perspective or context. Hence, "By so doing, contextual theology strives not only to gather the experiences that emerge in specific situations or contexts but

20. Budden, "The Necessity of Second People's Theology," 58.
21. Bevans, *Models of Contextual Theology*, 3.
22. Ibid., 4.
23. Okafor, "The Challenge of Contextual Theology," 2.

also strives to actively change the context, and making theology part of the process of cultural renewal."²⁴

Why should present human experience be added to traditional theological understanding of Christian faith? It is mainly because of 'meaning.' Meaning of faith is not the same in all places and at all times. We need to understand Christian faith basing on the way our context leads us to interpret it. This statement has been elaborated very clearly by Bevans when he says: "Reality is not just 'out there'; reality is 'mediated by meaning,' a meaning that we give it in the context of our culture or our historical period, interpreted from our own particular horizon and in our particular thought forms."²⁵ Bevans' stamen indicates that meaning itself is contextual; there is hardly a universal meaning exists.

We can summarize the meaning of contextual theology with Bevans by saying that "doing theology contextually means doing theology in a way that takes into account two things: First, it takes into account the faith experience of the *past* that is recorded in Scriptures and kept alive, preserved, defended—and perhaps even neglected or suppressed—in tradition. [. . .]. Second, contextual theology takes into account the experience of the present, the *context*."²⁶ Here Bevans insists that the lived experiences of people in a particular context are important in order to understand the Scripture and traditions inscribed in the Bible. This means that what is inscribed in the Bible (*i.e.*, Scripture and tradition) need to be understood in the light of our own individual collective experiences in particular contexts.

NEED AND CRITERIA FOR CONTEXTUL THEOLOGY

The Need for a Context-Based Theology

In the previous section we quoted the words from Bevans saying: "The contextualization of theology—the attempt to understand Christian faith in terms of a particular context—is really a theological imperative."²⁷ This statement capitalizes the need for contextual theology. A similar view is held by the theologian Lurdino A. Yuzon. Yuzon holds that doing theology in context is not a voluntary endeavor; rather, it is a mandate. Yuzon asks a question and provides the answer:

24. Ibid., 3.
25. Bevans, *Models of Contextual Theology*, 4.
26. Ibid., 5.
27. Ibid., 3.

Why should theology be contextual? Doing theology in context is not something optional. It is a mandate, an imperative which, as Bevans says, is based on external and internal factors. The external factors include a feeling in the Third World (and to some extent in the First World) of "general dissatisfaction with classical approaches to theology" [...] which do not make sense in non-western cultural patterns and thought forms and have been perceived to be irrelevant in Third World historical realities characterized by rapid changes brought about by western technological advances and the struggles of suffering people for justice, power-sharing and freedom from anti-life forces. Another external factor is the reaction to the "oppressive nature of older approaches" [...] to theology. For instance, individualistic and other-worldly theologies from the west have functioned to justify authoritarian governments and the exploitation and oppression of marginalized and powerless peoples not only in the Third World but also in the First World countries. Also, male-dominated theology and structures have served to exclude women from their rightful places in the life and work of churches the world over. In the Third World, there has been a growing awareness of the fact that a "colonial theology" has nothing to do with the real meaning of Christian faith.[28]

In order to state the need for contextual theology in Africa today basing on the statements provided by Bevans and Yuzon, we need to state more clearly the context into which the church in Africa finds itself.

Context of the Church in Africa in the Twenty-First Century

The Church in Africa is caught in the shackles of the twenty-first century ever-changing context—the context of globalization and its demands. Bevans elaborates in the following eleven points what type of Church is it.[29] First, *it is a Church of Great Diversity*. When we talk of "Church" we do not talk of buildings; we mostly talk of people that believe in Jesus Christ and his message of salvation. It is a collection of believers whereby the word of God is preached accurately and the Sacraments administered accurately. In this collection, believers are not the same everywhere. They are different in cultural orientation, political and economic orientations. The way worship is done differs from place to place; people are different in ways they understand sacraments, interpret Scriptures, *etc*. They also differ in their

28. Yuzon, "Towards a Contextual Theology."

29. Bevans, "What has Contextual Theology to Offer the Church."

experience of life. Taking an example of the African Church, the theologian Orobator states: "Ecclessiology in Africa is neither one nor homogeneous; an attempt to trace the historical trajectory and map the future course of the Christian community in Africa ought to take into account its fundamentally pluralistic and diverse nature."[30] Orobator's statement indicates that diversity is the real tune of the twenty-first century Church in Africa. As Orobator further notes: "Its nature, mission, and structure are variously understood by the different ecclesial bodies, denominations, groups, communities, etc."[31] So, this diversity calls for the need to understand Christian faith according to where we are.

Second, *it is a World Church*. The major dogmatically known petition in the Christian Creed is that the Church of Jesus Christ is universal. It is a Catholic Church. The Church of the Twenty-first century is a global church. This assertion means that the church is located in a varying population with varying challenges. Most Christians are from the so-called Third Worlds (Africa, Latin America) and Asia, especially Philippines, South Korea and China. However, the number of Christians increases in these worlds more greatly. Nowadays scholars talk of the North having a big theology but a small church, and the South having a Big church but a small theology. As a reader of this book, what is your opinion on this point?

In considering about the above question, look at statistics according to Bevans and compare with what scholars claim and your own opinion:

- In the year 1900, there were 521712000 Christians in the whole world.
- In the mid-2009, there were 2,149,761 Christians.
- The rate of increase of Christians in the South is larger than in the North.[32]

A theologian Straub, taking ideas from the Pew Charitable Trust study, adds the following demographic information: "The global Christian population has increased from 600 million in 1910 to the current levels. During these years, the center of global Christianity has gradually shifted from Europe and the Americas that claimed 93% of Christianity in 1910 down to 63% of the global whole as of 2010. Christianity in Africa jumped from just 9% of the African population to 63% in the same 100-year period."[33]

It is envisaged that in the above demographic information most of the Christians belong to the Pentecostal churches and charismatic renewal

30. Orobator, "The future of Ecclesiology in Africa," 37.

31. *Ibid.*

32. Bevans, "What has Contextual Theology to Offer the Church," 4; *cf.* Ferdinando, "Christian Identity," 121.

33. Straub, "The Pentecostalization of Global Christianity," 208.

movements within historical churches. Straub provides the definition and categories of Pentecostals:

> Scholars have attempted various divergent ways of defining Pentecostalism, some of which are ambiguous and of little use, while others attempt to demonstrate 'distinctiveness' and create unnecessarily strained relationships with other Christians as a result." Four similar and often overlapping strands of global Pentecostalism have been identified. *Classic Pentecostalism* emerged in the early 20th century out of the Azusa Street revival of Los Angeles. The largest group are the Assemblies of God, at 67.3 million globally. Second are a large number of unaffiliated groups that hold aspects of Pentecostal doctrine and practice called *Independents*. Examples would be churches called African Initiated Churches that emerged in Africa in the early 20th century in the post-colonial era. Third are the *Charismatics*, traditionally nonPentecostal groups that have come to adopt a measure of Pentecostal theology and practice, such as Charismatic Catholics. A so-called *second wave* of Pentecostal revival began in the United States in the late 1960s and touched the mainline denominations, reaching into the World Council of Churches. Finally, there are independent mega churches, neo-charismatics, and Prosperity Gospelers. These churches have sprung up across the global south in Africa, Latin America, and Asia. They have a huge impact on the changing shape of global Christianity, often exporting their theological particulars back to traditional Christian nations like the United States.[34]

According to the report from the Pew Research Centre on Religion and Public Life, the Pentecostal churches and charismatic renewal movements sum up a quarter of almost 2 billion Christians of the world now.[35]

In Africa, there has been a growing number of Pentecostal Christians since its inception in the early 20th century. Straub reports thus as he wrote in the year 2016: "Pentecostalism reached Africa in the aftermath of Azusa Street and now boasts about 200 million adherents, a staggering 63% of which are Neo Pentecostals. Nigeria has 84.5 million Christians out of 183.5 million people, 56 million who claim Pentecostalism. In South Africa, 24 million of 43.8 million Christians are Pentecostal in a country of 55 million. Similar

---

34. *Ibid.*, 210 (Italics for emphasis are in original). Straub reports that "The movement reached the World Council of Churches through David DuPlessis (1905—1997)" (see Straub, "The Pentecostalization of Global Christianity," 215). The detailed discussion of the Prosperity gospel and its tenets will be done in chapter five of this book.

35. Pew Research Centre on Religion and Public Life, "Spirit and Power—A 10 Country Survey."

figures could be listed for The Democratic Republic of Congo. Pentecostalism has become an African phenomenon that shows no signs of abating."[36]

What do the above statistics project? They most likely project the tremendous global changes in the centre of gravity of Christianity. The missiologist Samuel Escobar once stated: "around the world today there is a growing awareness that Europe and North America, the strongholds of Christianity at the beginning of the century, are rapidly becoming pagan territories where the Christian presence must take again a missionary stance."[37]

However, the dream of the shift of Christianity from the North to the South is addressed by the theologian Philip Jenkins. Jenkins in his well-received book *The Next Christendom: The Coming of Global Christianity*, published by Oxford University Press, suggested that the church lives in an extraordinary time whereby there are tremendous changes in the orientation of Christendom.[38] From the long-held Christianity that is Euro and North American-centred, transformation takes place towards a different loci. The centre of gravity of Christianity is now moving from the North to the South, to Africa, Asia and Latin America. In this book, Jenkins believes that Christianity and civilization that made the North to behave in a hegemonic way towards the southern poor nations is now the same Northern Christian civilization in the dying stages.

In his article, Jenkins states:

> In the world today, there are approximately two billion Christians. Of those, the largest contingent, about 530 million, live in Europe. Close behind is Latin America, with 510 million; Africa has 390 million; and Asia has 300 million. However, if we project that firm into the future, the numbers change quite rapidly. By 2025, the title of 'the most Christian' continent—the continent with the largest number of Christians—will be in competition between Africa and Latin America. If we move further into the future, however, there is no doubt that by about 2050, Africa will win. In terms of population distribution, Christianity will be a religion of Africa and the African diaspora, which will, in a sense, be the heartland of Christianity.[39]

36. Straub, "The Pentecostalization of Global Christianity," 217–218.

37. Escober, "The Search for a Missiological Christology," 200.

38. Several other scholars have advocated this idea of the shift in the center of gravity of Christianity. Gatwa reports that "Mbiti, Walls, Bediako, Jenkins and others suggested that the centres of the church's universality were no longer in Geneva, Rome, Athens, Paris, London or New York, but in Lagos, Buenos Aires, Kinshasa, Addis Ababa and Manila." (Gatwa, "The Cross-Cultural Mission," 84).

39. Jenkins, "The Next Christendom," 113–114; *cf.* Kombo, "The Past and Presence," 104–105.

In the above projection, Jenkins sees Christianity to be growing inversely between the Global North and the Global South. While Christianity decreases in the North, it grows large in the South.

Jenkins' prophecy focuses on the increase and decrease in the number of Christians without touching other aspects that significantly make the North remain central. We agree with Jenkins at least in this aspect of numbers. The number of Christians has been increasing in Africa making the continent possibly be in the lead in the Jenkins' projected year. However, Jenkins hardly considers the issues like the economic hegemony of the North which enhance them to publish more volumes than the South and the long history of their Christian civilization which the North has ever boasted of. These aspects still make the North outstanding. Through their economic power, the North makes their theology greater by increasing publications despite their smaller number of practicing Christians. Through their history, the name still remains as a region that has influenced the world Christianity for so long.

Moreover, Gathogo, quoting Mugambi, adds another challenge to Jenkin's projections:

> Christians cannot quantify the idea that the shifting has now come to Africa when there are only a few written books by African theologians. To add an insult to an injury, even some books that are already authored by African theologians, are published in the North Atlantic (cf. Orbis books in New York, Regnum in UK among others). This makes them too costly for African Christians to afford. Mugambi regrets that even the most outspoken advocates of indigenisation and inculturation are foreign missionaries to Africa—and not African Christians themselves![40]

Therefore, despite the small number, we would argue, the North has not totally lost its influence on the ongoing changes to world Christianity.

The worst challenge to Jenkin's proposal has been recently posed by Togarasei in the article: "Modern/Charismatic Pentecostalism as a form of 'Religious' Secularisation in Africa." In this article, Togarasei purports that despite that African churches are flocking with large numbers of Christians, this can hardly be taken as an ultimate measure for Africa being the center of gravity of the Christian religion in the current African context as is the western context. Since secularization was one of the major factors to make the number of religious adherents decrease in the western world in favor of the worldly aspects, leading to the less influence of religion in the public

---

40. Gathogo, "Historical Developments," 28.

sphere, this is hardly the same form of secularization in our current African context. Togarasei believes that there is a different form of secularization in Africa despite the resurgence of large churches with large number of adherents.

Togarasei calls the secularization in Africa as "Religious Secularization" with the connotation that religion (in this case Christianity) is the major cause of the secularization process. The emergence of Neo-Pentecostal Christianity in the middle of the twentieth century and its peak in the 1980s and 1990s and its emphatic preaching on the prosperity gospel, attracting the attention of poor people in Africa, has caused the secularization process to take root. It implies the dawn of a new era in the history of Christianity in Africa. It also indicates the break from the mainline Christianity and African Independent Christianity.[41]

Meyer explains this shift more clearly:

> If in the 1980s Independent Churches were found to be attractive, by African Christians as well as researchers, above all because they seemed to offer a more "authentic," Africanized version of Christianity than do the presumably Western-oriented mainline churches, current Pentecostal-Charismatic Churches (PCCs) appear to derive their mass appeal at least partly from propagating a "complete break with the past'. [. . .]. Dissociating themselves from both mainline churches and African Independent, or as they call them, "Spiritual" Churches, the new PCCs promise to link up their born-again believers with global circuits. Although PCCs gain an ever-increasing number of followers, also from the older AICs.[42]

The break which Meyer suggests above indicates the break from Christianity based on the cultural background of the African people towards Christianity seeking the life of secularism and prosperity, stressing on the economic dimension of being born-again.

It is agreed by most scholars that prosperity gospel and Neo-Pentecostalism as a whole are materialistic, individualistic, and this-worldly phenomena. Their major emphasis is the gains of prosperity in health and wealth in this world, not in the other world. Having this emphasis, most churches in Africa have embraced Neo-Pentecostal Christianity just because of the material and health prosperity it promises and not for the sake of God's worship in spirit and truth. Togarasei emphasizes this point when he says that "numbers and observation of religious functions cannot be used

---

41. Lewison, "Pentecostal Power," 33–37.
42. Meyer, "Christianity in Africa," 448.

on their own to measure levels of religiosity. Like in the days of Amos (5: 21–24), the eighth century Hebrew Bible prophet, people can throng places of worship as a matter of routine, yet without any religious convictions."[43]

According to Togarasei's article, religion has been an agent of secularization because it has accepted some secular aspects to be incorporated in religious practices. For example, the way in which modern means are used in music, the emphasis in health in the here and now, the emphasis on wealth in preaching and teachings, and the shunning of post-mortem doctrines and the *Parousia* which emphasize on the other-worldly life in favor of proximate (this-worldly) issues. Togarasei concludes that "the Church has unconsciously introduced secularism by promoting a privatised, departmentalised religion that does not effectively challenge the myths of economism."[44]

In fact, what Togarasei wants us to understand is that the secularization which emerged in the West due to the rise of materialism and individualism, also caused by religion (*i.e.*, the Protestant Reformation and its teachings—Luther's and Wesley's), the same secularization happens now in Africa, but in a different form and context. While the secularism which emerged in the West was characterized by the dwindling in number of people who embraced religion and who attended worship services, African religious secularism is characterized by the rise in the number of religious (Christian) adherents who join religion because of poverty, longing for divine uplift in health and material. In that case, the unbelief of people in the West and their turn to secular sphere is almost similar to that of Africa, but in a different guise.

Third, *it is a Multicultural Church which exists in a Multicultural World*. Despite the allusion of the Christian Church as being One, Holy, Catholic and Apostolic, it is located in a context of many cultures and many religions. What is becoming vivid is the homogenization of world cultures into a new culture, a culture that results from the blending of different world cultures. This homogenization of cultures is not something foreign. It has its origin from the Scriptures. The Bible itself is not a collection of books from one culture. It is a collection of books through which God revealed oneself in different cultures with different challenges and experiences. This multicultural nature of biblical books suggests that the Bible is a collection of different cultures which can either be accepted or challenged in our contemporary cultural orientations. And this challenge or acceptance is what makes dialogue between the Bible and our current cultural situation important and necessary.

---

43. Togarasei, "Modern/Charismatic Pentecostalism," 59.
44. Ibid., 61–62.

Another aspect which the multicultural nature of the church has its bases is the doctrine of God's Incarnation. God became a human being not in a vacuum, but in a particular culture. After his incarnation, Jesus lived in a highly multicultural Greco-Roman world. However, the message he preached went beyond the cultural orientations of his time. For example, Jesus' message to love God and one's neighbor is not limited to Jesus Jewish context. It transcends the Jewish cultural context to the Gentiles (cf. Matthew 15: 21–28; Mark 7: 24–30; Luke 10: 25–37; and John 4: 1–39). This incarnation of God indicates that God created cultural differences between human beings for God's own purpose and loves such cultural differences. Cultural differences exist for the fulfillment of God's wills.

During the Pentecost day, the multicultural nature of the church was vividly seen. People from various linguistic backgrounds (Acts 2: 1–13), which represented their cultural orientations, gathered at Jerusalem and were baptized as being members of the church. The gathering included both Jews and Gentiles from different corners of the Greco-Roman world. The multilingual worship in the Pentecost day indicates the various cultural differences which has existed in the church of God throughout its life until now, and will continue until Jesus returns in the second coming.

In regard to what happened during the Pentecost, Ayanga maintains that

> although there was a diversity of cultures, backgrounds and experiences present at the venue, there is no record of an attempt to translate or interpret what the Apostles were saying. [. . .] difference and diversity were not a problem at Pentecost. Instead, what happened was an opportunity to differences. These members of the new born church were united, not on the basis of sameness and uniformity; rather the basis of their unity was their ability to understand and accept God's gift of salvation and the power that comes from the Spirit of God.[45]

Therefore, Ayanga's words highlight that belonging to the One, Holy, Catholic and Apostolic Church does not mean that members of the Church belong to one culture. They are in different cultures and worldviews. Yet, they understand one another through the power of the Holy Spirit who unites the Church despite its members' differing worldviews and cultural backgrounds. As Ayanga puts it, "God uses difference and diversity to show the power that we can have with open channels of communication, not just

---

45. Ayanga, "Globalisation," 172.

between believers but with those who are different and outside of our immediate circle."[46]

The most fluorescent multicultural nature of the church is in the ministry of the Apostles after the Ascension of Jesus. Some ministered to Gentiles (*e.g.*, Paul) and others to people of Jewish background. Paul, though a Jew, preached the gospel to Gentiles being sensitive to the Gentile context, especially in the question of circumcision. It should be clear that the Apostles who preached to people of Jewish context emphasized circumcision as a prerequisite for belonging to the covenant of God's people while those who preached to Gentiles did not. These differences in emphasis among Apostles' preaching indicate that the Church of Jesus Christ belonged to people of all cultures. The early church was a multicultural church and continues to be a multicultural church until now.

Moreover, the multicultural nature of the church is vivid in the Great Commission of Jesus Christ. Before his ascension, Jesus commanded that the Good News be preached to people of all nations. It means that the cultural boundaries are not hindrances for salvation. The work of Jesus at the cross was not a monocultural event. It was a multicultural one. The good news of salvation needs to be preached to all people for them to hear and believe in Jesus their Lord. The multicultural nature of the Great Commission suggests for the work of the missionaries from Europe and North America towards other non-Christian nations in the word in the twentieth century. People from various cultural orientations become one people, a church of Jesus Christ.

Fourth, *it is a Church of the Young People.* The church of the 21st century belongs to young people. In other words we can say that this church belongs to the youth. The youth are the largest population in all churches. However, they are the ones who are highly affected by the effects of globalization. How does globalization affect youth? The effect of globalization to the youth is mostly on their thinking and worldview. Most youth are affected by the current Hip Hop music, and the current ways of worship which involve body movements. The lack of globalization flavors in churches cause most youth become inactive in those churches making them mostly nominal members leaving churches in the hands of old people. Since the youth are the largest population, it is a mandate that the Church adheres to demands of the twenty-first century globalization.

It is necessary to consider the youth in churches and societies. It is important to recognize their presence not only that they are the majority; rather, because they are both the most vulnerable group and the group

---

46. *Ibid.*

involved in the process of change engendered by globalization. However, as Ilie states: "Young people are not the only vulnerable to the vast changes brought on by the process of globalization, but can also be the key change agents. Despite this young people are often ignored both in the literature and in the sphere of political decision–making."[47] Their voices are not heard in the public sphere. Therefore, the most vulnerable group and most potential group for social change, the youth is an important group for the consolidation of the Church of the twenty-first century and its development.

Why should we consider the youth as being more vulnerable to the effects of globalization? It is mainly because of their ability to adapt to ongoing changes brought about by tools of globalization. Gidley puts this point clear when she states: "The Mass Media (such as Television, music), and in particular the New Media (such as the Internet) are important tools in the process of spreading the global culture to young people around the world and conversely can be used as a platform for the networking of resistance."[48] In that case, youth as change agents, can be both for the support or rejection of the effects of globalization in their local cultures and religious affiliations.

Fifth, *it is a persecuted Church*. In the introduction to her book *The Persecuted Church Devotional*, Beverly J. Pegues writes: "More Christians were martyred in the twentieth century than all previous centuries combined. All over the world men and women who heard about Jesus Christ and chose to follow Him were slaughtered for their choice. This onslaught has continued unabated into our new century."[49] As Pegues asserts in her book, most of the Christians that form the Church of the 21st century are persecuted in one way or another. They are racially segregated, gender persecuted, or are persecuted in one way or another because of bearing witness to the truth.

The resurgence of incurable diseases, such as AIDS, Ebola, and the current *Coronavirus disease 2019 (COVID-19)*[50] make the Church vulnerable and a suffering entity because most youth that form the main working force die of such diseases. The death of such youth leaves orphans, who become a burden to other members of the Church. In this case, the death causing diseases make the Church have a chain of suffering.

Sixth, *it is a Poor Church*. Poverty spreads throughout the whole church. Poverty is not only material (lack of enough money), but also lack

---

47. Ilie, "The effects of Golobalization," 66.

48. Gidley, "Globalization and Its Impact," 93, *cf.* Nwadialor, "Pentecostal Hermeneutics," 1283–1284.

49. Pegues, *The Persecuted Church*, xiii.

50. *Coronavirus disease 2019 (COVID-19)* is caused by the coronavirus named *Severe Acute Respiratory Syndrome coronavirus 2 (SARS-CoV-2)*. This virus was first detected in Wuhan China in December 2019.

of good relationship. In this case, all churches in the world have a poverty of some sort. In Africa, for example, we do not mostly speak of poverty in terms of relationship because, philosophically and etymologically, Africans are relational beings. The philosophy of "I am because we are" shows that the lives of Africans are characterized by relationship wherever they are. This means that the life of most Africans is not individualistic and solitary; and their poverty is not relational, but material. On the other hand, the poverty of people in the western world is mostly different from that of Africans. People in these states are rich materially (economically) but poor relationally. The scourges of individualism and secularism have made most people undergo solitary lives, each one fighting for his or her own survival. The poverty of relationship makes most people in these states undergo psychological torture and suffering despite their abundant wealth.[51]

Seventh, *it is a Church which is in a more Drastic Climatic Change*. Nowadays, climatic change is a reality. Rain seasons are not as they used to be. Change in sunlight intensity, change in air composition in the atmosphere, change in the atmospheric pressure, change in humidity, *etc*, are the reality of the present world. Diara and Christian have echoed this situation:

> The challenges of climate change to the human ecology are overwhelming. In the whole world today, there are clear evidences of increase in climate change induced environmental hazards that invariably militate against the natural as well as the socio-economic security of most nations of the world. Persistent droughts and flooding, off season rains and dry spells have become common phenomena today. For instance, in south eastern states of Nigeria, the impacts of change include heat stress, absence of harmattan, unpredictable rainfall patterns, heavier rains, gully erosion, flooding and landslides. In addition to other factors, these hazards have affected soil-fertility, water and forest resources, settlement infrastructure and farmlands [. . .].[52]

We agree with Diara that "there is no such thing as a 'normal climate' or average climate, for as the weather changes from day to day, so also does the climate change from year to year [. . .]."[53] Theology has to speak to this drastically changing climate.

The causes for the climate changes are categorized into two as Diara puts them:

---

51. Wafawanaka, "African Perspectives on Poverty," 495–496; *cf.* Kimilike, *Poverty in the Book of Proverbs*; Wyngaard, "In Search of Root Causes of Poverty."

52. Diara & Christian, "Theology of Climate Change," 85–86.

53. *Ibid.*, 86.

> Climate can change due to forces external to the climate system (e.g., arrangement of continents, volcanic eruptions, and changes in the intensity of sunlight). It can also change as a result of forces internal to the climate system (e.g., atmospheric composition, clouds), or because of anthropogenic (human-caused) changes (e.g., large-scale modifications of the land surface and atmospheric composition of greenhouse gases). Humans are however the major inducer and sufferers of climate change. In fact, the term 'Climate Change' commonly refers to influences on climate resulting from human practices. This is because increases in the concentration of greenhouse gases in the atmosphere resulting largely from burning of fossil fuels and deforestation, have led to an observed and projected warming of the earth, known as the enhanced greenhouse effect. This is why many scientists regard human-caused (anthropogenic) global climate change to be the most important environmental issue of our times [...].[54]

In this case, the human being stands at the centre of most of the climatic changes that occur in the world.

However, at the very early existence of humanity, it was recalled that the human being is responsible for the environment and the weather changes in it. God commissioned the human being as is written in the book of Genesis: "Then the Lord God took the man and put him in the garden to tend and keep it." (Genesis 2: 15) Therefore, it is the responsibility of human beings to respond to the current disasters caused by dramatic climate change in all their dimensions.

What does Contextual Theology Offer the Church in the Twenty-First Century?

Now, having discussed the context of the twenty-first century church above, we have to respond to the question: Why do we need contextual theology today in this twenty-first century? Bevans provides three main reasons for this need: First, *Contextual Theology provides us with a New Agenda for our Theologizing.* There have been different agendas in the life of the church from the first century until now. The church of the first century had its own agenda, the church of the Middle Ages, the church of the Medieval period, the church of the Reformation, *etc.* had their own agendas. Moreover, the present church has its own agenda that is different from the past agendas. For example, as

54. *Ibid.*

we write this book, the *Coronavirus disease 2019 (COVID-19)* has become an agenda, not only for world nations and their various affairs, but also for the church and its theology. *Coronavirus disease 2019 (COVID-19)* does not only affect human health, politics, aviation, social well-beings and economy, but also human spiritual well-being and religious affiliation.

Yet, we can still ask: Why were they different agendas in various stages of the life of the church? It is mainly because "Context not only shapes the content and method of our theologizing. It also determines the questions we ask and highlights the things we see as important."[55] This means that what was important in the first century, was not necessarily important in the 2nd century; what was important in the third century was not necessarily important in the Medieval or Reformation periods, and so goes the story until the present church. What was important during the fight for freedom among states in the 1960s is not the same as this time when the *coronavirus disease 2019 (COVID-19)* ravages humanity. What is seen as being important determines the type of questions we have to ask. What is narrated in Scripture was important to people of the first century. It is what provided their agenda. Since the church of the 21st century has its own important issues; and the questions it raises need to be related to the current agenda.

What is the agenda of the Church of the twenty-first century in Africa? The main agenda of the twenty-first century Church in Africa is to have a theology that honors the present experiences of its church members. "A theology that honors the experience of context will be one that is not tied to Western ways, themes, and methods of theology."[56] In contextual theology we deal with questions like: How can a Christian symbol of baptism be understood by the Maasai who conceives powering of water onto the woman's head to be a ritual that curses her to barrenness? How can the Maasai understand God as being more powerful than the lion? How does it mean to talk about God in the midst of a non-discriminating pandemic like the *coronavirus disease 2019 (COVID-19)* jeopardizing scientific advancements and human intellectual nature? What does it mean to "subdue the earth" in the midst of the *coronavirus disease 2019 (COVID-19)* and its devastating social, economic and cultural effects? All these questions and the like need to make people understand Christian faith in their own lived experiences.

Second, *Contextual Theology provides us a New Method of Doing Theology*. In the old method, theology was conceived as being for the clergy. As Morekwa observes:

---

55. Bevans, "What has the Contextual Theology to offer the Church," 12.
56. Bevans, "What has Contextual Theology to Offer the Church," 11.

> In the past theology was reserved for clergy. The Church and theology strongly supported the privileged position of the clergy as the first estate in the social set-up of the old order. That kind of attitude confined theology to the clergy's theories and ideologies. [. . .]. The study of theology at universities and colleges influenced people to hold the perception that the Bible belongs to the clergy and theological experts. This led to the belief that the clergy in the society are the only ones in possession of God's wisdom and people should only follow their interpretations.[57]

This perception means that the clergy were the ones who were eligible to speak about theology and the church, not the normal church members and their life experiences. In this case, theology became a coded language to be spoken and understood only by the clergy.

The main concern of contextual theology is to provide methods of doing contextual theology that take the real experiences of people seriously, not only clergy. It provides us with methods that enhance new thinking about the Christian faith through the guidance of contexts. A good example is the current situation where the *coronavirus disease 2019 (COVID-19)* has made people equal in terms of vulnerability to infection. The *Coronavirus disease 2019 (COVID-19)* hardly discriminates between clergy and lay, poor and rich, white and black, etc. The virus teaches the world that the method that values people who are mostly discriminated by the hegemonic methods is required in the midst of crisis. Some of the methods have been proposed by: Bevan's book *Models of Contextual Theology*, Mligo's book *Jesus and the Stigmatized*, West's book *Contextual Bible Study*, etc.

All the mentioned theologians emphasize that doing theology should go hand in hand with the inner transformation of the perspective of the theologian. They also emphasize that, methodologically, theology should start *from below*, from the lived experiences of untrained lay theologians, and not from the lofty and quiet offices of trained theologians and clearngy. They further emphasize that theology should be a dialogue between the experiences of the past (scriptures and tradition) and the experiences of the present (the current context and its lived questions). Therefore, the great interlocutor of contextual theology, as discussed before, is the normal person, who lives in a real context with real experiences of life in a context he or she is.

Third, *Contextual Theology provides us with New Voices*. The new voices provided will depend on the questions asked in particular contexts. The contexts of economic poverty will bring out new voices in that context and

---

57. Morekwa, "Doing Theology in the Post Liberation Era," 54.

the context of relational poverty will also bring out new voices in that context. Moreover, contextual theology challenges traditional theology on both methods of doing theology and reading the Bible. In this case, the voices raised are important treasures needed by the church of the 21st century.

In traditional theology, some of the biblical texts were silenced because they were thought to be unfit for the use in churches. Texts like that of the adulterous woman in the gospel of John, most of the book of Song of Songs, and the story of Tamar in the Old Testament are good examples of silenced text in the Bible. Moreover, the voices of some people in various contexts were silenced, for example those of children, women, people with albinism, old people with red eyes in some places in Africa, poor people are those people whose cultures humiliate them. In contextual theology, all these silenced voices are revived and listened because they have important contributions to offer. As the current worldly crises like the *coronavirus disease 2019 (COVID-19)* and the HIV and AIDS provide equal chances of infection among all people, contextual theology provides equal rights to all people to do theology, especially those who experience the real life. Basing on this equal provision of chances among various groups of people to reflect about the word of God in their own contexts, one can imagine the various branches of contextual theology discussed in this book, *i.e.*, liberation theology, minjung theology, black theology, *etc*.

Fourth, *Contextual Theology provides us with a New Dialogue*. The Theology done by the Church of the twenty-first century needs to be contextual. This assertion means that theology needs to take the experiences of particular contexts as points of dialogue. Most traditional theologians have challenged contextual theologians of being too contextual that they forget some global aspects. However, currently, we conceive of contextual theology as encompassing both the global and the local. This is what Robert Schreiter says in his book *The New Catholicity*. Schreiter is convinced that "Theology must also have a universalizing function, by which is meant an ability to speak beyond its own context, and an openness to hear voices from beyond its own boundaries. [. . .]. Theology cannot restrict itself only to its own immediate context; if the message of what God has done in Christ is indeed Good News for all peoples, then the occurrence of grace in any setting has relevance for the rest of humanity."[58]

Since the Church of God is One and lives in the diversity of cultures, this diversity makes the dialogue between the biblical text and the cultures inevitable. This is because the Bible and its message were not intended to the present cultures. They were intended to recipients of the message in the

---

58. Schreiter, *The New Catholicity*, 4.

respective centuries which the Bible texts were written. Therefore, in order for readers of the twenty-first century cultures to do justice to biblical texts of the first century they read, there must be a dialogue between the two distant cultures (the current twenty-first and the ancient culture located in the biblical texts).

Criteria for Contextual Theology

In the previous section, we discussed the nature of the Church that exists in the twenty-first century and what contextual theology offers the Church in its first century context. This section discusses the five criteria of doing contextual theology basing on Rose Donkor's analysis.[59] The first criterion is based on the starting point. Contextual theology starts from the specific to the general. It is inclusive in nature. It starts from specific lived experiences of people within particular cultures towards general theological formulations. This means that such theology takes in account the experiences of issues in the contemporary context and the implications such issues have to contemporary people.

A good example of this kind of inductive theologizing is found in the Korean *Minjung* Theology. Kim, quoting Park contends:

> The basic hermeneutical task of minjung theology is not to interpret the Bible (text) in the light of the Korean situation (the context), but to interpret the suffering experience of the Korean minjung (the context) in the light of the Bible (text). Minjung theology contends that the minjung do not exist for the authority of the Bible, but the authority of the Bible exists for the freedom of the minjung. This does not mean that the minjung are more important than the Bible; it means that the minjung are a starting point for a biblical hermeneutics.[60]

In this case, as just said before, contextual theology is inductive in its nature.

The second criterion is that contextual theology should focus on formulating and answering contemporary life questions. It should inquire about God's role on particular situations. This is because, in some situations, people in a particular situation hardly see God in their midst. Therefore, some important questions are like: Is there God in this situation? How can we establish the Kingdom of God in this situation? What is an appropriate Christian response to this situation? Is there any will of God for what is

---

59. Donkor, "Criteria for Developing a Relevant Contextual Theology," 15–17.
60. Kim, "Minjung Theology," 61; *cf.* Fernandez, "Towards a Theology of Struggle."

going on here, *etc*? These questions focus on exploring the existing situation in order to find possible answers for them in regard to God's dealings with people in particular situations.

Third, as Jesus did, contextual theology should focus on a particular group of people in society: the marginalized and needy people. The lived experience of this group does not leave aside the experiences of those who marginalize; rather, the knowledge and scrutiny of the experiences of the marginalized group provides a room towards knowing the experiences of those who marginalize as well. In this case, there is no group of people remains unattended.

The fourth criterion is the dialogue between experiences. The experience of the past documented in the Bible and transmitted from one generation to the other through the church should dialogue with the experience of the present as lived by people in particular contexts. This means that reading the Bible dialogically has to consider the tradition inscribed in it beyond what it says. It is questioning it to hear what it says in light of present experiences. Hence, as Rilloma rightly says: "Effective contextualization [of theology] calls for continuous dialogue between biblical text and the cultural context."[61] The missiologist Samuel Escobar, quoting Stott and Coote, has succinctly put it when referring to the work of evangelical theology in Latin America:

> Today's readers [of the Bible] cannot come to the text in a personal vacuum, and should not try to. Instead, they should come with an awareness of concerns stemming from their cultural background, personal situation, and responsibility to others. These concerns will influence the questions which are put to the Scriptures. What is received back, however, will not be answers only, but more questions. As we address Scripture, Scripture addresses us. We find that our culturally conditioned presuppositions are being challenged and our questions corrected. In fact we are compelled to reformulate our previous questions and ask fresh ones. So the living interaction precedes.[62]

We agree with Escobar when he quotes the words of Stott and Coote saying that theological imperialism and provincialism are the worst enemies of dialogue and should be avoided in all costs. He further notes: "A church's theology should be developed by the community of faith out of Scripture in

---

61. Rilloma, "Contextualizing Theological Education," 120.

62. Escobar, "The Search for a Missiological Christology," 201–202; *cf.* Kahakwa, "Interpretative Contextual Based Models," 67–68.

interaction with other theologies of the past and present, and with the local culture and its needs."⁶³

The fifth criterion has to do with those who do contextual theology and their attitude. Doing contextual theology requires commitment towards transformation of the existing situations. Contextual theology is not primarily a theoretical enterprise; it is mainly praxis involving actions and reflections. The action and reflection involves the community itself, depending on their lived experiences, with the commitment towards bringing change in the existing situation. Therefore, the trained theologian remains the facilitator of the community's action and reflection process when giving birth of theology out of their interaction with the experience of the past as they read the Bible.

WHO DOES CONTEXTUAL THEOLOGY AND HOW IS IT DONE?

Interlocutors of Contextual Theology

Having discussed the five criteria for doing contextual theology in the previous section, this section focuses more on the main interlocutors in the process of doing contextual theology. The above question inquires for the theologian in the process of doing theology. It is common in traditional theology that a theologian is trained and equipped with all the necessary skills in seminaries or universities. According to traditional theology, the trained theologian does theology by using the skills he or she acquired from the training. This way of doing theology is probably not the same in contextual theology because the theology that emerges from the theologian is of very little help to the community members that are to use that theology. The theologian in contextual theology is highlighted by both Schreiter and Bevans. Schreiter states that the resources of the professional theologian are not to be ignored, yet it should not be allowed to dominate the theologizing process because that will be most a traditional way of doing theology.

The community at which the professional theologian interacts should be allowed to theologize, but should not be allowed to ignore the resources of the inputs of the professional theologian. Schreiter states:

> To ignore the resources of the professional theologian is to prefer ignorance over knowledge. But to allow the professional theologian to dominate the development of a local theology seems to

---

63. *Ibid.*, 203.

> introduce a new hegemony into often already oppressed communities. In the development of local theologies, the professional theologian serves as an important resource, helping the community to clarify its own experience and to relate it to other experiences of other communities past and present. Thus the professional theologian has an indispensable but limited role. The theologian cannot create a theology in isolation from the community's experience; but the community has a need of the theologian's knowledge to ground its own experience with the Christian traditions of faith. In doing that the theologian helps to create the bonds of mutual accountability between local and world church.[64]

Moreover, Wielenga emphasizes: "Reading the Bible one [finds] so many answers to existential problems of everyday life that it [becomes] a much loved and revered Book. Without being aware of the original meaning of a text, not having the reading skills to discover the most plausible message of a passage, having no access to the peculiarities of the original languages of the Bible, in Africa the ordinary reader applies the Bible text directly, addressing the pressing problems of the moment."[65]

The expressions by Bevans and Wielenga put clear what is the role of the professional theologian. They put clear that contextual theology is not something that one seats in the office and does by constructing good expressions to convince people. Contextual Theology that comes out of ordinary readers of the Bible is experiential. It comes from their experiences of life: from their songs, worships, their relationships in various sectors, *etc*. It is from these aspects where contextual theology emerges, a theology which learned contextual theologians write. Therefore, the professional theologian is mostly the facilitator of the theologizing process because he or she has the skills of biblical interpretation. The professional theologian is not the main interlocutor in the theologizing process.

Bevans states similar views regarding the role of the trained theologian in the midst of his or her community members. He writes: "A number of contextual theologians insist that theology is not real done by experts such as (Rahner or Lonergan or Guterez) and then "trickled down" to the people for their consumption. If theology is truly to take culture and cultural change seriously, it must be understood as being done most fully by the subjects and agents of culture and cultural change."[66] Kanyoro further

---

64. Schreiter, *Constructing Local Theologies*, 18; *cf.* West, "Locating 'Contextual Bible Study.'"

65. Wielenga, "Bible Reading in Africa," 703.

66. Bevans, *Models of Contextual Theology*, 18; *cf.* West, "Locating 'Contextual Bible Study.'"

states: "Many simply do not have time to sit and write long papers with footnotes and quotations from numerous other scholars. Many cannot take time for academic study and pursuits. Many do not have access to books and libraries, and money is short and theological books are expensive."[67] Through their experiences of life in the various cultural and social lives, theology is born. Theology emerges through their claim of the Bible as their own and read it while appropriating it to their real lived situations. The Latin American theologian Carlos Mesters states this concern blatantly: "As the ordinary Christian Bible readers gain in confidence to claim the Bible as their own, dislocations or shifts in interpretation take place: from an upper class toward a lower class perspective, from biblical text to real life, from a text enclosed in itself to a text with meaning for us, from an abstract individualistic understanding to a community sense, from neutrality to taking sides in society, and from overly spiritualized concepts to the concrete meanings and demands of faith in a present lived situation."[68]

Mesters' words above put more emphasis on the ownership of the Bible and the theology that emerges from its reading, the process of reading the Bible and the main interlocutor of the Bible reading and doing theology. Mesters emphasizes that ordinary readers are the main interlocutors of the Bible reading process not professional theologians. Trained theologians are mere facilitators in the process of reading the Bible and theologizing. Bevans adds the following about the role of the trained theologian: "The role of the trained theologian (the minister, the theology teacher) is that of articulating more clearly what the people are expressing more general or vaguely, deepening their ideas by providing them with the wealth of the Christian tradition, and challenges them to broaden their horizon by presenting them with the whole of Christian theological expression."[69] Hence, according to Bevans, "'the people are the best contextualizers'; and the role of the theologian is to function as a midwife to the people as they give birth to a theology that is truly rooted in a culture and moment of history."[70]

The main question in this section has been why there is a need for contextual theology today. A simple response has been the following. We need contextual theology today because the existing traditional theology has been dissatisfactory. There have been great philosophies and ideas in the past, but such philosophies and ideas have greatly failed to resonate

67. Kanyoro, "Engendered Communal Theology," 174.
68. Mesters, "The Use of the Bible," 119.
69. Bevans, *Models of Contextual Theology*, 18.
70. *Ibid.*; *cf.* Trokan, "Models of Theological Reflection," 146–147; West, "Locating 'Contextual Bible Study.'"

with current people's lived experiences. In this case, they have been useless tools for answering people's current questions. We need contextual theology today because most of the past theologies have been oppressive. They have marginalized gender, race, and people's cultural orientations.

We need contextual theology today because "Theology must rather be an activity of dialogue, emerging out of mutual respect between 'faith-ful' but not technically trained people and 'faith-ful' and listening professionals."[71] This need highlights the fact that theology is not a monopoly of few elites in the academy; rather, it is a shared activity between the academy and the community.

How should Contextual Theology be Done?

In the previous lectures we defined contextual theology and explained the reasons as to why we need it in this 21st century. We said that contextual theology is a theology that takes a particular perspective, the perspective of current people's lived experiences. We also said that this kind of theology is needed because it provides the church of the 21st century with: a new agenda for doing theology, new voices, new dialogue, and new methods of doing theology. In short, we discussed that we need contextual theology today because the existing traditional theology has been unsatisfactory. It has failed to take the current experiences of people seriously.

The main question here is that: Why does the existing traditional theology has been unsatisfactory? In other words, what made traditional theology unsatisfactory? Bevans reports that "Since the Middle Ages and the beginning of scholasticism, theology has been regarded as a scholarly, academic discipline. Its location has been in university or seminary, and its main form has been discursive, whether in the classroom lecture or in the scholarly article or monograph. (. . .). The discursive form, for one thing, is something typically Western and the formal fruit of a visual, literate culture."[72] According to Bevans such way of doing theology is not needed in our current 21st century context.

Since traditional theology is regarded as scholarly and academic discipline to be done in universities and seminaries, "it understood the theologian to be a scholar, an academic, a highly trained specialist with a wide knowledge of Christian tradition and history of doctrine and with a number of linguistic and hermeneutical skills."[73] Bevans asserts that "Such

---

71. Ibid.
72. Ibid., 17.
73. Ibid.

a picture of theology and the theologian made sense as long as theology was conceived as being a reflection on documents that needed considerable background skills to understand."[74]

According to Bevans and other contextual theologians, contextual theology is not done by experts of particular documents. It is done by normal people in their experiences of life. Bevans says it more clearly: "when theology is conceived in terms of expressing one's present experience in terms of one's faith, the question arises whether ordinary people, people who are in touch with everyday life, who suffer under the burden of anxiety and oppression and understand the joys of work and married love, are not the real theologians [. . .]."[75] Sedmak further adds:

> Doing local [contextual] theology requires that we keep our feet on the ground. Doing theology is about making an option. Jesus paid attention to the poor, to the excluded, to the marginalized, to the 'little ones,' to the weakest members of society: the children, the sick, persons with handcaps. Theology is a way of following Jesus. That is why the theologian is called to pay special attention to the poor. This is challenging because we have to ask hard questions: Who are the weakest members of our society? Where are they? Why are they vulnerable and weak? Where is their strength?[76]

It means that theology is not only for the so called experts and elites in society. It is to be done collaboratively between trained experts and non-trained people mostly in favor of the poor and vulnerable. The theological skills of trained people should have a dialogue with the real experiences of life from the non-trained people. In this case, a model is needed in order to do such kind of theology. In this section we will concentrate much on the aspect of model as a tool for doing theology. We will summarize Bevan's suggested models and examine their relevance in various contexts.

The Notion of a Model

First of all we need to understand the notion of a model. What is a model? Scholars have defined it in various ways: Bevans defines it by quoting Avery Dulles's *Models of Revelation*: "a model is 'a relatively simple, artificially constructed case which is found to be useful and illuminating for dealing

---

74. Ibid.
75. Ibid.
76. Sedmak, *Doing Local Theology*, 99.

with realities that are more complex and differentiated."⁷⁷ According to this definition, models are constructions that are meant to express a certain existing reality.

Sallie McFague defines a model as a representative of relationship between the 'real' and the 'imaginative.' A model affirms something real, yet it does not capture that reality.⁷⁸ McFague further states that "models of God are not definitions of God but likely accounts of experiences of relating to God with the help of relationships we know and understand."⁷⁹ According to Fuellenbach, "A model is a conceptual and symbolic representation or system by which we try to grasp and express reality or part of reality."⁸⁰ Following Fuellenbauch's statement above, reality is vast and can hardly be grasped in its entirety. A model simplifies the understanding of reality because it represents it symbolically.

The above definitions indicate that a model is a tool used to express reality but does not capture that reality fully. A model is a constructed 'case' that makes the complex reality easy to explain it to the level of people's understanding. Even though that model does not help towards understanding that reality fully, yet it helps to cast considerable knowledge towards understanding it. Therefore, as Avery Dulles speaks of Models of the Church, and Models of Revelation, as Sallie McFague speaks of Models of God, and as Fuellenbach speaks of Models of the Kingdom, Bevans also speaks of Models of Contextual Theology.⁸¹ Models of Contextual Theology are constructions that illuminate us on the ways to do theology in the present context. In the following subsections we consider in detail each of Bevans's models of doing contextual theology.

Translation Model

The first question to be answered when looking at the translation model is: What really makes it a Translation Model? This is a crucial question because it states the distinction between itself and the other models. Bevans states that in one way or another "every model of contextual theology is a model

---

77. Ibid., 29.
78. See McFague, *Models of God*, 38–39.
79. Ibid., 39.
80. Fuellenbauch, *The Kingdom of God*, 61.
81. Spae discusses only three models of contextual theology: Translation Model, Liberation Model and Contextualization Model (see Spae, "Missiology as Local Theology," 481–482).

of translation."[82] What distinguishes this model and other models is "its insistence on the message of the gospel as an unchanging message."[83] According to scholars who practice this model of doing contextual theology, truth cannot be creatively constructed. The theologian practicing this model has to be faithful to what is conceived as being 'the truth,' as being the message of the gospel.

However, this model is interested in meaning of words and not just a mere translation of a word from one language to another, e.g., an English word 'consubstantiation' into Swahili, Bena, or Nyakyusa. Bevans himself asserts that "Any translation has to be a translation of meaning, not of word and grammar."[84] In this case, the translation of a particular doctrine, e.g., baptism, justification, grace, *etc*, is done by taking the culture of particular contexts seriously.

This model has the following presuppositions. First, the gospel, or the message of the Bible is supracultural and supracontextual. This means that the message is above culture and context. Theologians who practice this model claim that the message of the Bible is wrapped in a particular culture, the culture of the first century. In order for it to be useful, it needs to be removed from the husk to get a 'naked gospel' and then applied to a particular culture. At that culture where it is applied, it must be above that culture. The cultural aspects going on at a particular society need to be modified according to the message of the Bible. This is the major presupposition of this model of doing contextual theology

The second presupposition is concerned about the starting point for doing theology. According to this model, the theologian has to start with the supracultural and supracontextual teaching or doctrine of the Bible. The message of the doctrine is unchanging. The unchanging message shapes or molds culture and context. The 'naked gospel' is inserted into a culture where it influences the affairs of that culture while itself remaining unchanged. In this case, the naked gospel is more important than experience, culture and social change. According to this model, culture, experience and social change have to be evangelized so that they conform to the naked gospel.

Some strengths of this model are the following: First, the model takes the message of Christianity very seriously. It shows that Christianity has a special message to offer to the world. The model promises people that it is "truly one that can bring light and peace to a dark and troubled world."[85]

---

82. Bevans, *Models of Contextual Theology*, 37.
83. Ibid.
84. Ibid., 38; *cf.* Kahakwa, "Interpretative Contextual Based Models," 81–85.
85. Ibid., 42.

Second, despite emphasizing on the supracultural message, yet it recognizes the existence cultures, experiences of people and the social change. It is this recognition of these aspects which makes it a model of doing contextual theology. Third, any person can use this model in doing contextual theology provided that such a person commits oneself to a particular culture.

Some of the weaknesses of the model are the following. First, the so-called "supracultural message of the Bible" can capitalize on issues that are culturally different from those presupposed by the culture in question. For example, the question of polygamy, homosexuality, the status of women, *etc*. The second criticism is based on the supracultural message itself being separated from the particular cultural husk. There is no possibility of getting a so-called "naked gospel" because it is not possible to separate between a child (gospel) and its bathwater (context). What is considered as "gospel" is a human formulation, and that formulation depends on the context of the human being formulating it.

This model, because of the strengths and weaknesses mentioned above, cannot be accepted or rejected without examining it critically. There are times when it will be needed, especially when we want to emphasize on the efficacy of Christianity, and there are times when we need to reject it, especially when it claims to search for an impossible naked gospel and when we clearly see that the supracultural message claimed by the model claims superiority on issues that are conceived differently from one culture and another.

Anthropological Model

Anthropological model stands at the opposite end of the translation model according to Bevan's. While the preservation of the Christian tradition is the main concern of the translation model, the preservation of people's cultural identity is the concern of the anthropological model. The anthropological model maintains that a person is shaped by his/her culture; and every cultural background of people has a grain of truth in it. In that case, the task of Christianity is not to transform people from their cultural backgrounds towards Christianity and its foreign culture; rather, it is making people Christians within their own culture while maintaining their cultural identities.

The name—anthropological—used by this model is based on its main concern. Its main concern is the value and goodness of the *anthropos*, the human person.[86] God's revelation is not limited to only a particular culture but is in every culture. The revelation of God in that particular culture

---

86. Bevans, *Models of Contextual Theology*, 55.

becomes vivid as people experience the divine presence of God. By the use of the discipline of anthropology the model traces and understands the cultural relationships among people in a particular culture making the divine presence of God more manifest. Following the emphasis of the model in the human person and the use of the discipline of anthropology, this model is mainly centered on culture that consolidates people's relationship among themselves and in their faith to God.

Since the model emphasizes on cultural identity and the value of the human person in each culture, care has to be taken in approaching people of other religions cultures and nations. There is a great need of taking out ones shoes before entering that group because God's presence is there; the group is holy and is in people's cultures where they experience God's presence. The model is guided by "human nature and therefore the human context, is good, holy, and valuable."[87] The treasures of culture hides the insights which illuminates the gospel of God; the gospel does not come from outside to illuminate a particular culture. In that case, the normal people who live in a particular culture are the ones who contextualize the gospel. The person practicing this model has a midwifery role, not that of expert who imposes his/her knowledge to people without question; rather, it is to provide to people biblical backgrounds that will enable them develop their own theology basing on their cultural treasures. It means that the model values dialogue as the major means of approaching people of other cultures and traditions because they are not *tabula rasa*, *i.e.*, people without divine insight and experience.

The model is commended for three main aspects: first, "it regards human reality with utmost reality."[88] Second, it recognizes that Christianity, as a religion, is in constant dialogue with people's religions and cultural backgrounds; it is not just a reception of values as being the most valuable as compared to people's existing cultures and religions. Third, the model deals with peoples lived experiences and questions seriously, from their own contexts, instead of dealing with questions not asked by their contexts. However, the main problem of this model lies on its overemphasis on the non–existent culture. Culture is not static; it is always on the process of change. The romantic overlooks that that culture has been encountering with other cultures which made it undergo changes.

---

87. *Ibid*, 56.
88. *Ibid.*, 59.

Praxis Model

The praxis model is different from both the Translation and the Anthropological model, especially in what these models focus on. The translation model "seeks to reserve continuity with the older and wider tradition" while the anthropological model focuses on maintaining the cultural identity of Christians within a particular lived context. The praxis model emphasizes on words, actions and social change while looking at the future.

The concept of 'praxis' as used in this model entails a way of doing theology. It is a technical concept which has its roots from the philosophy of Karl Marx as articulated at the Frankfort School and the philosophy of the educationist Paulo Freire. In doing theology by following these philosophies, it becomes of paramount importance that theological expressions are accompanied by a commitment to Christian actions. In this way of doing theology, dialogue between theological expressions and the actions taken in regard to the expressions is provided and is continuous. Content and activity must go hand in hand in this model in order to lead towards the required social change.

In this model, there is an action and a reflection on the action taken. As Bevans says, during the process of action and reflection, "It is reflected-upon action and acted-upon reflection [...]."[89] The reflection is done on the experience of the past (Scripture and tradition) and the action is done on the reflection done following the experience of the present (present culture, present experience and the present changes in life). Bevans clearly affirms: "By first acting and then reflecting on that action in faith, practitioners of the praxis model believe that one can develop a theology that is truly relevant to a particular context. What becomes clear is that theology done in this way cannot be conceived in terms of books, essays, or articles. Rather than something concrete, permanent, and printed, theology is conceived more in terms of an activity, a process, a way of living."[90]

The main assumption of this model, as Bevans states it, is that most of the Bible stories speak about the liberation of mankind: "the Bible itself is a product of struggles for human freedom; that Jesus' message is a message not primarily of doctrines but of structure-shaking attitudes and behavior; that sin must be opposed not by compromise but by radical reordering of one's life."[91] The main privileged group of people which this model seeks social transformation are the poor and marginalized people in society. It is this

---

89. Bevans, *Models of Contextual Theology*, 72.
90. Ibid., 74.
91. Ibid., 73.

group which, through the action and reflection on theological expressions, is led to transformation. Therefore, a critical reflection on committed actions is a characteristic of this model and of liberation theology as a whole.

Synthetic Model

Bevans calls this model as "a middle-of-the-road model."[92] He conceives it as following the Hegelian dialectical nature in its attempt to work with the more traditional aspects of theology and the more contemporary ones. In working with the traditional and the contemporary, the model tries to preserve the gospel tradition, yet respecting fully the present experience as being important. This means that the model presents a way of doing theology that synthesizes the gospel tradition (the experience of the past) and the present experience (present social changes, culture, *etc*.). The main emphasis of the model is dialogue between cultures in order to reach mutual understanding. Every culture has elements that are *unique* to it; and elements that are *similar* to those of other cultures.

According to this model, dialogue opens up the possibility of one culture to learn from the other culture, yet remaining unique. Practitioners of this model believe that the riches found in various cultures are the capital for learning from each other. They believe that no culture is totally self-sufficient. In this case, the model rejects any kind of rigidity to particular cultures and ways of understanding and opens a way towards learning from other cultures and thought forms. It opens up a way for interaction between the experience of the past (the gospel and its tradition) and the experience of the present (the present culture and social change).

Transcendental Model

This model emphasizes conversion of the human mind. Bevans clarifies in his book: "What is important is not so much that a particular theology is produced but that the theologian who is producing it operates as an authentic, converted subject. In the same way that Bernard Lonergan speaks of metaphysics, a contextual theology will not appear primarily in books, but in men's and women's minds."[93] As Bevans puts it, the major focus of this model is the converted human person and his or her ability to generate knowledge. It sticks on the human person's new outlook on issues

---

92. Ibid., 88.
93. Bevans, *Models of Contextual Theology*, 103.

surrounding the world. It argues that one cannot understand the new without undergoing a radical change of mindset. Practitioners of the Transcendental model shifts in their understanding of reality. Instead of understanding it as "something out there," he or she understands it as something here, now experienced by the practitioner. Bevans's own words may put this statement clearer when he writes: "Transcendental method proposes a basic switch in the process of coming to know reality. Instead of beginning with the conviction that reality is 'out there' existing somehow independently of human knowing, it suggests that the knowing subject is intimately involved in determining reality's basic shape—and so one needs to begin one's quest for knowing what 'is' by attending to the dynamic of one's own consciousness and irrepressible desire to know."[94] This way of understanding is the one that enhances the shift or conversion. Therefore, as one approaches reality with this model, he or she has to be converted first.

According to this model, the starting point to theologizing is not the gospel, or the content of the tradition; rather, it is one's experience of reality around him or her. This experience is determined by one's context, a particular time and place. Hence, the main emphasis of this model is the Subject or the person or the community that does theology and its context and experience at a particular time. The strength of this model is that it affirms that any Christian trying to appropriate his or her faith participates in doing theology.[95]

Counter-Cultural Model

This model takes the present experience (*i.e.*, culture and social change) seriously. However, it believes that some cultures or traditions within a culture need to be *challenged* by the gospel. The model emphasizes that "the native soil of a particular context needs to be weeded and fertilized in order that the seeds can be planted."[96]

The model has the following major presuppositions. First, it presupposes human context is always insufficient and ambiguous in its nature. Human context is never enough. Second, according to this model, true contextualization of the gospel allows it to penetrate most aspects of the culture and speak within that culture while challenging its various aspects. Hence, the model emphasizes on the challenging and critical functions of the gospel.

---

94. *Ibid.*, 104.
95. Trokan, "Models of Theological Reflection," 146, 148.
96. Bevans, *Models of Contextual Theology*, 118.

What is the Best Model of Doing Theology?

At the end of Bevans's discussions of models of contextual theology, he poses the question in regard to suitability of models: which among the discussed models serves as the more adequate one for doing contextual theology? In response to the posed question, Bevans sums up his presentation of models with a brief statement that: "It depends on the context." This means that the careful practitioner of contextual theology will know when, where, and why, apply a particular model. The best application of a particular model will also indicate the way the practitioner is sensitive to the context where a particular model has been applied and the kind of theology needed by people at that particular time.

Criticisms of Bevans's Models Approach to Contextual Theology

Though Bevans's models presented above illustrate clearly what contextual theologians should do when doing contextual theology, it cannot survive criticisms. Contextual theology embraces an array of contextual theologies and methodologies, which makes it necessary for anyone using Bevans's models to be cautious about them as models may be confusing and limiting, contrary to what is considered as justice to the existing plethora of contextual theologies and methodologies. This means that romanticizing and using them uncritically Bevans's models hardly removes the romanticizing person from the shackles of traditional ways of understanding theology and theologizing because they will be seen to be beyond criticism in a similar way as traditional theology is conceived. In other words, Bevans's models are not to be considered as unchanging or forms of theology to be embraced by theologians without critical evaluation. Despite the above observation, Bevans's work remains, and will most likely continue to be, vital and groundbreaking for this kind of theology.[97]

Contextual Bible Study

In the previous subsection, we discussed in detail about the role of a model in enhancing the process of doing contextual theology. In this subsection we discuss the way in which the Bible can be read by taking into account people's contexts and lived experiences.[98] We look closer at three ways of reading the

---

97. *Cf.* Pears, *Doing Contextual Theology*, 20.

98. West, "Contextual Bible Study in South Africa." Contextual Bible Study is located within the larger context of reader-response criticism and has been in the academy

Bible and which way among them takes into account the existing context and lived experiences of people. Therefore, through this section we will be able to distinguish between the traditional and contextual readings of the Bible.

We should state at the outset that the Bible is a huge forest where every reader can survey as much as he or she wishes. This is what has been done by those who brought Christianity into our African soil. For a long time, the Bible has been used to protect weak people from humiliating situations they face, or humiliating and subjugating them. The theologian Miguel De la Torre testifies about the way in which the Bible has been being used when he says: "Historically, the Bible has been used to justify such acts as genocide, slavery, war, crusades, colonialism, economic plunder, and gender oppression. Bible verses were quoted, sermons preached from pulpits, and theses written in theological academic centers to justify barbaric acts that were labeled 'Christian missionary zeal' or 'righteous indignation.' Millions have unjustly died and perished in the name of Jesus and by the hands of those who call themselves his followers."[99] The words of De la Torre indicate the way in which the Bible has been misused for a long time to justify humiliation and the perversion of human rights. What De la Torre emphasizes in his words is that, to a large extent, the Bible has been used as a tool for liberation and as a sword for humiliation. Hence, we can say that for the Bible to be a tool for liberation or a weapon for humiliation depends solely on who reads it and at which perspective.

In this subsection, we examine two important aspects: the three ways of reading used by readers of the Bible, and the differences between the traditional and contextual Bible studies. Hence, the main argument of this subsection is that in the contextual bible study, the reader of the biblical text is the owner of the meaning of the text being read because he or she is the one who has the lived experience of the particular context enabling him or her to have a dialogue with the biblical text being read and observes the way that text displays itself to him or her.

Three Ways of Reading the Bible

There are three ways of reading biblical Scriptures: *reading behind the text mode, reading the text mode,* and *reading in front of the text.*[100] Basing on

---

since 1989. It is just a newly evolving way of reading the Bible which is now being done in various parts of the world, including South Africa (*cf.* Muneja, *HIV/AIDS and the Bible,* 50–51).

99. De la Torre, *Reading the Bible,* 38.
100. West, *Contextual Bible Study,* 27–29.

the reading behind the text mode, the reader examines the historical background of what is said; it concentrates on the *historical and sociological life behind the text*. In this mode of reading, the reader seeks, in whatever way, to excavate the real meaning of the original author of the text, the meaning which was intended to his or her readers. The reader endeavors to excavate this meaning through reading the witnesses of various scholars and the witness from commentaries about the respective text in order to understand the way in which various scholars have understood the text being read. In laboring on the various possible historical interpretations of the text, the reader believes the meaning obtained is the one intended and should be construed universally.

Despite that the reader labors greatly in surveying the various historical texts about the text being read, yet one can still note a problem with this mode of reading. One main problem with this mode is that the reader builds his or her faith on a false hope of obtaining the author's intended meaning through the search of historical and sociological texts around the text being read. De la Torre echoes about this problem:

> All too often we approach the biblical text assuming that it contains only one meaning that existed in the mind of God and was revealed to the original person who verbalized this revelation to those who first heard or read the message. The task of the present-day reader of the Bible is to apply linguistic and historical tools to the text in order to arrive at the original meaning, which is submerged in centuries of commentaries and church doctrines. By applying this methodology, the reader believes he or she will be able to ascertain the original universal meaning that remains applicable to all peoples in all times.[101]

Following De la Torre's statement above, the meaning of the text is only one coming from the conscience of God, and which the author of the text was provided by God to inform his or her intended readers. To our view, it is not easy to obtain the meaning of the original author of the text just by searching the historical and sociological literature behind the text being read. What is your opinion as a theologian and reader of this book in regard to this mode of reading? Is it possible for the theologian of today, who was not present when the text was being written, to obtain the only one meaning intended by the author of the text?

Another mode of reading is the reading the text mode. Basing on the *reading the text mode*, the reader concentrates much on examining carefully the way characters interact in the respective text being read. The reader

---

101. De la Torre, *Reading the Bible*, 3.

examines carefully to determine the main character, minor characters, the way characters interact, the plot of the story, time, and the way the interaction of characters conveys meaning to the reader. Hence, in this mode of reading, the reader focuses mainly on the linguistic aspects used by the author of the story: types of words used, special phrases, *etc*, and how the various linguistic aspects convey meaning to the reader.

This mode of reading presents the development in the process of searching for meaning from the text being read. Here, the reader focuses on the interactions of characters and the linguistic aspects that accompany the interactions, which eventually enables the reader to consider the meaning of the interactions to him or her.

The problem we encounter in this mode of reading, according to our view, is that it hardly matches with the reality of the two worldviews. Though the reader may be able to analyze the interactions of characters within the text, and determine the linguistic aspects used by the author, he or she can hardly bridge the two worldviews between the author of the text and the current reader of that text. The author of the text had his or her own worldview, faith standpoints, and philosophy of life and so is the current reader who tries to find meaning in the text being read. All these are important aspects to enable the reader understand scriptures being read in his or her perspective and are discussed in the third mode of reading below.

The third mode of reading looks at what is in front of the text being read. It is referred to as the *reading in front of the text mode*. This kind of reading looks at the experiences of the reader and how such experience can build the meaning of the text being read depending on the current life situation. In this reading, the reader constructs themes from the text being read which enable him or her to discern the meaning of the text as a whole. Therefore, readers using this mode of reading believe that the meaning of any biblical text being read resides in the reader himself or herself. Every reader constructs meaning from the text being read depending on the real lived experience in a particular context. There are no two readers of the same text will have the same meaning because they differ in experience of life within the same context. In most cases, this mode of reading is known as *reader-response criticism* because the meaning of the text being read does not sorely depend on the historical background of the author of the text, nor on the interaction of characters within that text, but on the reader himself or herself and the way in which his or her experience will lead to constructing themes which elucidate the meaning of the text.

Despite its efficacy, the third mode of reading also has some weaknesses. One of such weaknesses is that there is a possibility for the reader to romanticize his or her lived experience more than allowing it to have a dialogue with the experience of the past as embodied in the text and the tradition within it. Moreover, there is a possibility of confusing between the meaning of the text and the reader's experience. The reader can take for granted that the experience he or she has reflects the meaning of the text he or she reads. In so doing, the reader will hardly do justice to the scriptural text being read and the experience he or she has.

The question here is: Which among the three discussed models of reading exactly represents a contextual reading of Scriptures? Looking closely at the way each mode works, we can conclude that each of the modes discussed above represents a contextual reading of the Bible. The reading by taking into account the *historical and sociological aspects behind the text* is contextual because it analyzes the context that existed before the text was written, and which most likely prompted the emergence of the text. Reading the text mode is contextual because the meaning of the text depends on the context that appears within the text itself, especially the context of interaction of characters within the story. The reading in front of the text mode is contextual because it considers the experience of the reader in a particular context he or she lives and the way that context can dialogue with the context of the text and the context behind the text. The reader constructs meaning of texts read basing on his or her lived reality in the time of reading the text. This is because there is hardly a meaning without a context. De la Torre clearly says: "The interpretation of Scripture can never occur apart from the identity of the one doing the interpreting."[102] Hence, following De la Torre's words many contextual theologians consider the reading in front of the text mode as being closer to real meaning of contextual theology because the meaning which emerges as a result of this kind of reading corresponds to the real lived situation of the reader at the time of his or her reading of the text. Moreover, the reader is the one who constructs the meaning of the text depending on his or her experience of life.

Traditional and Contextual Readings of the Bible

As there are differences between traditional and contextual theologies, there are also differences between traditional and contextual readings of the Bible. This issue is discussed at a great length in Mligo's book called *Jesus and the Stigmatized*.[103] In this book, it is put clear that the traditional reading of the Bible considers the trained theologian as the one who has to read scriptures and the lay Christians as the ones who are to receive the meaning of the

---

102. De la Torre, *Reading the Bible*, 3–4.
103. See Mligo, *Jesus and the Stigmatized*, 136–142.

texts from trained theologians passively. In other words, lay Christians, who are considered to know nothing, are to be fed meaning by the trained theologian, who is considered to be knowledgeable. In that book, Mligo called this traditional way of reading and the notion behind it as "banking" education as proposed by the educationist Paulo Freire in his book *Pedagogy of the Oppressed*. Mligo writes in *Jesus and the Stigmatized*: "The 'banking' terminology, according to Freire, refers to the type of teaching that does not allow participants to have any kind of reflection on what teachers have taught them."[104] This statement means that trained theologians are the ones who know the whole truth about theological issues while lay Christians do not know anything about theological issues. Lay Christians are considered to be empty containers which require to be filled with theological ideas and meanings of texts construed by the trained theologian. In this way of reading, lay Christians have no any chance and any contribution to the ongoing process of reading the Bible and theologizing. Lay Christians are supposed to listen and take into account what the trained theologian tells them. It also means that what the trained theologian tells them is an absolute truth which the lay Christian is ought to adhere to without questioning it. As a reader of this book, what is your opinion in regard to this perspective underlying this traditional way of reading the Bible? Do you accept that lay Christians know nothing and have no contribution to searching for meaning from biblical texts, and require receiving passively from the reading and theologizing done by trained theologians?

Contrary to the traditional reading of the Bible, contextual reading focuses on all readers, of the text whether lay or trained, and the experience they have within their context when approaching the biblical text. This way of reading takes into account the contribution of lay Christians and their experiences which dialogue with scriptures to emerge a compromised meaning of the text being read. By the use of Freire's terminology, the trained theologian in this way of reading uses *problem-posing pedagogy* to enable lay Christians to discern the meaning embodied within the text they read. The trained theologian provides the tools that help lay Christians find meaning from the text they read. The tools provided are the questions (problems) which help lay Christians think around the text and re-question it in their own ways so that it brings the intended meaning according to their current experiences. While quoting from Freire, Mligo wrote in *Jesus and the Stigmatized*: "In problem-posing education, people develop their power to perceive critically *the way they exist* in the world *with which* and *in which* they find themselves; they come to see the world not as a static reality, but

---

104. Mligo, *Jesus and the Stigmatized*, 137.

as a reality in process, in transformation."[105] This statement clearly shows that lay Christians are capable of reading the Bible and theologizing; and in so doing, they are also capable of bringing change in the existing worldview and in their own understanding of scriptures they read.

In a similar way to what we said regarding lay Christians and their capabilities to work with biblical texts in their contexts and experiences, the theologian Gerald West in his book *Contextual Bible Study* writes: "So readers merge or fuse their world with the world of the text through a process of dialogue with the text. In this process of dialogue between the questions, needs, and interests of the readers and the themes, metaphors, and symbols of the text both the reader and the text are transformed."[106] What does West mean by dialogue between the reader and the scriptures he or she reads, and about the changes that emerge to the reader and to scriptures being read? To our view, here is where the core of contextual reading is. The reader dialogues with the texts being read; and in such dialogue, the reader contributes his or her experience depending on the questions (problems) existing in his or her time. And to its side, the text being read contributes the experiences of the past, the experience that led to the production of the text. Through the dialogue between the experience of the past located in the text being read and the experience of the present which the reader has, the text being read acquires a different meaning from the one intended by the original author to his or her original audience. This is the meaning of change of scripture when engages in dialogue with the reader. At the same time of dialogue, the point of view of the reader can be changed by the experiences of the past. In this case, the dialogue between the reader and the text being read is the most important interface in the process of reading scriptures contextually.

Major Premises of Contextual Bible Study

In this part we summarize the major tenets of Contextual Bible Study. Contextual Bible Study, being shaped by community involvement and the scholarship (the academy), has the following premises as reported by Muneja:

1. The Bible study begins and ends with community consciousness;
2. The Bible study belongs to the community and is therefore authoritative;
3. It equalises power relationships (this includes gender inequalities);
4. It is a collaboration between both critical readers and ordinary readers;

---

105. Ibid., 165.
106. West, *Contextual Bible Study*, 44; cf. Mbuvi, "African Biblical Studies," 152.

5. It owns local embodied theologies;
6. It reads the Bible for individual and social transformation (pragmatic) through the See-Judge-Act Method;
7. Modes of reading include: behind the text (past), the text itself, and in front of the text (present);
8. It recognises the interpretation as a dynamic process: the reader is active and not passive;
9. It reads the Bible from the perspective of the poor, working class and the marginalised;
10. It includes literary interpretation against the backdrop of historical and sociological construction."[107]

Following the above premises, and as discussed in this chapter, contextual Bible study does not mainly belong to the academy. It predominantly belongs to the community, to normal people and their daily lived context which must be taken seriously when doing contextual theology.

In concluding this section, we should put clear, as we began in the introduction that contextual theology emphasizes that the meaning of a biblical text resides to the reader. His or her contemporary context provides an identity to him or her when reading a particular text and the meaning that comes out of that text. The theologian De la Torre echoes about this issue blatantly when he says: "All biblical interpretations are valid to the one who does the interpretation."[108] To a lager extent, De la Torre's words above are the ones that consolidate the content of the whole discussion in this chapter.

When we speak about the difference between the traditional and contextual readings of the Bible, we focus on the question of ownership of meaning: who exactly owns the meaning of the text being read? In the discussion within this subsection, it has been obvious that the trained theologian is the owner of everything: the reading process, the meaning produced (which is considered to be universal), and the theology produced. In the traditional reading, the trained theologian labors greatly to find the original meaning of the text, the meaning of the text intended by the author to his or her intended audience. The trained theologian searches for this universal meaning through reading literature that survey the historical and sociological context behind the text, surveying the linguistic and constructions of story within the text itself, and surveying the inherited traditional teachings of the Church. The trained theologian imparts the meaning and knowledge gained from his or her endeavor to lay Christians who have to receive it passively as he or she understands it. It has been clear in the

107. Muneja, *HIV/AIDS and the Bible*, 50–51.
108. De la Torre, *Reading the Bible*, 1.

discussion within this chapter that the owner of the meaning of the text is the trained theologian who believes to have found the universal meaning through his or her study.

In contextual reading, the long silenced voices of the marginalized lay Christians are heard. The silenced biblical texts are revived to have voiced to the Christian community. When reading, Christians march their reading with their current lived experiences with the experiences of the past and allow a dialogue between the two experiences. In so doing the owner of the reading process and the meaning obtained is the reader of the text, the lay Christian who has not undergone theological training, who makes the experience obtained in his or her life determines the meaning of the text being read.

In this subsection, we have also seen that all the three modes of reading take into account the context of reading. However, all the three types of reading are contextual readings in the perspective of this book each depending on its own focus. The reading that considers what is in front of the text *(reading in front of the text mode),* is the one closer to the contextual theology advocated in this book because it uses the experience of the reader in the time when he or she reads the text in order to engage in dialogue with the text being read. In that case the reader begets meaning and theology from the text being read, a theology which is useful depending on the context of people and their current life questions. It is the theology generated by the twenty-first century African reader of the text that becomes relevant to questions asked in this century within the African continent.

CONCLUSION

The main aim of this chapter was to introduce readers to contextual theology and its urgent need in the contemporary African context. We started by defining contextual theology on the bases of the wider context of theology and discussed the question of the relationship between theology and context. In this discussion, we noticed that there is no theology that is without context. However, what differentiates between what we call traditional theology and what we call contextual theology is the question of method and perspective, or point of view. While traditional theology is mainly based on the Bible and its tradition (the past experience), contextual theology takes the present experience more seriously. While traditional theology provides universal answers to old questions, contextual theology raises contextual questions to both the old answers and the new reality. This means that it brings the two experiences (the experience of the past narrated in the scriptures and their tradition and the experience of the present as lived by contemporary people at their own contexts) in dialogue.

In this chapter, we also discussed about the need for contextual theology in this era of globalization. We pointed out that this kind of theology is needed in this era because we live in a world which is subject to change. The world is not static; rather, it is dynamic. In this case, the Church of Jesus Christ in Africa lives in the world with great diversity, the world where there is an asymmetry between the rich and the poor, the world where people are stigmatized due to their differences in body, character, and sense of belonging. In all these situations, contextual theology provides us with a new agenda, a new method, new voices and new dialogue partners in our theologizing process.

One major issue of concern in this chapter, among others, was how contextual theology is done. We have analyzed some models of doing contextual theology basing on Bevans's book. Some of these models were the following: the translation model whose emphasis is on the sapra-cultural message of Jesus; the anthropological model whose emphasis is on the efficacy of human culture; the praxis model whose emphasis is on the action and the reflection on that action; the transcendental model whose emphasis is on the ability of the human being to use his or her experience; and the synthetic model whose emphasis is on the collecting together of various ideas and experiences in order to make the whole. In closing the discussion of models, we provided a caution that the romantic use of models makes the one using them to be limited to them and possibly be confused because the arrays of contextual theologies continue to grow which may likely not be accommodated by such models.

Moreover, we discussed contextual Bible study as one of the ways of reading the Bible in order to obtain meaning from this ancient text. We discussed the three modes of reading the Bible (the behind the text, the text, and the in front of the text modes of reading) and their efficacy. Therefore, in the modes of doing contextual Bible study and the models of doing contextual theology, we laid down the methodological part of doing contextual theology and reading the Bible contextually.

The disturbing question as we end this chapter has been raised by Kahakwa: "does African contextual-based interpretation need global church approval, recognition and acceptance of our theological expertise as true interpretation of the gospel?" In response to this question, Kahakwa quotes Mwombeki's words, which he also quotes from Oduyoye, with an emphasis "that Africans' interpretation of the biblical message does not need to be justified 'before the courts of European and American judges [. . .].'"[109] Ilomo further adds: "To want to measure contextual theologies by the criterion of Western academic theology will not do justice to them, since these [Western academic theologies] are theologies from which they [contextual theologies] seek emancipation."[110]

We agree with the above responses because they emphasizes the fact which De la Torre points out, that the validity of meaning of any biblical text and the theology in it reside to the ones who interpret the respective text and do theology, not to the ones who consider their interpretations and theological reflections as being more useful and valid than those of others.[111] The response indicates the efficacy of contextual theology emanating from people's reading of the Bible according to their own places, and the universal theology of the universal Church. At this point, Ilomo is right when he states:

> The postulate of a contextual theology is not to be understood as the denial of the universal claim of Christianity; it means, rather, the determination to reach all potential hearers of the word in the most sociocultural situations. Such a theological attitude is the consequence of the realization that not every language, including theological language, can be understood everywhere. In the long run, only on the foundation of such behaviour can the message of the Gospel be expressed in the diversity of languages, thought and behaviour patterns of the world without losing its universal claim.[112]

Therefore, while the Bible has been interpreted differently in various places of Africa and the world at large, using various methodological perspectives, yet universal meanings of some biblical aspects can hardly be ignored and abandoned because contextual theology does not exist in a vacuum.

---

109. Kahakwa, "Interpretative Contextual based Models," 74.
110. Ilomo, *A Relevant Christian Eschatology*, 90–91.
111. De la Torre, *Reading the Bible*, 1.
112. Ilomo, *A Relevant Christian Eschatology*, 90.

3

Contextual Theology in Africa

INTRODUCTION

In the previous chapter we surveyed the meaning of contextual theology, its need and the way this kind of theology is done in general. We looked at the models which can be used in doing this theology by considering the experience of the past (the gospel and its traditions) and the experience of the present (culture and social change). Moreover, we surveyed the various modes of reading the Bible in order to link the past experiences with the current experiences. In this chapter, we stick much on the way Contextual theology is done in the African context. We concentrate much on the following aspects: the culture of the African people, their religion, their conception of Jesus Christ, and the meaning of African Christian Theology. The main aim of this chapter is to survey contextual theology in Africa in order to make readers aware of the context in which Africans are doing theology.

TAKING AFRICAN CULTURES SERIOUSLY

Africa is a place, a dwelling place of people with varied ways of life—people with different cultures. Speaking of contextual theology in Africa can hardly deviate from considering the various cultures into which theology should be exercised. The theologian Okofor states in regard to theology and culture: "contemporary contextual theologians take culture into account in a conscious and explicit way in their theologizing. They assume that local and particular situations are the locus of truth, and therefore take them into account explicitly as a source of their theological enterprise. This is the understanding of what contextual theology stands for in our contemporary period of history."[1] The words of Okofor above indicate that culture and theology are inseparable entities; and that it is impossible to theologize in a vacuum.

However, culture itself is an amalgamation of many things. The attempt to define culture can end up with frustrations because there are as many definitions of it as the number of people interested in it. Culture stands above all what people can try to explain. In other words, culture involves the totality of human life. The way people behave, the way they eat, the language they speak, the clothes they put on, the way they relate to each other, their various art and craft work, their various ceremonies, their literature, their religion, their political and economic orientations, their worldview, *etc.*, are some of the elements of culture. African people have all these aspects, and even more than these mentioned ones. Theology needs to take into account all the cultural aspects of a place in order to be contextual. It needs to value people's ways of life and ways of behavior in that particular place.

Some scholars have attempted to define culture. The first one is Edward B. Taylor. Taylor is credited as being the pioneer of this attempt. Taking ideas from Taylor's definition, Idang states: "Taylor saw culture as that complex whole which includes knowledge, belief, art, morals, law, customs or any other capabilities and habits acquired by man as a member of society. This definition captures the exhaustive nature of culture."[2] Idang adds: "Culture embraces a wide range of human phenomena, material achievements and norms, beliefs, feelings, manners, morals and so on. It is the patterned way of life shared by a particular group of people that claim to share a single origin or descent."[3] Clemens Sedmak also writes: "Culture is the way we live and at the same time the framework within which we live as social beings. [. . .]. Culture marks the difference between human and nonhuman forms of life [. . .].[4] In this case, theologians are prompted to doing theology because of the various burning questions that arise in their cultural surroundings.

However, a more lucid attempt at defining culture is done by Walligo. Waligo defines "Culture, meaning the sum total of all people's traditional religions, customs, traditions, rites, ceremonies, symbols, art, wisdom and institutions, has been booming in all parts of Africa. It is based on a people's worldview, the way they relate to the Supreme Being, to the supernatural powers and phenomena, to their fellowmen and women, to

1. Okofor, "The Challenge of Contextual Theology," 6.
2. Idang, "African Culture," 98.
3. *Ibid.*
4. Sedmack, *Doing Local Theology*, 74.

the world of other living beings and inanimate beings, and to the world underground."⁵ Waliggo's definition emphasizes on the previous definitions that culture is not something different from people's lives, both in times of joys and times of peril.

Moreover, in his article "Taking Culture Seriously," Laurent Magesa illustrates the way African culture is held strongly during the time of sickness. A person that suffers from HIV/AIDS does not accept to be suffering from any other kind of disease except witchcraft. For example, Mangena and Mhizha have this statement in regard to witchcraft beliefs in Africa: "there is a spiritual view of life whereby everything is given a religious interpretation, with witchcraft being considered to be an invariable problem in Africa. This belief in witchcraft affects Africans of all socio-economic classes; rich or poor, educated or uneducated [. . .]. The overarching belief is that witchcraft hinders human and social development in the continent [. . .]. For this reason, Africans have developed a witchcraft mentality-which is a permanent condition of living helplessly in fear, mental torture, intimidation and spiritual insecurity [. . .]."⁶ The above-stated witchcraft belief situation indicates that African culture affiliates calamities with witchcraft and the breach of strongly held taboos. In other cases, calamities are associated with the dishonor of ancestors. In this case, ancestors are thought to be punishing people because of their disobedience.⁷

In African context, apart from sickness, issues related to sexuality are important matters geared towards procreation. This is mainly the purpose of marriage as far as African cultures are concerned. A person that reaches a marriageable age is expected to get married. A person who is not married carries with him/her a stigma. Moreover, a married person who does not get children carries a stigma, and a married person that gets only female children gets a stigma. In this case, marriage in African context focuses on the continuation of life, a thing that can prove to be contrary to other cultures. Since African sexual orientation mostly focuses on the preservation of life force, most African traditional marriages are polygamous aiming at increasing the number of children.

Some practices and rituals are culturally inevitable in delving within the African cultural orientation. Widow cleansing is one of the rituals practiced in some African societies. In this practice, the widow "is required to have sexual relations with one of her diseased husband's male relatives."⁸

---

5. Walligo, "Making the Church," 27; *cf.* Idang, "African Culture," 98–101.
6. Mangena & Mhizha, "The Rise of White Colar Prophecy," 134.
7. Magesa, "Taking Culture Seriously," 76–79.
8. Magesa, "Taking Culture Seriously," 80; *cf.* Maurice, "Levirate Unions," 287;

Inheritance of widows and levirate marriages are also some of the encouraged customs embraced by Africans. African traditional medicine men and women are influential in the African context. They are said to play a great role in the healing process. People consult these medicines for the cure of their various illnesses, including HIV/AIDS. Their main function is not only healing the physical suffering of people, but also their broken relationship. In the healing process, the broken relationship between them and their ancestors is restored. Hence, these and other many unmentioned cultural practices, customs and traditions form the African context where the theologian has to theologize. They form the bulk of a context where burning questions about the authenticity of God of life are discussed against the idols of death.[9] It is within this context which theology has to take root if is to be African at all.

African Traditional Religion as Part of African Culture

We cannot be fully just if we bypass the reality of African Traditional Religion in the African Context. We need to discuss ATR as part of our contextual Theology book. This is because it is part and parcel of people's life. Beyers puts it: "The nature of African religion lies not in dogmatic constructs or philosophically (theologically) formulated doctrines, but, rather, African Traditional Religion lives in the hearts and lives of people who practice it [. . .]."[10] Bayer's statement above has a handful of truth which we endeavor to illustrate in this section.

Now let us first answer these two questions: What is ATR? Why study about ATR while we belong to a very magnificent Christian Religion? Religion forms the most important part of life of every African. From the beginning, before the coming of Christian missionaries, Africans had a religion. They had their own way of relating to the Supreme Being. Christianity is secondary while ATR is primary in the African continent. African people are religious by nature. Each African has his or her religious way or system of relating to God and with the neighbor which permeates throughout his or her life. As Sundermeier rightly states, "The traditional religions [*sic!*] of Africa are 'human' in the deepest sense, because they focus on people. The way earlier researchers portrayed them—as 'primitive,' 'barbaric,' and so on, is one of the greatest misunderstandings of former generations, and can only be explained by the arrogance of the Western attitude to mission.

Baloyi, "The Christian View of Levirate Marriage," 284–285.

9. Cf. Richard (ed.), *The Idols of Death and God of Life*.
10. Beyers, "What is Religion? 6.

Blind to its weakness, it portrayed other cultures as inferior in order to justify colonialist adventures and claims to sovereignty."[11] Hence, it is not easy to separate the religious life with the real "human" life of an African which was ignored by their missionaries due to their ignorance and claims to own cultural superiority.

When we talk of African Traditional Religion we refer to the religious system embraced by Africans that characterizes their totality of life. This religious system consists of beliefs and practices towards the recognition of the Supreme Being who is known through different names for every ethnic group. African Traditional Religion is the strongest element in the thinking and living of African people. Even after Christianity, ATR continues to have influence over the converted Christians. Theologian Awolalu provides the following explanations regarding the influence of ATR:

> When we speak of African Traditional Religion, we mean the indigenous religious beliefs and practices of the Africans. It is the religion which resulted from the sustaining faith held by the forebears of the present Africans, and which is being practiced today in various forms and various shades and intensities by a very large number of Africans, including individuals who claim to be Muslims or Christians.[12]

This means that wherever the African is, there is his or her religion. ATR is not limited to Temples and churches. In the Traditional African society, there are no irreligious people, and to claim one as irreligious is to excommunicate oneself from the entire life of the African society. It is this link with the entire life of the African that makes ATR important to study it.

Rationale for Studying African Traditional Religion

The reasons to why should we take time and energy to study African Traditional Religion (ATR) are manifold. Some of these reasons are the following: First, as Christian ministers, we study ATR in order to understand our context into which we minister. Other people say that ATR is irrelevant in the 21st century of modern science and technology. They say that it does not go with modern time and its questions. The reality is that whether we like it or not, the knowledge of ATR is unavoidable if we are to understand and minister in this 21st century African context.

---

11. Sundermeier, *The Individual and the Community*, 1.
12. Awolalu, "What is African Traditional Religion?" 1.

We agree with Sundermeier that "If you do not know anything about the person you are talking to, misunderstandings will arise."[13] The knowledge of ATR enables us to understand the life and culture of people to whom we minister. It enables us to understand the background and identity of Africans in their various ethnic groups. Knowledge will enable us to find appropriate ways to communicate the gospel without offending or abusing the African cultures and lifestyles. As Stinton, quoting the Pan-African Conference of Third World Theologians, clearly puts it: "In Africa the traditional religions are a major source for the study of the African experience of God. The beliefs and practices of the traditional religions in Africa can enrich Christian theology and spirituality."[14] If one wants to understand about the strength and weaknesses of a particular plant, he or she has to know its anchor; one has to know its roots. If one wants to know the strengths and weaknesses of Africans he or she has to know ATR because it is the root of African life. In this case, as Van Eck rightly says, "African traditional religion came to be seen as 'Africa's Old Testament', a kind of *praeparatio evangelica*, a fertile ground for sowing the gospel message."[15] It is a background for Christianity to anchor its roots and can hardly be ignored if Christianity is to take roots in Africa.

Second, we need to study ATR because it is one of the world religions. It is a religion with great people and great past. As we said previously, Africans are religious. Their religiosity begins with the beginning of the first African person. In this case, ATR has a long history that is rooted in the culture of Africans and their total life.

Third, since ATR forms the culture of African life, there is a need to study it in order to bridge the gap between Christianity and ATR. Christianity has its own cultural background and so is ATR. If Christianity has to take roots in Africa, then ATR needs to be understood thoroughly well. Among the Rangi of Haubi in Kondoa District Tanzania, bridging the gap between Christianity and ATR through the proper teachings of the Bible and ATR is the main cause of syncretistic life of Rangi Christians. Cox reports:

> "Rangi Christians suffer from a lack of solid Biblical teaching. Often the priests or nuns do not know the Rangi words for certain subjects and so resort to the Swahili terms, which do not carry much weight with the Rangi. They also teach the people in a 'western' way, as that is how they themselves have been

---

13. Sundermeier, *The Individual and Community*, 1.

14. Stinton, "Africa's Contribution to Christology," 19.

15. Van Eck, "The Word is Life," 681; *cf.* Shorter, *African Christian Theology*, 23; Bowers, "African Theology," 117.

taught. Finally, certain topics are not addressed whatsoever by the ministers of the church. Teaching concerning initiation rites, traditional rituals to appease the spirit world and other components of ATR is simply non-existent. Due to this lack of teaching, Rangi Christians simply substitute the knowledge that ATR provides for the areas of life that the Church's instruction does not address."[16]

The above quotation in regard to the syncretistic life of the Rangi Christians in Tanzania indicates that we need to start from the known (ATR) to the unknown (Christianity) informed by proper teachings in a language that Africans can understand. Mokhoathi states it more clearly:

"Christianity needs to communicate with the African cultural and religious heritage. This means that it needs to be couched in a language that Africans can understand and appreciate, and further be presented in a manner that does not require the alienation of Africans from their cultural heritage. But in that endeavour, all aspects of the African cultural and religious heritage must be considered, not only the positive and negatives. These include the pragmatic nature of the African cultural and religious heritage, as well as the methods that Africans use to respond to moments of crises."[17]

Mokhoathi further states the reason for couching Christianity in the language of the African religious heritage:

African Christianity is the amalgamation of Christianity and African Traditional Religion. [. . .] It is a form of Christianity that draws from both the Christian faith and African Traditional Religion for some ethico-spiritual principles. It is evidenced by the reverting of Christians back to African traditional practices and the consultation of traditional healers3. In this narrative, it becomes difficult for Africans to plainly choose between Christianity and their African traditional practices. Christianity connects them to God while African traditional practices provide a lasting bond with their ancestors.[18]

Hence, understanding ATR helps Africans to do African Christian theology in an African context. It helps African theologians describe Christology that values African people and their context.

16. Cox, "Why Rangi Christians continue to practice African Traditional Religion?" 6.

17. Mokhoathi, "From Contextual Theology," 11.

18. Mokhoathi, "From Contextual Theology," 3.

The Unity and Uniqueness of ATR in Africa

ATR is a one unified religion, a religion that unifies Africans and their various cultures wherever they are. This religious unity is not based on their cultural identities, which are many and varied; rather, it is based on the philosophy of their cultures. Culturally, Africans have multiple identities, yet these identities have the same philosophy, *i.e.*, they represent a similar worldview. Therefore, as Mugambi conceives, "though there are many ethnic groups in Africa, their cultural and religious heritage has sufficient homogeneity to justify their being studied as a topical entity."[19]

We speak of ATR as African Traditional Religion, not as "African Religion," "African Religions," nor "African Traditional Religions" as once conceived by some African scholars.[20] It is only one religion embraced by Africans based on the philosophy of their cultural orientations, not many religions characterized by the various African tribes as Mbiti and some earlier scholars initially conceived it.[21] Rather, this religion is only one as Christianity remains one despite the many denominations and sects within it. Hence, despite the many denominations and sects within Christianity, all have only one philosophy, and so applies to African Traditional religion.

When we say that the traditional religion is one, we are aware of the various ways of practicing this traditional religion in the various ethnic groups within Africa. We are aware that Africa is not one country and neither is it having only one ethnic group with similar culture and religious practices. We talk of it as being only one religion when we look at the commonly held world view of Africans despite their ethnic disparity. This common world view or religious philosophy is the one that keeps the unity and uniqueness of ATR as a religion of the Africans. Awolalu states it rightly:

> We speak of religion in the singular. This is deliberate. We are not unconscious of the fact that Africa is a large continent with multitudes of nations who have complex cultures,

---

19. Mugambi, *Christianity and African Culture*, 140; *cf.* Ilomo, *African Religion*; Mligo, *Elements of African Traditional Religion*.

20. See for example Kato, *Theological Pitfalls*, and Mbiti, *African Traditional Religions*. Moreover, Diaz intentionally states: "African religion is not one thing, but something that belongs to each particular ethnic group so that we need to speak of African religions, Ghanaian religions, Ashanti religions, and Dagonba religions. It is African religions." (Diaz, African Traditional Religion," 54) which gives its followers a sense of security in life.

21. Mbiti, *African Traditional Religions*, 1; Mbiti, "Christianity and Traditional Religions," 430–431 & Sundermeier, *The Individual and Community*." Later, Mbiti changed his view and conceived ATR as one unified religion, see Mbiti, *Introduction to African Religion* & Mbiti, "A Person who Eats Alone," 83.

innumerable languages and myriads of dialects. But in spite of all these differences, there are many basic similarities in the religious systems—everywhere there is the concept of God (called by different names); there is also the concept of divinities and/or spirits as well as beliefs in the ancestral cult. Every locality may and does have its own local deities, its own festivals, its own name or names for the Supreme Being, but in essence the pattern is the same. There is that noticeable "Africanness" in the whole pattern.[22]

Another theologian Aylward Shorter states succinctly about the singular conception of African Traditional Religion: "Although they (African religious systems) were separate and self-contained systems, they interact with one another and influenced one another to different degrees. This justifies our using the term African Traditional Religion in the singular to refer to the whole African religious phenomena, even if we are, in fact, dealing with multiplicity of theologies."[23] Following the above statements by Awolalu and Shorter, we should differ with all scholars, including the initial conception of Mbiti, who conceive of ATR as a collection of religions embraced by the various ethnic groups within Africa as just noted above.[24] Those who hold on the idea of Africa having a collection of religions believe that Africa is composed of 'multiple identities' making it difficult to identify one religion embraced by all cultural identities of the Africans. Beyers states it clearly: "It is generally accepted that there are many religious systems in Africa [. . .]. It therefore is impossible to talk of one type of religion as being uniquely African. There is diversity in religious concepts and practices in Africa and it will therefore not be incorrect to talk about different African religions (plural) [. . .]."[25] However, this view does not consider religion as a philosophy of life; and, mos unfortunately, most scholars who hold this view are doing it from the "outsider's" point of view. Though Africans have different religious systems, all contribute to the one African philosophy of life which forms the main religious belief—belief and reverence to the one Supreme God.

Concerning the unity of ATR despite its diverse beliefs and practices, we concur with Bayers, quoting Kruger, when he opines: "'religions of black

---

22. Awolalu, "What is African Traditional Religion?" 1.

23. Shorter, *African Christian Theology*, 1.

24. Though Mbiti initially conceived ATR in the plural (African Traditional Religions), he later revised it to the singular. As quoted in Mokhoethi, Mbiti states: "in the first edition I spoke about 'African religions' in the plural to keep alive the diversity of African religiosity [. . .]. I now use the singular, 'African religion,' more than the plural expression." (Mokhoethi, "Towards Contextual Theology," 3).

25. Bayers, "What is Religion?" 3.

Africa are similar enough to talk of African Religion in a generic sense. They also share a sufficient number of characteristics'. There seems to be a coherent philosophy underlying the different expressions of religion in Africa. The expressions of thought may vary and differ, but they still remain expression of basic belief [. . .]."[26]

This African Religion is "traditional" in its real sense. When we speak of this one religion of the Africans being "traditional" we mean that the religion is inherently African as distinguished from other imported religions which are within Africa. Awolalu clarifies this point:

> We need to explain the word "traditional." This word means indigenous, that which is aboriginal or foundational, handed down from generation to generation, upheld and practiced by Africans today. This is a heritage from the past, but treated not as a thing of the past but as that which connects the past with the present and the present with eternity. This is not a "fossil" religion, a thing of the past or a dead religion. It is a religion that is practiced by living men and women.[27]

Therefore, as Mokhoethi asserts, "The word 'traditional' is included 'to indicate that these religions [sic!] emerged among traditional communities in specific regions before they came into contact with other world religions and cultures'[. . .]."[28]

Distinguishing Features of ATR as a Religion

ATR, as a religion has its own distinguishing features as compared to other world religions. The distinguishing features of ATR, according to Awolalu, are the following:[29] first, it is not a missionary religion. This means that its adherents are neither obtained through proselytizing nor dialogue; they are born into ATR background, reared into it, grown into it and pass it to the following generations. This assertion means that its transmission from one generation to another is done orally. There are no sacred scriptures written in papers regarding this religion. The chapters of ATR are embedded into African people's lives and practices; and are handed from one generation to another through oral and practical teachings.

---

26. *Ibid.*
27. Awolalu, "What is African Traditional Religion?" 1.
28. Mokhoethi, "Towards Contextual Theology," 3.
29. Awolalu, "What is African Traditional Religion? 2.

Second, contrary to other religions which have founders, such as Buddha, Muhammad, Jesus Christ, *etc*, ATR has no founder. It is a life-lived religion. ATR informs the African people's culture and a way of being. Its origin is as old as the African people themselves.

Third, ATR has religious officials or leaders who preside over religious matters, such as ceremonies, sacrifices, prayers and divination. Before they assume such leadership activities these leaders are trained by their predecessors. As Diaz asserts, "In many cases they are trained men and women. They know more about religious affairs then [*sic!*] other people, and are highly respected by their people. They hold offices as priests, rain-makers, ritual elders, diviners, medicine men, and even as kings and chiefs."[30]

Fourth, ATR as a religion has its specific belief. Diaz stating in regard to ATR's belief system: "shows the way people think about the universe and their attitude toward life itself. African religious beliefs are concerned with topics such as god, spirits, human life, magic, the hereafter, witches, etc."[31] These aspects are important in every well-organized religion.

Fifth, ATR as is any other religion has its specific way of expressing the faith it has. Again, Diaz writes that ATR expresses its beliefs in "*practices, ceremonies and festivals.*"[32] According to Diaz, it "is here where religious practices show how beliefs are expressed in more practical terms, such us: prayers, making sacrifices and offerings, performing ceremonies and rituals, *etc*. Festivals are generally festive occasions when people sing, dance, eat and celebrate a particular occasion or event. For example, there are festivals to mark harvest time, the start of the rainy season, the birth of a child, and victory over enemies."[33] Therefore, it is in the mentioned practices where one notices the theology of ATR.

Having the above distinguishing features, ATR has been an important background for Christianity and the interpretation of the gospel as Meiring rightly notes: "Not only have African theologians interpreted the Gospel in ways to address the specific context(s) of Africa, but many would (in my opinion, rightly) add that African Traditional Religion (which often informs African Theology), is quite compatible with the message and worldview of the Bible and can enhance our view of God."[34] We conclude this section with the words of Craford that "if Christianity could [not] find a new identity in the African context, become a place for African Christians to feel at

30. Diaz, "African Traditional Religion," 54.
31. *Ibid.*
32. *Ibid.*
33. *Ibid.*
34. Meiring, "As Below, so Above," 733.

home, speak a language that appeals to Africans and still remain true to the essentials of the gospel, it will be nothing less than a miracle of God's power to evangelize the cultures of humankind."[35] Craford's statement means that the relevance of Christianity in Africa will solely depend on the extent it respects the religious context of ATR.

Despite our focus on the concept of African traditional religion as a singular unified religion in Africa, we are aware of the challenge posed to it, especially in the use of the word 'religion..' The challenge facing it is that African traditional religion lacks compartmentalization of the various aspects in it that qualifies it to being a religion which can be evangelized and believed by any person of any culture as is in other religions such as Christianity, Islam, Buddhism, *etc*. African traditional religion can hardly be separated from African people's life. It includes the totality of their philosophy and practice of their lives. In that case, a person belongs to the religion not by evangelization as one can belong to Christianity and Islam, rather by being born in the cultural world view of Africans. Therefore, African traditional religion can hardly be identified apart from the African culture where it originates as Christianity, Islam and Buddhism can be.[36] However, despite this criticism, one can hardly deny that African traditional religion is a way of Africans to relate to the Supreme Being, which primarily makes it a vital religious system taking it into account. It is in the context of this religion where Jesus Christ was and is being preached in Africa. It is in this context where Christianity and its practices in Africa have to be rooted.

JESUS CHRIST IN AFRICAN CHRISTIANITY

After discussing the religious context of Africans into which Christianity has to take into account for it to take root, we should ask: how can Jesus be contextualized within Africa to yield an African Christianity. We should state at the outset that there is a difference between the contextualization of Christianity and the contextualization of theological articulation of Christianity in Africa. The contextualization of Christianity has to do with the contextualization of the practices of faith–Christian faith, while the contextualization of theology has to do with the articulation and reflections on the practices of faith. Mokhoathi states that there has been conspicuous move among scholars to advocate for the African contextual Christianity, yet there has been no agreed way on which Christianity should be practiced contextually in Africa. Mokhoethi opines:

35. Craford, "The Church in Africa," 173.
36. Mugambi, *Christianity and African Culture*, 140–141.

> A great number of African scholars contend for the contextualization of Christianity, which aims at providing a link between the African cultural and Christian underpinnings. But what seems to be lacking in this debate is the critical evaluation of how Christianity can fully be expressed or practiced within the cultural context. Even though it is apparent that Africans yawn to experience Christianity within their cultural setting, it still remains to be established how Christianity can best be communicated within an African cultural context.[37]

Mokhoethi further states that the endeavor to contextualize Christianity has ended up with the production of what Mokhoethi calls "African Christianity," which is a syncretism between Christianity in the western understanding and African Traditional Religion.[38] This means that the Christianity produced in this endeavor mixes some elements of Christianity and some elements of African Traditional Religion. In doing that, Mokhoethi states: "The amalgamation of Christianity and African Traditional Religion appears to overlook the essence of both religions, as the elements of one religion are expressed through the other."[39]

In the previous section we discussed about ATR as part of the culture of Africans and as the foundation of understanding any other foreign religion, including its practices. In this section we endeavor to understand Christian theology in Africa in light of people's culture. African Christian Theology is mostly centered on Jesus and his dealings with human beings in the various contexts or places of the African continent. It is contextual because it deals with unique difficult theological questions that face people in their daily lives. Jesus who dealt with issues in his ministry needs to speak today in current African people's lives. This way of understanding Jesus is what it means by rediscovering Jesus in our own places as advocated by the title of this book.

In most cases, African theology is *resonance theology*. It means that Africans, in their endeavor to rediscover Jesus in their own places, try to see the way in which the experiences of the past resonate with the experiences of the present. Doing theology in this way is trying to see how some of the

---

37. Mokhoethi, "Towards a Contextual Theology," 1.

38. One of the criticisms to the notion of 'African Christianity' is that it jeopardizes the universality of Christianity reducing it to being 'African' without having any recognized history to justify its identity. Since it emerges due to the amalgamation between western values which came with the missionaries and ATR, it is charged of having no convincing evidence to show its truly Africanness (Mokhoethi, "Towards Contextual Theology," 4).

39. Ibid.

deeds found in the Bible correlate with the deeds that are done by people in the current African world. Therefore, as van Eck believes, African theology is by nature a theology of protest. As a theology of protest, "It should protest, on a Biblical basis, against everything in its context and social life that is not Biblical: Corruption, poverty, crime, not caring for the sick (especially those with HIV/Aids), nepotism, misuse of (political) power, the abuse of women, to name but a few. It must, however, also attend to the spiritual needs of people."[40]

The major question in doing this kind of theology is the identity of Jesus in each particular place and experience of people. The question of identity of Jesus has been a burning question for centuries. Jesus asked his disciples: "Who do people say that I am? And "Who do you say that I am?" These questions are questions about the identity of Jesus in relation to the situation of people at a particular time and in a particular context. These questions indicate that Jesus has a specific identity in every place and situation facing a human being. The sick people have a specific answer for the above questions. The poor, the rich, the stigmatized, the travelers, the Sangu, the Bena, the teachers, the Muslims, the Hindus, *etc.*, all can provide different answers to the above questions. The way Jesus is perceived and understood depends very much on what is experienced in that particular context. Hence, the unchanging Jesus and his message is understood and experienced very differently in particular changing contexts. This explains why some questions are important in some places, not all places. For example, the questions of divorce and remarriage, polygamy, widow inheritance, female genital mutilation, etc are important to most African churches and not to churches of other continents. In whatever the case, Jesus is the same God in all continents and contexts. People in all continents, countries and regions within those countries rediscover the role of Jesus to them according to what those people experience in their real lives.

Who did New Testament people say Jesus was? In the New Testament, Jesus is identified with various names. These names were given to Jesus according to their perception of him in their own contexts. For those who believed in him, Jesus was Lord, Messiah, Rabbi, King, *etc.* All these names explain the way people who believed in him experienced his presence in their midst. His deeds upon them bore witness to the name he deserved to be given by his contemporaries. To those who did not believe in him, Jesus was a 'sinner,' the 'one with a demon,' 'son of a carpenter,' *etc.* All these names reflected the way they perceived him in their interaction with him.

40. Van Eck, "The Word is Life," 694.

Who do Africans say Jesus is in their current context? Africans identify Jesus with various names that reflect their experience of him in their various interactions with life questions. To Africans, Jesus is King, chief, ancestor, widow, elder brother, Age-Set Herald (Maasai of Northern Tanzania), Rain Maker Priest (Ilyamba of central Tanzania), Prophet, priest and potentate,[41] Master of Initiation,[42] African Chief,[43] Ancestor and Elder Brother,[44] Healer,[45] Liberator,[46] *etc.*, all reflecting on what people experience of him. In this case, some of the titles of Jesus in the New Testament are resonated with the life experience of the present African context in order to see the way they can explain people's experiences of Jesus today.[47] Anne Nasimiyu-Wasike, as quoted in Stinton, confirms this assertion when she asserts: "each cultural context has come up with its own understanding of who Jesus Christ is for them in their given cultural, religious and political reality."[48]

Now to you, readers of this book, as members of the Church, who do you say that Jesus Christ is to you? Why do you call him in these names? It is our conviction that the name you provide upon Jesus reflects your primary experience of him in your own context. Your context is unique and should provide a unique experience of Jesus to you and to each member in your context. Therefore, the questions you ask in your context have a unique meaning in your encounter with Jesus.

AFRICAN THEOLOGY AS CONTEXTUAL THEOLOGY

After looking at some of the Christological reflections to try explain who Jesus is in our various African contexts in the previous paragraph, we turn to considering African theology as a theology that emerges when people rediscover the role of Jesus in their local contexts. In this subsection we discuss briefly what African theology is, its importance, the three main theological trends and their origins, and concentrate much on African Indigenous Churches as a response of Africans to an unsatisfactory brand of Christianity brought by missionaries. What is African Theology? In fact it

---

41. Waruta, "Who is Jesus Christ for Africans Today?"
42. Sanon, "Jesus, Master of Initiation."
43. Kabasele, "Christ as Chief."
44. Kabasele, "Christ as Ancestor and Elder Brother."
45. Colie, Jesus as Healer."
46. Magesa, "Christ the Liberator and Africa Today."
47. Mafu, "The Impact of the Bible"; Kabasele, "Christ as Chief"; Mligo, *Jesus and the Stigmatized;* 362–371; Mafico, "The biblical God of the Fathers."
48. Stinton, "Africa's Contribution to Christology," 18.

is not easy to define or explain what African Theology really is, especially at this context now, due to the various conceptions among scholars about this kind of theology. Meiring outlines the various conceptions among scholars: "it is hard to establish a single common denominator in their writings. Some would typify African Theology as theology of liberation, either from colonialism (as in Black Theology) or from physical and spiritual affliction (as many AIC theologians might say). Others, such as Gabriel Setiloane, see African Theology as a theology of solidarity, or as a theology of healing, even of ecology and of harmony. It seems that African Theology may mean a number of different things for different theologians [. . .]."[49] Moreover, it is not easy to find a theology that is truly African, a theology that is not influenced by other theologies from other cultural worldviews.

However, despite the great debate among scholars over the first use of the concept of an African oriented theology in publications, there is a growing consensus among scholars that the term "African Theology" was first used in the book called *Des Pretes noirs s'interrogent (Some Black Priests Wonder)* in the year 1956. This book comprised of the African Roman Catholic priests' plea to the Church to articulate theology having the flavor of the African people in terms of context, experience, and culture.[50] Therefore, if we are to define African theology, we would propose the following as working definitions for the sake of developing this chapter:

1. "African theology [is] the study that seeks to reflect upon and express the Christian faith in African thought-forms and idiom as it is experienced in African Christian communities, and always in dialogue with the rest of Christendom."[51]
2. "By African Theology we mean a theology which is based on the Biblical faith and speaks to the African 'soul' (or is relevant to Africa). It is expressed in categories of thought which arise out of the philosophy of the African people."[52] This definition means that "African theology has been motivated by the desire to make Christianity a truly African religion, contending that African converts must feel that the religion addresses their deepest needs and fears. If Christianity fails to do this, it will continue to be experienced as a foreign religion, the religion of the white man."[53]

49. Meiring, "As Below, so Above," 734; cf. Sawyerr, "What is African Theology?" 17–23.
50. Chitando, *Troubled but not Destroyed*, 9.
51. Kurewa, "The Meaning of African Theology," 36.
52. AACC as quoted in Mpanga, *Towards a Catholic Theology*, 33.
53. Chitando, *Troubled but not Destroyed*, 13.

3. "I will use the term 'African Theology' [...] without apology or embarrassment, to mean theological reflection and expression by African Christians."[54]

What do the above definitions tell us about this kind of theology? The above definitions tell us that the theologies that were imported from the North do not meet the requirements of people as Africans. This deficiency in meeting the requirements necessitates the quest for a theology that can meet people's needs, a theology grounded upon people's questions and world views. It means that African-oriented theology should not be based on the philosophical grounding of the Western philosophers but on the lived reality of people at the grassroots and articulated in the writings of the academy.[55]

There are three affirmations from African theological scholars for the above assertion: Tshibangu, the Pan-African Conference of Third World theologians and Okullu. In his part, Tshibangu affirms: "African theology will not necessarily be a theology based on the philosophy of the Greeks and their neighbors. It will be one that validly operates on the basis of the cultural and religious experience of the African peoples, a theology responding to the questions posed by African society in its contemporary evolution."[56] Here, Tshibangu emphasizes the importance of African religious background as a fertile soil for raising questions relevant to people's needs.

The Pan-African Conference affirms:

> We believe that African theology must be understood in the context of African life and culture and the creative attempt of African people to shape a new future that is different from the colonial past and the neo-colonial present. The African situation

---

54. Mbiti, J. "The Biblical Basis for Present Trends," 83.

55. Pioneers for this quest for a theology that can meet African people's needs include scholars such as Vicent Mulago from Bukavu, Kivu in the Democratic Republic of the Congo (see Bujo, "Vincent Mulago," 13–38), Engelbert Mveng from Enam-Nagal in Cameroon (see Hebga, "Engelbert Mveng," 39–46), Tharcisse Tshibangu Tshishiku from Kipush near Lubumbashi in the Democratic Republic of Congo (see Ntakarutimana, (MSGR Tharcisse Tshibangu," 47–63), Alphonse Ngindu Mushete from Tshilundu in the Eastern Kasai in the Democratic Republic of Congo (see Ntakarutimana, "Alphose Ngindu Mushete," 64–72), Sidbe Sempore from Ouagadougou in Burkina Faso (see Afan, "Sidbe Sempore," 73–94), Oscar Bimwenyi from Bena-Moyo near Luebo in the Democratic Republic of Congo (see Ozankom, "Oscar Bimwenyi," 95–106), Benezet Bujo from Drodro in the Democratic Republic of Congo (see Muya, "Benezet Bujo," 107–149), Barthelemy Adoukonou from Abomey in Benin (see Sempore, "Barthelemy Adoukonou," 150–166) and Elochukwu Eugen Uzukwu from Umuzu in Nigeria (see Gaise, "Elochukwu Eugen Uzukwu," 166–175).

56. Tshibangu in Mpanga, *Towards a Catholic Theology*, 35.

requires a new theological methodology that is different from the approaches of the dominant theologies of the West. African theology must reject, therefore, the prefabricated ideas of North Atlantic theology by defining itself according to the struggles of the people in their resistance against the structures of domination. Our task as theologians is to create a theology that arises from and is accountable to African people.[57]

The Pan-African Conference affirms in the above statement that African Theology must be based on people's rediscovery of Jesus in their own places, not on pre-fabricated formulations from the western world.

In his part, Okullu affirms:

"When we are looking for African theology we should go first to the fields, to the village church, to Christian homes to listen to those spontaneously uttered prayers before people go to bed. We should go to the schools, to the frontiers where traditional religions meet with Christianity. We must listen to the throbbing drumbeats and the clapping of hands accompanying the impromptu singing in the independent churches. We must look at the way in which Christianity is being planted in Africa through music, drama, songs, dances, art, [and] paintings. We must listen to the preaching of a sophisticated pastor as well as that of the simple village vicar. [. . .]. Can it be that all this is an empty show? It is impossible. This then is African Theology. This is not a racialistic theology, but an expression of the Christian faith in the African language."[58]

Here, Okullu views African Traditional Religion and its practice by the local people as the important context for the development of African Theology. The rediscovery of Jesus in an African context emanates nowhere apart from the cultural worldview of African people.

Conquering with Okullu's affirmation, Mbiti categorizes African Theology into three categories as practiced in African local churches and societies:

Written theology, Oral Theology and symbolic theology. According to Mbiti, Written African theology is the privilege of a few Christians who have had a considerable education and who generally articulate their theological reflection in articles and (so far, few) books, mostly in English, French, German or other

---

57. Pan African Conference of Third World Theologians, December 17-23, 1977, Accra, Ghana, "Final Communiqué," 193.

58. Okullu, *Church and Politics*, 54.

European languages. Oral theology is produced in the fields, by the masses, through song, sermon, teaching, prayer, conversation, *etc*. It is theology in open air, often unrecorded, often heard only by small groups, and generally lost to libraries and seminars. Symbolic theology is expressed through art, sculpture, drama, symbols, rituals, dance, colours, numbers, etc.[59]

According to Mbiti, all the three types of theologies are genuinely practiced in the various contexts within the African continent.

The problem is that theology has mostly been equated with writings of trained professionals. This problem is clearly echoed by Geheman: "All too often theology is equated with professional scholars writing books on theology for one another. A measure of a theologian is his [her] ability to interact with philosophers and theologians who write in many different languages."[60] Geheman further adds: "But theology is more than that. Theology not only can be done but in actual practice is done by all believers, whatever their educational level may be, when they reflect and think about their Christian faith and communicate that to others."[61] Therefore, as stated in the above paragraphs, African theology, as is any other contextual theology, is not a monopoly of a few trained people; rather, it is a theology accessible to all African people, lived and articulated in various spheres of their lives.

The words 'African Theology' and 'African Christian Theology' are used interchangeably in this book.[62] Each one of them means a theology that reflects on the Gospel as good news for salvation, the Christian tradition, the African reality of life experience according to the African worldview. Each of them indicate "the study that seeks to reflect upon and express the Christian faith in African thought forms and idioms as it is experienced in African Christian communities and always in dialogue with the rest of the Christendom."[63] Hence in considering the two concepts the challenge

---

59. Mbiti, "The Biblical Basis for Present Trends," 83–84.

60. Gehman, *Doing African Christian Theology*," 27.

61. *Ibid*.

62. In a real sense, the words "African Theology" imply an articulation of beliefs and practices of Africans in African Traditional Religion before the emergence of other religious faiths such as Christianity, Islam, *etc*. Though there is a diversity among ethnic groups and their beliefs and practices, the theology of ATR portrays some sort of religious identity for Africans (cf. Gathogo, "Liberation and Reconstruction," 86–88). In recognition that African Theology has a connection with ATR, other scholars have used the term *Theologia Africana* (see Dickson, "Towards a Theologia Africana"; Sawyerr, "What is African Theology?" 17–23) and others have added the word "Christian" in the middle to qualify for the kind of theology practiced in Africa after the coming of missionaries (see Mugambi, *African Christian Theology*).

63. Gathogo, Liberation and Reconstruction," 89.

of Mbiti to African theology need not be ignored. Mbiti, as quoted in Gathogo, poses the following challenge: "Christianity has made a real claim on Africa [. . .] the question is: Has Africa made a real claim on Christianity? Christianity has Christianised Africa, but Africa has not Africanised Christianity."[64] What Mbiti portrays in this quotation is that Christianity has monopolized Africa through its rampant spread and the great number of adherents; however, most of such adherents have not taken such Christian religion seriously in their real daily lives. Christianity has not entirely been African.

In whatever we can talk about African theology and its synonyms, we have to bear in mind that African culture and its African traditional religion are the main originators of African Theology. And, as Chitando insists, "African theology mainly promotes continuity between the old and the new. Its key goal is to ensure that Christianity in Africa reflects an African ethos, outlook and flavor."[65] This means that despite the Christian attitude of the missionaries, African theology tries to distinguish between the gospel and western culture and "rewrap the Christian faith indigenously" in order to prevent Africans from losing their cultural identities and promoting people's cultural continuity after conversion to Christianity.[66] This cultural continuity is the possible alternative for Africanizing Christianity making it relevant to the lives of people within the continent.

In response to Mbiti's challenge above, we can at least say that for a long time since African countries regained their independence from their colonial masters, the main emphasis has been that African churches and their theologies must have their own stamps. They should not adhere to the way their colonial masters did it when they earlier propagated the gospel in the African soil. African Traditional Religion must be taken seriously because it is the religion of the people that forms the roots of people's lives, people's worldview and practice. Hence, that is what is meant by African Theology being contextual.

Van Eck exemplifies the main criterion for a truly African Theology as being the following: "African Theology must be Biblical and contextual."[67] This means that African people have needs that depend on the African context they are. If the theology that purports to be African speaks to the real needs of African people and their respective contexts, yet remaining faithful

---

64. Gathogo, "Liberation and Reconstruction," 89; *cf.* Maddox, "African Theology," 25.

65. Chitando, *Troubled but not Destroyed*, 12.

66. Kurewa, "The Meaning of African Theology."

67. Van Eck, "The Word is Life," 696.

to Christian Scriptures, that kind of theology is truly African Theology. Hence, African theology is by nature not different from Western theology in terms of their origin (Bible and context). Both have the same criteria: being biblical based and context based. Their main difference is the types of contexts and the way they are done.

The Africanness of African Theology

The major problem facing African Theology is its attribution to Africa as a continent. Africa, as a continent is large, with many ethnic groups in it, with various cultural values and backgrounds. Is it legitimate to speak of theology as being African? Mugambi begins explaining this idea from the roots of theology itself. According to him, theology is the discourse about God. The concern of theology, as it is of philosophy, is about three major aspects: where does life come from (the origin of being), what is the purpose of life (purpose of being), and where is life going (the destiny of being)[68] Mugambi sees the problem of ascribing the discourse about God (theology) as being 'African' because of the nature of the continent. Africa is the large continent, with "an area of about eleven and a half squire miles, a population of more than five hundred million and ethnic identity comprising more than one thousand groups."[69] Moreover, Africa has "nearly fifty nations [. . .] with different constitutions and varying histories."[70] "The complexities of Africa," Michael L. Cook writes, "are compounded by the fact that there is an ancient and distinctive history of Christianity in Ethiopia (Acts 8:26–39), Egypt (e.g., Origen, Athanasius, Antony, *et al.*, along with the later Coptic tradition), and northern Africa (e.g., Tertullian, Cyprian, Augustine), and that South Africa has a distinctive history of its own. Moreover, the contemporary scene is complicated by 'a triple heritage' represented religiously by African traditional religions, Islam, and Christianity."[71] Therefore, taking the varying aspects within the continent, it is hard to discern what is real 'African'.

However, Mugambi proposes that when talking of theology as 'African' (*i.e.*, African Theology), two implications must be considered: first, "the phrase may refer to the discourse which Africans conducted among themselves before their contact and influence by Christians and Muslims. Secondly, it may also refer to the discourse which is being conducted by

68. Mugambi, *African Christian Theology*, 7.
69. Ibid., 3.
70. Ibid.
71. Cook, "The African Experience," 671.

Africans, in order to relate their own cultural and religious heritage to Christianity."[72] Mugambi's two proposals have been focal points of discussions and disagreements among scholars since the concept of African theology emerged. The major discussion among scholars is centered on whether theology in Africa should be known as African Theology, or African Christian Theology.

Despite the disagreements among scholars in regard to what the phrase 'African Theology' really means, the phrase has been recognized as 'African Christian Theology' in the context of organizations such as the World Council of Churches (WCC), World Student Christian Federation (WSCF), the All Africa Conference of Churches (AACC) and the National Council of Churches (NCC). An example of this recognition can be picked from one organization (the AACC) when it states: "African Theology is 'a theology based on the Biblical faith of Africans, and which speaks to the African soul. It is expressed in categories of thought which arise out of the philosophy of the African people. This does not mean it is narrow in outlook (syncretistic). To speak of African Theology involves formulating clearly a Christian attitude to other religions [. . .]."[73] In these organs, the phrase 'African Theology' has been used to refer to the way Africans express and experience God in their midst as Africans. Using in that way indicates that in Africa theology is not only verbalized, but also lived. The concept of God, who is the essence of the African theological discourse, is a reality that pervades throughout the life of Africans not just a philosophical concept. Mugambi concludes that "'African Theology' may thus imply (1) African Christian Theology (or African Muslim Theology); (2) African Religious Tradition (referring to non-christian and non-Muslim African tradition)."[74]

Gathogo, taking ideas from Mugambi, also sees the idea of the Africanness of theology as being problematic because of the homogeneous and heterogeneous nature of the various contexts within the African continent. Gathogo states that speaking of the Africannes of theology is difficulty, first because the African continent is not monolithic. Second, the African continent comprises a vast number of cultures which influence theology. Cultures include religions such as Christianity, Islam, African Traditional religion and the European culture inherited from the western missionaries. Third, there are cultures from out of Africa which have now made Africa as their home of residence and have great influence to theology. The homogeneity

---

72. Ibid., 9.

73. AACC in Shorter, *African Christian Theology*, 23.

74. Mugambi, *African Christian Theology*, 10; cf. Kunhiyop, "Challenges and Prospects," 65–66.

of the African large community of people can be viewed in the African concept of family as almost similar for all Africans, as compared to Europeans, Arabs, *etc*. The common history of colonization makes African people have similar backgrounds. Moreover, the concept of God and the whole divine worldview portrays similar main elements of the various cultures within Africa. The homogeneity and diversity of cultures and worldviews of the various communities within Africa need to be taken seriously when addressing the Africanness of theology.[75] We conclude this section with van Eck that "The Africanness of any theology (that purports to be Christian) should be measured by the degree to which it speaks to the needs of Africans in their total context, and be judged by the degree to which it is faithful to the Christian Scripture."[76]

Phases of African Theology

After discussing the Africanness of theology and its problems, we now consider the phases of development of African theological thinking. The development of African Theology has passed into several phases. In this section, we use Ezra Chitando's ideas to categorize the phases. The first phase of African theology, according to Chitando, is roughly estimated to last from 1956 to 1973. Its main concern was "the call to adapt Christianity to the African context. Catholic and Protestant African theologians demanded that the church in Africa be truly indigenous and also queried the interpretation of African cultures and religions as primitive."[77] It means despite the missionaries' endeavor to bring Christianity to Africa, Africa had no theology to boast as its own while some other continents had their own theologies apart from the hegemonic theology of the western missionaries. This concern is clearly stated by Akao: "The pathetic theological situation in Africa was calling for concern in that after more than a century of existence on the African soil, the church was still to come to grips with a theology it could proudly call its own. While the Latin Americans were fine-tuning their Liberation theology and the Asians romanticizing their fledging theologies, the Africans had nothing, even a heresy, to show to the world."[78]

Some Catholic priests that involved themselves in publishing manuscripts to reinforce the above emphasis include the following: Placide Temples who insisted on the 'vital force' of African indigenous religions,

75. Gathago, "Liberation and Reconstruction," 68–81.
76. Van Eck, "The Word is Life," 969.
77. Chitando, Troubed but not Destroyed, 16.
78. Akao, "The Task of African Theology," 341.

Alexis Kagame and Vincent Mulago whom, being influenced by Temples insisted on the value of African culture and the need for it being integrated together with the imposed foreign Christianity. Moreover, other scholars in this first phase are John S. Mbiti from Kenya and E. Bolaji Idowu from Nigeria who were considered key proponents towards this theology, especially in emphasizing on African beliefs and practices (Mbiti) and the possible indigenous church (Idowu). Therefore, the first phase is commendable "in that it represents the period when African intellectuals articulated the need for African theology and took decisive steps to frame its identity."[79] Their emphasis was on abundant resources in the African culture to make the Christianity brought by missionaries be experienced as African Christianity instead of being foreign.

The second phase is considered to last from 1974 to 1989. It is in this phase where the world witnessed the confident experience of the Church in Africa, more predominantly in the mid 1970s which followed the death of the Soviet Union and communism in the late 1980s. The demise of communism brought a turn in the world's landscape causing the witness of transformation in political, economic and technological orientations. In the second phase, theologians addressed the issues of the first phase without diverging that theology needed to be contextual for it to be relevant to people's worldviews and questions.

As Chitando puts it, "The second phase of African Theology saw more University Religious Studies departments establishing courses on ATRs and African Theology, along with an increasing acceptance of, and emphasis on, these new areas of academic inquiry."[80] Moreover, it is in this phase whereby more attention was paid to the concept of God in various contexts and indigenous religious experiences. The concept of Christology received its utmost attention. Scholars like Charles Nyamiti and Adrian Hastings expressed their concerns more emphatically than was in the first phase. The various beliefs and practices which were pointed out in the first phase, such as rites of passage, marriage issues, ancestral beliefs, issues of polygyny and polyandry received greater attention from scholarly articulations. Hence , the various discussions of terminologies to name the kind of theology being articulated in Africa, such as indigenization, translation, adaptation, Africanization, *etc.*, indicated the deepening concern of theologians on making theology attuned to people's realities.

According to Chitando, this phase is commended for several important aspects. One such aspects is that there was a high spread of African

79. *Ibid.*, 17.
80. *Ibid.*, 18.

theology in most parts of the sub-Saharan African area. This means that despite having contributors from West, East and Central Africa alone as being dominant contributors, contributions from Southern Africa also emerged as contributors in various theological articulations, which further ensured the expansion of African theology within the African continent. The expansion of African theology to South Africa led to the gain in momentum in this phase towards the fight against the dehumanizing apartheid regime.

Despite the intensified liberation struggle in the Southern Africa, the sense of community in African theology was highly amplified in this phase. Scholars struggled against the teaching of the salvation of the individual within Christianity blended with the western individualism. They emphasized on the sense of African community centered on *Ubuntu* philosophy of 'I am because we are.' Hence, contrary to the first phase that was a *call* towards African theology, the second phase moved towards *doing* African theology.

The third phase of African theology is considered to last from 1990 to the present day. The gain in independence for most Southern African countries and the demise of the dehumanizing apartheid regime in South Africa made the 1990s a period of hope and optimism. The church's efforts on the democratization process, the emergence of the fatal HIV and AIDS, the consolidation of the Circle of Concerned Women Theologians, and the emergence of Reconstruction Theologies made the phase more challenging. In this case, the third phase is commended for the greater expansion of African theology maintaining the focus on the intimate relationship between Christianity and African culture building on the themes of earlier phases.

Some important issues in the third phase include: the increase in the reflection on the theme of Christology which caused the emergence of "African Christological titles like Chief, Healer, Ancestor, Elder Brother, and others to interpret the significance of Christ in Africa,"[81] the increased reflections on the theme of ecclesiology emphasizing on the church having a structure attuned to the African context hence an African contextually relevant church, the increase in publications on Africa and the Bible, e.g., that of Hannah Kinoti and John Mary Waliggo on "the Bible in African Christianity" and that of Gerald West and Musa Dube on "the bible in Africa." Through these publications, and others not mentioned, the importance of the Bible to African context was highly amplified. Moreover, the amplification of African theology in this phase is vivid in that many students of theology pursuing Masters and Doctoral degrees within African Universities and abroad have reflected on various themes on African theology such as

---

81. *Ibid.*, 22.

"ethics, points of convergence between ATR and Christianity, the contribution of African creative writers and others."[82]

Challenges facing African Theology

Despite the above-discussed phases of African theology, yet it faces various challenges. In this part we use Waweru's article to illustrate these challenges.[83] First, though there is a large increase in the number of Christians in Africa, yet African Theology has mainly been scientifically articulated in the academic arenas leaving Christians divided on what is to be contextualized. This challenge means that the real practice of African Theology should be realized both in academic and non-academic contexts. Therefore, the major challenge here is how to bridge the gap between the professional theologians and normal believers of the Christian faith.

Second, African theology is practiced in the context of tragic social, political, economic and religious situations that ever pose challenges to it. Some examples of such situations include, but not limited to, bad governance among states, violence in all its sorts, incurable illnesses, poverty and the manipulation of differences in religion and ethnic belonging leading to abject poverty among Africans. African theology has hardly managed to end such devastating situations resulting into Africa being a good place to live only for the few people. As Waweru has reiterated, "Many African Christians have been cheated and mislead, leaving them confused, discouraged, and betrayed."[84]

Third, in the midst of evaluators, "African theology portrays Africa as sick, starved, bleeding, and crippled both economically and spiritually."[85] Moreover, evaluators see that reports produced by African theology proponents indicate the many active conflicts among Africans waged between ethnic groups, leaders who manipulate constitutions, various forms of violence, *etc.*, leading to human rights abuses. The failure of Africans to fully end these catastrophes poses a heavy task to reconstruction theology proponents within the African society.

Fourth, despite the existence of African Theology, the African church exists in the mult-religious context. In this context, the major question is how African Christian theology has co-existed with other living faiths. In

---

82. *Ibid.*, 23.
83. See Waweru, "African Theology," 222–223.
84. *Ibid.*, 222.
85. *Ibid.*

most cases, African Christian theology has not honored the respect and integrity of other faiths adequately.

Fifth, Africanization is one of the urgent priorities if the church is to take root in an African context. The challenge is whether African theology has taken the Africanization process serious for the church to be live and for the African people.

In summary, the whole process of African theology in its above-discussed phases and challenges is a process of resistance. It is a resistance against the missionaries' urge to change African people to western culture in order for them to be true Christians. Mbiti, as quoted in Chitando, clearly states about the notion of western missionaries which is highly resisted by all the above phases: "It was very unfortunate, therefore, that Africans were told by the word and example, by those who brought them the gospel that they first had to become culturally circumcised before they could become Christians (according to the form of Christianity developed in the home country of those missionaries)."[86] Therefore, African theology began, continued and continues as a theology of defense for the value and dignity of African people and their respective African cultures, reaffirmation of the black race, and the struggle against dehumanization of any kind.

However, why did Western missionaries force Africans who converted to Christianity to be circumcised from their African traditional cultural world view and practices as they became Christians? Togarasei provides a nuanced answer as she states: "Christianity has existed in the West for close to two centuries now resulting in Westerners seeing no difference between Christianity and their culture."[87] What Togarase says in this statement is that the understanding of Christianity among missionaries was totally bound to their culture. Anything out of their culture, which was embedded to Christianity for many years, was considered to be heathen and pagan. Therefore, Togarasei urges Christendom that Christianity in Africa should be understood within the framework of African culture. In contrast to the Western culture where traditional religion does not account for the lives of people, in Africa the traditional religion holds a great deal of meaning to the life of people in such a way that it can hardly be abandoned in whatever setting the African people will reside.[88]

---

86. Chitando, *Troubled but Not Destroyed*, 24.
87. Togarasei, "The Conversion of Paul," 117.
88. *Ibid*.

Criticisms to African Theology

Despite its reputable contribution, African theology has been criticized in two ways: Its legitimacy, and its syncretistic nature. The inception of African Theology was not smooth among some theologians in Africa. Byang Kato, for example did not find legitimacy for African theology to replace the contemporary Christian theology. Kato was suspicious with this kind of theology and considered it illegitimate and not genuine kind of a theology. Kato's notion is most likely still shared by some European and American theologians to date.[89]

Another criticism directed to African theology is based on the way African people practice their faith. There are still thoughts among some African theologians that African theology is not at all Christian, but an amalgamation of traces of Christianity and traces of African traditional religion. Morekwa, quoting an Apostolic Mission Church pastor in Botswana, attests this thought: "*African theology is just a mixture of African traditional religion with Christianity. Christianity should not be mixed with anything. African theology believes that a person can go to the traditional healer and still go and partake on the Holy Communion sacrament. That is a sin in front of God's eyes. Therefore if African theology condones these kinds of practices, it is not a Christian theology.*"[90] Therefore, this criticism makes African theology and African Christianity to be viewed as not being pure Christianity in the way it is supposed to be, especially as portrayed in African indigenous churches discussed below.

African Indigenous Churches (AIC)

Being a theology of defense, as discussed in the summary of the above subsection, African theology has manifested itself its various African forms and sub-forms of theologies. The most prominent emerging African theologies are those of the African Indigenous/Instituted/Independent/Initiated/International Churches (AIC).[91] According to Ngong, the emergence of these theologies was due to a response to the western Christianity which appeared in three phases:

> "The first was the establishment of the Ethiopian churches, the second was the rise of the prophet-healing or spirit churches,

89. Morekwa, "Doing Theology in the Post Liberation Era," 90.

90. *Ibid* (Italics is in original).

91. Chitando, *Troubled but not Destroyed*, 15; cf. Chitando &Mateveke, "Shifting Perceptions," 129–130.

and the third is the current Pentecostal-Charismatic Christianity that is spreading like wildfire on the continent. All these churches fall under what has variously been called African Independent Churches, African Instituted Churches, African International Churches or African Initiated Churches (AICs) and Apostolic Churches, but the Pentecostal-type churches belong to the second and the third responses. The second response, known as the prophet-healing or spirit churches, have variously been referred to as Zionist (South Africa), Aladura (Nigeria) or Roho (Kenya) Churches, among other names. These churches started in the 1920s and 1930s, propelled partly by the healings which their charismatic founders were believed to have wrought during the 1918 influenza epidemic in Africa."[92]

Adamo further elaborates about these churches: "African Indigenous Churches have been given so many names such as Aladura Churches (praying churches), Pentecostal Churches, African Independence Churches, Zionist Churches, White Garment Churches, Ethiopian Churches and others."[93] They are called Aladura Churches because they put more emphasis on prayer; they are called Pentecostal churches because of the way they pray and the way they put much emphasis on the Holy Spirit.[94] They are called African independent churches because they claim to be free from the control of western influence and from the influence of the western mainline churches. The name Zionist is because of their Pentecostal praying and emphasis on spiritual healing. They are called White Garment churches simply because of the white robs which most members of these churches wear. They wear these white robes believing that such garments are used by angels in heaven, and are called Ethiopian because their establishment is thought to be because of political nature and maintain much of the structures of the mission churches from which they came.[95]

---

92. Ngong, "Theology as the Construction of Piety," 357; cf. Bayer, *Religions in Global Society*, 143, Sawyerr, "What is African Theology?" 10–13 & Manyonganise, "African Independent Churches," 161.

93. Adamo, *Reading and Interpreting the Bible*, 23. The question is whether these churches are independent from mainline churches as they claim to be. Some scholars see that these churches are still in relationship with the mainline churches and still depend on mainline churches in various aspects (Olowola, "Introduction to Independent African Churches," 22–23).

94. Beyer states that "The dominant bond which identifies Pentecostalism is [. . .] the presence of *individualized* demonstrations of religious power in ritual settings, especially ecstatic utterances (prophesying, glossalaria), other bodily possessions and ritual healing." (Bayer, *Religions in Global Society*, 147, italics is in original)

95. Adamo, Reading and Interpreting the Bible, 23–24; cf. Hastings, *A History of African Christianity*, 67–85 & Vengeyi & Mwandayi, "Dress as a Mark of Differentiation,"

In the opening of his article, the theologian M.L. Daneel puts it clear about the theology and practice of the above churches which distinguish them from Western-oriented Christianity. Daneel affirms: "The Theology of African Initiated Churches (AICs) [...] can hardly be described as systematized, written theology based on abstract reflection as is common in the West. Instead, it is an enacted theology, written in the song and dance, in the rhythm of dancing feet, in serving hands of healing and exorcism, where worship and proclamation give expression to the presence of God, to His kingdom already manifest in black 'Jerusalems' and 'Zion Cities' under the blazing skies of Africa."[96]

Why did AICs emerge? Waliggo provides a nuanced answer to this question: "These churches have an important lesson for us all today. In one real way they have come into being because of what they saw as the failure of the main Christian Churches to accept and promote the principle of inculturation. They are the evident signs that not all is well within the major churches. Although we should realize that some of those churches sprung up as a result of personality conflict, racism within the church ranks, disagreements on some central issues of doctrine and morality, the general lesson should not be forgotten."[97] Therefore, it is only when the main churches have undergone a proper inculturation that they will acquire lasting identities among Africans and quenches the hunger and thirst of Africans making them join the AICs.

Another reason for their emergence is political. Monyonganise, writing in the Zimbabwean context, asserts that the rise of nationalism among African nations kindled the urge among Christians to participate in what was going on outside the church. Since the mainline churches hardly criticized the political activities of the colonizers, Christians initiated churches where they used as an arena to criticize the unjust political conduct of the colonial governments. It was an arena for them to free from the western influence and the influence of missionary mainline churches. The experience within churches that was not different from the experience outside the church made Christians long for participation in the critique of both the conduct of mainline churches and of the colonial powers. In this situation, where mainline churches shunned participation in politics making

---

203–204.

96. Daneel, "Holistic African Theology," 1.

97. Waliggo, "Making a Church that is Truly African," 21; cf. Gunda, "African 'Biblical' Christianity," 145&148.

Christians have a similar experience from what was outside the churches, initiation of more African oriented churches was inevitable.[98]

Another reason was the failure of some ambitious Christians to acquire leadership positions within the mainline churches. Such Christians broke away from mainline churches they belonged and initiated their own churches where they fulfilled their ambitions. According to Machingura: "the radicalism commonly found in apostolic sects has its origin in the conflict between white missionaries and their black congregations resulting in a number of apostolic independent sect leaders like Johanne Marange and Johane Masowe breaking away from the mission churches due to accounts of frustrated ambition to positions of leadership within the mission churches. Most of the apostolic sects were founded and supported as a result of racial hostility against blacks."[99] Therefore, the formation of African initiated Churches is mainly associated with the missionaries' racial hostility against the blacks and the paternalistic habit of mainline churches.

What are the characteristics of African Indigenous Churches? Adamo lists nine of the distinguishing features of these churches:[100] First, they put much emphasis on the African worldview in the way they read and interpret the Bible. They preach the message of the Gospel taking into account the existence of ancestors, spirits and evil spirits that can cause harm in people's lives. They also engage in the interpretation of dreams, trances and visions encountered by their members."[101] This is what Adamo calls as a "corporate responsibility in African healing system."[102]

Second, they put much emphasis on divine healing. Prayers for healing are prayed upon those who are sick and special days are set because of this purpose and those healed provide testimonies before the other congregations. Falaye emphasizes that "The AICs are often on the television today claiming the divine power of God to heal people of all manners of infirmities as they come to believe in Jesus Christ the Saviour. Healing of the medical incurable illness such as HIV&AIDS, cancer, diabetics and others have been claimed to have been healed by these AICs."[103]

Machingura provides an example of one AIC sect in Zimbabwe—the Johane Marange Apostolic Church (JMAC)—and its strict dependence on

---

98. Monyonganise, "African Independent Churches," 162.
99. Machingura, "The Martyring of People," 179.
100. Van Zyl, "Holistic Healing," 318.
101. Adamo, Reading and Interpreting the Bible, 48.
102. Ibid., 48.
103. Falaye, "The Relevance of African Independent Churches," 14; cf. Machingura, "The Martyring of People," 190–194.

healing prayers putting aside all western medicines. While the JMAC strictly rejects all kinds of family planning as being against God's plan for humanity causing the bearing of a huge number of children among its members, it has caused the death of a large number of innocent souls through its jettison of western medicines. In his own words, Machingura substantiates: "The JMAC proclaim a holistic gospel of salvation that includes deliverance from all types of evil oppression like sickness, barrenness, sorcery, evil spirits, unemployment and poverty [. . .]. The JMAC's beliefs have been labelled in the media as retrogressive since their beliefs result in the martyring of innocent souls.[. . .].What is interesting is that, their radical beliefs don't take into consideration the disturbing number of JMAC children dying from: polio, measles, diphtheria, Tetanus, and Pertussis (whooping cough)."[104] In some cases, healers of these "churches allow the use of certain rituals such as bathing in a flowing river, use of palm front, use of oil and others in the healing of sick people. Some of them also make use of the local herbs to cure sickness such as prostate cancer, stroke and paralysis successfully."[105]

Third, they put more emphasis on Prayers. The main task of church members is mostly fasting and praying for the sick and the need to regain their normal situation. For example, Falaye reports that some Aladura churches in Nigeria prefer to go to mountains for praying. Falaye, quoting Oshitelu, says that going to the mountains for prayers is one of the "'features of African traditional religion: the belief that the abode of *Olodumare* is in the high places.' Their prayers include the use of psalms, fasting which they believe hastens answers to prayers. They also believe in special prayers: for breaking ancestral curse, for the unemployed to get job, for overseas travelers to gain visa from the embassies, for the waiting mothers and others with some common spiritually induced social problems."[106]

Fourth, they put more emphasis on spirituality. Every event that happens is provided a spiritual interpretation be poverty, barrenness, sickness, *etc*. The events of problems emerging are provided spiritual solutions, and the spirits are seen to be working through whatever the individual attempts. In this case, the whole life of the Christian is believed to be guided by the spirit world. Hence, their incorporation of the spirit world in the Christian faith and practice affirmed the African communal life as opposed to the western individualistic Christianity that stressed on the individual and his

---

104. Machingura, "The Martyring of People," 190–191.
105. Falaye, "The Relevance of African Independent Churches," 14.
106. *Ibid*.

or her own responsibility. In African communality, both the living and the departed come together in relationship to form one community.[107]

Fifth, they put more emphasis on Evangelism and Revival. Most leaders and members of these churches are enthusiastic evangelists who preach at various open air meetings to win converts. Their preaching emphasizes more on personal revival and living the life of renunciation and faith through the work of the Holy Spirit in their lives. Moreover, the early prominent leaders of AICs insisted that they were led by the Holy Spirit to break from the mainline Christianity preached in mainline churches.[108]

Sixth, they put much emphasis on flexible worship services. Their worships are not guided by rigid Eurocentric liturgies, but flexible forms of liturgy full of dancing singing, clapping of hands, chomping of feet, etc., using traditional musical instruments like drums. These kinds of worship make members of these churches more active and enthusiastic worshipers.

Seventh, they emphasize on an elaborate role of women. In these churches, women are provided an elevated position contrary to missionary churches that proclaim equality between men and women while leaving most of the positions of authority being in the hands of men. In fact, "In these churches women are more possessed, they prophesy, they dance, they sing, clap, and give more testimonies than men. They are always in the majority and are more active. In fact they are church founders."[109] The question is that why are they the majority in these churches? Quoting Mwaura, Kasomo responds to this question: "Women want to remain in the Church but when the patriarchal hierarchy puts obstacles on their way and they cannot attain spiritual fulfillment, they leave to express their spirituality in a new Church or an accommodating one [. . .]."[110] For example, in the Akurinu church among the Gikuyu of Kenya women denied leadership positions in the church opted to form a group of *Anabii* (prophets) in order to affirm their presence and contribution in the life of the church.[111]

---

107. *Ibid.*, 10.

108. See Chitando, *Troubled but not Destroyed*, 15.

109. Adamo, *Reading and Interpreting*, 40; *cf.* Kasomo, "The Role of Women," 135–137. Kasomo, quoting Mwaura, asserts: "Women want to remain in the Church but when the patriarchal hierarchy puts obstacles on their way and they cannot attain spiritual fulfillment, they leave to express their spirituality in a new Church or an accommodating one." (Kasomo, "The Role of Women," 132) Mwaura's words account for the flocking of women in African Indigenous Churches where they feel welcome to express their God-given talents.

110. Kasomo, "The Role of Women," 132.

111. Ndug'u, "The Role of the Bible," 246.

Despite the greater participation of women in these churches, Oduyoye affirms that this prominence hardly guarantees women from not being excluded by men. She states: "In African instituted Churches women are most visible in the structures of authority. However, even here traditional taboos still exclude women, including women founders of churches, from sacramental roles."[112] In order to substantiate her claim, Oduyoye provides an example from the Aladura church: "In the Aladura church, for example, four categories of people are not allowed to enter into a house of prayer for fear that their presence might desecrate the holy place. They include a woman who has just delivered a baby, a menstruating woman, men and women who have remained unwashed after sexual intercourse, and a woman with uncovered hair."[113] Hence, this exclusion of women within Christianity means that the Christianity which is embraced by people is not an emancipating religion. It is still used as a weapon of subjugation even within the AICs, apart from the mainline churches. Rosemary N. Edet cements this statement when she avers: "The Christian proclamation of human liberation and the equality of men and women is indeed good news for women, but [in Christianity] this teaching is more theoretical than practical. If it were practical, Christianity could have emancipated women from adverse rituals."[114]

Eighth, they put more emphasis on the power of the Words. These churches believe greatly on the power of potent words spoken by their prophets to effect what the words are spoken for. They also believe on the power of the words recited from the Bible to effect what the words promise to fulfill. Adamo says that because of its potency, "The Word of God may be prescribed to be read seven times during midnight and while naked [. . .]."[115] For example, Adamo illustrates: "For success or good-luck in winning court cases, Psalms 13, 35, 46, 51, 77, 83, 87, 91, 110, 121, and 148, with specific instruction are recommended. [. . .]. Psalm 4, 108 and 114 are special Psalms for success in any venture one embarks on, such as laying the foundation of a house, promotion in government work, or embarking on a business trip. These Psalms are to be read with prescribed instructions and prayers to accompany them."[116] Therefore, for the AICs the power of the word, especially the use of psalms with prescribed instructions, hold important position in the life and practice of Christians.

112. Oduyoye, "Women and Ritual," 10.

113. *Ibid.*

114. Edet, "Christianity and African Women's Rituals," 35; *cf.* Ndug'u, "The Role of the Bible," 246.

115. Adamo, *Reading and Interpreting*, 40.

116. Adamo, "The Use of Psalms," 344–345.

The above mentioned characteristics of African Indigenous Churches indicate that these churches are deeply rooted in the African worldview. They try to mix African culture and the message of salvation from the Bible. In other cases, they can be considered to be a protest from what the main line churches are doing in their Western-oriented theology and practice. It is an endeavor by Africans to regain their identity jeopardized by mainline churches which imposed western inconceivable values. Atuahene puts it: "This religious and cultural imposition created awareness in the African people of the need to struggle for an African Christian identity and African way of worship. It is an undeniable fact that the AICs emerged to challenge the attempt by the Europeans to control and eliminate Africans' identity."[117] Instead of leaving the African culture aside, they incorporate it in the life and practices of their Christians as Chitando here emphasizes: "They have sought to ensure that their followers encounter Christianity as an African religion and for the most part manage to inculcate a sense of belonging amongst their members. They address existential issues that confront their members and have extended healing services to other African Christians and traditionalists."[118]

As we said in the beginning of the discussion about the AIC, their emergence was just a response to the western Christianity which accompanied the missionary or mainline churches. However, there has been a decline in followers to these churches in the 21st century. Their place is being taken by the Pentecostal/Charismatic churches. Ngong clearly states it: "prophet-healing and spirit churches have been declining in much of Africa in recent years. Their place is now being taken by the Pentecostal-Charismatic churches. What used to be said of the prophet-healing and spirit churches is now being said of the Pentecostal-Charismatic churches, namely that people are fleeing from the mission created or mainline churches (and in some cases from the older prophet-healing or spirit churches) to them because these mission churches cannot adequately address their needs."[119] Therefore, this movement of Christians from mainline and classical AIC churches to Pentecostal/Charismatic churches indicates the nature of Neo-Pentecostalism which spreads in the world like fire as a form of globalization. This kind of Pentecostal movements will be discussed in more detail in the following chapter.

---

117. Atuahene, "A Comparative Study of the Prophets," 21.
118. Chitando, *Troubled but not Destroyed*, 16.
119. Ngong, "Theology as the Construction of Piety," 358.

Criticisms against Activities of African Indigenous Churches

Despite the initiatives of these churches, one among the criticisms directed to them is the morality and training of most of their leaders. Most of their leaders, the "white robed," "spirit-type," or "Apostolic" prophets,[120] lack theological training and have been accused of leading immoral lives in the course of their ministry. Atuahene reports on what happens in Ghana:

> Many Ghanaians are searching for answers to the kind of training, and the contents and duration of training of AIC prophets because they are of the opinion that many of the AIC prophets do not go through any structured form of training like the pastors of the mainline churches such as the Methodist, the Presbyterian, the Anglican and the Catholic [. . .]. Unfortunately, a day hardly passes in Ghana without a prophet being alleged to have been involved in an immoral act, ranging from rape, defilement, duping, stealing, using black powers and ritual murder.[121]

In fact, when such immoral issues face these religious leaders, they leave questions to adherents and the community at large regarding the nature of God whom they claim to serve.

More badly, any ministerial leader that emerges adds the title "prophet" to it as Atuahene reports: "More disturbing is the fact that 'many men of God' are now adding 'Prophet' to their existing titles—Pastors, Elders and Bishops. There are even cases where every leader in the ministry is given the title 'prophet' with the founder or leader being the 'Presiding Prophet'. The man who preaches the sermon is a prophet, the one who leads the praises and worship is called a prophet; and the pastor is a prophet; so is the one who administers healing and deliverance."[122] The lack of elaborate training to leaders of these churches makes it legitimate for another criticism of their being syncretistic, the incorporation of incompatible cultural values which go against Scriptures as Olowola clarifies it: "One can safely conclude that while some are trying to be biblical Christians, others are clearly cultic. Some are actually traditional worshipers in Christian colour. Hence, their doctrines and practices are not biblical."[123]

Most of the above-stated prophets are alleged of being modern *sangomas* in the guise of reading the Bible as a tool for their *sangoma* activities.

---

120. Chitando, "Prophets, Profits and Protest," 98.

121. *Ibid.*, 2; Olowola, "An Introduction to Independent African Churches," 45, cf. Magezi & Banda, "Competing with Christ?" 1.

122. *Ibid.*, cf. Gunda & Machingura, "The 'Man of God'," 22–26.

123. Olowola, "An Introduction to Independent African Churches," 45.

Pastor Shoko, quoted in Marongwe and Maposa, alleges these prophets in the Zimbabwean context: "It's pretty obvious. In Zimbabwe we have too many false prophets than any other country but the major ones are well known. Zimbabwe's false prophets are even more advanced, in terms of prosperity and even technology. They can do anything for you, but if you are so spiritual you will see that they are just modern day *sangomas* who wear suits and read the bible. We all know these false prophets."[124] Prosperity gospel churches which Marongwe and Maposa mention in their statement are turned into hospitals or, more accurately, places of work for advanced *sangomas* (prophets).

These prophets are mainly engaged in what Marongwe and Maposa call '*gospreneurship*,' not in the real gospel portrayed in the Bible through reading it responsibly.[125] The gospel has become an industry, the Jesus industry, where the "white collar prophets"[126] engage themselves in invading the majority Christians who are not able to interrogate the legality and efficacy of their false actions. Their clandestine or open involvement into immoral issues questions the authenticity of what they preach and teach despite ascribing to themselves huge religious titles. These types of "white collar prophets" and the prosperity gospel they embrace will be considered in detail in chapter five below.

However, the problem with pastor Shoko's allegation stated in the above paragraph is that it hardly considers the criteria used to discern the true and the false prophet. What exactly is the basis for the prophet to be

---

124. Marongwe & Maposa, "PHDS Gospreneurship, Globalozation and the Pentecostal 'New Wave' in Zimbabwe," 16.

125. The term '*gospreneurship*' was introduced by Jonathan Mbiriyamveka in his article published in *The Heralds* of 27 July 2013. Mbiriyamveka introduced this term "in specific reference to the works of the emerging trend where Pentecostal churches were being perceived as lucrative financial ventures and where the 'prophets' and their wives who were also turning out as 'prophetesses' were exhibited opulence. Thus [. . .] gospreneurship can be taken to mean the setting of the gospel mission as a platform for profiteering as in a business venture that is as a 'latter day, money-spinning family enterprise' [. . .] This occurs when 'street wise'[. . .] charismatics who were driven by money, fame and fortune 'get into the ministry for money after observing how others have had a mixture of fame and fortune, having made lots of money'" (Marongwe & Maposa, "PHDS Gospreneurship, Globalozation and the Pentecostal 'New Wave' in Zimbabwe," 15).

126. By definition, these are "those prophets who are motivated by the desire to professionalize the word of God through monetizing it. In other words, white collar prophets put emphasis on money and prosperity as pillars of deliverance and salvation. They believe that poverty, misfortune and disease are caused by evil spirits and that God wants people to be prosperous and disease free in this world." (Mangena & Mhizha, "The Rise of White Colar Prophecy," 136).

true or false while all of them are labeled as prophets? The debate about who is true prophet and who is false is as ancient as and as complicated as the institution itself and the society that faced the institution. In the Old Testament times, for example, prophets performed miracles in a similar way as the contemporary prophets perform in various African countries. If one examines the Bible carefully, it can be noted that it hardly indicates clear cut criteria for a true and a false prophet in Israel. Vangeyi states that an "attempt at establishing criteria of authenticity of prophets in Israel is captured in literature by Deuteronomist theologians/editors (Deut 13:1–5; 18:15–22), Jeremiah (23:9–32) and Ezekiel (13). However, rather than solving the debate as regards to who exactly was a true prophet and who was a false one, the criteria set by the Deuteronomist theologians only provide very important insights into the dilemma that befell the society of Judah in trying to fish out false prophets from true prophets."[127]

A similar dilemma faces prophecy in Africa in our contemporary context. Criteria such as that of speaking in the name of Yahweh (Deuteronomy 13: 1–5) and that of prediction and fulfillment (Deuteronomy 13:1–5; 18:21–22) set by the Deuteronomistic scholars can hardly be used to distinguish between false and true prophets both in Israel and in contemporary Africa.[128] For prophecy in Israel, it was plausible to distinguish between prophets of Yahweh and prophets of Baal because those of Yahweh spoke in the name of Yahweh and those of Baal spoke in the name of Baal. In the contemporary Africa, all prophets speak in the name of God, use the same Bible as a source of their prophetic inspiration and sometimes their messages contradict. How can one distinguish between them?

Moreover, the question of predictions made by prophets and their fulfillment can hardly be a criterion for true and false prophets, especially in the current African context because that is not prophecy. Biri and Togarasei, basing on 1 Corinthians 14: 3 in a Zimbabwean context, argue that

> "the common and popular understanding of prophecy as foretelling [. . .] is misleading and has resulted in many people in Zimbabwe being deluded by the contemporary prophetic bandwagon of popular prophets [. . .]. These male prophets have deeply divided the nation, with some following them and others

---

127. Vangeyi, "Zimbabwean Pentecostal Prophets," 33.

128. Vangeyi discusses the strengths and weaknesses of several criteria for discerning true and false prophets in the Old Testament and contemporary Africa such as speaking in the name of Yahweh, predictions and fulfillment, morality, *pro-status quo* and *anti-status quo*, professionalism, ecstasy and prophetic call (see Vangeyi, "Zimbabwean Pentecostal Prophets," 32–54). However, for the sake of this section we have discussed only the first two criteria.

describing them as nothing but charlatans bent on enriching themselves through claiming prophetic inspiration. We argue that, though some New Testament prophets had abilities to perceive the thoughts and background details of other people and to predict future events as done by the likes of Prophets Makandiwa, Angel and many other prophets of the same guild, neither of these is necessarily the primary function of the gift of prophecy. By definition, "prophecy is an inspired word of instruction and/or exhortation that addresses the community in the language of the people [...]." According to Paul, prophecy edifies, encourages and consoles (1 Cor. 14:3).[129]

Biri and Togarasei, taking ideas from Hargreaves' comments on 1Corinthians 14, further elaborate

- "That prophets were a group of Christians within a congregation who taught the people
- That they were responsible for up building, encouragement, consolation, convict and call to account
- That they were not foretellers, but rather people who were fully aware of the will of God and the situation in which they and their contemporaries were living."[130]

As just indicated by Biri and Togarasei above, it becomes obvious that the sole concern for prophets in the Old Testament time was to preach to people for them to change their evil behavior, not just providing future predictions. Prophets were understood or likely understood themselves as being critics of society in order to enhance social, political, cultural, religious and economic reforms. The predictions they made were warning to people they preached of what would happen should they not change their behavior. Vengeyi clearly confirms: "Prophets were first and foremost preachers, whose preaching was intended to cause change of attitude and change of action from the audience [. . .]. 'certainly the (Israelite) prophet did predict the future [. . .] but prediction (of the future) was not the larger part of prophecy; it was as much the prophet's responsibility to interpret correctly the past and the present."[131] This statement means that prophecy cannot be equated with mere predictions and fulfillment, and neither can predictions and fulfillment be used as sole criteria for discerning true and false prophets

---

129. Biri & Togarasei, ". . .but the One Who Prophesies Builds the Church," 89.
130. *Ibid.*, 90.
131. *Ibid.*, 37.

in contemporary Africa because even false prophets can predict what can come to pass.

As said above, in the Old Testament times prophets conveyed contradicting messages and sometimes arising conflicts among themselves which made it difficult to distinguish between true and false ones. In regard to this issue, Vengeyi reports: "The clashes between Elijah and the 450 prophets of Baal (and 400 prophets of Asherah) at Mt. Carmel (1Kgs 18: 16–40), that of Micaiah ben Imlah and Zedekiah (1 Kgs 22:24) and the one between Jeremiah and Hananiah (Jer. 28) are convincing evidence not only to the fact that in Israel conflicting theological convictions between prophets was the source of contradictory messages but also that this ideological clash in most cases ended up in real physical clashes/fist-fighting and death."[132]

Most of these clashes among prophets are vivid in our contemporary African context making the attempt to distinguish the true and the false ones even more difficult just by using the Bible as a sole criterion because both parties use the same Bible to justify their prophetic activities (see texts like Mark 16: 17–18; 1Corinthians 2: 9; and John 14: 12).[133] And sometimes, true prophets face divine deception, where God provides a false message to a true prophet for a particular purpose (see for example 1Kings 22).[134] Hence, it is possible that both true and false prophets are used as mediums of the same God, being not responsible for the message they deliver; and the Bible can hardly be the only solution to distinguishing between true and false prophets in the increasing population of prophets in our contemporary African contexts.[135]

CONCLUSION

In this chapter we have discussed about African theology as contextual theology. The major emphasis in this discussion has been the way we need to value African culture as a prerequisite context in doing theology. By using Magesa's article, we discussed the African worldview in relation to various issues such as widow cleansing, widow inheritance and their effects in this era of HIV and AIDS. We discussed in detail the role of ATR in shaping African lifestyles in various areas of the African continent. Moreover, we

---

132. *Ibid.*, 32–33.

133. *Ibid.*, 81–83.

134. The concept of divine deception and that of divine repentance are both fount in the Bible (see Amos 3: 6, 7 for divine repentance. God repents to do what was planned to be done).

135. *Ibid.*, 36–39.

discussed why most Africans remain Christians during the time of joy and resume to ATR during the times of sorrow; and why most Africans are Christians during the day and ATR followers during the night.¹³⁶ We showed that this double life embraced by Africans indicates that Christianity has managed to Christianize Africa, but Africans have hardly managed to Africanize Christianity. Christianity, though widely resurgent and with great number of adherents in Africa, yet has remained foreign.

We also discussed in this chapter about the various Christological reflections that are done by African theologians doing African theology. In this discussion, we emphasized that African theology is mostly "resonance theology" because it tries to resonate issues found in the Bible with issues found in the real life of Africans in their own contexts. Christologies such as Jesus Christ as African chief, African king, African ancestor, African master of initiation, African Divine Chameleon, African Healer, African Black Messiah, *etc.*, are some of the resonance Christologies depicted in Christological reflections in doing African theology.¹³⁷ These Christological titles clearly indicate the way people come to rediscover Jesus' role in their places, depending on the questions they ask and find them important.

Moreover, even the theology of inculturation mostly done in Africa north of the Limpopo river which centers on people's cultural worldviews, the theology of liberation done in various parts of Africa which centers on the question of poverty, and black theology practiced in the southern part of Africa centering on the questions of race and class are all resonance African Theologies.¹³⁸ These Christological reflections make African Christian theology contextual theology because they depict the role of Jesus Christ in particular African contexts depending on people's experiences of God in those contexts.

We ended the discussion of this chapter by looking closely at the theology and emphasis of African Indigenous Churches. Basing on Adamo's book, we stated the reasons for their emergence, and their major characteristics in relation to mainline or missionary churches. Moreover, we deduced the dilemma facing true and false prophets both in the Bible and in

---

136. *Cf.* Togarasei, "The Conversion of Paul," 111–114.

137. Akao, "The Task of African Theology," 342.

138. *Cf.* Ukpong, "Current Theology," 501–502. There are tendencies for some scholars to view African Theology as being distinct from Black Theology mostly done in South Africa and North America (see Mokhoethi, "Towards Contextual Theology," 2n2) To my view, since both theologies address the concerns of Africans and their contexts wherever they are found, they should be referred to as African Theologies. However, we should recognize inculturation and Black Theologies as distinct theologies due to their location—north and south of the Limpopo River respectively.

contemporary African context by surveying the Deuteronomistic criteria. It has been clear that both false and true prophets use the same Bible and claim for truth in the message they deliver. Speaking in the name of Yahweh and predictions and fulfillment are hardly sole criteria for true prophecy. In this case, the chapter has successfully provided a brief survey of some issues of African theology in Africa with the aim of kindling zeal to readers to explore much about this kind of theology and its practice in Africa. The chapter has successfully managed to survey the African context through which Christianity has to anchor its roots if it is to be relevant to African people in the twenty-first century.

4

Practical Theology as Contextual Theology

INTRODUCTION

One of my students in a Practical Theology class asked a question: "We confess in the Apostolic Creed about the Church being One, Holy, and Apostolic, where can we see the *Oneness* of the Church in the twenty-first century?" The student continued, "There is no one way of worshiping God throughout the world. There is no one way that people experience about God in the various places of this world, and neither is there one way of practicing faith. People practice faith according to their various experiences of God in their own places. How can we claim that the Church is One?" The student pronounced his faith: As an African, "I believe in the One God who is experienced in the multiple churches of Jesus Christ in various contexts of our continent." The confession of this student raised a hot discussion in class regarding the third article of the Apostles' Creed. In the discussion, the student seemed to be unaware of the meaning of the ever-confessed article of the Apostles' Creed in regard to the implied aspects of the Oneness of the Church.

However, the question of the student went beyond the hot discussion of the class. As one could see, the student's question pointed to the practices of the Church in Africa where people could experience the presence and activities of God in their real lives. The experience of the Church about God cannot be expressed in terms of the Church in its general sense but within churches in their particular sense. It is within churches where Jesus the founder of the Church is visible with all his activities: healing the sick, consoling those who mourn, feeding them when hungry, providing hope to those economically stricken by the globalizing forces, and counseling and caring them through the ministers of such churches. In that case, the practice of the Church in Africa is visible through the various practices of particular churches within their particular places.

If the practice of the Church in Africa is visible through the practices of particular churches in their respective places, what is the role of practical theology to the Church in Africa as an academic discipline? Though this question will be explored further within this chapter, we better introduce it here in order to make it clear about our conceptualization of Practical theology as a theology of place. Osmer in his article called "Practical Theology: A Current International Perspective" argues that the role of Practical Theology is based mainly on four aspects:

- "Descriptive-empirical: What is going on? Gathering information to better understand particular episodes, situations, or contexts.
- Interpretive: Why is this going on? Entering into a dialogue with the social sciences to interpret and explain why certain actions and patterns are taking place.
- Normative: What ought to be going on? Raising normative questions from the perspectives of theology, ethics and other fields.
- Pragmatic: How might we respond? Forming an action plan and undertaking specific responses that seek to shape the episode, situation, or context in desirable directions."[1]

The above-highlighted tasks are done by Practical Theology in relation to the practice of the Church through particular churches. Osmer calls the four tasks as a "paradigm" in Thomas Kuhn's understanding of paradigm. He further calls this paradigm as "a paradigm of reflexive practice" whose historical root comes from modernity in Europe.[2]

The four tasks highlighted above indicate that Practical Theology appeared as an academic discipline in universities in European context posing challenges to "traditional medieval patterns of life, including religion."[3] Osmer further notes: "In the context of modernity, it was not enough for Christian leaders simply to hand on the traditions and practices of the past. Nor was it enough for theologians simply to hand on the Christian cultural

---

1. Osmer, "Practical Theology," 2.
2. *Ibid.*
3. *Ibid.*

heritage of the West along the lines of the liberal arts tradition of the Renaissance and Reformation universities. In both the church and academy, the challenge of developing new forms of Christian practice in a modernizing world and providing good reasons to justify these practices was front and centre."[4] These words by Osmer indicate that the task of Practical Theology as a discipline was to evaluate the practices of the Church through the practices of churches in their particular places and developing theories of how things should be done and rules which leaders of churches can be guided towards better actions.

Osmel's tasks above clearly show that Practical Theology can hardly escape from the notion of place as put forth in this book. The above tasks indicate that practical theology is theology in practice within particular churches. Churches undergo their practices in particular places and the reflective actions done by Practical Theology hardly focus on the Universal Church directly, but mostly on the practices of particular churches. Therefore, this chapter argues that since the reflections of Practical Theology are done focusing on the actions of churches in particular places in the African continent, is contextual theology in its own sake. After discussing the context which contextual theology requires to take into account in the previous chapter, this chapter purports that contextual theology in Africa should be done in the form of practical theology, i.e., as actions and reflections on theology. In order to justify these propositions, various issues are discussed: the meaning, the contextual nature, and the history of practical theology as a discipline in theology which provide the basis for chapter five, a chapter that surveys the real contextual issues practiced within the Church in Africa, and which Practical theology endeavors to reflect as a contextual theology in Africa. We agree with Dames' position that "Suffice it to argue that practical theology is deeply *contextual* in terms of ecclesial, social, cultural interconnections, relationships and systems [. . .]."[5] In that case, as it will be noted clearly in chapter five, the commitment of practical theology to particular contexts of people's lived experiences is what leads it to being a theology of place, a contextual theology.

---

4. Ibid.

5. Dames, "The Dilemma of Traditional and 21st Century Pastoral Ministry," 1 (italics added). There is an agreement among some scholars that Practical Theology, with its infinite scope embracing issues of contemporary human concern, is contextual theology in its practice (see *e.g.*, Woodward & Pattison, *The Blackwell Reader*, 8, 13–16; Pears, *Doing Contextual Theology*, 33–34).

PRACTICAL THEOLOGY AND ITS CONTEXTUAL NATURE

Before defining Practical Theology and describing its contextual nature, we need to repeat what it entails by the concept of "theology" as defined in chapter one in order to have a better foundation for the definition of provided to practical theology. Etymologically, the word or concept of theology is formed from two Greek words: *theos*, which means God, and *logos*, which means word, study or discourse. Following this etymology, theology can be understood as a "word, study or discourse about God." However, as we saw in chapter one the definition of the concept of theology has been expanded by scholars to cover a wide range of meanings more than the etymological meaning of the two concepts. Theologians Gullet, quoting Orton and Culbertson, expands the definition of theology: theology is "the science of God and divine things, based upon the revelation made to mankind in Jesus Christ, and variously systematized within the Christian Church [. . .]."[6] Here, Gullet considers theology as Christian Theology. However, it should clearly be conceived that theology is not only Christian. Basing on this understanding, theology can be defined in various ways depending on the ways various religions understand the relationship between humankind and the Supreme Being they worship and adore.

Basing on Christian Theology, Gullet further subdivides theology in various branches: "historical theology, biblical theology, philosophical theology, and systematic theology."[7] Gullet further lists the theologies that emerge when the word 'theology' is attached to other sociological concepts: "the Theology of Work, the Theology of Homelessness, the Theology of Disability, the Theology of Sports [. . .]."[8] Some more place-based theologies can be mentioned: the Theology of Compassion, the Theology of HIV/AIDS, the Theology of Inculturation, the Political Theology, the Feminist Theology, to mention just a few of them. These sub-divisions of theology indicate the wide range of meanings of the concept of theology in the Christian perspective. Similar sub-divisions may be provided to other religious theologies making theology a vast terminology and hard to grasp its totality. However the subdivisions of theology as a concept indicate the various conceptions of the role of God to different situations. It reflects people's endeavors to rediscover God's dealings with human beings in their various experiences of life.

---

6. Gullet, *Practical Theology*, 1.
7. Ibid.
8. Ibid.

Basing on the above description, what then is Practical Theology? Gullet defines it as follows: "Practical Theology is a discipline [within the vast understanding of theology] that seeks to explore the deeper levels of human experience with and about God. It involves a critical reflection on the praxis of the Church in the world focusing on scripture, Christian traditions and other relevant knowledge. Christian praxis is the place where theology becomes embodied and acted out in everyday living [. . .]."[9] Being the place where theology is located and acted upon in people's lives, "the church's praxis should illuminate the Kingdom of God. The actions of the Christian community in addressing contemporary social issues should be a witness to God's abundant love for the world and all humanity."[10] In that case, focusing on Gullet's assertion in an African context, Practical Theology becomes contextual theology and a useful tool to examine the way Scriptures and traditions are used in order to respond to contemporary issues facing the Christian community such as gender relations, HIV/AIDS, homosexuality, female genital mutilation, globalization, alcoholism, *etc*. However, despite considering the question of 'tradition' in a more conservative way, Gullet's definition is useful as it recognizes the critical nature of theology in relation to the praxis of the church to society.

On another endeavor, a position more useful to the discussion of this book, Sinton and Mowat define Practical Theology: "Practical Theology is critical, theological reflection on the practices of the Church as they interact with the practices of the world, with the view to ensuring and enabling faithful participation in God's redemptive practices in, to and for the world."[11] In this definition, Swinton and Mowat identify four aspects: first, the critical nature of Practical Theology. The faithfulness of this theology to the revelation of scriptures depends greatly on the 'honest critical reflection' on those scriptures and the experience of faith in the real lived life. This critical reflection is echoed by Dames: "Pastoral hermeneutics is a critical action-reflection-action process on *how* to shape faith practices in transforming life-threatening context [. . .]."[12] It is in this critical nature of this theology to scriptures and its reflection on the lived experiences of people that is considered contextual. As it will be noted in the following chapter, Practical Theology in Africa needs to be critical the churches' practices on various issues pertaining to its their lives.

---

9. Gullet, "Practical Theology," 1; *cf*. Mwenisongole & Mligo, *Pastoral Counseling*.
10. *Ibid.*, 2.
11. Swinton & Mowat, *Practical Theology*, 6.
12. Dames, "The Dilema of Traditional and 21st Century Pastoral Ministry," 3.

Second, despite having a critical reflection on scriptures and real life experiences, Practical Theology is also theological reflection which uses other sources of knowledge in order to enrich itself towards understanding the way the faith in scriptures can be described in the wider context of human life. Third, the practices of the Church should interact with the practices of world in order to enhance a better understanding of faith a "performed practice." Here, as the theological reflection looks for other sources, e.g., from social sciences, the practice of the church links with that of the world to make a real meaning of Practical Theology as contextual theology that is both universal and local. It is in this reason that Swinton and Mowat write: "The practices of the Church cannot be understood as ontologically separate or different from the practices of the world. Both occur within God's creation and both are caught up in God's redemptive movement towards the world."[13]

However, the difference between the Church practices that recognize the presence and initiatives of Jesus, and those of the world that hardly recognize the presence of Jesus' initiatives should not be ignored. Therefore, one of the major tasks of Practical Theology, according to Swinton and Mowat, is to play the role of reminder, that though the practices of the Church have to interact with the practices of the world, the practices of the Church have to sincerely remain faithful to the originator of the Church—Jesus Christ. Fourth, since Practical Theology involves faithful practice, it should ensure and enable the effectiveness of that practice. In this case, Practical Theology should "enable faithful living and authentic Christian practice."[14]

The faithful living and the authentic Christian practice lead to the real experience of the lived faith in Jesus Christ the founder of Christianity. Christianity and being Christian alone hardly matter; what actually matters is the way the experience of being a Christian is transformed into actions. Yet, actions alone hardly matter, but reflective actions (praxis). This is what Swinton and Mowat call "faithful performance" of the Christian faith.[15] They rightly state: "Practical Theology takes seriously the idea of performing the faith and seeks to explore the nature and in particular the faithfulness of that performance."[16] The action and reflection of theology will be amplified in the discussion of specific contextual issues in the following chapter.

The major basis of Practical theology, according to Swinton and Mowat, is the human experience, the experience of God working in the lives of human beings as Christians. This means that Practical Theology takes

13. Swinton & Mowat, *Practical Theology*, 8.
14. Ibid., 9.
15. Ibid., 4.
16. Ibid., 4.

seriously the way the human being experiences and lives the good news of Scripture. Swinton and Mowat put this more clearly: "Practical Theology acknowledges and seeks to explore the implications of the proposition that faith is a performative and embodied act; that the gospel is not simply something to be believed, but also something to be lived. Human experience is a 'place' where the gospel is grounded, embodied, interpreted and lived out."[17] It is in this way has contextual theology in Africa been conceived; it is in this way that this book presents practical theology as a theology based on African people's lived experiences.

HISTORICAL BACKGROUND OF PRACTICAL THEOLOGY

In order to understand Swinton and Mowat's above statement above, we need to trace the historical background of practical theology before concluding the chapter with the role played by practical theology. The history of Practical Theology, as a form of contextual theology, does not start from the nearest ages of the Church. Rather, it starts with the Early Church. The whole current understanding of Practical Theology derives its formulations from the conceptions of theology from the Early Church. The early Church did not have the sub-divisions of theology we currently have; rather, theology was just conceived as theology in its totality. However, the conception of theology as a whole ended in the thirteenth century, when the university was introduced in the western world whereby theological scholars distinguished theology into two branches: "speculative or theoretical theology" regarded as a theology done inside the university, and "practical theology" a theology done outside the university dealing with people's spirituality in their daily Christian lives. Therefore, the distinction of theology as speculative and practical dominated universities in the western world until the seventeenth century when was considered the peak of this distinction.

In regard to the above point, Maddox says: "By the seventeenth century it became more typical to use 'Practical Theology' (capitalized because now a distinct university discipline) to designate the academic study of Christian *actions*, as distinguished from Theoretical (or Speculative) Theology," which dealt with Christian *beliefs*."[18] At this time, Practical Theology was now an "academic" discipline in a similar way to theoretical theology. What was considered "academic" theology was not only one thing, but a differentiated number of disciplines or sciences producing knowledge depending on their

17. Ibid., 5.
18. Maddox, "Practical Theology," 160.

methods. Such disciplines were the following: "Biblical Theology, Historical Theology, Systematic Theology, and Practical Theology."[19]

However, scholars trace the background of modern Practical Theology from the German movement in the eighteenth century. It is in this century when the German universities incorporated the practical theological discipline in their curriculum. They considered Practical Theology as a discipline among the four disciplines. The other disciplines of theology, according to the sub-divisions done by the Germans universities were: Biblical Theology, Church History or Historical Theology, and Systematic Theology. These disciplines were considered as "theoretical theological disciplines." Practical Theology was considered an applied or practical discipline of theology.[20]

The pressure from students in the German universities caused the change in the previous notion of Practical Theology which focused on "shepherding" to a practical theology that transcended the clerical limits to include all members of the Church apart from the clergy and their clerical functions. Maddox states that the "broader definition of ministry soon encouraged the rejection of the title 'Pastoral Theology' preferring the previous 'Practical Theology.'"[21] Maddox mentions the major proponents of the German notion of Practical Theology to include Karl Rahner, as being the greatest proponent. Others were the following: "Alistair Campbell, Ebehard Hubner, Mafred Jossutis, Wolfhart Pannenberg, Dietrich Rossler, and Gerhard Sauter." Hence, all the proponents mentioned above pioneered the rejection of the "clerical paradigm" of Practical Theology" in favor of the general Christian praxis theology based on the whole community. It is in this line of conceiving practical theology as Christian praxis that we have the discipline in universities to reflect on the actions of churches.

CONCLUSION

The task of this chapter was to introduce practical theology in Africa as a theology of praxis based on actions and reflections—the actions of churches are critically reflected in theological colleges and universities. The chapter defined practical theology in light of the wider understanding of theology and traced its historical background to reach the essence of the conception of it as a theology of Christian praxis. We have noted from this chapter that the option from the previous concept of 'Practical Theology' over 'Pastoral

19. Ibid.
20. Petta, "In Search of a Contextual Pastoral Theology," 171; *cf.* Mwenisongole & Mligo, *Pastoral Counseling*, 29.
21. Maddox, "Practical Theology," 163.

Theology' prompted for the need to consider the task of the emerging notion of Practical Theology. The Practical Theology that existed before the emergence of Pastoral Theology emphasized and focused on the relationship between theory and practice. Practical Theology was considered as an "application" of the theoretical or speculative theology.

In the new debate about Practical Theology as conceived by the German tradition, the question of whether practice is derived from theory, or whether theory is a reflection from practice were highly contested. The debate focused on the need to incorporate human *actions* on the reflections being made. In that case, the concept of praxis was "retrieved to capture this dialectical relationship between action and reflection."[22]

As Maddox, quoting Dermot A. Lane, expresses it, the concept of praxis is not a mere practice emerging from theory; rather, it is a "creative action, inspired by critical reflection, that gives rise to both change and insight."[23] In this case, change and insight are the major results of praxis which were not in the normal practice of theory as was conceived by the Practical Theology of universities before the shift to Practical Theology as a study of Christian actions.

Creative action inspired by critical reflection was "the application of the Church of theories previously developed by Systematic Theology."[24] The contemporary interest of Practical Theology in Africa and other parts of the world is in the development of a comprehensive and integrated understanding of the Christian life of faith. Practical Theology provides an understanding on the way in which faith can guide action in today's circumstances lived by members of the Church. Therefore, as Swinton and Mowat state: "The fundamental [task] of Practical Theology is to enable the Church to perform faithfully as it participates in God's ongoing mission in, to and for the world. As such, it seeks to reflect critically and theologically on situations and provide insights and strategies which will enable the movement towards faithful change."[25] With a similar concern, Ballard emphasizes: "The special task of Practical Theology is to start with the concrete, historical, immediate reality critically evaluating and enabling the practical life of the Church in all its many forms, drawing on the findings of fundamental, historical and systematic theology."[26] It is in light of this task that we turn to discussing the role of practical theology to some contemporary contextual issues facing the Church in Africa.

22. Maddox, "Practical Theology," 165.
23. *Ibid.*, 166.
24. *Ibid.*, 166.
25. Swinton and Mowat, *Practical Theology*, 25.
26. Ballard, "Can Theology be Practical?" 29.

5

Contemporary Practical and Contextual Issues in Africa

INTRODUCTION

In the previous chapter we defined Practical theology as a study on Christian actions. As a study (reflection), it is praxis on the Church's daily activities. This chapter ventures on a critical examination of some of the contextual practices of the Church which challenge the contemporary Church in Africa: the question of alcoholism, the prophetic role of the Church in various contexts, the resurgence of prosperity gospel, the question of violence, and the issue of homosexuality. These practices will clearly demonstrate that Practical Theology is contextual when it involves itself in the critical reflection upon the mentioned aspects.

Since the mentioned issues are found in various places within the church in Africa, this chapter presents a general discussion of them without basing on a particular one place. In this case, it considers the church in Africa with its varied cultural backgrounds as a context where the issues are practiced. Of course, there are many other pressing issues in Africa, probably more pressing than the ones discussed in this section, such as poverty, HIV and AIDS, divorce and remarriage, relationship between church and state, strikes, corruption, procreation and fertility, the use of contraceptives, widows and orphans, polygamy, rape, incest, female genital mutilation (FGM), prostitution and sex trafficking, abortion, early marriages, teenage pregnancies, drug abuse, sorcery and witchcraft, street children, land clashes, break down of the rule of law, debt crises, peoples' insecurity and vulnerability, and the existence of evils, to mention just a few of them.[1] However, the issues discussed in this section are not selected by their importance, rather randomly to just illustrate the role of practical theology as contextual theology. Therefore, through the intensive discussions on each of the mentioned issues, it will become clear the way practical theology encounters challenges as it evaluates the practice of the Church in Africa in the midst of pressing issues in the twenty-first century.

THE CHURCH AND ALCOHOLISM

We commence our discussion with the issue of alcoholism. Alcoholism and/or alcohol abuse is one of the complex issues facing the Church in Africa throughout its life. Why is alcohol use so a complex issue in the life of the Church in Africa? It is mostly due to its multifaceted associations accompanying it. Christopher C.H. Cook highlights the various associations of alcohol use:

> Alcohol has many and contrasting associations. A glass of wine with a meal can symbolise love, friendship, relaxation and enjoyment of a special occasion. It can represent romance, coming of age, success, beginnings and endings, good news and good company. At a Christian Eucharist or Jewish Passover, where wine is also shared, thanks are given to God for divine salvation from all that enslaves, restricts and condemns. In drinking the wine, Christians participate with the first disciples in their last supper with Christ, and Jews participate with the ancient Hebrews in their exodus from enslavement in Egypt. But sadly, the sacredness and redemptiveness of these occasions contrasts with the associations of alcohol with drunken violence in our towns and cities, cirrhosis of the liver on our medical wards, debt in families, and death on our roads. It contrasts also, and more especially, with the enslavement that is alcoholism, or alcohol addiction."[2]

Hence, despite its multifaceted associations, alcohol is the most widely consumed substance occupying the lives of most of the members and non-members of the Body of Christ in Africa, making them vulnerable to unacceptable behavior and unnecessary sufferings. For instance, thousands of

---

1. For discussions on some of these issues, please see Kunhiyop, *African Christian Ethics*.
2. Cook, *Alcohol, Addiction and Christian Ethics*, 1.

innocent passengers perish in road accidents yearly owing to the fact that thousands of drivers on the highways consume alcohol up to the high-risk levels. In spite of knowing the danger of driving under the influence of alcohol, most drivers of commercial and private vehicles do not mind using alcohol."[3]

Mydze and Rwomire justify the above assertion when they state:

> "Historically, Africans have always been accustomed to the consumption of fermented beverages which, as a group, have less alcoholic content that distilled beverages. These beverages are obtained from ripe bananas, millet or honey and sorghum. In Botswana, brewing and beer consumption have generally been an integral part of village life while sorghum, a staple food throughout southern Africa, was a primary ingredient in the production of traditional alcoholic beverages. [. . .]. Usually, the consumption of alcoholic beverages was restricted to elders of the community and drinking was social rather than an individual activity. Women were generally excluded from drinking parties but not entirely."[4]

However, in drinking alcohol of any kind as stipulated in the above quotation, Africans have their own purpose depending on their social, economic and psychological contexts different from people in the Western countries.

While alcohol is used for recreational purposes for people in most Western countries, in Africa it is used as means to release tensions emerging from daily social, economic and domestic problems facing people. Talking about the relationship between poverty and alcoholism, Chukwu states that "In Africa, most alcoholics do not indulge in alcohol use as a means of spending a part of their high wages or income. On the contrary, the majority of users engage in alcohol use as a way of easing the stress, frustration and tension pertinent to low wages and income."[5] Due to its uncontrolled consumption, "Alcohol consumption has been identified as the leading risk factor for death and disability in sub-Saharan Africa and the leading risk factor for disability-adjusted life-years [. . .] among African male adolescents aged 15–24 years."[6] In this case, the abuse of alcohol in African societies has been the source of various atrocities ranging from family to societal levels rather than being a thing for enjoyment and pleasure.

---

3. Chukwu, "Alcoholism in Africa," 121.
4. Mydze & Rwomire, "Alcoholism in Africa," 4.
5. Chukwu, "Alcoholism in Africa," 127.
6. Ferreira-Borges, Parry & Babor, "Harmful Use of Alcohol," 3.

Alcohol is the drug commonly used in the world to the extent that most people do not recognize it as being one of the harmful drugs.[7] Strictly speaking, alcohol "is in fact an addictive psychoactive substance that acts as an intoxicant, depressing the central nervous system. It can cause temporary loss of physical and metal control. When taken in large quantities, it becomes a poison."[8] It is medically recognized as one of the legal drugs, a chemical which when taken enters the blood stream and is easily transported to the brain changing the way the human being perceives of oneself and the world around him or her.[9]

There are different ways of using drugs depending on the type and nature. There are drugs injected into the blood stream directly through injections. There are those drugs which are smoked, sniffed, swallowed and snorted. In whatever way they are taken, their function is to alter the normal functioning of the brain for some time. Alcohol is one of the drugs which are swallowed and enter the blood stream through the normal digestion and absorption of food materials. Therefore, it is important to note that excessive alcohol use leads the user to addiction, an individual's strong desire to use it frequently without missing.[10]

Morgan poses a subtle question: "what precisely is the role, the unique contribution, of Christian faith communities in the contemporary struggle with chemical abuse and addiction?"[11] Morgan provides the following response to the above question: "Many of the major denominations publish educational programmes, pastoral guide books, and practical strategies to address the prevention and abuse. Many churches and a variety of Christian and non-Christian congregations already host Twelve Step and other

---

7. Drug abuse involves the "use of illegal substances such as marijuana, cocaine, heroin and misuse of legal drugs such as, alcohol, cigarettes, prescription drugs or fumes from household products." (Agumba, "The Effect of Alcohol," 17; *cf.* Konchellah, "Effects of Alcohol Abuse," 12–13.) Obaga defines a drug: "A drug is any chemical substance that, when taken into the body, changes how a person thinks and feels by altering one's mood. It produces physical, mental, emotional, behavioral, or spiritual changes in the user. Cocaine, heroin, marijuana, *etc.* are examples of other drugs or mood-altering substances." (Obaga, "Understanding the Nature and Impact of Alcoholism," 4n6.

8. Kunhiyop, *African Christian Ethics*, 366.

9. Chukwu, "Alcoholism in Africa," 117.

10. *Ibid.*

11. Morgan, "Practical Theology," 35. The word 'addiction' is derived from Latin a*ddicere* which means 'being enslaved.' Following Kunhiyop's definition, as quoted from the clinical neuroscientist Joseph Frascella, "addiction is 'repetitive behaviors in the face of negative consequences, the desire to continue something you know is bad for you.'" (Kunhiyop, *African Christian Ethics*, 359) Hence, an addict is a person who is enslaved to using a certain substance; this person is a willing and devoted slave knowing the harmful effects of that substance (*Ibid.*).

'self-help' meetings. Several communities of faith have addressed policies or instructions to be faithful about the pastoral challenges of abuse and addiction. Yet, there is still an impression that churches, synagogues of worship have yet to respond fully and adequately."[12]

Despite the above efforts done by faith communities, yet alcohol abuse and addiction remain a problem in Africa to both individual people and society at large. Alcoholism is problematic to health and economy, to family relationships, peer-relationships, safety and academic issues; and in that case, it becomes a pastoral problem that still needs to be addressed.[13] Broadly speaking, alcohol abuse brings harmful effects to the user. If Christians turn to alcohol abuse, which are likely cases to most churches in Africa, that stance can likely destroy their strong adherence to faith and to Christian ethics. In turn, it can lead such Christians to backsliding, making the task of evangelization less fruitful. It becomes less fruitful because it is, in most cases, hard to evangelize someone by trying to address issues affecting the evangelist personally.[14]

Moreover, alcohol abuse causes the user to suffer from alcohol related diseases and other unnecessary situations. Chukwu asserts that "Other disastrous consequences of alcohol abuse include diseases that may damage the liver, kidney, heart and brain. Alcohol may cause loss of appetite and restlessness. It can cause bankruptcy, family disintegration, poverty, physical aggression, decreased efficiency and low productivity in the work place, and wastage of national wealth."[15]

There are other effects that face innocent community members through someone abusing alcohol. As an example, Chukwu reports that "thousands of innocent passengers perish in road accidents yearly owing to that thousands of drivers on the highways consume alcohol up to high-risk levels. In spite of knowing the danger of driving under the influence of alcohol, most drivers of commercial and private vehicles do not mind using alcohol."[16] Following this reckless behavior of drivers, passengers travel with uncertainty whether their journeys may be safe throughout their travels.

In trying to reflect on alcoholism as a pastoral problem to the Church, Morgan poses a question in relation to biblical texts: "What narrative resources, texts and metaphors can be brought to bear in formulating a practical theology of alcohol abuse, addiction and recovery?" Then he states that

12. Morgan, "Practical Theology," 35.
13. Kgabe, "Abuse of Alcohol by Anglican Clergy," 88–92.
14. Chukwu, "Alcoholism in Africa," 120.
15. *Ibid.*
16. *Ibid.*, 121.

the consensus had been some time in the past in regard to the biblical point of view about the use of alcoholic related drinks. He further summarizes the consensus with two points: "First, in the Hebrew Bible the production, commerce and consumption of wine is described as an accepted fact of life. Wine was/is a gift of God, a joyous symbol that can 'gladden' life. (Ps. 104: 14–15; Amos 9: 13–14; Joel 12: 24 & 3: 18) and a normal part of Israel's daily rituals. 'Wine' was, in short, an accepted part of Israel's daily life and religious observance [. . .]."[17] In doing that Morgan recognizes the Bible as being the authority through which theology and church practices base on its life and practice.

Alcohol in the Old Testament

However, Morgan in the above quotation is aware that the Old Testament writers were aware of the possible abuse of alcohol. This awareness of the Old Testament writers is vivid in their condemnations within "the Hebrew Bible (Gen 9.20ff; Gen 19. 20–38; Proverbs 20.1; Proverbs 23.29–35; Sirach 31.25–31; Is 5: 11–12; Hosea 4.11). Leaders (e.g., kings, priests, prophets) who abuse are the objects of special admonition (Is 56.11–12; Hosea 7.5; Is 28.7; Lev 10. 8–9; Ez 44. 21). And, while abstinence is not advocated as a general rule anywhere in the Bible, particular groups which practice it voluntarily are praised. [. . .]. The Nazarites (Numbers 6: 2–4; Judges 13. 5–7) and Rechabites (Jer 35), as well as John the Baptist (Mt 11. 18) [. . .]."[18] Following the above texts, Morgan concludes that the Hebrew Bible did not prohibit Israelites from the use of alcohol in their daily lives. However, the Hebrew Bible condemns excessive use of alcohol and praises the voluntary abstinence of alcohol.

Alcohol in the New Testament

The second point is that the New Testament also reflects on the use of alcohol. "Jesus' own practice indicates approval of the moderate use of wine (Jn 2.1–11; Mk 14.23–25; Mt 26.29). Paul prescribes wine in small amounts for medical purposes (1 Tim 5.23). They both accept alcohol as a fact of life."[19] However, in the New Testament, Morgan notes some condemnations of excessive drinking of alcohol and its danger. In the New Testament,

17. Morgan, "Practical Theology," 39.
18. Ibid.
19. Ibid., 40.

> Jesus himself condemned drunkenness (Lk 21.34) and Paul is clear about the danger of it. [. . .]. This vice also appears in several of Paul's lists of common sins to be avoided (Rom 13: 11–14; 1Cor 6:11 and 11.17–22; Gal 5.21; Eph 5.18). Drunkenness could exclude one from the Kingdom of God in Paul's view (1Cor 6.10) and drunkards were to be avoided, even 'excommunicated' from the early Christian community, along with idolaters (1Cor 5.11) . . . the 'pastoral' letters specifically warn against alcoholic excess among Christian leaders (1Tim 3.3; Titus 1.7; 1Tim 3.8).[20]

Following the above examination, the New Testament hardly prohibits the use of alcohol; it prohibits an excessive use of it.

Alcohol in the African Context

Turning to the African context, for example, before the coming of missionaries and Christianity, drinking was not something condemned by society. It was something honored and respected. Quoting from Eide *et al*, the situation sounds: "Drinking in traditional African setting was not seen as evil. Drinking beer as a beverage was respected because it played an important social, economic and religious role. Traditional society had its drinking ethics. They limited people from excessive use of alcohol. For instance, only mature adults and old people were allowed to drink alcohol. The youth, children and women were not allowed to take alcohol even when a feat was for them. Drinking was done at home and only during traditional festivals in public."[21] They further write: "Alcohol was treated with respect as a refreshment and blessing. Society strongly opposed drunkenness to the extent that a person who misused beer could be banned from using it. A person who drunk, quarreled, fought and insulted other people was given a reprimand. If the person persisted in this behavior, the community was ordered to deny him/her any offer of beer. The social controls on drinking alcohol limited problems such as domestic violence, divorce and extramarital children."[22]

The availability of beer in the current African society is not very much different from that of traditional society described by Eide *et al* above. The only difference is that of technology. Technology has enhanced the different and easier ways of preparing and distributing alcohol. The questions here are the following: What makes alcohol more harmful to current African

20. Morgan, "Practical Theology," 40.
21. Eide, *et al.* (eds.), *Restoring Life*, 50.
22. Ibid., 51.

societies as compared to traditional societies? Basing on the biblical and African society's conception of beer described by Eide *et al* above, is it legitimate to consider drinking beer as being sinful or contrary to God's wills for humanity?

In fact, the use of alcohol is one of the pressing issues for churches and ministers in Africa. The problem faced mostly base on the way the Bible is interpreted. As noted above, the Bible does not directly prohibit the use of alcohol (cf. 1Tim 5: 23; Eph 5: 18). But the different interpretations of biblical texts within the various denominations within the Body of Christ to prohibit alcohol drinking create a great pressure to some denominations which favor its use. What should be done in this situation of confusion in regard to the use of alcohol? The question facing ministers and normal Christians in current churches in Africa is the following: Who is right, the one preaching and teaching against, or the one in favor of the use of alcohol with precautions and in a minimal amount as the biblical tradition teaches?

In the midst of this dilemma, Eide *et al* opine: "Arguing for or against the use of alcohol is not necessarily helpful when trying to see the issue from a Christian ethical perspective . . .. A deeper theological reflection is necessary."[23] By the use of a text from Romans 14: 14, Eid *et al* argue that the use of alcohol as depicted in Scripture is contextual. When Paul writes to the Romans, he deals with foods and drinks as problematic to the Roman congregation. The members of the congregation had entered into a dilemma in regard to foods and drinks in a similar situation to our modern dilemmas within churches in Africa. The main dilemma was about the cleanness or uncleanness of some foods offered for sacrifice to the Roman gods. Paul's argument to the Romans is that drinks and foods as creations of God are clean, irrespective of their type. Alcohol itself as a creation of God is clean. What makes a drink or food clean or unclean is the individual's perception about it. Therefore, the prohibition of alcohol use is illogical and inconsistent with the teaching of Scriptures because it is created by God for use as a drink. The problem, however, is not the use of drinks and foods but the amount and purpose of its use. Paul writes to the Romans: "I am fully convinced that no food is unclean in itself. But if anyone regards something as unclean, then for him it is unclean." (Romans 14: 14 NIV) What is your opinion about this reflection?

It is because of Paul's stand point stated above that some scholars have stated questioning the use of bread and wine as symbols of the Eucharist in the African context. The problem raised is this: Do Africans really need to use the bread and wine, which were used in the first century Church in

---

23. *Ibid.*, 52–53.

order for them to be true Christians who hold the accurate commemoration of Jesus' Last Supper? Togarasei's opinion, which we find it plausible, is that African traditional foods and drinks available in the African context were provided by God to African's as wine and bread were provided to the context of people in the early church and can serve a similar commemoration purposes if we want to make the Holy Communion truly African. Togarasei states: "I am thinking of why we should not use *sadza* and *maheu* (common food and drink, respectively, for most people in central and southern Africa) as symbolisms of the flesh and the blood of Jesus in the same way the early church used bread and wine. Bread and wine were the most available food items of the time and surely bread and wine are scarce commodities among many ordinary Africans."[24]

To our opinion, Eide *et al* are right when they consider the question of drinking alcoholic drinks or not drinking in the direction of love for the neighbor. Every food is clean before God; but it may be clean or unclean in the eyes of an individual person. When one takes a particular food or drink, including alcohol, he/she should ask oneself whether that partaking brings someone to fall off or stand in faith, brings harm to someone physically, psychologically, *etc.*, or not. Moreover, one should ask oneself if the partaking of a particular food or drink makes him or her live a life of glory to God or not.[25]

THE CHURCH'S PROPHETIC ROLE

The first subtle question we need to ask as we venture into the prophetic role of the Church in Africa is about the term 'prophecy' itself. What is it and how can we understand it in our contemporary world? On the one hand, according to Ankrah, "Prophecy is *the proclamation beforehand of events that are to come in the future*. It is an utterance of an event to come at a certain time, or a succession of unpleasant events or conditions which are surely to occur—a coming of judgement and suffering or a series of hardships or joy. It is often a supernatural work and act of God, a process with external consequences."[26] On the other hand, "to prophesy [. . .] involves predicting sometimes, unpleasant consequences for authorities in the man-controlled world [which] appear to have higher physical and legal power to destroy the prophet."[27]

24. Togarasei, "The Conversion of Paul," 116.
25. Ibid., 54.
26. Ankrah, "The Church and National Development," 34.
27. Ibid.

Moreover, Tishken avers:

> Prophecy is the process by which a person claims a personal connection with supernatural forces that is unavailable to the average member of the community. This link is manifested in ways accepted as tangible and credible by members of the community. A prophet or prophetess is one who engages in this process."[28] Therefore, prophecy, in this sense, is not only a mere soothsaying—"the esoteric fortune-and-future telling type"; rather, it is a *critical prophecy* that "allows a religion to contribute meaningfully and fundamentally to a society's progress [. . .] by being vigilant and critical of inhuman conduct.[29]

Critical prophecy plays a chastising role of leaders and the society as a whole towards the required ethical behavior. At best, a "prophet is primarily a teacher of conscience—a counsellor."[30]

The above definitions indicate that prophecy was not confined only to Israel and did not end in the Old and New Testament times.[31] It still persists provided that human beings persist and is found in all religions. It persists because of situations which human beings encounter in their contexts and religions in terms of their leaders. Abioje puts it clear that prophecy emerges when "bad leaders ignore the rule of law and the courts, and abuse the security resources at their disposal."[32]

Prophecy in the Old Testament

In the Old Testament, for example, bad situations and actions of leaders which existed in the Jewish context forced God to rise up prophets in order to prophesy against such situations and actions. Prophets in the Old Testament who mostly prophesied against the existing political situations of kings at their time included for example, prophets Gad and Nathan who prophesied under the kingship of David (2Sam 24: 10–25; 2Sam 7 & 11),

---

28. Tishken, "The History of Prophecy," 1468.
29. Abioje, "Critical Prophecy," 790.
30. Nyiawung, "The Prophetic Witness," 4.
31. Quoting Blenkinsopp, Abioje states: "The Hebrew Bible itself attests that prophecy was not confined to Israel. In the early years of the reign of Zedekiah, last king of independent Judah, Jeremiah is reported to have urged rulers from the neighbouring lands of Edom, Moab, Ammon, and the Phoenician cities, meeting in Jerusalem, not to heed their prophets, diviners and other intermediaries who were backing the planned rebellion against Nebuchadrezza (Jer. 27:1–3)." (Abioje, "Critical Prophecy," 792).
32. Abioje, "Critical Prophecy," 790.

Prophets Elijah and Elisha prophesied under the kingship of Ahab who was married to Jezebel, a Phoenician woman, who wanted to do away with the faith in Yahweh among the Israelites. The message of most prophets who preached against the existing political situations was mostly of warning and condemnation to those who wanted or used their power for their personal gains against the wills of Yahweh.

Other prophets prophesied a message of condemnation and judgment not only to kings, but also to the whole nation of Israel due to their transgression of the covenant with Yahweh. Prophets like Micah, Zephaniah, Nahum, Habakkuk, and Jeremiah were prophets who prophesied to Israel before the Exile warning people about their forthcoming judgment due to their breach of the covenant. Prophets condemned them for the failure to abide to the covenant with Yahweh telling them about the consequence of their failure—that they would be deported to Babylon and exiled there.

Other prophets, especially exilic prophets, prophesied hope to people in destitute situations. People in exile in Babylon were provided hope that despite their situation in exile, Yahweh would remember the covenant with them and return them back to their homeland in Israel. Prophets who prophesied in exile include Ezekiel. Other prophets prophesied after the exile, when Israelites had returned to their homeland. Their message was of consolation and a call to reconstruction of Israel and their land, and rebuilding the Temple and its cult. Prophets who prophesied during the post-exilic period include Nehemiah and Haggai. Therefore, as just overviewed, each of the prophets above had a specific message depending on a particular situation. Ankrah states that "the prophets, especially Amos and Micah, were nevertheless fearless in their acts for God, bold in crying aloud His word. They denounced the sins of individuals and kingdoms, they often proclaimed the nearness of punishment and made it quite clear in no uncertain terms that God, who is just, loving and righteous, requires men [*sic!*] to deal justly with one another."[33]

Prophecy in the New Testament

In the New Testament, situations also dictated the emergence of prophets. John the Baptist, for example, prophesied about the coming of the one mightier than him (the Messiah) and warned people of the judgment that would befall those who were not baptized and could not repent their sins, He also prophesied against the king's wicked behavior . Jesus as prophet (Matthew 13: 57; Luke 13: 33; Hebrews 1: 1; Matthew 16: 16; 21: 11, 46

---

33. Ankrah, "The Church and National Development," 33.

prophesied about the down of the Kingdom of God through his presence on earth, and urged people to repent and adhere to the ethics of the Kingdom. Jesus also prophesied against the political situation of rulers of his time warning them not to use power for their own personal gains. A good example of Jesus' prophecy against the worldly powers of his time is found in his inaugural address found in Luke 4: 18—19 when he said: "The spirit of the Lord is upon me. He has appointed me to preach the good news to the poor. He has sent me to proclaim liberty to the captives. And recovery of sight to the blind, to set free the oppressed, to announce the year when the Lord will save his people."

Jesus' words at the inauguration of his worldly ministry did not indicate the existence of peace in his society but conflict and misunderstanding. Jesus makes it clear that it is hard for a prophet to be welcomed in his own community. As Ankrah, quoting Downey states, Jesus' proclamation in his own community "displayed many of the characteristics of a prophet. He was critical of accepted values and hypocrisy and pharisaism of contemporary practice."[34] Furthermore, Abioje, quoting Ramsay states: "Jesus was more than a prophet, but he was a prophet," and "the New Testament tells us that there continued to be prophets in the early church," for instance "the prophets Agabus, Simon called Niger, Manaen, and others whose names we will never know, spoke for God to the first Christians"[35] Therefore, it is vivid that the New Testament Prophets, as were the Old Testament prophets, also prophesied in particular situations that forced them to deliver the messages they delivered to respective leadership authorities.

Prophecy in the Current Church in Africa

As was in the Old and New Testaments, the current Church has never ceased, and should never cease, to provide prophetic messages to rulers in various situations. This is because, as was in the Old Testament times, "most problems faced by African societies [today] are related to issues of moral crisis. Most of these societies have gradually been established on pillars of mistrust, treachery and moral degradation."[36] The establishment on such pillars has led to African societies having stagnated development because of "turncoat politicians and soldiers who have perpetuated themselves in office by manipulating the system."[37] Therefore, the Body of Christ—the

34. Ibid., 34.
35. Abioje, "Critical Prophecy," 797–798.
36. Nyiawung, "The Prophetic Witness," 4.
37. Ibid., 4.

Church—has to prophesy to its members who are also members of current societies in Africa

Since the Church is the body of Christ, and has to prophesy, it needs to be as critical as Jesus was to rulers of his time speaking out on behalf of those without voice. Sedmak, quoting the U.S bishops, echoes this concern: "The example of Jesus poses a number of challenges to the contemporary Church. It imposes a prophetic mandate to speak for those who have no one to speak for them, to be a defender of the defenseless, who in biblical terms are the poor. It also demands a compassionate vision that enables the Church to see things from the side of the poor and powerless and to assess lifestyle, policies, and social institutions in terms of their impact on the poor."[38]

The Church in Africa, through its theology as an instrument, is called to exert influence in various issues to ensure that human dignity is restored and lived among its members. We suggest contextual theology should be an instrument of the Church in Africa to cater the challenging issues in this time of globalization. Some of such issues are the following: respect to human dignity as beings made in the image of God, rebuke to favoritism and nepotism in governmental bodies, ecclesiastical bodies and civil services, equality of genders, violence of all sorts in society and any kind of stigmatization and discrimination. In being prophetic, the Church in Africa, will assure its members that the world is a better place for life intended by God for them.

Contextual theology is suggested because it is itself prophetic. As Rodriguez reiterates, "Contextual Theology is usually referred to as 'prophetic theology' because it depends upon biblical 'exegesis'—or critical interpretation—and places its emphasis on the biblical themes of liberation and the prophets' teachings. The biblical prophets appeared in times of social, spiritual, and political turmoil. In this regard, Contextual Theology also studies the current times with regard to the gospel teachings. Therefore, 'the gospel becomes contextualized in an attempt to understand its meaning in the situation of crisis and conflict.'"[39] Hence, a contextualized theology in the situation of crisis, changing as the context changes, adoptive to signs of the time is what the Church in Africa should embrace.

By the use of contextual theology as its tool, the prophetic voice of the Church in Africa requires being critical for it to be prophetic. However, its critical nature will not leave it without retaliation from whom it is directed. Koonthanam states in regard to prophecy: "Every prophet is a

38. Sedmak, *Doing Local Theology*, 100.
39. Rodriguez, "Confrontational Christianity," 1–2.

critic, but not every critic a prophet. A prophet may criticize and condemn at times the entire nation of Israel; but whenever he specifies certain groups, it is always those classes or individuals in the country who wield power, social military or religious. Kings, priests, judges, generals and the rich fight against a prophet (Jer. 1: 18), because they are the targets of his attack (Jer. 22.13–19; Mic. 3.1, 9–12; Amos 5.12; Hos. 4. 4–10 etc.)."[40]

Similarly, the challenge which faces the Church in its prophetic messages is the resistance of rulers to receive the prophetic messages delivered by the Church in Africa and their urge to retaliate. Despite that the Church prophesies in the African context to respond to contemporary issues, yet recipients, especially Christians in political leadership, have been reluctant to receive the prophetic messages delivered to them. A Practical Theology scholar Wilma Gallet states this more clearly: "There are some Christians who argue that church leaders should not be intervening in the political arena, strongly asserting that politics is the sole domain of elected officials. While it is safe to assume that church leaders from most denominations respect the legitimate role of government. Nonetheless Scripture exhorts Christians and Christian leaders to make the church's prophetic voice known, particularly in matters of injustice."[41] Gallet adds that the prophetic voice of the Church is made known when Christians and Christian leaders challenge "unjust laws and structures that oppress the poor and marginalized. The words of the Old Testament prophets and the teachings of Jesus make clear God's concern for the poor, the widow, the orphan and the stranger."[42] Therefore, since the Church of Jesus Christ in Africa encompasses both the clergy and the lay, Gallet's words indicate that the prophetic task of this Church is not only entrusted to Church leaders, but also to lay Christians. The Church in Africa as a whole has a critical prophetic task against the horrible existing situations.

Resistance to the Church's prophetic messages is expected of current African leaders mostly because the messages they receive touch their comfortable zones. They touch what Christians or people in leadership consider to be what should conventionally be. In Africa, for example, Abioje rightly puts it:

> The continent of Africa is thus perceived as plagued by corrupt and selfish leaders who propagate widespread poverty, in spite of the abundant human and material resources in many African countries. [. . .] '[t]he lack of moral will and ethical strength by

---

40. Koonthanam, "Yahweh the Defender of the *Dalits*," 229.
41. Gallet, "Practical Theology," 1.
42. *Ibid.*

leadership in Africa has been identified as the most serious issue and problem facing Africa today." There is no ulterior motive to say that Africa has no excuse for its lack of advancement several decades after achieving political independence from foreign colonialists, apart from the moral laxity of those who assume their leadership positions, and their resultant inability to work for the general good of their people.[43]

It is in this situation of leadership in Africa and the world that makes prophecy inevitable in order to challenge selfish pursuits and promote those of the majority. However, Abioje echoes that "whoever cannot endure persecution, may never be a critical prophet, as enjoined by biblical and African traditions. Yet, there seems to be no doubt that Africa needs such prophets for conscientisation and rebuke, with particular reference to political leaders who control both the human and material resources that can be harnessed for the development of the continent."[44]

However, the major problem in our time within the African continent is how to distinguish between true and false prophets among the many who identify themselves by the name "prophet." The definition of a prophet is clear, the one with a message to warn, to console or to admonish people about their way of life. Sometimes the prophet may have a message of judgment to people about their sin. Abioje further elaborates about prophecy and prophets in the current churches in Africa, especially Independent Churches (AICs) and prosperity gospel churches: "They claim to give oracles and perform miracles. Prophets among them give visions and interpret dreams. They use holy water, sacred oil, ashes, candles and incense to heal and to prevent diseases. The cross has acquired a power which is almost magical. They offer prayers with persuasive, evocative and emotive language."[45]

In the Zimbabwean context, for example, Chitando lists the types of miracles performed by prophets: "In the period 2010 to 2013 in Zimbabwe, this included 'miracle money' where money was said to enter into peoples' pockets mystically, gold 'raining' on congregants, 'miracle weight loss,' healing of all kinds of ailments, 'miracle babies' that were (putatively) delivered three months after conception, and others."[46] The question that remains is this: Since all prophets, true and false ones, have a message, how then can we distinguish between true prophets from false ones in our current

43. Abioje, Critical Prophecy," 789.
44. Ibid., 807.
45. Ibid., 801.
46. Chitando, "Prophets, Profits and Protest," 100.

churches in Africa where prophets are widespread and all claim to prophesy in the name of God? We now examine the teachings of these prophets in a more detail below.

PROSPERITY GOSPEL TEACHINGS AND PRACTICES

After surveying the prophetic role of the Church in Africa and the way it has hardly fulfilled it, we now turn to considering the gospel of the Neopentecostal era, the resurgence of its prophets, and the danger this brand of gospel poses to mainstream Christianity in Africa. Julius Gathogo, quoting an anonymous communicator, states: "Christianity began as a personal relationship with Jesus Christ. When it went to Athens, it became a philosophy. When it went to Rome, it became an organisation. When it went to Europe, it became a culture. When it went to America, it became a business."[47] What happened when Christianity went to Africa from North America, especially in the Neopentecostal brand? We concentrate on this question within this section.

In fact, one of the pressing issues in Practical Theology as contextual theology in the current Church in Africa is the wide spreading of prosperity gospel preaching and theology. We live in an economically competitive, materialistic and consumer society, a society where people of every age are forced by physical and spiritual problems in lives. In this situation, people find solutions to their problems from whatever means possible. Under this situation, the

> majority of the youth [and people in general] want to find a solution for their problems and [. . .] seek solutions from churches that preach prosperity gospel, a gospel that promises goodies and claiming to reverse situations. It is so vivid and clear that so many have a mindset of receiving blessings instead of true worship to God; seeking first the Kingdom of God. Prosperity, being seen as a gospel that solves daily life problems [. . .] tends to win more populations that are faced by a decreasing quality of life, by insecurity of modernity, by feelings of isolation hence will be chosen by many as a last resort, after trying 'everything else.'[48]

Moreover, Groody speaks more blatantly about the nature of the current consumer society which human beings find themselves in, more enshrined

---

47. Gathogo, "The Challenge of Money and Wealth," 133.
48. Milemba, "The Influence of Properity Gospel," 6.

in the love of money. Money has become a solution of every problem facing human beings. Groody explains:

> In place of understanding human life in light of a monotheistic faith that inverts the current world order through the economy of grace, the consumer culture fosters the notion that the answers lie in a 'money-theistic' faith that baptizes the status quo and finds its redemption only through the economy of our current global system. Money-theism, idolization of capital expressed as the worship of the gods of the marketplace, is often practiced through the rituals of the stock market and the liturgies of global capitalism. The idolatry of money not only greatly contributes to global injustices, but it is also anchored in a fundamental theological and anthropological error precisely because it measures people in terms of material wealth and financial metrics, often at the expenses of people's human dignity and spiritual endowments. It is more concerned with the size of one's bank account than one's spiritual capital.[49]

It is in this consumer society where the prosperity gospel finds its fertile soil.

Meaning of Prosperity Gospel

What then is prosperity gospel? Togarasei is right when she says: "By their nature, definitions are misleading, since they tend to box 'things', taking those in the box as 'the things' and those out of the box as not."[50] The same possibility can be noted when we try to define the concept of prosperity gospel. Here, we can just say that prosperity gospel is a brand of theological stance. It is a brand of theological discourse that has a significant role in the life of those who follow it. The Wikipedia attempts a better definition of it: "Prosperity theology (sometimes referred to as the prosperity gospel, the health and wealth gospel, or the gospel of success) is a religious belief among some Christians, who hold that financial blessing and physical wellbeing are always the will of God for them, and that faith, positive speech, and donations to religious causes will increase one's material wealth."[51] For them, the death of Jesus on the cross has already made them healthy and wealthy; what they have to do is to claim possession of this health and

---

49. Groody, "Globalizing Solidarity," 263–264; cf. Nwonkwo, "African Christianity," 17.

50. Togarasei, "Modern/Charismatic Pentecostalism," 58.

51. See Niemandt, "The Prosperity Gospel," 210; Kasera, "Biblical and Theological Examination," 33–34)

wealth. This theology is centered on the dictum of "name it" and "claim it" or that of "blab it" and "grab it" being regarded as the "positive confession theology" or simply put "prosperity gospel."

As Mashau and Kgatle, quoting Togarasei, write: "The gospel of prosperity [. . .] teaches that all resources are there for people to claim them [. . .]."[52] Health and wealth are seen as being divine rights for all those who believe in the word of God inscribed in the Bible and can claim it by faith positively hoping to receive them abundantly. Two quotations from the very practitioners of prosperity gospel will suffice to illustrate this point. First, Young quotes Idahosa saying: "No one in God's family was ever destined to exist in sickness, fear, ignorance, poverty, loneliness or mediocrity. God's abundant goodness will be enjoyed and utilised by those who discipline themselves, become decisive, bold, adventurous, believing, daring, risking and determined."[53] Second, Young quotes William F. Kumuyi saying: "It is God's perfect will that a believer should enjoy perfect health, spiritual and material blessings, victory, promotion, peace, joy and satisfaction throughout his sojourn on earth. There are thousands of promises in the word of God that should make a believer remain blessed all the days of his life."[54] Following the above quotations, "Prosperity theology views the Bible as a contract between God and humans: if humans have faith in God, he will deliver security and prosperity."[55] Claiming without receiving abundant health and/or wealth is the sign of lack of faith or the sign of the devil's intervention.

Its Distinguishing Features

Some important features are notable in the prosperity gospel as a prevailing brand of theological movement. First, it "is neither a standardised movement nor does it hold a clearly expressed theological position [. . .]."[56] Second, the "movement is fundamentally a hybridisation of various doctrines and philosophies promoted by multiple voices. Thus, its 'teachings are neither systematic nor do all the proponents teach the same precepts of this theology. Depending on the persons, the teachings vary and there is no uniformity [. . .].'"[57] It means that prosperity gospel is formed from a cluster of unrelated concepts with no clear theological position to stand on.

52. Mashau & Kgatle, "Prosperity Gospel and the Culture of Greed," 2.
53. Young, "Prosperity Teaching," 5.
54. Ibid.
55. Niemandt, "Prosperity Gospel," 210.
56. Kasera, "Biblical and Theological Examination," 6.
57. Ibid.

In that case, the unstandardized nature of the teachings and their hybridization from various doctrines indicate that it is not possible to hear similar messages in the texts used to enforce the gospel among preachers. In other words, there is no checking among the proponents to ensure that the theology propagated is not distorted. Each individual preacher interprets and propagates the preaching at his or her wish, coming up with a meaning that favors his or her intentions.[58]

Third, prosperity gospel spreads very fast throughout the world in the name of churches which embrace that brand of Christianity. Three important reasons for their rapid spread include "First, their messages appeal to the needs of the majority especially people coming from poor backgrounds. Secondly, these churches provide simplistic but appealing practical advice to their audience. [. . .]. Thirdly, these churches do preach the message of repentance and are evangelistic in orientation. Besides preaching the message of prosperity, they preach the message of salvation from sin and eternal punishment."[59] Being more evangelistic oriented, these churches and movements carry out evangelistic crusades with large masses of people in stadiums and obtain adherents in hundreds of thousands of people who turn to their churches through altar calls; and who are further subjected to more seminars and teachings on the doctrine.

Fourth, it has an emphasis on the here and now, the main emphasis of Neopentecostalism. Neopentecostalism and prosperity gospel preach that salvation, satisfaction and victory is within reach, here and now. It means that faith of individuals is expected to provide concrete results instantly, now! The preaching and exhortations of Neopentecostal leaders is mainly on what the world can offer instantly: financial prosperity, good health, happiness here on earth, abundant wealth, *etc*. What this world offers indicates the individual's good relationship with God. This good relationship with God is the one that provides a right to one to own all which he or she did not own before.

Unlike the traditional Pentecostalism's emphasis on the role of the Holy Spirit, speaking in tongues, strict pietistic morals, miracles, the second coming of Jesus, and salvation (being saved), Neopentecostalism, and prosperity gospel in particular, emphasizes on spiritual warfare, exorcisms, immediate healing and personal prosperity in this world. In this case, since traditional Pentecostalism had its origin from Protestantism, in the Neopentecostal movement one can easily not that there is a profound shift in emphasis from rationality to experience, from making sense of the faith to

---

58. *Ibid*.

59. Zacka, "Prosperity Theology," 9–10.

sensing the faith, from arguments to sentiments and emotions. The main aspects that characterize Neopentecostalism, as stated above are emphasis on the immediate satisfaction of desires, in the present moment, and the sacrificial theology and practice. These aspects which characterize Neopentecostalism indicate that its origin is not Protestantism; rather it emerges from somewhere else.

The satisfaction of the claims made is demonstrated by the provision of testimonies by believers in the prosperity gospel. A specific time is set in the worship service for testimonies whereby believers testify what they named, claimed and received. However, Mashau and Kgatle, quoting Gifford, say: "The testimonies almost invariably focus on the material realm, on finances, marriage, children, visas, jobs, promotion, [and] travel. Only a small fraction, perhaps 10%, refer[s] to moral reform or deliverance from laziness or drink. Testimonies support the contention that these churches are about success [. . .]."[60] Hence, testimonies are the ones used as motivating agents for people to continue flowing to these churches hoping to acquire success in terms of healing and material wealth.

Pioneers of Prosperity Gospel in North America

The preaching and teaching about prosperity is not a recent phenomenon. It has its origin and must be understood in line with the emergence and resurgence of Pentecostalism;[61] however, its emergence is complex and disputed. It is thought that the preaching about prosperity gospel was pioneered by the American Pentecostal preacher Kenneth Erwin Hagin (1917—2003) after obtaining influence from Essek William Kenyon (1847—1948) (who was also influenced by Christian Science and New Thought, but was not a Pentecostal and opposed Pentecostalism). The teachings were perpetuated by Hagin's followers Kenneth Copeland, Benny Hinn and Joel Osteen. It is thought that Kenneth Copeland was the one responsible in preaching about these teachings to a large extent and ensuring its wide spread.[62] Hagin founded a College by the name Rhema Bible College in 1974 and mentored other prosperity gospel preachers there.[63] Therefore, the main

60. Mashau & Kgatle, "Prosperity Gospel and the Culture of Greed," 3.

61. Niemandt, "The Prosperity Gospel," 206; cf. Chitando, "Prophets, Profits and Protest," 97.

62. See McTavish, "Pentecostal Profits," 12–23; Niemandt, "The Prosperity Gospel," 205–206; Hagin, *The Believer's Authority*; Copeland, *The Laws of Prosperity*; Milemba, "The Influence of Prosperity Gospel," 12–13 & Straub, "The Pentecostalization of Global Christianity," 216–217.

63. Kwateng-Yeboah, "A Re-appraisal of Prosperity Gospel," 16.

origin of prosperity teachings, as will be further discussed below, is from Neo-Pentecostalism which mainly differed from the classical Pentecostalism which emphasized on anti-materialism and holiness.[64]

Situation that led to the Rise of Prosperity Gospel in America and in Africa

As Kwanteng-Yeboah, quoting Dan Lioy, writes: "'prosperity gospel in the American type emerged in "the days when living standards were visibly increasing [. . .] and success through a positive mental attitude' was the creed. It was in 'an economy of superabundance where the craving for material rewards became a fetal addiction for which there was no cure."[65] As Niemandt further notes: "The core of the prosperity gospel is a spiritualisation of materiality and raising classic symbols of surplus excess (such as expensive motorcars, private jets, and other symbols of affluence) as symbols of holiness and God's blessing."[66] In this case, prosperity gospel "places the individual as the subject of consumerism" making the benefits of the gospel to be not for the church, but for individual believers.[67]

According to Christman, while materialism entails overvaluing material objects more than human beings, consumerism goes further than that. Christman, quoting Miller, says that consumerism involves a "high level of consumption." Consumption that yields consumerism is not an act committed once, *i.e.*, when a consumer buys a good; rather, it is a repeated act and occupies the thinking and mind of those who are involved in it. As Christman says, it is a process that involves "dreaming, shopping, buying, personalizing and disposing of a good."[68] This process of consumption creates a consumer culture whose assumption is based on the endless human desires. A consumer continues to consume materials without being satisfied by what he or she consumes.[69] In this case, "Consumerism focuses on the self and pursuing one's own individual desires. The difficult aspect of consumerism is that people do not deliberately and selfishly choose to ignore the needs and lives of others."[70] This statement means that desire is insatiable. Desire does not desire to satisfy one's desire; but always desire desires desire. The

64. *Ibid.*, 8.
65. Kwateng-Yeboah, "A Re-appraisal of Prosperity Gospel," 16.
66. Niemandt, "The Prosperity Gospel," 215.
67. *Ibid.*; *cf.* Gbotoe, "Commercialized Gospel," 63–64.
68. Christman, "Consumerism and Christianity," 10.
69. See *Ibid.*, 26.
70. *Ibid.*, 38.

consumer's consumption does not long to quench the desire completely; instead, it creates a thirst for more to consume.[71] In this case, in the consumer culture, the production of materials is not primarily about satisfying human needs, nor is it about satisfying human desires. Being competitive in nature, production is primarily the production of desires for temporal satisfaction without quenching it completely. As Staalset asserts, the "*Homo consumens* is a restless creature, always drifting, always on the move, from one moment to another moment of unsatisfactory satisfactions."[72] In this movement, the winners are the ones who prevail and the losers lose completely without one to blame but themselves.

Apart from the American prosperity gospel which emerged in the context of the rise in the living standards and the craving for success among Americans, the African prosperity gospel emerged in the context of poverty at "the wake of Pentecostalism"[73] to provide hope to most desperately poverty stricken people in Africa. Killian's statement is more helpful to explain this scenario: "widespread poverty among many ordinary people has compelled them to search for alternative ways to tackle their problems."[74] Quoting from Amaladoss, Killian emphasizes: "in a context of increasing poverty and marginalization, prayer caters to the needs of the poor—physical, psychic, and spiritual and often takes the form of exorcism [. . .]."[75] For example, Chitando explains about what happened to Zimbabwe during what she called "the crisis" decade: in Zimbabwe, *i.e.*, years between 1998—2008. Chitando, quoting Brian Raftopoulos, restates: "A key aspect of the crisis was the rapid decline of the economy, characterised by, among other things: steep declines in industrial and agricultural productivity; historic levels of hyperinflation; the informalisation of labour; the dollarisation of economic transactions; displacements; and a critical erosion of livelihoods."[76] She adds: "As the crisis deepened, many citizens sought solace in religion. In particular, Pentecostal prophets proclaimed that God had grand plans for Zimbabweans. If they would commit themselves, pray and fast, their fortunes would be transformed in a very profound way."[77] It was in this period of acute poverty and hopelessness that prosperity churches and prophets flocked in Zimbabwe

---

71. See, Bauman, *Globalization*, 79–85, *cf.* Staalsett, "Discovering Jesus," 7; Christman, "Consumerism and Christianity," 26–30.

72. Staalsett, "Discovering Jesus," 7.

73. Niemandt, "The Prosperity Gospel," 207.

74. Killian, "Intra-denominational Conflicts," 278.

75. Killian, "Intra-denominational Conflicts," 278

76. Chitando, "Prophets, Profits and Protest," 98.

77. *Ibid.*, 99; *cf.* Mangena & Mhizha, "The Rise of White Collar Prophecy," 137.

promising people better life from existing structural economic challenges caused by the neo-liberal economic policies of the Structural Adjustment Programme imposed in the country.

Another example is the introduction of the Marian Faith Healing Ministry (MFHM) within the Catholic Church in Tanzania. Killian reports that Father Felician Nkwera of the Diocese of Njombe introduced the healing ministry whose main emphasis was the role of the Blessed Virgin Mary and the Eucharist contrary to the emphasis of the mainstream Catholic Church emphasizing the Holy Scriptures and the Eucharist. The Marian teachings on the Holy Eucharist emphasized on receiving it while kneeling and on the tongue and not otherwise contrary to the Roman Catholic church's teaching that it can be received while standing or kneeling and on the hand or on the tongue.[78] Further Nkwera, the founder of the MFHM, emphasized on the revelations from the Blessed Virgin Mary as being the ultimate authority while the Roman Catholic Church authorities emphasized on the hierarchy of the church, especially the bishops, as having the ultimate authority.[79] However, the introduction of the ministry caused most Christians of the Roman Catholic Church, Protestants, and even Muslims, mostly the poor and marginalized from various places he visited (*e.g.*, Songea, Iringa, Tabora and Arusha) and where the ministry centres were opened (in Dar es Salaam, Mahenge, Tabora, Sembawanga, *etc.*), to find solace in this group while remaining Catholics.[80]

Father Kwera claimed to receive a call "to pray for the sick and those overwhelmed by various problems of life" seven months after he was ordained to the ministry of priesthood in the Roman Catholic Church. Father Kwera's Marian Faith Healing Ministry group is characterized among the prosperity teachings because of its emphasis on people's physical well being and the use of instruments in the healing process "claimed to be given to him by the Blessed virgin Mary and the Lord Jesus Christ—a Holy Ring, Holy Oil and a Holy Host," including the holy water for exorcising the demons from the possessed ones.[81] Hence, this ministry caused the emergence of extraordinary conflicts and mixed feelings between Father Nkwera's healing ministry and the Roman Catholic Church in Tanzania since its beginning at Madunda Parish in Njombe Tanzania on the 7th May 1969. It reached its peak in 1999 when the TEC excommunicated the group from church membership and participation in various public activities of the Roman Catholic Church.[82]

78. Killian, "Intra-denominational Conflicts," 276.
79. Tambila & Sivalon, "Intra-denominational Conflict," 242.
80. See Killian, "Intra-denominational Conflicts," 280–281, 288–290.
81. See *Ibid.*, 280–282.
82. Killian, "Intra-denominational Conflicts," 280, 283–287.

Furthermore, Ehioghae and Olanrewaju state that "from time immemorial, Africans [in general] have had a longing for freedom from poverty, sickness and demon possession. These longings have found expression in their tales, stories, proverbs, prayers, sacrifices, and wishes. Unfortunately, the mainline churches failed to address these problems, while condemning the solution offered by traditional religions. Worse, some of the evangelical churches conceived the intense suffering of the poor in Africa as a mirage or at least played it down as though it was nothing to attract much attention."[83] In this case, "classical Pentecostalism and conservative evangelicals could be accused of being concerned with winning souls for heaven (to the extent of forgetting that believers are still living in this world)."[84]

Unfortunately, when Christianity moved to Africa by Christian missionaries, classical Pentecostal and conservative evangelical churches encouraged what is called "poverty theology" while looking at material possession here on earth as being a curse for a committed Christian. Churches preached greatly and emphatically that Christians should get rid of worldly attachment seeking the heavenly kingdom than any other thing.[85] This failure of churches (both classical Pentecostals and mainline evangelicals) to provide answers to problems of life among Africans here on earth and, yet condemning the solutions provided by African Traditional Religion created a room for the prosperity gospel, a form of Pentecostalism which Togarasei calls 'religious secularization' whereby "religion (in this case, the church in Africa) begins to be influenced and itself begins to promote 'secular' values over the traditional/historical Christian values."[86]

Prosperity Gospel and Secularization in the Western World and in Africa

As will be unveiled below, while secularization in the Western world was associated with the decline in the numbers of religious adherents and the increase of atheists or nominal religious adherents, this measure can hardly be used to determine secularization in Africa. In Africa, secularization has

83. Ehiogae & Olanrewaju, "A Theological Evaluation," 71; Mussana, "Interpretation, Message and Challenge," 87.

84. Togarasei, "Modern/Charismatic Pentecostalism," 64.

85. Chinkwo, "Poverty, Prosperity and Faith," 28. "Poverty theology" is the teaching about the evilness of the world and any kind of riches emerging from this world, and that people should not succumb to it in order for them to attain ultimate salvation in heaven. In this case, poverty is seen as the ideal for heavenly citizenship (see Chitando, "Prophets, Profits and Protest," 100).

86. Togarasei, "Modern/Charismatic Pentecostalism," 64.

penetrated within religion (Christianity in this case) in the guise of the larger populations of religious adherents in crusades, normal and mega-churches. This is what Togarasei has named as religious secularization above. In this kind, "secularization involves people's concern with proximate (this worldly) issues rather than ultimate (post-mortem) issues. [Hence] modern [or charismatic] Pentecostalism has secularized traditional Christian values, allowing us to see it as some form of religious secularisation."[87] Niemandt reports that "A survey done by PEW Research Centre found that in sub-Saharan Africa, 'in most countries more than half of Christians believe in the prosperity gospel—that God will grant wealth and good health to people who have enough faith [. . .]."[88] However, as Togarasei avers: "Like in the days of Amos (5: 21–24), the eighth century Hebrew Bible prophet, people can throng places of worship as a matter of routine, yet without any religious convictions."[89] Therefore, we can say that Pentecostal churches in Africa, though flocked with adherents, demonstrate secularism in the following aspects: "the search for health; the search for wealth (consumerism); the search for pleasure (music and dance); and inattention to post-mortem doctrines."[90]

What Togarasei states in the above quotation is what happens in most African churches of the contemporary time greatly challenging the practice of the Church. The post-colonial economic and traditional life situations, beliefs, and worship in Africa played a great role as fertile soils in enhancing the development of prosperity gospel and the flocking of adherents in churches. This situation is clearly articulated by Niemandt:

> Post-colonial times, with its emphasis on economic transformation, material independence, and self-actualisation, proved to be a fertile context to reshape African religious landscapes [. . .]. The economic and political situation in many African countries represented an opportunity to the followers of this theology. Rather than orientating itself along the lines of liberation theology with its option for the poor, it theologised wealth and simultaneously kept spiritual control over money by spiritualising richness and wealth [. . .].[91]

---

87. *Ibid.*, 59.

88. Niemandt, "Practical Theology," 206–207; Kasera, "Biblical and Theological Examination,"

89. Togarasei, "Modern/Charismatic Pentecostalism," 59.

90. *Ibid.*, 60.

91. Niemandt, "The Prosperity Gospel," 207; *cf.* Kasera, "Biblical and Theological Examination," 46.

Therefore, prosperity gospel is highly commercialized. Quoting Ayegboyin, Mashau and Kgatle, state that "Apart from the 'give and prosper messages' in some of the prosperity gospel ministries, there is full-scale commercialization of the Gospel through the sale of 'break-through handkerchiefs' (called mantles), anointing oil, prayer books and vow-making."[92] They also sell water, pieces of cake, tooth sticks, soda, soil, salt, photos of respective prophets, ear rings, underwear, pieces of soap, pens, shoes, cups, *etc.*, which they name them as being "anointed," to obtain more money from their followers. The gospel has become a business as was in the American consumer society; but, in this time, to the poverty stricken majority of Africans. As a result, superstition has invaded the church, a lazy generation that long for prosperity without working is increasing in societies, and a miserable poverty greatly dominates adherents of the commercialized gospel teachings.

Ukoma, Nnachi and Oji have captured very well the concept of commercialization of the gospel in the in Africa as the write:

> The word Commercialization is derived from commerce connoting the ideology of managing a business basis for profit, developing commerce to exploit for profit, or to debase in quality for more profit. [. . .]. The idea projected is that the Church is fast turning to a market place where all manner of people and winds of doctrines are displayed for the purpose of making money and not the making of souls for eternity. Many preachers today rather see in Christ an avenue of making money and acquiring wealth. In the case of the Church, commercialization simply means to run church meetings and programmes with the view of making money or garnering material substances in the name of giving to God hence every meeting must end in offerings and seeds of faith. The underlining intent and content of this type of propagation is all about personal wealth acquisition but in the name of God.[93]

Hence, according to Ukoma, Nnachi an Oji, the name of God has become a tool to enhance the success of the the intended business; and the contemporary church has turned to being more a market place than a place for adoring God, a place where believers are made commodities of trade than a place where they are made to hear the comforting and healing gospel.

The commercialization of the gospel highlighted above is noted in the way most people turn to the ministry of prophecy. Prophesies are on the

---

92. Mashau & Kgatle, "Prosperity Gospel and the Culture of Greed," 4; *cf.* Nwadialor, "Pentecostal Hermeneutics," 1271.

93. Ukoma, Nnachi & Oji, "The Problem of Prosperity Preaching," 153.

hands of business people who use the titles to perpetuate the 'culture of greed and consumption,' as Mashau and Kgatle put it.[94] Mashau and Kgatle further emphasize:

> Some rush into business situations based on such personal prophecy because they believe such prophecies are harbingers of prosperity. However, quite a number of them end up giving out the little they have only to wait endlessly for a hundred-fold multiplication of what they have given. Some prophets are later discovered to be charlatans who are just making merchandise of the gift of God. Kgatle [. . .] mentions some of these prophets, namely, Lesego Daniel, Lethebo Rabalago, Penuel Mnguni and Paseka Motsoeneng, who have abused church members in the name of religion.[95]

Therefore, this quotation indicates that most of the so-called men and women of God in the current consumer culture are hardly servants of the living God, but of their own bellies.

They are servants of their own bellies because, as Magezi and Banda write, their mediatory role is riddled in competition with that of Christ they purport to serve. Magezi and Banda state:

> The mediatory role of the Pentecostal prophets is riddled with competition against the mediatory role of Christ between God and humanity (1 Tm 2:5) as it tends to usurp Christ's role over the church. Instead of being channels that lead people to depend only on Christ for their spiritual security, prosperity Pentecostal prophets present themselves as super spiritual authorities who must be relied upon by the believers in addition to Christ. [. . .]. As super spiritual authorities, Pentecostal prophets project themselves as uniquely anointed by God. This places them closer to God than other people and, in turn, they receive spiritual power and authority over other believers. The prophets mediate their presence in the lives of their followers through anointed objects such as their personal pictures, anointed oil and armbands.[96]

---

94. Mashau & Kgatle, "Prosperity Gospel and the Culture of Greed," 4.

95. Ibid.

96. Magezi & Banda, "Competing with Christ?" 1; *cf.* Magezi & Manzanga, "Prosperity and Health Ministry."

Pioneers of Prosperity Gospel in Africa

The main founder of prosperity gospel teachings in Africa, according to Kwateng-Yeboah, was the late Pentecostal Nigerian Archbishop Benson Idahosa (1938—1998) of Benin city in Nigeria, once trained among the Salvation Army and Methodists before turning to Prosperity preaching. Straub reports: "In 1971, he attended Christ for the Nations Institute of Dallas, Texas, founded by Gordon Lindsay (1906–1973). After only one semester he returned to Africa with a burning desire to impact Nigeria for Christ. Idahosa founded the Church of God International Mission. Oral Roberts University conferred an honorary doctorate on him in 1984, a sign of their approval of his theology."[97] Kwateng-Yeboah further reports: "Idahosa was trained in the Rhema Bible College of Kenneth Hagin in Oklama. When Idahosa returned to Nigeria, he started his own Bible School and later established the 'Church of God Mission International', headquartered in Benin City."[98] Idahosa's theology and influence led him to planting more than 600 churches in Nigeria and Ghana.[99]

Following the introduction of his ministry, several other Neo-Pentecostal pastors were trained including the Archbishop Nicholous Dunkan Williams—who founded the first charismatic church in Ghana by the name of "The Christian Action Faith Ministry International," and the famous prosperity gospel preacher in Nigeria and founder of the church by the name of "Living Faith World Outreach" or "Winners' Chapel" under its motto 'I am a winner' which is "sported on stickers adorning cars, shops, and houses in Lagos and Accra."[100] Hence, from the above pioneering prosperity gospel

---

97. Straub, "The Pentecostalization of Global Christianity," 219.

98. Kwateng-Yeboah, "A Reappraisal of the Prosperity Gospel," 17; cf. Habib, "A New Paradigm of Leadership," 80–82; Olofinjana, 20 *Pentecostal Pioneers*, 98–113 & Straub, "The Pentecostalization of Global Christianity," 219. Some scholars ascribe the pioneering work of prosperity teachings in Africa to Reinhard Bonnke, an American preacher through his "Christ for All Nations" crusades established in various parts of Africa (see Young, "Prosperity Teaching," 4). Straub, writing in 2016, reports: "Among the most significant is the preaching ministry of Reinhard Bonnke (b. 1940). His African ministry commenced as AFM missionary in Lesotho in 1967. There he claimed a vision in which God told him that Africa would be saved. Bonnke began an itinerate ministry that has carried him around Africa and across the globe delivering the Pentecostal message, claiming 74 million converts in the past 41 years, most of them from Africa."(Straub, "The Pentecostalization of Global Christianity,"224.

99. Straub, "The Pentecostalization of Global Christianity," 219.

100. Kwateng-Yeboah, "A Re-appraisal of the Prosperity Gospel," 17. In Lagos Nigeria is where the largest church auditorium in the world is situated with ca. 50,400 seats. The Winners' Chapel has more than 400 branches within and outside Nigeria (see Gifford, "The Bible in Africa," 208).

preachers, prosperity gospel spread throughout Africa causing the emergence of preachers and prophets pioneering churches and ministries.[101] Mashau and Kgatle mention some other richest prosperity gospel preachers in Africa: "Nigerian pastor Temitope Balogun Joshua (TB Joshua) of The Synagogue, Church of All Nations (SCOAN), Nigerian-born pastor Chris Oyakhilome of Christ Embassy, South African televangelist pastor Paseka Motsoeneng (Mboro) of Incredible Happenings, South Africa–based Malawian prophet Shepherd Bushiri of the Enlightened Christian Gathering (ECG) and many others."[102]

Niemandt further asserts that "many of the African recipients of American 'prosperity theology' received their theological education in North American Faith Gospel milieus, and that they evolved as prosperity megastars of their own, closely modelled on their mentors. These early adapters again mentored a new generation of African prosperity theologians."[103] Basing on the foundation of those who studied in North America, a North American type of prosperity gospel developed in different parts of Africa. It means that these theologians themselves were the foundation for the African prosperity gospel movement prevailing now in most African parts.

Principles Governing Prosperity Gospel

African prosperity gospel and Neo-Pentecostalism as a whole, according to Kwateng-Yeboah, is built upon three major principles: hard work, prayer, and giving.[104] Prosperity gospel teachings and Neo-Pentecostalism emphasize that adherents have to use their own hands in order to earn their living. They are encouraged to engage in various profitable activities in order to get income, for example petty trading, farming, vending cheap food staffs, *etc*. However, the physical struggle for income alone does not make someone prosper, according to the Neo-Pentecostal teachings. The adherent has to engage in giving, which is done in various forms: "*offering, tithes,* and gifts to men and women of God termed *sowing* and *reaping* [. . .]. Sowing and reaping comprises the giving of money, land, cars, time, abilities, and one's possession for God's work (evangelism, missions, and church projects) and to God's servants in expectation for divine blessing."[105] In this case, giving,

---

101. Kwateng-Yeboah, "A Re-appraisal of the Prosperity Gospel," 18.
102. Mashau & Kgatle, "Prosperity Gospel and the Culture of Greed," 3.
103. Niemandt, "The Prosperity Gospel," 215.
104. See Kwateng-Yeboah, "A Re-appraisal of the Prosperity Gospel," 19.
105. Kwateng-Yeboah, "A Re-appraisal of the Prosperity Gospel," 19; Kasera, "Biblical and Theological Examination," 15.

as advocated by the prosperity gospel teaching is "reciprocal and 'transactional' as adherents are taught to expect appropriate redemptive uplifts (e.g., money, jobs, promotions, good health, and breakthroughs) from God when giving obligations are faithfully fulfilled."[106] The above activities of hard work and giving are accompanied by words of prayers to God for prosperity because thoughts, words and actions of the believer are believed to have formative effects towards his or her prosperity.

Major Emphasis of Prosperity Gospel Teachings

Following the three principles outlined above, the main emphasis of prosperity gospel is the accumulation of wealth here on earth, physical well-being, and success in life. These aspects, as said above, are obtained through sowing seeds in the heavenly account, and through positive confessions of faith basing on Mark 11: 22–24. Positive confession is uttering positive statements about the things which the prosperity gospel adherents would like them be improved, with the faith that they will be improved as per their confessions. As Ehioghae and Olanrewaju put clear, "Proponents of prosperity gospel believe that Christians can decide what they want, confess and claim it and presto it is theirs! What this means is that believers can obtain the longings of their hearts by naming and claiming them by faith. In essence, God is glorified when those who confess him are rich and happy in every conceivable way."[107] Kasera further emphasizes: "The speaking must be loud as it is believed that God can only hear us if we say the words loud and our circumstances can also hear our word and as a result will conform to what we want them to be."[108] In that case, people tend to connect with archaic narcissistic elements more easily due to vulnerability of self they have because of what they have suffered for a long time. As part of their spiritual healing, it is common to see in worship gatherings prosperity gospel adherents express their sentiments, shouting to God with loud voices, saying: "I don't accept poverty [. . .]. I don't accept that [. . .]. I determine that I will be victorious and prosperous! I determine that I will have so and so at my disposal! God, you did not create me to be poor, but to be rich [. . .]!" In fact, the above confession is a typical resistance from an unacceptable life condition and a claim from God what the prosperity gospel adherent believes should have. It is an expression of one's desire for material, not spiritual abundance.

106. Kwateng-Yeboah, "A Re-appraisal of the Prosperity Gospel," 19.
107. Ehioghae & Olanrewaju, "A Theological Evaluation," 71.
108. Kasera, "Biblical and Theological Examination," 56.

By the use of the two ways stated above, followers of prosperity gospel are made to believe that the much they provide to God what they have through their ministers, especially those holding the prosperity gospel perspective, the much they will receive from God in return (Mark 10: 29–30). Basing on this teaching, followers of prosperity teachings who need to prosper (or to be rich) are emphasized to "plant their seeds" through giving what they have to God in churches or to God's representatives who are here on earth directly. It means that they can send directly to churches, directly to servants, or send through social media, e.g., M-Pesa, Tigo Pesa, Airtel Money, *etc* (in Tanzanian context) for them to receive abundant blessings from God—for them to receive a hundred times (Mark 14: 1–9).[109] Quoting from Akoko, Kasera emphasizes: "In some of the new Pentecostal churches [. . .] members are sometimes urged to borrow money [take loans or open insurance policies], if necessary, in order to give to the church; they are told that they thus qualify for supernatural monetary blessing [. . .]."[110]

Cementing on the concept of sowing seeds in order to prosper, Akoko, quoting from Fomum, writes: "you prosper by planting a financial seed in faith, the return on which will meet all your financial needs."[111] Akoko further asserts:

> This theology teaches that the spiritual and material fortunes of a 'believer and are dependent on faith and on how much he gives spiritually and materially to God or his representative in the world. Though this applies not only to material but also to spiritual giving—and similarly not only to material but also to spiritual prosperity in biblical sense—most groups emphasize the importance of financial prosperity and financial giving here and now. The aspect of spiritual giving and prosperity seems to have been pushed aside because Pentecostal leaders use the emphasis on financial gift as a springboard to raise money for the church and also for themselves.[112]

Following Akoko's words above, the material or spiritual prosperity depends solely on the individual himself or herself. The individual becomes poor not because God wants him or her to be poor, but because that individual lacks faith and does not give offerings and tithes as is supposed to give. The sowing of seeds discussed in the above paragraphs is enforced by giving

---

109. See Akoko, *"Ask and You will be given,"* 1–5; Kwateng-Yeboah, ""A Re-appraisal of the Prosperity Gospel," 8.

110. Kasera, "Biblical and Theological Examination," 57.

111. Akoko, *"Ask and You will be Given,"* 5.

112. Akoko, *"Ask and You will be given,"* 5; *cf.* Copeland, *The Laws of Prosperity.*

tithes and offerings. Tithing is giving the tenth part of one's earning in order to receive a hundred times in this world. Therefore, according to the prosperity teachings, the major emphasis is "this-worldly" property and not the "other-worldly."[113] As Ehioghae and Olanrewaju state, "prosperity gospel preachers have moved beyond traditional Pentecostal practices of speaking in tongues, prophesying, and healing to the belief that God will provide—money, cars, houses, and even spouses—in response to the believer's faith—if not immediately, then soon."[114] Togarasei emphasizes this point: "With its teaching that wealth is a sign of God's blessings upon an individual, the gospel of prosperity is indeed a departure from the traditional Christian teaching of *hatina musha panyika* (Shona: we have no home in this passing world). Prosperity preachers are very much 'this-worldly' in their approach to wealth and consumer materialism in general. Owning cars, houses, successful businesses and other material possessions is not only accepted but expected of those who have the right dosage of faith."[115]

Biblical Texts mostly used to enforce Prosperity Gospel Teachings

In order to enforce the prosperity gospel teachings in regard to "physical well-being, financial fortunes, and material progress"[116] preachers use various techniques, including the use of the Bible as a source of their messages. Kwateng-Yeboah identifies those texts:

> "Several biblical texts are cited in support: 3John 2ff (God's will for believers is to prosper and to be in good health); Philippians 4: 19ff (God supplies all your needs according to His glorious riches in Christ); 2Corinthians 9: 8ff (Jesus Christ, though rich, became poor for our sake so that through his poverty, we might be rich); Luke 6: 38ff (Give and it shall be given unto you, a good and overflowing measure); Deuteronomy 8: 18ff (God gives power to become wealthy); and John 10: 10 (God gives abundant life characterized by wealth)."[117] Such texts are mainly used by what Kasera calls "militant proponents of prosperity gospel" (who make radical claims) such as Kenneth Hagin, Kenneth Copeland, Benson Idahosa, Fred Price, *etc* whose radical claims

---

113. Koch, "The Prosperity Gospel," 31; *cf.* Koch, "Who are the Prosperity Gospel Adherents?"

114. Ehioghae & Olanrewaju, "A Theological Evaluation," 69.

115. Tagarasei, "Modern/Charismatic Pentecostalism," 60–61.

116. Kwateng-Yeboah, "A Re-appraisal of the Prosperity Gospel," 14.

117. *Ibid.*

are "'God's will is healing,' 'God's will for you is wealth,' "poverty is of the devil,' or 'God is a rich God and all His children ought to be rich' etc.[118]

The above-mentioned proof texts for the teaching are faultily interpreted as if they stand alone without any relationship to other texts and without caring about the original meanings to intended readers. However, with this fault interpretations provided to the above texts, prosperity gospel remains an utopian promise that *"feeds the greed of its peddlers [and] emasculates the spirituality of believers."*[119]

North American and African Prosperity Gospels—Continuity and Discontinuity

There is a continuity and discontinuity between the American and African Neo-Pentecostalism and prosperity preaching in general. According to Kwetang-Yeboah, what most African prosperity preachers and prophets practice is just a duplication of that which was done by the American prosperity preachers. As Neimandt has put it, "it seems as if the myriad of churches that can broadly be categorised as part of the prosperity gospel, continue the fundamentalist approaches of North American Pentecostalism."[120] Most of the African prosperity gospel proponents "teach adherents that 'God wants his children to be rich. He wants them to be buoyant, and so He blesses with prosperity, not poverty.'"[121] In such way of teaching African prosperity gospel preachers still stick to the "North American elements of conspicuous consumption, extreme materialism, and an extravagant lifestyle [. . .]."[122]

Moreover, the use of media as one of their major means of promoting the prosperity gospel preaching used in America (televangelism) is also notable among the African prosperity gospel preachers and prophets. African prosperity gospel preachers use the modern media means of communication such as radios, televisions, magazines, *etc.* to propagate their prosperity gospel preaching.[123] In the South African context, that may be similar to other African contexts, television "Viewers are not only promised abundance

118. Kasera, "Biblical and Theological Examination," 25.

119. Ehioghae & Olanrewaju, "A Theological Evaluation," 69.

120. Niemandt, "The Prosperity Gospel," 216; *cf.* Kasera, "Biblical and Theological Examination," 7–8.

121. Kwetang-Yeboah, "'A Re-appraisal of the Prosperity Gospel," 20.

122. *Ibid.*

123. Niemandt, "The Prosperity Gospel," 211; *cf.* Kasera, "Biblical and Theological Examination," 16.

in terms of material gains and or health, they are also encouraged to 'touch the screen' and connect with the 'anointed man of God' for them to receive their anointing or blessings. Those who benefit from these services are encouraged to contribute financially towards the sustenance of such ministries."[124] However, the difference between the American and African prosperity gospel is based on the worldviews of their origin. American prosperity gospel was built upon people's longing for more wealth and material gains due to the rise in living expenses, while African prosperity gospel, though originates from America, is anchored on people's poverty situation. Since most of the poor lack education, it is possible that they easily accept the preachers' prosperity teaching without question. They are directed to dealing with their own lack of faith in God the giver of everything to those who believe with outstanding faith. In this case, African prosperity gospel is rooted "in the African religion-cultural concepts of *well-being*, the *dualistic view of life*, and the *role of religious functionaries*[125] (the primal African worldview) making it have a unique language.

Criticisms to Prosperity Gospel Teachings

As Sharpe puts it, "The widespread embrace of Prosperity [Gospel] and Pentecostalism among the most insecure and economically impoverished is seen here as compensatory response to socio-economic helplessness. [. . .]. Pentecostal Christianity is an opiate for the poor, disinherited and displaced of the earth, inevitably created by the rapid export of dynamic, multinational capitalist economies into the developing world."[126] In fact, "prosperity gospel is fundamentally a theology that explains way luck. It is a pragmatic, result-based, and a therapeutic set of beliefs that explain why some believers rise to the top and others plummet to the very bottom."[127]

Despite its popularity and strong adherence, especially in low income parts of the world, prosperity gospel has been heavily criticized in various ways—positively and negatively. Positively, prosperity gospel critics see that prosperity gospel preaching enhances self-worth to those whom it is preached. Mangena and Mhizha write that "In Africa, preaching a message that promised solutions for present felt needs like sickness and the fear of evil spirits, makes the prophet's 'full gospel message' to be readily accepted by ordinary African people. They develop a type of oral

---

124. Mashau & Kgatle, "Prosperity Gospel and the Culture of Greed," 3.
125. Kwateng-Yeboah, ""A Re-appraisal of the Prosperity Gospel," 20.
126. Sharpe, "Name It and Claim It,"172.
127. Bowler, "Blessed," 11.

liturgy and ministry in which poor people take an active part and thus find a new human dignity."[128]

The sermon below further illustrates this point:

> If you will believe the gospel, the Lord will immediately break the power of sin in your life and you can be filled and empowered by the Holy Spirit to speak in tongues, cast out devils and evangelize the world. You can instantly be set free from your addictions to alcohol, tobacco, sexual promiscuity and drugs, and Jesus will make you into a healthy, honest member of society. God is not against you. There is no virtue in being poor just for the sake of being poor. So God will also bless you materially as you work hard, live honestly, save your money and give a portion of your income to others.[129]

It is in a similar vein as of self-worth among adherents, Bishau echoes: "We agree with many who argue that when we look at the basic import of the Prosperity Gospel per see, it is difficult to find anything wrong with it. [. . .]. From the point of view of sociology, it is known that wealth and success in general contribute towards a high social status. An analysis of group dynamics also shows that people in general tend to listen more to, and tend to congregate more around, the affluent than ordinary lowly members of society."[130] In this case, prosperity gospel is considered by proponents as a holistic approach to human life and his or her well-being. According to proponents of prosperity gospel, "those who oppose this theology are believed to be opposing the move of the Holy Spirit, just like the first century Pharisees did."[131]

Negatively, prosperity gospel is criticized of several aspects: first, it is criticized of being exploitative to the most vulnerable populations. Sharpe notes these exploitative charges: "Critical theological and social scientific perspectives express concern that Prosperity [Gospel] exploit growing numbers among the world's most vulnerable populations, taking the tithes from

---

128. Mangena & Mhizha, "The Rise of White Collar Prophets," 137.

129. Sharper, "Name It and Claim It," 175. A drug is "any substance in a pharmaceutical product that is used to modify or explore psychological systems or pathological states for the benefit of the recipient." (Kunhiyop, *African Christian Ethics*, 360–361) This section deals with drugs called 'psychotropic drugs' or 'psychoactive drugs' which affect the psychological functioning of the human brain to cause "seduction, 'stimulation, or change in mood or behavior." These drugs can be taken into the body of a person in various ways: through "drinking, smoking, injecting, swallowing, sniffing and chewing." (Kunhiyop, *African Christian Ethics*, 360–361)

130. Bishau, "The Prosperity Gospel," 69.

131. Kasera, "Biblical and Theological Examination," 6.

the poorest and offering in exchange only false hope and inflated promises of miracle healings and untold economic abundance."[132] For example, Chitando, analyzing the song by Fungisai Zvakavapano that criticizes the greedy life of pastors, quotes: "(we have given our Talents, we want to see God here). Pastors may no longer continue to exploit their members: they must live up to their calling."[133] Chitando further explains the state of ministry in churches where pastors worship money instead of God: "the preoccupation with prosperity has corrupted the church and weakened its pastoral ministry. Pastors no longer want to visit church members who are poor or who live in less affluent suburbs. Worse still, the appointment of deacons and elders is no longer guided by qualifications that are laid out in the Bible, but by the perceived financial clout of the prospective candidates. Those who own Mercedes Benz vehicles receive preferential treatment, while members of the Zimbabwe Footers Association (the car-less) are brushed aside."[134] This situation indicates that the greedy of pastors and prophets in churches is not only prominent in Zimbabwe, but also everywhere in Africa where prosperity gospel is preached. Goliama further reports that "Experiences and research reports from Africa and other continents have indicated that some Prosperity Gospel members eventually become disillusioned by it. They are disappointed by its unfulfilled promises and as a result some decide to completely stop practising any religion in their lives."[135]

In emphasizing on the greed of pastors and prophets highlighted above, Mashau and Kgatle states: "The prophets of this movement put emphasis on individual success but are silent about or have not developed a systematic theological analysis of economic injustice and social marginalisation that accompanies prosperity gospel."[136] They further add: "The bluff with prosperity gospel is that African Christians who have embraced this message continue to 'name it', whilst their pastors are the ones 'claiming it'. Prophets of prosperity gospel continue to live conspicuous materialistic lifestyles in affluent suburbs and drive the most expensive cars on the market, whilst their congregants are drowning in the triple unholy alliance of

---

132. Sharpe, "Name It and Claim It," 174; cf. Hinn, *God, Greed, and the (Prosperity) Gospel*, 15.

133. Chitando, "Prophets, Profits and Protest," 107. Members of Pentecostal churches are encourages to pay or give Talents. "'Talents' refer to the money that one gets from buying and re-selling different goods or products such as vegetables. Talents are meant to empower the individual believer financially." (Mangena & Mhizha, "The Rise of White Collar Prophets," 144)

134. Ibid., 106.

135. Goliama, "The Gospel of Prosperity," 5.

136. Mashau & Kgatle, "Prosperity Gospel and the Culture of Greed," 1.

poverty, unemployment and inequality '[t]hey [the poor] continue to hope against hope, even in their hopelessness.'"[137] In this case, prosperity gospel is considered to be predominantly more anthropocentric than Christocentric which mostly milks people it serves and disadvantages further those who are disadvantaged by encouraging them to give beyond measure in hope to receive more.

Second, it is criticized of being individualistic, and a property of the few who use it for their own material gains. Sharpe states this point more clearly when he writes: "Prosperity [Gospel] is charged with promoting self-centred individualism and diverting converts' attention away from the lasting causes of their deprivations [. . .]."[138] To illustrate this point, Sharpe quotes the words of the Nigerian Bishop of the Winners' Chapel Bishop David O. Oyedepo praising God for his prosperity saying: "There was a time in my life when I was known as a failure [. . .]. The only car my family had before then was stolen [. . .]. But to the glory of God in October 2000, He gave me a Mercedes Benz car. I have also been able to dedicate a new mansion God blessed me with to the glory of His Name. To crown it all, another car was recently added to my family. I have every reason to celebrate the faithfulness of God."[139] Despite his own attestation, Straub affirms: "Begun in 1983, [Oyedope's] movement boasts 300 churches across Nigeria and around the world. Recently, Oyedepo was listed in *Forbes* as the wealthiest pastor in Nigeria."[140] It is in this way that prosperity gospel is considered an opiate of the poor that hinders them from recognizing the causes of their destitute situations. As Mashau and Kgatle, quoting Umoh, write: "religion appears to be the most lucrative business today."[141]

Third, prosperity gospel and the search for wealth create a world of hate, lack of trust and hypocrisy. It creates the world where people hunt material things in whatever expenses, even leading to what Neal calls "economic violence." Donald Trump, as quoted in Neal states it succinctly:

> The world is a vicious and brutal place. We think we're civilized. In truth, it's a cruel world and people are ruthless. They act nice to your face, but underneath they're out to kill you. You have to know how to defend yourself. People will be mean and nasty and try to hurt you just for sport. Lions in the jungle only kill for food, but humans kill for fun. Even your friends are out to

---

137. Ibid., 3.
138. Sharpe, "Name It and Claim It," 175.
139. Sharpe, "Name It and Claim It," 166.
140. Straub, "The Pentecostalization of Global Christianity," 219.
141. Mashau & Kgatle, "Prosperity Gospel and the Culture of Greed," 3.

> get you: they want your job, they want your house, they want your money, they want your wife, and they even want your dog. Those are your friends; your enemies are even worse! My motto is, 'Hire the best people, and don't trust them.'[142]

In such situation, the prosperity gospel and its tenets turn the world into being an insecure place to live despite its promises.

Fourth, it is criticized of being careless in its methodology of interpreting scriptures used to enforce the teachings. There is an abuse of scriptures and the commercialization of the gospel being preached. Criticizing the stance of prosperity gospel, a well-known prosperity gospel preacher Benny Hinn is quoted in Nwankwo's article denouncing prosperity gospel and acknowledging it as being erroneous. In his own confession, Hinn says: "I don't want to get to heaven and be rebuked. I think it is time we say it like it is: the Gospel is not for sale and the blessings of God are not for sale; and miracles are not for sale and prosperity is not for sale."[143] Hinn's confession criticizes the way in which the gospel is used as a commodity for economic purposes, preaching neither message about Jesus nor his suffering on the cross but abundant material possession here on earth. In that case, prosperity teachings are de-linked to the cross and are hardly Christian.

Due to its careless in interpreting scriptures, the prosperity gospel preaching is developed from dogmatic assertions of the preachers not from appropriate, well-grounded, and sound methods of interpreting the Bible. They are developed from the preachers' own interests in order to back up their precooked dogmas which are materially beneficial to them. Bishau clearly explains the dogmatic approach this way:

> The dogmatic approach [...] is an approach where the meaning of the text is broken down into key terms, phrases or isolated verses that are lined up as proof-texts to validate a particular dogma; in this kind of interpretation the interpreter begins with a set of dogmatic positions and then gets into the Bible to find proof for the positions. The key terms, phrases or isolated verses are lined up as probative evidence for the dogma without any due respect for the historical context, literary form or theological purpose of the verses because they are suitable to prove a point and not because of their meaning within the larger context of the chapter.[144]

142. Neal, "Christian Implications," 70.

143. Nwankwo, "African Christianity," 12.

144. Bishau, "The Prosperity Gospel," 71; *cf.* Ehioghae & Olanrewaju, "A Theological Evaluation," 72–73; Young, "Prosperity Teaching," 10–12.

This is the careless approach to the Bible found in most prosperity gospel teachings throughout the African continent.

Moreover, with the carelessness of the prosperity gospel in grounding prosperity gospel into sound methods of biblical interpretation, "there are differing views as to whether prosperity gospel may properly be regarded as gospel. The thinking in some quarters is that prosperity gospel is a ruse, another clever ploy deployed by self-serving preachers to take advantage of the gullibility of religious people."[145] Mussana outlines the point which scholars stress for the well-grounded interpretation: "A point which is stressed by theologians is that God's self-revelation is through created realities and human culture. In the Bible, it is the Israelite culture which is used to speak to us across thousands of years. If God revealed himself in the Israelite culture, it must also be in the present; God revealing himself through other cultures, including the African culture."[146] Following this emphasis of scholars, as pointed out by Mussana, one can conclude that the mere reading of texts and applying them to the African context as if they were written to Africans as original recipients, as done by prosperity gospel preachers, hardly does justice to both the texts being preached for and the current African culture to which the texts are being preached.

Fifth, Sharpe states that "The very emphasis Prosperity [Gospel] places on physical and economic flourishing, while it downplays the realities of structural oppression [. . .]. [This emphasis] differentiates the movement from older, more other-worldly forms of Pentecostalism and Christianity."[147] A good example of the negligence of existing reality done by the prosperity gospel in Africa is found in the analysis of the theology of Bishop David Oyedepo done by Gifford. Niemandt reports: "Although it made itself at home in many African countries and in countless African faith communities, Gifford found—in his careful analysis of the theology of David Oyedepo—that Oyedepo's particular Prosperity Theology is not '[. . .]African in the sense of having some special focus on Africa'. Oyedepo very seldom focuses on African or Nigerian realities, and does not attempt to address it [. . .]."[148] In that case, "Despite all its claims to restoration and the utopian image it presents prosperity gospel has only succeeded in muzzling the witness of the Christian church because it is based on wrong-headed theology

---

145. Ehioghae & Olanrewaju, "A Theological Evaluation," 69.

146. Musanna, "Interpretation, Message and Challenge," 87.

147. Sharpe, "Name It and Claim It," 176. Moreover, prosperity gospel does not take into account the eschatological teaching of the Bible. Jesus second coming (the *parousia*) is not emphasized in the prosperity teachings. Prosperity teachings emphasize the individual's well-being here and now (see Young, "Prosperity Teaching," 12–13).

148. Niemandt, "The Prosperity Gospel," 207.

and faulty hermeneutical principles. It feeds on the greed of its peddlers, leaving their acolytes worse off, materially and spiritually."[149]

Sixth, the activities of white collar prophets who preach prosperity gospel are suspect in regard to public morality. Mangena and Mhizha summarize the following issues which make them suspect:[150]

1. They sometimes side with and participate in the policies of the *status quo*, even oppressive ones. This habit is contrary to the way prophets of the Old Testament were acting. Dietrich clarifies the main concern of prophets in the Old Testament: "The prophets spoke out clearly about injustice. They blamed the corrupt leaders of their time, and advocated for the poor and marginalized. At the same time, they were concerned about the people's faithlessness in relation to God. The love of God and the love of 'your neighbour' were connected in their prophecies. The neglect of God was, according to the prophets, intertwined closely with the neglect of humankind in need."[151]
2. They do not have the courage to challenge the existing authorities for fear of losing their lives.
3. They diverge from the message of salvation centered on the cross of Jesus Christ and concentrate on the prosperity message about health and wealth here on earth. God's call for prophets is not centered on the performance of miracles and predictions about the future; rather, it is centered on preaching about the good news of salvation and its ethics.
4. Though they use the Bible and do all what they do in the name of God, yet their followers join them not with the motive of spiritual enrichment, but with the motive of material gain and health well-being. Most of them have suffered from various physical, spiritual and mental problems in their lives and need deliverance. Prosperity teachings are their last resort after trying everything else without success.
5. The source of their power to perform miracles is questionable and controversial. Most of them have been forced to visit traditional healers in order to expand their ministries by the practice of magical activities contrary to the teachings of mainstream Christianity. Others have consulted the so called "men of God" in West Africa to acquire power to perform miracles from them. All these endeavors indicate that the source of their power is not from God worshiped in Christianity, but from occultism. They perform miracles to just let their

---

149. Ehioghae & Olanrewaju, "A Theological Evaluation," 74.
150. See Mangena & Mhizha, "The Rise of White Collar Prophecy," 148–149.
151. Dietrich, "For thus says the Lord," 153.

followers believe and trust them as being true prophets with ability to perform extraordinary deeds, but not true prophets in the real sense.

Generally, the above negative criticisms can be summarized by the quotation from Kasera with only three points as to why prosperity gospel is considered as being critically deficient and less appealing to mainstream Christianity: "1) it is a man-centred theology. 2) It teaches a counterfeit theology of giving. 3) It opposes social and economic equality and encourages materialistic excessiveness and by so doing, it sets up a theological superstructure of oppressing the poor and even taking from them [. . .]."[152]

Bishau further notes in regard to what makes the prosperity gospel not appealing to orthodox Christianity:

> An analysis of the definition of the Prosperity Gospel shows that there is nothing intrinsically sinister about the gospel itself. Its basic tenets and what it is said to stand for show that the Prosperity Gospel has its foundations from the Bible; there is no doubt that it is biblically based and what it promises, nobody can refuse to accept. Nobody wants to be poor and nobody wants ill health and if taken positively there is no doubt that it can be an ideological basis for industry and an overall economic policy that empowers the Christians [. . .]. However, it seems the gospel has been and is [still] being manipulated to suit other people's selfish ends.[153]

The above quotation means that despite the fact that prosperity gospel preachers use the Bible and preach about tangible issues of wealth and health, what makes the prosperity gospel unappealing to mainline and orthodox Pentecostal Christianity is the reckless way in which the Bible is used.

Due to their recklessness in interpreting Scriptures pointed out in the fourth criticism above, the prosperity gospel preachers and their materialistic stance are the possible destructive agents of the gospel and its value. As Ehioghae and Olanrewaju echo: "Prosperity gospel teaches people to focus on getting, not giving. At its core it is a selfish and materialistic faith with a thin Christian veneer. It is true that God promises to reward those who give to him generously (2 Cor 9:6–11) but this should not be understood as putting God under the obligation to materially bless the giver. Divine largesse, like other blessings, is received by grace."[154] In its conception that human beings can have absolute control of everything through faith and putting

---

152. Kasera, "Biblical and Theological Examination," 10.
153. Bishau, "The Prosperity Gospel," 73.
154. Ehioghae & Olanrewaju, "A Theological Evaluation," 73.

God under obligation to respond to the desires and wills of human beings, prosperity gospel overlooks the reality of the Fall that plundered humanity and the sovereignty of God over the existing creation.[155]

Seventh, in a sad way, Kasera quotes a statement from the Lausanne Theology Working Group to provide an overarching criticism to the prosperity gospel in Africa and other developing parts of the world:

> We recognize that Prosperity Teaching flourishes in contexts of terrible poverty, and that for many people, it presents their only hope, in the face of constant frustration, the failure of politicians and NGOs, *etc.*, for a better future, or even for a more bearable present. We are angry that such poverty persists and we affirm the Bible's view that it also angers God and that it is not his will that people should live in abject poverty. We acknowledge and confess that in many situations the Church has lost its prophetic voice in the public arena. However, we do not believe that Prosperity Teaching provides a helpful or biblical response to the poverty of the people among whom it flourishes [. . .].
>
> (a) It vastly enriches those who preach it, but leaves multitudes no better off than before, with the added burden of disappointed hopes.
> (b) While emphasizing various alleged spiritual or demonic causes of poverty, it gives little or no attention to those causes that are economic and political, including injustice, exploitation, unfair international trade practices, *etc.*
> (c) It thus tends to victimize the poor by making them feel that their poverty is their own fault (which the Bible does not do), while failing to address and denounce those whose greed inflicts poverty on others (which the Bible does repeatedly).
> (d) Some prosperity teaching is not really about helping the poor at all, and provides no sustainable answer to the real causes of poverty [. . .].[156]

Eighth, Abackle cements on the above criticism when he further criticizes by stating the reasons for the uncontrollable flourishing of prosperity gospel. According to him, Pentecostalism, and prosperity gospel in particular, flourishes because of the following reasons: "It has the ability to offer people *immediate* hope that there are solutions to their problems within the intense chaos of urban poverty; if there is no success they can blame the

---

155. Kasera, "Biblical and Theological Examination," 9.
156. Ibid., 97.

devil or their own lack of faith in the Spirit. Wealth is a sign of God's blessings [. . .]. '[Pentecostalism] doesn't oppose consumerism. It embraces it. It *imports meaning* into consumerism.'"[157] Therefore, the stated reasons make prosperity gospel attractive and a solution to most African people heavily struck by acute poverty related problems.

Nineth, we need to pay attention to Jones's words. After his discussion of the five errors of prosperity gospel, *i.e.*, the bases on Abrahamic Covenant as a Christian entitlement for material prosperity, the atonement of Jesus as a source for physical healing and economic well-being and the misconception of the life of Jesus as a whole, Christians giving done in order to receive compensation from God, and prayers done in order to force God to respond to their human health and wealth needs,[158] Jones concluded:

> In light of Scripture, the prosperity gospel is fundamentally flawed. At bottom, it is a false gospel because of its faulty view of the relationship between God and man. Simply put, if the prosperity gospel is true, grace is obsolete, God is irrelevant, and man is the measure of all things. Whether they're talking about the Abrahamic covenant, the atonement, giving, faith, or prayer, prosperity teachers turn the relationship between God and man into a *quid pro quo* transaction. As James Goff noted in a 1990 *Christianity Today* article, God is "reduced to a kind of 'cosmic bellhop' attending to the needs and desires of his creation."[159]

According to Jones and Woodbridge, the erroneous nature of prosperity gospel is based on the fact that its teachings are not in harmony with the orthodox Christianity advocated by both mainline churches and the orthodox Pentecostalism. Jones and Woodbridge highlight a few points to illustrate the erroneous nature of prosperity gospel:

- Prosperity gospel presents a distorted view of God. It hardly accepts the orthodox view of the Holy Trinity, a fact not realized by most adherents. Most believers of the prosperity gospel hardly realize that their teachers present a distorted and unbiblical doctrine about the nature of God.[160]

---

157. Abackle, *Culture, Inculturation, and Theologicans*, 135 (Italics for emphasis is in original).

158. *Cf.* Ukoma, Nnachi & Oji, "The Problem of Prosperity Preaching," 148–149.

159. Jones, "5 Errors of the Prosperity Gospel."

160. See Jones & Woodbridge, "Health, Wealth & Happiness," 57–59; *cf.* Gbotoe, "Commercialized Gospel," 11.

- Prosperity gospel elevates human mind over matter through its belief in the word, both in thought and spoken forms, and its creative power.[161]
- In the relation between humankind and the Creator, humankind is elevated to the level of the Creator. The humankind is deified and stands at the centre of the universe; and God is there to serve the needs of the created human being claimed through prayers and positive confession.[162]
- Prosperity gospel emphasizes health and wealth instead of the atonement message of Jesus Christ. It emphasizes more on this-worldly materials that the other-worldly matters.[163]
- Some prosperity preachers diverge from the orthodox view of salvation through Jesus Christ and his work on the cross.

Hence, following the above listed aspects and the entire discussion in this section, prosperity gospel needs to be treated with caution because it is held suspect by mainline churches and orthodox Pentecostalism as possibly being not Christian; it is thought to be corresponding more to the New Thought movement than the orthodox Christianity.[164] This is because "Both New Thought and prosperity gospel exhibit a distorted view of God, an elevation of mind over matter, an exalted view of people, a focus on health and wealth, and an unorthodox view of salvation."[165]

What then should practical theology do in this disappointing situation, where prosperity gospel claims to provide hope to people in the situation of poverty within African context? What should practical theology do in a context where the new brand of Christianity has caused the exodus of Christians from mainline churches to Pentecostal churches in search of cheap answers to problems of their daily living, in search for new spirituality and economic emancipation? These and many similar questions still need further reflections.

However, the materialistic nature of the prosperity gospel discussed in Abackle's criticism above is enshrined within people's hearts. Daniel G. Groody, taking ideas from Donald Gelpi, writes that the "political and social injustices in the world are connected to fundamental psychological,

---

161. See Jones & Woodbridge, "Health, Wealth & Happiness," 59–62.
162. See *Ibid.*, 63–64.
163. See *Ibid.*, 64–69.
164. Chimuka, "Reflections on the Morality of Some Prophetic Acts," 119.
165. Jones & Woodbridge, "Health, Wealth & Happiness," 71.

intellectual, personal, moral and religious distortions within people."[166] It is a distortion within people's hearts manifested through their actions towards others. Putting more emphasis to the notion of the heart as the source of all human potentials, Groody says:

> the biblical notion of the heart deals with inner wealth: the quality of people's characters, the endowment of their souls, and the treasure within them. The heart symbolizes the whole process of human understanding that can only be grasped from the depths of one's being, the place where the human and the divine interact. It is the place from which flow one's values, one's relationships, and it is intimately connected with how one responds to the most vulnerable members of the human family. Therefore, the work of global transformation has its origin in a more rudimentary inner transformation.[167]

The reflection on prosperity gospel in relation to the practice of the Church in Africa should focus on the transformation of people's hearts; it should focus on the liberation from the spirit of materialism onto which the prosperity gospel anchors to spirit of real Christian gospel embraced by mainstream Christianity.

The transformation of the materialistic society, the consumer society to which prosperity gospel has enshrined, depends solely on the inner transformation of society in general. It is liberation of society. As Groody further contends, the major means for being liberated from the heartily-rooted spirit of materialism is through "conversion," and about turn (*metanoia*). Succinctly defined, conversion is "not simply a movement from one religious belief to another but more fundamentally as a movement from irresponsibility to responsibility."[168] It is movement from valuing materials more towards valuing the dignity of human beings and from valuing worldly health more towards valuing the heavenly treasures.

We strongly agree with Gathogo's assertion that in whatever the case Africans should not curse their God and turn to theologies of prosperity that exacerbate suffering to people more tormented by poverty, incurable diseases, violence, angry spiritual beings and unjust leadership regimes as he clearly states:

> While Africa [. . .] must reject the temptation to curse God despite its sufferings, a theology that encourages more suffering

---

166. Groody, "Globalizing Solidarity," 262.
167. *Ibid.*
168. *Ibid.*, 263.

should be resisted. Similarly, Africa must resist the temptation to believe that there must be something wrong with the continued belief in a God who seems to be totally insensitive to the suffering of the people supposedly created by God's will, as Friedrich Nietzsche (1844—1900), the son and grandson of a family of Lutheran Pastors in Prussia, held. For Nietzsche, since God seemed not to care for His creatures, he was either absent, dead or irrelevant to the immediate needs of the suffering people.[169]

It is in the midst of suffering and hopelessness where God reveals power and presence. It is in the midst of the resurgence of materialist theologies of our post modern world where God calls the true Church in Africa to grasp the real purpose of the death and resurrection of Jesus Christ.

THE CHALLENGE OF VIOLENCE

After a detailed examination of the concept of prosperity gospel as practiced within the Church in Africa in the previous section, we now turn to another more intriguing issue of *violence,* its various manifestations in the practice of the Church in Africa and some possible theological reflections about it. The notion of violence is universal. Alexander John Malik explains about the universality of violence: "Violence is not restricted to one country or continent, one region or religion. It is universally used as a means and a strategy to achieve certain objectives; sometimes brutally as sheer naked aggression, or at other times subtly, covered in the garb of legislation and legitimacy as a tool to maintain law and order."[170] Malik adds: "No nation or people in the whole world could claim, in all honesty, that it has not committed violence at one time or other in its history."[171]

It is now common phenomenon in Africa to hear about people killed, young children thrown by their mothers after birth, women raped by men, children forced to work in difficult jobs, people bitten, insulted, or denied rights to enter a certain country. Whatever we can hear, which causes harm to humanity psychologically, mentally, physically and any other aspect of human life entails violence. Violence shatters human ambitions, retards human aspirations and causes sufferings to people in all levels: individuals, families, and or entire societies. In this case, the concept of violence is too wide and can hardly be comprehended by just liming oneself to a few aspects of it. However, violence always occurs in situations where there is

169. Gathogo, "The Challenge of Money and Wealth," 149.
170. Malik, "Religion and Violence," 23.
171. *Ibid.*

unequal power relation between the actor of violence and the one to which it is acted. The major aim of violence is to establish control. The actor wants to control the one to whom it is acted.

There are good examples of physical violence against humanity such as the carnage of September 11, 2001 in the United States of America, the machete killing of one another among the Hutu and Tutsi tribes in Rwanda,[172] the killing of people with albinism in Tanzania,[173] the killing of elderly people with red eyes in some regions in Tanzania,[174] and the demolishing of mosques, churches and pork butchers in Dar es Salaam Tanzania in 1993 and 1998 due to the Christian-Muslim conflict.[175] Other Violence deeds in Africa involve the assassination of individual state leaders such as Samuel Doe of Liberia, Muamar Khadafi of Libya, and the recent attack and shooting of the Member of Parliament Tundu Lissu in Tanzania to mention just a few of them. Hence, looking at all these, one can see that the victims are mostly harmed physically.

As just pointed out above, violence is a wide phenomenon and can hardly be expressed in just a single form. It can be noted in various places of human life: at homes, work places, in public buses during travels, religious gatherings during worships, schools, colleges and universities during studies, *etc*. As Nyaundi says, whenever it happens, "Violence causes immeasurable anguish to individuals, families, communities and nations in general. Violence damages moral probity, destroys property, and leads to loss of life."[176] Moreover, violence breaks relationship between the actor and the one upon whom it is acted.

Meaning of Violence

Having explained the general occurrences of violence in the above paragraphs, we need to answer the disturbing question: What is violence? This question longs for the meaning of the concept of violence. There are various definitions of the concept of violence and no single definition suffices. De

---

172. Longman, "Church Politics"; Court, "The Christian Churches"; Nikuze, "The Genocide"; Le Roux, "The Role of African Christian Churches"; Benda, "The Test of Faith."

173. Uromi, "Violence against Persons"; Mutungi, "The Killing of Albinos" Salewi, "The Killing of Persons" & Stensson, "The Social Stratification."

174. Uromi, "Violence against Persons."

175. Poncian, "Christian-Muslim Relations," 57; Nguruwe, "Called to Harmony" 13; Tetti, "What went Wrong,"506; *cf*. Nkoko, "Accounting for the 1990—2013 Christian-Muslim Conflicts."

176. Nyaundi, "The Phenomenon of Violence," 123.

Haan says that there is even no beginning of agreement among scholars on what the concept of violence really is.[177] It is difficult to define the concept of violence because of its many forms and manifestations. De Haan says about the definition of violence:

> Violence is multifaceted because there are many different forms of violence, which are exhibited in a wide range of contexts. It may, for example, be distinguished in 'youth violence', 'gang violence', 'school violence', 'street violence', 'teen violence', 'dating violence', 'intimate violence', 'domestic violence', 'workplace violence', 'suite violence' [. . .], 'urban violence', 'interpersonal violence', 'random violence', 'racist violence', 'media violence', 'mimetic violence', 'systemic violence', 'symbolic violence', 'structural violence' or even 'apocalyptic violence' [. . .]. Violence can be physical ('aggression', 'abuse' or 'assault'), but it can also be verbal ('bullying', 'humiliation' or 'intimidation'). It can be overt but also covert like in language and literacy, abstraction, interpretation and representation, and in the violence of 'censure' [. . .]. Violence can be individual or collective, interpersonal or institutional, national or international, symbolic or structural. The context may be private or public and the victims may be family members, acquaintances or strangers. Based on the offender's motive, violence may be angry, impulsive, hostile, expressive, dispute-related, instrumental, or predatory. "Some incidents occur, more or less, 'out of the blue', whereas others occur within some form of relationship in which conflict escalates. Some incidents are concluded in a few moments, whereas others evolve into long-term conflict relationships. Non-physical attacks can be made against the gender, race or sexuality of the victim, or—as in some of these cases—their professional integrity." [. . .]. Instead of or in addition to physical injury; violence can have mental ('psychological'), social and/or material consequences and there is seems no simple relationship between the apparent severity of a violent act and the impact it has upon the victim.[178]

Following de Haan's statement above, how can one define violence? How can one find a definition that encompasses all the above-mentioned aspects properly represented in that definition. The multifaceted nature of this concept is the one that makes it difficult among scholars to have a one agreed definition.

---

177. De Haan, "Violence as an essentially Contested Concept," 27.
178. De Haan, "Violence as an essentially Contested Concept," 28.

However, some scholars have attempted at defining the concept of violence, and their definitions include the following:

1. *Nehemia M. Nyaundi*: Violence is "An act of aggression that inflicts harm on an individual or community. In whatever the case, violence can be planned or unplanned. It can be small or large in scale. At the individual level, violence may cause physical disfigurement or death, while at the societal level, psychological discontent, residential displacement, or large scale carnage."[179] Nyaundi's definition conceives that there should be an act directed upon a person who in turn is harmed by that action, whether planned or not.
2. *World Health Organization*: Violence is "The intentional use of physical force or power, threatened actual, against oneself, another person, or against a group or community, that either results in or has a high likelihood of resulting in injury, death, psychological harm, maldevelopment or deprivation."[180] The main component of this definition is the 'intentional use of force' upon a person in order to harm such a person or group of people.
3. *Martyn John Smith*: "*violence is a potentially irresistible force (whether physical, mental, spiritual or verbal) exerted to achieve a desired end. Exertion can be positive or negative depending on various factors: the context of the exertion; the reason for it; who is exerting and upon whom the exertion is occurring.*"[181] Here, Smith's definition conceives that force is used, but should be irresistible and having various forms: physical, mental, spiritual or verbal.
4. *Henry, as quoted in De Haan*: Violence is

    'the use of power to harm another, whatever form it takes'[...]. In this case, harm is not only physical pain and suffering. It "can also occur along many dimensions beyond the physical to include psychological or emotional, material or economic, social or identity, moral or ethical, and so on. Within each dimension, the harm can be of two kinds: 'harms of reduction' and 'harms of repression' [...]. Harms of reduction remove something from a person's existing status as a human being. For example, physical harms or reduction produce bodily pain or loss (of blood, organs, limbs, physical functioning). Material harms of reduction remove some of the [...] economic status (property, wealth, money). Psychological harms of reduction have destructive

---

179. Nyaundi, "The Phenomenon of Violence," 124.
180. World Health Organization, "Violence-A Global public Health Problem," 5.
181. Smith, "Divine Violence," 11.

effects on the human mind and weaken a person's emotional or mental functioning (such as in posttraumatic stress syndrome). Social and symbolic harms of reduction lower a person's social status (by violating their human rights, sexuality, social identity). Moral or ethical harms of reduction corrupt standards of concern for the well-being of others (as in hate, pressure to cheat, and the like). In contrast, harms of repression reveal how the exercise of power acts to systematically limit another person's capability of achieving higher levels accomplishment along any of these dimensions [. . .]. Violence, then, is the exercise of power over others by some individual, agency, or social process that denies those subject to it their humanity to make a difference, either by reducing them from what they are or by limiting them from becoming what they might be.[182]

Haan's definition conceives violence not only as the use of force to bring about physical harm, but also as power exercised upon individuals taking various forms apart from physical harm.

5. *Terence E. Fretheim:* Violence is "any action, verbal or nonverbal, oral or written, physical or psychical, active or passive, public or private, individual or institutional/societal, human or divine, in whatever degree of intensity, that abuses, violates, injures, or kills."[183]

Fretheim's definition limits violence to actions which lead to abuse, violation and killing of the one whom actions of violence are executed.

As we just said above, none of the definitions stated above encompasses all the aspects of the concept of violence. However, what is common in the above definitions is that all point to something unpleasant or something or act that brings harm to the side of the one whom violence is inflicted. That unpleasant thing or act can be physical, or psychological or emotional harm. Moreover, violence can be a self–violence done by one person to oneself, or an interpersonal violence done by one person to another person. Fretheim's definition above will mainly be taken into account in this lecture because it encompasses both the human and divine violence. In the following sub-title, we focus on the theological reflection on violence.

Theological Evaluation of Violence

The concept of violence is not only a legal, anthropological, sociological, physical, or biological problem, it is also a theological problem. Violence is

182. De Haan, "Violence as an essentially Contested Concept," 32.
183. Fretheim, "God and Violence," 19.

a theme running throughout the Bible if one reads it carefully. Malik states that the sacred texts of the Old Testament, for example, have stories about violence. Malik puts it: "The religious history of the Old Testament aside, even the secular histories of other nations are full of murders, rapes, killings, massacres, and violence. These nations/civilizations include the Egyptians, the Babylonians, the Romans, the Persians, the Chinese, the Japanese, and many others. All of them have used violence as strategy and tactics to overpower their enemies and keep their own people under control."[184] Therefore, it is not surprising to see in the Old Testament stories about wars and between Israel and its neighboring nations leading to acute violence whether Israel won or lost the war.

In the Bible one encounters with both *human* and *divine* violence. Speaking on human violence, Fretheim points it out: "Violence—from robbery to rape to homicide to war—appears near the beginning of the Bible and does not let up along the way. Gen 6:11–13, reporting the violence of 'all flesh' that led to the violence of the flood, tells the story of our own—and every—time: 'Now the earth was corrupt in God's sight and the earth was filled with violence.' We should be thankful that God has promised never to visit the earth in flood-like ways again (Gen 8: 21)!"[185] What Fretheim refers to in the above quotation is human violence as depicted in the Bible. According to Fretheim, human violence is not only physical; it is also in the form of words. In the Bible, "the use of words, e.g., slander, false charges, character assassination, and gossip. Such language has the capacity to promote distrust, disrespect, and enmity, which often lead to physical violence (e.g., Ps 140: 3, 11; Prov 10:6, 11; 16:27–30; Jer 9:2–8; note the link between 'peace' and violent speech in Ps 34:13–14)."[186]

Moreover, several other texts in the Bible demonstrate that God hates the violence of one person to another. The concept of *"namas"* used in the Hebrew Bible show how God is against human violence against another human being (Psalms 11: 5); Jeremiah 22: 3; Ezekiel 45: 9; Habbakuk 2: 8). The violence of a human being is also directed to nonhuman matter. Feretheim provides the link of this kind of violence: "Hos 4:1–3 establishes a clear link: human swearing, lying, murder, stealing, adultery, and bloodshed have highly adverse effects upon the land, animals, birds, and fish."[187] And, eventually, the violence of nonhuman creatures to other creatures is also portrayed in the Bible (Genesis 9: 5; Exodus 21: 28). Therefore, human

---

184. Malik, "Religion and Violence," 24.
185. Fretheim, "God and Violence," 20.
186. *Ibid.*
187. *Ibid.*, 21.

violence as depicted in the Bible raises normal questions of concern for the failure of the Almighty God to intervene in order to bring harmony among human beings and between nonhuman creatures and human beings.

The most problematic violence depicted by the Bible is divine violence where God is involved. Fretheim notes: "The most basic theological problem with the Bible's violence is that it is often associated with the activity of God; with remarkable frequency, God is the subject of violent verbs: From the flood, to Sodom and Gomorrah, to the command to sacrifice Isaac, to the plagues, to all the children killed on Passover night—and we are not yet through the book of Exodus!"[188] In the midst of divine violence, the overarching questions are the following: Why divine involvement in violence? Where should human race build trust, if God, who is ontologically love is involved in extraordinary violence? It is clearly stated in the biblical text: "Whoever does not love does not know God, because God is love." (1John 4: 8; cf. 4: 16) Should Marcion and his followers be blamed for rejecting the Old Testament and some parts of the New Testament because of the divine violence they portray?

What can we say about the theological importance of the divine violence depicted in the Bible? In most cases, God uses human and nonhuman agents to administer violence as a consequence for something done by humanity. This means that the divine wrath that leads to divine violence is a consequence of human violence. Without human violence, there is no divine violence. Therefore, divine violence is the result or arousal from human violence. The sin of humanity is the one which arises consequences. The divine violence is intrinsic to the deed of humanity, not forensic to it.[189]

Moreover, God is incomprehensible. God used the means amicable for human deliverance. Violence is one of such means used by God for deliverance or salvation of humanity. For example, the violence of God to Pharaoh and his people in Egypt was used as a means of delivering Israelites from the bondage of slavery (Exodus 15: 1–3; cf. Isaiah 45: 1–5). Therefore, as Fretheim states, in the Egypt event "God uses violence in order to save Israel from the *effects of other people's sins*"; and can also in whatever time use "violence in order to save God's people from the *effects of their own sins* [. . .]."[190] The main purpose of God's use of violence is to subvert human violence; that it should not prevail any more in the life of God's creation. Contrary to human violence, divine violence is "counter-violence,"

---

188. Ibid., 21.

189. Ibid., 24; *cf.* Strijdom, "Violence in the Christian Bible," 2–3; Smith, "Violence and the Christus Victor Model," 41–43.

190. Fretheim, "God and Violence," 25.

used purposely and with a non-violent end. Some examples provided by Fretheim can suffice to illustrate the salvific nature of God's use of violence: "the deliverance of slaves from oppression (Exod 15:7; Ps 78:49–50), the righteous from their antagonists (Ps 7:6–11), the poor and needy from their abusers (Exod 22:21–24; Isa 1:23–24; Jer 21:12), and Israel from its enemies (Isa 30:27–33; 34:2; Hab 3:12–13)."[191]

Having looked at judgment and salvation of God as being theological reflections towards divine violence, there are some texts in the Bible that do not fall in the two issues. There are texts which there is no divine wrath inherent in the deeds and no salvific implications for humanity. For example during the conquest of Kanaan, God commanded Israel to kill people who dwelt in the land. The text so states: "But in the cities of these peoples that the Lord your God gives you for an inheritance, you shall save alive nothing that breathes, but you shall utterly destroy them" (see 1 Sam 15:3). The Israelites implemented God's command to execute violence to the Canaanites in order to occupy the land (Joshua 6–11). What can be said in regard to texts such as these? Human judgment can be critical to unanticipated divine actions. Yet, it can be said that God executes divine violence in order to accomplish a loving purpose for humanity.

Violence in the Name of Religion

In the previous paragraphs we discussed the disturbing question of divine involvement in violence. We ended with the solution that divine violence is mostly motivated by human violence, is salvific in its end, and its purpose is love for humanity. This section discusses the relationship between human violence and religion. The important questions in this section are the following: What is the relationship between religion and violence? Is religion involved in the various violence forms encountering human beings, and other living and non-living beings?

Volf in his lecture "Christianity and Violence" argues against the ascription of violence to the contemporary resurgence of religion. For him, the contemporary religiously legitimized violence are not due to the resurgence of religion, but to what he calls "thin" religion. Volf distinguishes between "thin" and "thick" religion. Moreover, Volf further distinguishes between "more" and "less" religion as far as violence is concerned. For religion being "thick" does not depend on "religious zeal." Despite its zeal, religion can be "thin." This is what he calls "blind religious zeal" which is not helpful but harmful. According to Volf, "approaching the issue of religion and violence

191. *Ibid.*

by looking at the *quantity* of religious commitment—more religion, more violence, less religion, less violence—is unsophisticated and mistaken."[192] What is important in a religion, according to Volf, is "the *quality* of religious commitments within a given religious tradition."[193]

In clarifying these concepts, while using Christianity as a case, Volf notes: "The more we reduce Christian faith to vague religiosity which serves primarily to energize, heal, and give meaning to the business of life whose content is shaped by factors other than faith (such as national or economic interests), the worse off we will be. Inversely, the more the Christian faith matters to its adherents as faith and the more they practice it as an ongoing tradition with strong ties to its origins and with clear cognitive and moral content, the better off we will be."[194] In this case, religion is not the factor that contributes to violence, but the way people are committed and use religion and its content. By the misuse of religion to legitimize violence, religious adherents claim God to be in their side while the adherents see themselves as shoulders of God to fulfill transcendental goals.

Volf elaborates why the idea that religion is involved in violence spreads more than its non-involvement. He ascribes this widespread of religious involvement in violence to what he calls "*self-inflation of the negative, the tendency of the evil to loom larger than the comparatively much larger good.*"[195] Quoting from Avishai Margarit, Volf writes: "It takes one cockroach found in your food to turn the most otherwise delicious meal into a bad experience [. . .]. It takes 30 to 40 ethnic groups who are fighting one another to make the 1,500 or more significant ethnic groups in the world who live more or less peacefully look bad."[196] Volf proposes that the cure for the resurgence of violence is not "less religion" but "more religion," not only in the sense of people being zealous, but by the high quality of religious commitment.[197] The question is: Can one agree with Volf's argument? Why?

Another assertion in regard to the relationship between religion and violence is given by Mark Juergensmeyer, in his book *Terror in the Mind of God: The Rise of Global Violence.* He calls his book as "a book about religious terrorism. It is about public acts of violence at the turn of the century for which religion has provided the motivation, the justification, the organiza-

---

192. Volf, "Christianity and Violence," 5.
193. Ibid.
194. Ibid.
195. Ibid., 15.
196. Ibid.
197. Ibid., 5, 8.

tion, and the worldview."[198] Juergensmeyer says that despite terrorism being done by human beings, religion is its justification. He provides some examples from some terrorist acts which he calls "state terrorism" used to subdue disenfranchised people in those states. Juergensmeyer provides the following examples: "the pogroms of Stalin, the government-supported death squads in El Salvador, the genocidal killings of the Khmer Rouge in Cambodia, ethnic cleansing in Bosnia and Kosovo, and government spurred violence of the Hutus and Tutsis in Centre Africa [. . .]."[199] By using these examples, he argues that "Most people feel that religion should provide tranquility and peace, not terror. Yet in many of these cases religion has supplied not only the ideology but also the motivation and the organizational structure for the perpetrators."[200] As we can understand Juergensmeyer, religion is the one responsible in motivating people to do acts of terror against other people. In this case Juergensmeryer is against Volf's view that violence is caused by "thin" religious adherents to justify their violent acts. For him, religion is not used by adherents; rather, it is the one that motivates adherents to commit violent acts. It is itself that is nature by violent.

Juergensmeyer rejects any efforts to put religion aside from being involved in violence. He says clearly: "Although some observers try to explain away religion's recent ties to violence as an aberration, a result of political ideology, or the characteristic of a mutant form of religion—fundamentalism—these are not my views. Rather, I look for explanations in the current forces of geopolitics and in a strain of violence that may be found at the deepest level of religious imagination."[201] Juergensmeyer's point of view is based on the ancient questions of scholars of religion who wrestled the divine legitimization of violence and the involvement of religion in violence.

One of the important questions embraced by great scholars like "Emile Durkheim, Marcel Mauss, and Sigmund Freud—is [. . .] Why does religion seem to need violence, and violence religion, and why is a divine mandate for destruction accepted with such certainty by some believers?"[202] He further states about what puzzles him more: "What puzzles me is not why bad things are done by bad people, but rather why bad things are done by people who otherwise appear to be good—in cases of religious terrorism, by pious

---

198. Juergensmeyer, *Terror in the Mind of God*, 7.
199. Ibid., 5.
200. Ibid.
201. Ibid., 6.
202. Ibid., 6–7.

people dedicated to a moral vision of the world."²⁰³ Humanly speaking, this question can be disturbing to any critical human mind!

Juergensmeyer's book is composed of interviews of religious activists involved in the "culture of violence" in various places. As he states, his book

> contains chapters in recent acts of terrorism related to almost all the major religious traditions—Christians in America who supported abortion clinic bombing and militia actions such as the bombing of the Ocklahoma City federal building, Catholics and Protestants who justified acts of terrorism in Northern Ireland, Muslims associated with the attacks of the World Trade Centre in New York City and Hamas targets in the Middle East, Jews who supported the assassination of Prime Minister Yitzhak Rabin and the attack in Hebrons's Tomb of Patriarchs, Sikhs identified with the killing of India's prime minister Indira Gandhi and Punjab's chief minister Beant Singh, and the Japanese Buddhists affiliated with the group accused of the nerve gas attack in Tokyo's subways.²⁰⁴

With these case studies from different religions, Juergensmayer justifies his argument that religion is involved in justifying, motivating, and organizing violent acts. He justifies his claim that religion is by nature violent. And in whatever done, the perpetrators of violence do not call themselves as terrorists; rather, they see their acts to be legitimate according to their religious worldviews and claims. The question here is: Can one agree that religion is the major interlocutor in enhancing, justifying and organizing violence? In the following subsection we focus our discussion on Africa. We discuss domestic violence in African context as an example to demonstrate the way violence works and the attitude of the church about it.

Domestic Violence in the African Context

In African context, domestic violence is any behavior of one spouse in the family to perform abusive acts with the purpose of gaining power and control over a spouse, partner, girl, boyfriend, or intimate family member. Domestic and family violence include different types of abuses exerted by the perpetrator. Thobejane and Luthada, for example, note that domestic violence relating to gender "comes in different forms such as physical abuse; sexual abuse; emotional, verbal and psychological abuse; economic abuse;

---

203. *Ibid.*, 7.
204. *Ibid.*, 14.

intimidation; harassment and stalking."²⁰⁵ It can be noted in this definition that the urge to gain and maintain power and control in domestic relationships is the heart of all acts of domestic violence in African societies.

As already noted by Thobejane and Luthada above, domestic violence includes, but not limited to, sexual, emotional, economic, or psychological actions or threats of actions that influence another person, and the use of hostile behavior such as gestures and words to cause emotional damage or harm to the victim. However, a person does not need to experience all of these types of abuse for it to be domestic. One of such actions is enough to account for the experience of domestic violence.

In most cases domestic violence consists of behaviors, a pattern of abusive and threatening behaviors comprising of physical, emotional, economic, sexual violence, as well as exerting intimidation and isolation of the victim. Hence, on the basis of the above definitions, the main purpose of domestic violence is to *establish* and *exert* power and control over another person within the domestic relationship. In most cases, men use violence against their intimate partners, such as current or former spouses, girlfriends or dating partners in order to establish power and control over them. However, all the above acts are against the very first Article of the the Universal Decleration for Human Rights which states blatantly: "All human beings are born free and equal in dignity and rights. They are endowed with reason and conscience and should act towards one another in a spirit of brotherhood."²⁰⁶

In order to substantiate the claim that the urge for power is the source of domestic violence, we describe some examples of researches and findings. A research done by Vyas and Mbwambo in Dar es Salaam and Mbeya Tanzania in 2017 to determine the behavior of help-seeking among women abused by their physical partners indicated that domestic violence is exerted in the two cities to a great extent. As the report says,

> Respondents were asked detailed questions about themselves and their community [. . .] their current or most recent partner and their experiences of violence [and] injuries they may have sustained because of violence [. . .]. The questionnaire recorded responses for each woman on her experience of six different acts of physical violence by her partner (whether she had ever been slapped or had something thrown at her, pushed, hit with or something that could hurt her, kicked or drugged, chocked or

---

205. Thobejane & Luthada, "An Investigation into the Trend of Domestic Violence," 11.

206. See Weavers: Women in Theological Education, *The Church and Violence*, 77.

burnt, or threatened with a knife, gun or other weapon). Of the women who had ever been partnered (1442 in DSM and 1256 in Mbeya), 474 in DSM and 586 in Mbeya had experienced at least one act of physical violence by a male intimate partner in their lifetime.[207]

However, domestic violence is not only limited to Dar es Salaam and Mbeya cities within Tanzania. Domestic violence exists in almost all urban and rural places of the country. Moreover, domestic violence exists in all countries of the African continent being exerted in various ways. In this case, basing on the example of research done in Mbeya and Dar es Salaam Tanzania and the reasons for domestic violence stipulated above, it is our contention that there is a need for African Church ministers, and lay Christians to use their God-given opportunity to providing helpful resources against the abuses of domestic violence through sermons, prayers, education, and pastoral care.

Moreover, domestic violence cases are noticed in other countries of East Africa apart from Tanzania. In Kenya, for example, Gathogo reports that cases of *kuchapa wanaume* (men battering) are rampant in various places of the country. Taking the Central region of Kenya as a example, Gathogo reports that "by February 2012, there were 460,000 cases of domestic abuse. Of these, 150,000 had reported undergoing emotional abuse while 300,000 cases had been physically assaulted. 300,000 men were battered by their spouses, making the region the worst place in the country for men in wedlock."[208] Therefore, the listed data above indicate that domestic violence, and men battering in particular, is a wide spread phenomenon in Kenya despite the long silence of men to disclose it due to fear of being loughed at and ridiculed by community members.[209] Moreover, Thobejane and Luthada, writing in the South African context, add: "The justice system, African cultural norms, patriarchal societal expectations are all compounding complex issues that causes [sic!] men to be reluctant to report cases of being emotionally, psychologically, [and] physically abused at the hands of their female partners."[210]

---

207. Vyas & Mbwambo, "Physical Partner Violence," 3, *Cf.* Fumbo, "The Moravian Church Response to Domestic Abuse."

208. Gathogo, "Kuchapa Wanaume," 45.

209. Similar views were provided by research participants in the research conducted by Thobejane and Luthada in the South African context (see Thobejane & Luthada, ""An Investigation into the Trend of Domestic Violence," 17).

210. Thobejane & Luthada, "An Investigation into the Trend of Domestic Violence," 13.

Major Reasons for Domestic Violence

What makes domestic violence acts resurgent in Africa apart from spouses' urge for power and control stated above? Domestic violence does not emerge spontaneously. There are root causes for its emergence based on respective contexts. In this part, we will use Kunhiyop's ideas to explain some of the major reasons or causes for the execution of domestic violence in various African contexts.[211]

1. *Demonstration of Power and Control*: As stated in the above paragraphs, power and control is at the heart of domestic violence. African traditional beliefs often hold that a woman is a man's property. This means that a man will not permit any insubordination by his wife or children in the family. In order for the man to remain powerful and in control of his members of the family he resorts to physical and verbal violence as a means to assert his control over them. In other cases, a woman demonstrates power over the man. Gathogo reports a good example of women showing power to their husbands, especially among Christian families. Basing on his interviews, he reports: "seventy percent of my interviewees pointed out that men battering is more rampant among Christians than among Muslims. In other words, it is very rare to find a Muslim woman battering her husband."[212] One reason for the battering of men according to Gathogo is their *failure to provide for the family*. Families where wives are chief providers, they show superiority over their husbands through battering them whenever they are dissatisfied with even trivial things.

2. *Learned Behavior*: Children learn how to behave through watching at the behavior of their parents. The behavior of their parents may be good or bad ones to the measure of the society they are in. If a male child grows up in an abusive home, where the male parent threatens them and exerts power and control over the whole family, he is likely to be abusive himself when is grown up. Therefore, the environment in which the child grows up in his childhood continues during his own adulthood and marriage, and the vicious circle is maintained to further generations. Cherlin says that Children learn from what they see happening around them, they learn violence as they watch their fathers beat and molest their mothers. Many young men have expressed their

---

211. Kunhiyop, *African Christian Ethics*, 244.
212. Gathogo, "*Kuchapa Wanaume*," 49.

fear that they will become like their fathers in terms of wife battering, while young girls have expressed fear of marrying an abusive man.[213]

3. *Social Tolerance of Violence:* Social tolerance of violence is perpetuated by words of encouragement and religious language. In most African context, marriage is something precious which needs to be safeguarded in all costs. Family members such as parents, uncles and aunts do not encourage women to leave away from violent and abusive relationships. Instead, they urge them to stay in the marriage, particularly when there have young children because they cannot be allowed to take the children with them. Religious language bases on Scriptures of each religion. Christianity, for example, uses Scriptures that encourage submission of wives to their husbands (Paul), creation stories (especially the first creation story), marriage is a contract made between the wife and the husband for life until God separates them by the death of one partner, emphasis on forgiveness as an important Christian virtue, *etc.*, to make women internalize their inferiority before their male partners. Religious language has been used by pastors in their counseling sessions in their attempts to protect marriages from parting.[214]

Instead of using religious language to try maintaining marriages from parting, it is better to direct the couples' attention to the love of God as portrayed by Jesus. Men should be taught that Jesus should be their example when it comes to the way they treat women, children and other members of their families. Wives and children should be loved and cared for as Jesus loves and cares for the church he initiated. Where wives are loved as Christ loved the church, there can hardly be any scope for physical and psychological violence against them. When children are treated in the same way that Jesus treated them, there may hardly be child abuse. Loving and caring families produce loving and caring members of society.

4. *Alcohol Abuse:* As just discussed in the previous subsections within this chapter, alcohol is among the recognized drugs. If abused, it is likely to bring effects to the health, economy and the relationship between the alcoholic and the surrounding members of the community. Some African men abuse alcohol and other drugs. In their drunken state, they are unable to tolerate any disagreements from their spouses, children, and other relatives within the home. Intoxication with alcohol makes them, liable to interpreting any action as insulting; hence, responding

---

213. Cherlin, *Public and Private Families*, 68.

214. Westenberg, "'When She Calls for Help.'" 4–5; Weavers: Women in Theological Education, *The Church and Violence*, 130–131; Kenge, "Towards a Theology of Peacebuilding," 82.

to it with physical or verbal violence. In some cases, Gathogo reports, women batter their husbands who take excessive alcohol and deny providing conjugal rights to their wives.[215]

Types of Domestic Violence

There are four types of domestic violence. For the sake of clarity, we list and briefly describe each of them in the following paragraphs:

1. *Physical abuse*—this type includes, but not limited to, slapping or throwing harmful things to the victim, pushing, hitting with or using something (a weapon) that can hurt the victim, kicking or drugging, chocking or burning the victim and homicide. For example, Gathogo writes in Kenyan context of men battering that when it happens that one between the couples, the faithful to the marriage wedlock (the wife), is infected a venereal disease by the unfaithful husband, it is likely for her to butter her husband as a result of her anger and cause great physical injuries upon him.[216]
2. *Verbal abuse*—this is an abuse by the use of words of mouth. It deals with such issues as swearing and continual humiliation, in private or public, verbal attacks on issues pertaining to intelligence, sexuality, body image and capacity as a parent and spouse.
3. *Psychological abuse*—this type of abuse attacks one's mind. It includes, but not limited to, the following aspects: "bullying, jealous behaviour, humiliation, verbal abuse such as ridiculing and blaming."[217] Examples of psychological abuse include abusing pets in front of family members, making threats regarding custody of children, saying to the pet that the police and courts will not help, and abandoning support.
4. *Emotional abuse*—this type includes blaming the victims for all problems in the relationship, and withdrawing all interest and engagement in the relationship.

The Role of Church Leaders to Existing Domestic Violence

How should the church in Africa respond to domestic violence? Malik has a convincing advice in regard to violence: "Violence, even though it

---

215. Gathogo, "*Kuchapa Wanaume*," 50.
216. Ibid.
217. Watson, *Preventing and Responding*, 19.

is universal and present in all societies, is neither inherited nor genetic. It belongs to our 'fallen' (animal) nature perverted by sin and self-assertion, by the desire to control and dominate; as such, humankind stands in need of recreation and rebirth."[218] This statement means that in order to deal with violence the church in Africa has a role to deal with the animal nature of humanity towards rebirth or transformation. It has to transform the fallen humanity into being sons and daughters of God that do not conform to this world but born again creatures (John 3:3; Romans 12: 1–2).

Taking domestic violence as an example, church leaders, religious stakeholders, and other organizations in Africa have a unique opportunity to help families suffering from it because it is a moral and humanitarian issue confronting the church and people of faith. It is important for church leader in Africa to understand that the collective approach of the church toward domestic violence, sexual misconduct and abuse, and the value placed on women in the home directly correlates to the church's reputation as a place of safety. Therefore, as they may be asked to provide spiritual guidance and counseling to both the victim and the perpetrator Church leaders must seek guidance and support from God to understand and change behaviors of couples within families towards the example of Jesus.

The church in Africa needs to educate men and women in the roles of husbands and wives basing on their respective African context. They can also emphasize love and respect in marriage. Women need to be taught how to apply assertiveness and boundaries in their relationships. Hence, the church must teach women the proper meaning of forgiveness and urge to continue forgiving their husbands despite the unfaithfulness of their husbands. This forgiveness teaching will be successful if church elders train the younger women to love their husbands and children, to be self-controlled and pure, to be busy at home, to be kind, and to understand what it means to be subject to their husbands in an African context. Similar teachings should be directed to male spouses towards their respective wives.

Moreover, Charlin states that, Pastors and Bishops have an opportunity to provide helpful recourses on domestic violence through seminars, prayers, education and pastoral care to various groups in the homes. An important function the church can serve is to tell the truth about women's experiences of domestic violence, to give a voice where there has been silence.[219] Hence, a victim of domestic violence hearing a prayer for all those living with abuse in the home breaks the silence.

---

218. Malik, "Religion and Violence," 28.
219. Cherlin, *Public and Private Families*, 366.

In summary, this section surveyed the broad concept of violence. We saw that one can hardly provide a convincing definition for it due to its multifaceted nature. We also attempted to provide some definitions as conceived by scholars, each touching some aspects of it. More important, the lecture has touched the pressing questions that face the concept when looked it theologically. A theological look at the concept has unveiled difficult questions which philosophers have wrestled with over the centuries. The questions were based on not the human involvement in violence; rather, on the divine involvement in the violent acts. We have highlighted some examples from the Bible where God seemed to be legalizing and even enacting violent acts. We have also discussed the role of religion in relation to violence. The main questions in all these aspects were directed to the nature of God and the nature of religion. While God is love, and is conceived as being intrinsically good, the divine legitimization and performance of violent acts seemed to be irreconcilable with the nature of God being worshiped. Moreover, while religion is conceived as being the source of peace and harmony among people in societies, the legitimization of violence has been irreconcilable with the nature of religion.

However, it has been noted in the discussion that divine involvement in violence has a human source. The sin of humanity is the initiator of God's violence as a response. God does not involve in violence for just acting violently; it is a response to human violent behavior. In whatever the case, the violent acts of God, as has been noted in the above discussion, have a salvific purpose. They are directed towards human redemption.

In regard to religion, one can note that though God is only one, religion is not one. We speak about 'religions'. Though all religions focus on reverence to the Supreme Being (God), they are not the same. Each religion is made in a particular culture, and with particular experiences. In this case, religion can be used by the owners of that religion in whatever purpose, even legitimizing and organizing violence.

Among the social problems confronted by the church, domestic violence is surely one of the most misunderstood and mismanaged by church leaders. For the church to be well acquainted by this challenge, leaders and church members need education on various aspects of it including what constitutes domestic violence, the signs of domestic violence, characteristics of abusers, the nature of dating violence, God's perspective on violence, what scriptures teach about gender equality, the dignity of women, and how believers can respond to domestic violence. Church leaders and Christians need this education because they are the first stakeholders having the work of protecting domestic violence victims in the houses and the whole church community. Hence, domestic violence is a very complex, destructive reality in many Christian homes. Clergy have not always responded in helpful ways to domestic violence in the past, but this can possibly change through their struggle to educate themselves about what constitutes domestic violence. If they educate themselves, they will have the courage to condemn domestic violence from the pulpit, breaking the cycle of violence and leading the body of Christ to being a place of safety and divine presence.

Furthermore, "Churches and theological institutions need to address the importance of liberating cultures, beliefs, theologies and interpretations of scriptures. The central concepts must also be examined, including the need to view violence as a public, not private issue; to explore the root causes, not symptoms of violence only; and to develop action strategies with all stakeholders to avoid duplication of efforts and resources [. . .]."[220] Delving into the root causes will possibly make church leaders in Africa touch the appropriate facets of domestic violence in their messages when preaching and teaching the word of God.

THE CHURCH AND HOMOSEXUALITY

The previous section examined the issue of violence within the Church in Africa, the African society at large, and the role of the Church and of Practical Theology towards this pressing issue. This section moves to another delicate issue in the life of the Church in Africa—the issue of *homosexuality*. The earliest records of African sexuality were produced by colonialists in the 1800s. In those records, African sexuality was presented on the bases of the imperial culture of the West as being superior and the African culture as inferior as compared to the Western culture. African sexuality was considered to be animal-like, savages and primitive as compared to a more civilized European sexuality. In the words of Sivertsen, "Colonialist perspectives on African sexuality included Africans as 'natural and instinctive beings,' a perspective in sharp contrast to sophisticated Europeans."[221] In the colonial view, African sexuality was seen to be centered on reproduction; in that case, they could not report on the existence of same-sex practices that existed in Africa when they arrived. Their reports denied the existence of homosexuality in Africa until later.[222]

The concept of homosexuality is of recent origin; however, its practice is as ancient as human beings are. According to scholars, the concept

---

220. Weavers: Women in Theological Education. *The Church and Violence against Women*, 43.

221. Sivertsen, "Homosexuality in Perspective," 6.

222. Ibid.

of "homosexuality" first appeared in the nineteenth century mostly in the European modernity. Sivertsen, taking ideas from Norton, asserts that "the term homosexuality was first used by Austrian Karl-Maria Kertbeny in 1869. Kertbeny used the term in several pamphlets, arguing that male same-sexuality was inborn and unchangeable."[223] However, homosexuality as a practice is as old as humanity itself. Ilikbaev asserts that "The first officially registered records of homosexuality date back to a pre-history, Mesolithic era: depictions of male intercourse were found in Mesolithic rock art in Sicily and date back to 9660 BCE. In addition, drawings and sexual depictions of the Neolithic and Bronze Age, like human figures of a third sex (e.g., with female breast and male genitals) were discovered, for example, in Neolithic Greece and Cyprus."[224]

This term "homosexuality" was coined to differentiate between its counterpart concept of "heterosexuality." In order to understand what exactly homosexuality entails, we need to explore both of the two concepts. The concept of "heterosexuality" is derived from two words: *hetero*—which means different and *sexuality* which refers to sexually related erotic behavior. The concept of "homosexuality" also evolves from two words: *homo*—which means "the same" and *sexuality* which refers to "sexually related erotic behavior. In this case, heterosexuality refers to sexually related erotic attractions between people of different sex orientations, while homosexuality refers to sexually related erotic attraction between people of the same sex.[225]

Homosexual relationships are commonly known in their two forms: lesbianism and guy relationships. Lesbianism is a form of homosexuality whereby one female has a sexually related erotic relationship with another fellow female; while guy relationship is a sexually related erotic relationship whereby one male has a sexually related erotic relationship with another male.[226] In both forms of homosexuality, the practitioners consider what they do as being legitimate. However, in the year 1980s the American activists introduced the abbreviation LGBT as an inclusive abbreviation for the whole homosexual identity. The abbreviation stands as a representative of lesbians, guys, bisexuals and transgender relationships, which are also homosexuals in nature. Hence, the introduction of the abbreviation and its later developments indicated the politics of inclusion or exclusion in the homosexual community in the Western world and had nothing to do

---

223. *Ibid.*, 7.
224. Ilikbaev, "A Great Divide," 4.
225. Mkumbo, "Homosexuality," 14.
226. *Ibid.*

with homosexual experiences in Africa.[227] In the following paragraphs, we concentrate much on the background and development of this practice in ancient world before looking at it in the African context.

Background of Homosexuality

In ancient times, during the Greek time, the form of homosexuality commonly practiced was pederasty.[228] Pederasty is the sex penetration of the elder male to young boys (Swahili: *ufiraji*). Scholars assert that this type of homosexuality was done as an educational means. The young boy was initiated to manhood and became a mature member of society under the tutelage of the older man. Balcha, quoting from Crompton, writes:

> The ancient Greeks had no word that corresponds to our 'homosexual.' *Paiderastia,* the closest they came to it, meant literally "boy love," that is, a relationship between an older male and someone younger, usually a youth between the ages of fourteen and twenty. The older man was called the *erastes* or lover. Ideally, it was his duty to be the boy's teacher and protector and serve as model of courage, virtue, and wisdom to his beloved, or *eromenos*, whose attraction lay in his beauty, his youth, and his promise of future moral, intellectual, and physical excellence.[229]

As for the Greeks, Mkumbo clearly concludes: "Pederasty therefore implied a homosexual relation in which the partners were not homosexuals in the modern meaning of the word. Pederasty was a social, educational, and moral development, in which cultural identity was more important than sexual identity."[230]

After the Greeks, the same sexual attitude was practiced to the Romans. However, pederasty in the Roman society was different from that of the Greek society in the sense that it was done between the master and the slave. Mkumbo asserts that "Even though one could well have sex with his

---

227. Sivertsen, "Homosexuality in Perspective," 8.

228. In ancient time several other places of the world practiced homosexuality without condemnation from their kings. Ilikbaev confirms this when he states: "elsewhere in the ancient world homosexuality was generally widely accepted in the ancient world and neither ancient kings nor pagan religions found any reason to persecute and condemn homosexuals. Thus, male cult homosexual prostitutes were quite popular in Ancient Mesopotamia. But the most notable fact is probably that Assyrian men prayed to their gods to bless their homosexual love." (Ilikbaev, "A Great Divide," 4)

229. Balcha, "Homosexuality in Ethiopia," 4–5 & Ilikbaev, "A Great Divide," 5.

230. Mkumbo, "Homosexuality," 15.

wife at home, a man in the baths, a prostitute in the brothel, and a slave in a dark corner, he would have only been challenged if he were not able to keep everything in its place. Prostitution, including male homosexual prostitution, was a common, legal, and tolerated behavior in the Roman streets and baths."[231] However, this was not for educational purpose as was in the Greek society. Homosexuality in the Roman society between the master and the slave aimed at showing power relation between the two parties, and was being practiced in pagan societies even during the beginning of the Christian era.[232] Balcha, quoting Crimpton, affirms this notion: "Homosexual relations were perceived primarily as a form of dominance, an extension of the will to power [. . .]. Same-sex intrigues are not between men and freeborn youths but exclusively between masters and slaves [. . .]. For the Romans, homosexual relations were not in themselves good or bad. But to submit to penetration was to be feminized and humiliated."[233]

Why was Homosexuality condemned in the Western World?

Scholars have been concerned with the source of the condemnation of homosexuality which was widely accepted among pagan societies in the ancient Western world. They have asked: If homosexuality was so widely accepted in the ancient Western world, where was the source of its condemnation? Ilikbaev confirms that "It came together with Judeo-Christian monotheistic religions, Christianity and Islam in particular."[234] The rejection of homosexuality by these religions was mainly due to the nature of their Holy Scriptures, the Bible and the Qur'an. In the Bible, homosexuality is considered as being 'idolatry', the mother of all sins (see Leviticus 18: 22; 20: 13; Romans 1: 26–27). Moreover, several passages in the Qur'an mention homosexuality as being a 'sin' (see Surat Al-Araf 80–81; Sura Ash-Shura 25:165–166). However, no punishment is pronounced by the Qur'an to those practicing homosexuality.

The more strict verses are found in the Hadith. The Hadith verses pronounce what punishment should be executed to those found guilty of homosexuality:—"Narrated Abdullah ibn Abbas: The Prophet (peace be upon him) said: If you find anyone doing as Lot's people did, kill the one who does it, and the one to whom it is done." (Sunan of Abu-Dawood— Book 38 Hadith 4447)—"Narrated Abdullah ibn Abbas: If a man who is not

231. Ibid.
232. Ilikbaev, "A Great Divide," 4.
233. Balcha, "Homosexuality in Ethiopia," 5.
234. Ibid., 5.

married is seized committing sodomy, he will be stoned to death." (Sunan of Abu-Dawood—Book 38 Hadith 4448).[235] However, in the 6th century AD the Roman society, being influenced by other cultures and the resurgence of Christianity, abolished homosexual activities and those who were caught practicing earned a death penalty.[236]

As stated above, in the Western world, the term homosexuality was introduced in the year 1869 showing that same-sex relationships were being practiced in the West during that time. However, up until 1970s homosexuality was not tolerated. It was condemned as evil. The views on homosexuality in the West has changed in the recent time from not tolerating towards tolerating and accepting the practices in most Western countries. In this case, the current trends and ideas about homosexuality in the West as practices to accept and tolerate are just recent ones.[237] Goldingay, et al. state:

> Modern Western societies in North America and Europe are increasingly moving toward the acceptance of same-sex relationships. At first people were challenged to accept lesbian and gay partnerships on a political and legal level; but recently and more problematically, Christians are being asked to accept a redefinition of the institution of marriage itself. No longer is marriage to be regarded essentially as a bond between one man and one woman, but as a sexual relationship in which two men or two women may also be committed to each other. They ought to be recognized to have the corresponding rights of support, parenting, adopting, inheriting, divorcing, and the other privileges and obligations that spouses in a marriage expect.[238]

Why is the once condemned Homosexuality now accepted?

The question about the Western acceptance of homosexuality and the rights of homosexuals is the following: Why do the West once highly influenced by Christianity to reject homosexuality now accepts it despite the existence of Christianity in those Western countries? Why in most Islamic countries is homosexuality still criminalized and homosexuals severely persecuted? Ilikbaev argues "that it is because in the West the church has been separated from the state with the establishment of a secular legal system with

---

235. Ilikbaev, "A Great Divide," 5–7.
236. Mkumbo, "Homosexuality," 15–16.
237. Sivertsen, "Homosexuality in Perspective," 7–8.
238. Goldingay et al. "Same-Sex Marriage," 1.

respect to human rights, while in the Islamic world many countries still live under religious, —sharia law, and church and religious leaders still have a huge influence over society."[239] It means that the situation which existed in the ancient world of the Greeks and Romans, which hardly prohibited homosexual acts, is now back in the western world due to secularization. The influence of Christianity, a religion which prohibits same-sex erotic relationships, is currently minimal. The situation is different in the Arab world. Since the influence of Islam is still visible in Islamic world, it is hard to practice homosexuality openly.

Homosexuality in African Context

In case of Africa, Mkumbo asserts that there have been documented occurrences of homosexual practices in North Africa. He believes that since the Northern part of Africa had some contacts with the Greek and Roman cultures since a long time in antiquity there is a possibility that it adapted some of the cultural values from those cultures, including the issue of homosexuality. However, Mkumbo does not see any traces of homosexual activities in Sub-Saharan Africa. In this case, he believes that there was a possibility for such practices to be imported to this part of Africa by colonialism when the Arabs and Europeans entered the region and spread in various parts and tribes of Africa. Despite its resurgence, it was practiced secretly because was not approved by such societies as a decent means of erotic relationship.[240]

A similar view held by Mkumbo in Tanzania is also held by Ethiopia. Balcha states that "For many, homosexuality is non-existent in Ethiopia simply because it is not an Ethiopian culture. If any Ethiopian becomes gay, then it is viewed as an acquired behaviour or disease due to an association with white men and their culture."[241]

Sivertsen presents a different view from the one presented by Mkumbo and Balcha about homosexuality in Africa. Sivertsen believes that homosexuality has been in the African soil since time immemorial. Sivertsen says: "Some of the oldest known depictions of or references to same-sex sexuality in the world come from Africa, including cave paintings dating back at least two thousand years in Zimbabwe, and in Egyptian myths and written histories [. . .]."[242] Sivertsen concludes on the bases of these oldest depictions

239. Ilikbaev, "A Great Divide," 9.
240. Mkumbo, "Homosexuality," 17–18.
241. Balcha, "Homosexuality in Ethiopia," 6.
242. Sivertsen, "Homosexuality in Perspective," 9.

of African same-sex practices that "one can argue that homosexuality has been practiced on the African continent since the dawn of human age."[243]

Currently, homosexuality has spread in various parts of Africa and the world as a whole. In East Africa homosexual prostitution is common. Since East African region was dominated by Arabs and was some trade interaction between this region and Oman, it is believed that homosexuality (in its both forms) was introduced in this region by the Arabs. Lesbian homosexuals are called *wasagaji* (grinders) and guy homosexuals are called *mashoga*. The singular word *wasagaji* is *msagaji* (grinder) and the singular word for *mashoga* is *shoga*. The word *mashoga* is commonly used to mean two women friends. If used to show the relationship of two men, it denotes guys. The East African countries do not legalize homosexuality. Therefore, most of the homosexual acts are practiced secretly. And, as just noted, it is practiced among homosexual prostitutes based on payments. The passive partner (who is always a young poor person in need of finance) receives some payments to practice homosexuality with the active partner (who is older rich person).[244]

Similar to Mkumbo's above assertion, Muneja confirms the existence of homosexuality in Tanzania (east Africa) despite the existence of legal prohibitions when he writes:

> the following tribes do not endorse homosexuality. These include but are not limited to the Makonde, Makonde Malaba, Maasai, and Nyakyusa [...]. The idea that a homosexual lifestyle is unacceptable is an indication that it exists, though not seen in public. Male homosexuals or gays are called *Wasenge* (meaning behaving like a woman). Female homosexuals or lesbians are called *Wasagaji* (meaning grinding—they need to 'grind' each other to attain sexual arousal). Tanzanian lesbians are less prominent than their male counterparts. Tanzanian law forbids homosexuality in its penal code as a criminal offence punishable up to 14 years in prison. However, this law is rarely enforced since it is very difficult to establish valid proof that a certain person is a homosexual [...].[245]

Muneja's statement above indicates not only the existence of homosexuality in Tanzania, but also its stigmatization as not belonging to people's worldview.

---

243. *Ibid.*
244. Mkumbo, "Homosexuality," 20–21.
245. Muneja, *HIV/AIDS and the Bible*, 22.

Moreover, Mkumbo expresses the concept of sexuality as conceived by African culture. According to him, sexuality is the property of the community and its members. Culturally sexuality, though belongs to the community, is not for public show up; it is private and only for those who practice it. Mkumbo further argues that since homosexuals often come public for recognition, they indicate that their homosexual acts are not originally African. Mkumbo explains:

> In traditional African perspective sexual matters are not for public consumption, they are done in the privacy, therefore the homosexuals by the way of "coming out," displaying and expressing their sexual preference, seeking to transport homosexuality into the public arena, as a way of being recognized, is contrary to the traditional African culture. This being the African perspective, homosexuality hence does not qualify to be labeled African. So then homosexual persons who attempt to force the Community to notice them and their practices are behaving in an unAfrican way. Such manifestation of homosexuality is therefore not an African.[246]

Mkumbo further concludes that "The attitude of many Africans towards homosexuals is that homosexuality is not part of African culture and traditions, it is against African moral values, set laws, culture and regulations, therefore it is unacceptable."[247] How is the practice of homosexuality conceived by the Church in Africa? This is the question which we focus our attention in the following subsection.

Homosexuality and Christianity in Africa

Globally, Christianity has shown a varying attitude towards homosexuality in its various denominations. In Africa, despite its high growth in the number of Christians, most of them belonging to Pentecostal and charismatic churches, Christianity has been viewed as being against homosexuality. Its growth has been seen as being directly proportional to anti-homosexuality.[248] However, due to secularism, as Ilikbaev has argued above, Christianity in the Western world has had some changes in the view of homosexuality. Others have recognized the rights of homosexuality while others have not yet to recognize. In this case, following the secularism argument posed by

---

246. Mkumbo, "Homosexuality," 22.
247. Ibid., 23; cf. Bongmba, "Homosexuality, Ubuntu, and Otherness," 24–25.
248. Sivertsen, "Homosexuality in Perspective," 14.

Ilikbaev above, African societies have strong holds of Christianity and Islam and their teachings against homosexuality. The secularism sweeping African societies (the imposition of secular values in the growing religious adherence) is different from that which swept Western countries (the dwindling of religious influence in the public sphere) which in turn allowed room for homosexuality and respect for homosexual rights. The room was created because the religious teaching against homosexuality had no more influence in the public sphere where religion had no influence any more.[249] In the following paragraphs we illustrate the influence of Christianity in the criminalization of homosexuality and denial of homosexual rights in Africa. We also show the exclusive attitude of the Church in Africa against homosexuals despite the African culture based on *Ubuntu* philosophy of compassion to humanity it claims to uphold.

One case that touched the global attention in the life of Christianity in the Western world, and which evoked vehement responses from African churches and political spheres, was the consecration of a guy priest of the Anglican Church into the office of bishop. Bongmba explains this event: "The Anglican Church's Episcopal cousin in the U.S. on August 5th, 2003, took the opposite stand when, at the Triennial General Convention of the Episcopal Church USA, it announced the ordination of the Reverend Gene Robinson, an openly gay priest, to be the presiding bishop of New Hampshire. Robinson was consecrated the presiding Bishop of New Hampshire November 2, 2003."[250] Hence, the consecration of Robinson to this office of bishop marked the beginning of divisions about the issue of homosexuality within the Anglican church.

Bongmba adds about the consequence of this consecration:

> this event heightened the crisis and threatened the unity of the Anglican Communion. [. . .]. Anglican clergy in Africa have criticized Western churches for promoting homosexuality and caving in to liberalism and accommodating Western social pressures. The former Anglican Archbishop of Nigeria, The Most Reverend Peter Akinola, took a stand on homosexuality by opposing the election and consecration of the Reverend Gene Robinson by the Episcopal Church in the United States [. . .]. Akinola announced that the Episcopal Church of the US "had chosen the path of deviation from the historic faith [describing homosexuality as] an aberration unknown even in animal relationship" [. . .]. 'The church that prided itself on unity amid

---

249. Ilikbaev, "A Great Divide," 10–11.

250. Bongmba, Homosexuality, *Ubuntu* and Otherness," 22; *cf.* Goldingay et al. "Same-Sex Marriage," 2.

diversity faced the threat of division. The crisis over homosexuality became a crossroads for the Anglican world".[251]

Hence, the pressure of time that forced the consecration of Robinson, the openly guy priest, threatened the unity of the Anglican Church in Europe and other continents, including Africa.

Despite the criticism of homosexuality as being against African culture posed by Mkumbo above, Christianity and other religions in East Africa also find homosexuality inconceivable and incompatible with their Scriptures. Taking Tanzania as an example, most people in the country are predominantly Christians who are exposed to the Bible and its tenets: they can read it and have their own moral judgment in regard to the issue of homosexuality. We illustrate this example in the following subsection.

Homosexuality and Christianity in Tanzania

The ELCT Bishops' Statement

In recent time the Bishops of the Evangelical Lutheran Church in Tanzania (ELCT),[252] one of the largest churches in Tanzania, have rejected the interpretation of the Bible by scholars in favor of any form of homosexuality. In their statement, they say:

> This Church, (ELCT), stands firmly on the foundation of the Word of God; that marriage is as taught in the Bible through the texts described in section 1.3.1 above [Gen.1: 27–28, 2:24; Mt.19:5–6a; Rom.1:26–27a and Gal.3:28]. These texts are being given perverse interpretations, which we cannot accept. All of us in this church, and elsewhere in the world, who reject same-sex marriages, believe that the Bible is self-interpreting; and does not need imposition and wishes according to certain people, certain place, or certain authority. Holy Scripture is accurate, fixed and unchangeable.[253]

They further state: "The Evangelical Lutheran Church in Tanzania vehemently refuses misinterpretations and scandalous use of Holy Scripture to legalize same-sex marriages."[254]

251. Ibid., 22–23.
252. The ELCT is the largest Lutheran church in Africa and the second largest in the Lutheran World Federation.
253. ELCT, "Dodoma Statement."
254. Ibid.

They warn Christians of their church to read the Bible and find wisdom from it about the issue of homosexuality because it is self-explanatory and should avoid being held pray of foreign interpretations that favor unbiblical interpretations. In the words of the Statement: "We have to signal the warning to every ELCT member to be vigilant; stand up, study the Word of God, and refuse strange teachings which can easily devour, new as well as old, believers in this globalized setting."[255]

Furthermore, the ELCT bishops stick on the Bible and its teachings and not on any other interpretations from any other authority. Mkumbo states "approving same sex marriages undermines the foundation of the Word of God for continuing procreation. Although the advocates of the same sex marriage use the Word of God in their teaching to justify their position, the ELCT rejects them because of their improper and incorrect representations of scripture."[256]

Mkumbo further elaborates that the ELCT bishops do not deny the existence of homosexuals in their churches and the Tanzanian society as a whole. Rather, they do not endorse it as being legitimate because it goes against the biblical attestation as recorded in 1Corinthians 6: 1–10 and Romans 1: 26–27. Bishops also appeal to the African culture of morality where marriage is only for men and women, not for people with same-sex orientations. Concluding the stand of the bishops of the ELCT, Mkumbo lists biblical texts considered to be weapons to defeats homosexuality and its proponents: Gen 19:1–11; Judges 19; Leviticus 18:22; 20:13; Romans 1:26–27; 1Corinthians 6:9–10 and 1Timothy 1:10. "These texts," Mkumbo says, "are the so-called deadly weapons against which homosexuality cannot survive. Weapons that prove once and for all, that the Word of God knows about homosexuality and God has taken a step on the matter."[257] The ELCT bishops see that "there is need for homosexuals to repent and be restored."[258] Therefore, according to Mkumbo, the ELCT bishops are of the position that "the Church's responsibility is not to agree to the wishes of homosexuals rather to help them accept their condition as a spiritual and physical problem. [...] the true Church of Christ would fail in its obligation if it were to surrender to the pressure from homosexuals and sodomites."[259] Hence, this position of the ELCT bishops indicates that the church hardly recognizes homosexuality as being a human condition that can be tolerated.

255. Ibid.
256. Mkumbo, "Homosexuality," 25.
257. Ibid.
258. Ibid.
259. Ibid., 28.

Homosexuality is a behavior to be vehemently rejected and condemned. In most cases, the ELCT bishop's stance serves as a representative of the stance upheld by most, if not all, churches in Africa. What is the position of critics towards this stance of the ELCT's bishops, and of churches in Africa towards the issue of homosexuality?

Criticisms to the ELCT Bishops' Statement on Homosexuality

Despite the firm standpoints of the bishops of the ELCT stipulated above, they can hardly go without criticisms. However, these criticisms are not exclusively directed to the ELCT bishops alone; rather, they are inclusively directed towards all churches in Africa which hold a similar view towards the issue of homosexuality. The major criticism which faces the ELCT and the African Christianity as a whole in its critical view to homosexuality is its failure to stick to the African culture it tries to defend.[260] In defense of African culture, the bishops' Statement firmly says: "In addition, cultural or societal changes in some areas such as Europe or America should not be construed as directives to other areas worldwide. And such societal changes should not be forced on to countries outside of the immediate culprit locality; because in other locations people have their own values and cultures they may wish to protect and perpetuate. We as Tanzanians/Africans have our own values and cultures, built over the years, that have guided our lifestyles and which accept only marriages between man and woman. Hence, while some areas may have their circumstances changed to accept same-sex marriages, it should be clearly understood that our conditions (cultures and values) do not allow such marriages."[261]

The African culture which church leaders and government leaders claim to be violated by the intrusion of homosexuality is built on the philosophy of *Ubuntu*. According to Bongmba, *Ubuntu* is "characterized by sympathy, consideration for others, compassion or benevolence. [. . .]. [It is] used to refer not only to an individual but to social relations and points specifically to the self and other, emphasizing the importance of the other for the self and sense of interconnectedness and interdependence [. . .]."[262]

---

260. This criticism, and the following criticisms to the ELCT bishops and the African Church, does not mean that the author endorses homosexuality; rather, it considers the human worth of homosexuals and the way Jesus, whom the bishops serve, handled people considered as sinners in the Jewish society (*cf.* Muneja, HIV/AIDS and the Bible, 22–23).

261. ELCT, "Dodoma Statement,"

262. Bongmba, "Homosexuality, Ubuntu and Otherness," 25–26; *cf.* Tarus & Lowery, "African Theologies of Identity," 306, and Taringa, "Possibilities and Limitations,"

Bongmba further argues, since homosexuals, in all its forms, are Africans and reside in African communities which are grounded in the *Ubuntu* philosophy of life, it is an obligation for such African community to show compassion, love and concern to them if they at all adhere to Ubuntu philosophy they claim to belong.

The philosophy of Ubuntu is clearly amplified by the African (Nigerian) novelist and poet Chinua Achebe in his ground breaking book *Things Fall Apart*. Achebe states that "A man who calls his kinsmen to a feast does not do so to save them from starving. They all have food in their own homes. When we gather together in the moonlit village ground it is not because of the moon. Every man can see it in his own compound. We come together because it is good for kinsmen to do so."[263] These are the words of one of the oldest member of the group of kinsmen (*umnna*) whom Okwonko invited to a feast in gratitude to their generosity. In this quotation, Achebe amplifies the African strength gained in community. Achebe means that an African gains identity as an individual when is in community; when members of the community come together in various activities including the participation in meals (such as the one Okonkwo called them together), dances, worship gatherings, wedding ceremonies, initiation rituals, *etc*. In that case, Achebe's statement above cements that, in African understanding, life attains its utmost meaning when one belongs to a particular community. The life of an individual is devoid of sense and meaning outside the community.[264]

Moreover, the philosophy of *Ubuntu* is not only for one African ethnic group; rather, it is a shared philosophy. Quoting the words of Gathogo, Mashau and Kgatle echo it:

> As a spiritual foundation of African societies, Ubuntu is a unifying vision or worldview enshrined in the Nguni maxim *Umuntu ngumuntu ngabantu*, that is, 'a person is a person through other persons'. This Ubuntu concept is also found in other African communities, even though there are different vocabularies and phrases that are used to describe it; and it will suffice to illustrate it by citing a few examples. The equivalent of it is seen in a Kikuyu idiom, which says: *Mundu ni mundu ni undu wa andu*, that is, 'a human being is a person because of the other people'. The same can be said of the Sotho whose idiom says: *Motho ke motho ka batho ba bang*, and with similar translations to those

---

188–190.

263. Achebe, *Things Fall Apart*, 118.

264. *Cf.* Stinton, *Jesus of Africa*, 166–168.

of other African communities. It is also the same, as: *munhu munhu nekuda kwevanhu*, used among the Shona people of Zimbabwe.[265]

In fact, this philosophy is based on scriptural assertion when one refers to the life of Christians in the Early Church. In the book of Acts, Luke writes: "Now the whole group of those who believed were of one heart and soul, and no one claimed private ownership of any possessions, but everything they owned was held in common. There was not a needy person among them, for as many as owned lands or houses sold them and brought the proceeds of what was sold. They laid it at the apostles' feet, and it was distributed to each as any had need." (Ac 4:32–35) Hence, being of 'one heart and soul' indicates the sense of mutuality and solidarity in terms of human value which depended sorely on what they were, not on what they did. It is a mutuality and solidarity that preserves life instead of destroying it.

Bongmba further contends that Christianity, being a foreign religion imposed by colonialism can hardly promote *Ubuntu* as a relational philosophy of African culture in the midst of homosexuals because missionaries considered African culture as being inferior compared to the imperial Western culture imported together with the Christian religion into the African soil. Despite the Christianity embraced from the hegemonic culture of the missionaries, Bongmba is of the opinion that the philosophy of *Ubuntu* should be a yardstick for African churches and people to relate with homosexuals who are considered 'other.'[266] He insists in this philosophy because it "prioritizes persons and the face of the other which resists possession and control. When one stands in the face of a sexual monitory, that face forbids violent speech and actions, regardless of one's perspective on same sex relations. The face of the other also forbids murder, which Levinas calls total negation. [...]. [Hence as] a dynamic ethical concept, *ubuntu* recognizes our ability to shift the ways in which we relate to the other. *Ubuntu* relationships welcome others, and more profoundly they resist violence."[267] According to Bongmba's above criticism, African homosexuals, though members of the African community guided by the philosophy of *ubuntu* are stigmatized, segregated and excluded by their fellow community members in the name of religious norms inscribed in sacred religious texts. What is your opinion about the above-criticism?

---

265. Mashau & Kgatle, "Prosperity Gospel and the Culture of Greed," 4; *cf.* Tarus & Lowery, "African Theologies of Identity," 306.

266. See *Ibid.*, 25–31; *cf.* Chimhanda, "Black Theology," 440.

267. Bongmba, "Homosexuality, Ubuntu and Otherness," 29; *cf.* Chimhanda, "Black Theology," 440.

The second criticism facing the ELCT bishops and the African Church is that of misinterpretation of biblical texts to support their standpoints. Masango asserts that most African fundamentalists misquote biblical texts out of context just to support their views against homosexuality. Masango says: "Fundamentalists also coin phrases and misquote certain passages of Scriptures, in their attempts to condemn homosexuals. No more divisive an issue faces the churches in Africa today than the question of homosexuality, with the underlying issue of the misquoting of scriptural passages in order to condemn it."[268]

Goldingay and LeMarquand state clearly what entails interpreting Scriptures: "Interpreting the Bible involves reading an ancient text in a contemporary context, establishing a dialogue between very different cultures and life situations. Awareness of both ancient and modern situations and properly balancing them enables the biblical message to be clearly understood and applied."[269] As Postmodern interpreters, "There is a certain ethical obligation in interpretation: we owe it to the author to try to understand what he or she meant; we also owe it to our forebears in the faith communities who took these writings into their Scriptures and invited us to live by them; and we also owe it to ourselves and to the consistency principle."[270] The main question facing people of our current time is about the extent at which they heed to the principles of interpretation in order to avoid fundamentalistic approaches that can impose our own prejudices to the sacred scriptures.

We are actually not sure to what extend has the bishops of the ELCT and the African church as a whole have taken precaution to get rid of fundamentalist approaches to biblical texts, or misquoting them without due responsibility to the current context as such texts were written to cultural contexts of more than 2000 years past? According to Masango, "African Churches are challenged to respond to this contentious issue. [. . .]. The church will not solve this problem by chasing homosexuals out of churches. This stance adds more confusion to the role of the church, a church that used to minister to people. We are called to minister to God's children."[271] Masango's quotation insists that a self-righteous church is no church, is no body of Christ and neither is it working on behalf of Christ. Jesus Christ, the author of the Christian church ate and drank with sinners; and of course he came because of them, so that they can be God's children. The above statement by Masango admonishes current leaders of churches in Africa to

---

268. Masango, Homosexuality," 957–958.
269. Goldingay *et al*, "Same-Sex Marriage," 50.
270. *Ibid.*, 16.
271. Masango, "Homosexuality," 159.

be truly servants of Jesus Christ who greatly hated sin but not sinners; who became light where there was darkness, and saw not light where there was pretention and hypocricy.

The third criticism to the ELCT bishops and the African church as a whole is their putting more attention to homosexuality than the other obvious sins, such as squandering church finances, uttering abusive languages to other people, adultery among heterosexuals, *etc.*, which carry similar weights in the eyes of God as homosexuality is.[272] Masango reiterates that we need "to consider the issue of sin in human nature, which needs to be addressed from a perspective of forgiveness. In dealing with the sinfulness of human nature, other sins and sinful issues, which merit similar treatment need to be considered along with homosexuality, in order to get a balanced perspective of this issue. The African Church tends to emphasize one kind of sin above others."[273] In this case, the ELCT bishops and the African church as a whole have been more Puritan in their approach to sin trying to separate sin in human degrees of sinfulness, forgetting the universality and equality of sin and human dependence on the grace of God obtained through faith alone without deeds of law. They forget that the consequence of any sin is to separate the one committing it from entering heaven irrespective of the weight of the sin committed! Are homosexuals and sodomites not within God's grace? Let us now illustrate the way homosexuality is viewed in other African countries apart from Tanzania.

Homosexuality and Christianity in Zambia

In Zambia, the question of homosexuality came into public scene in 1998 after the public announcement of a guy by the name of Francis Yabe Chisabisha, and after the establishment of the Lesbian, Guys, Bisexual, and Transgender Persons Association (LEGATRA). Van Klinken reports the consequence of the two events clearly:

> These actions sparked a 'mammoth scandal', with church leaders, NGO officials, students and professors, government ministers and politicians all voicing their horror of homosexuality [. . .]. President Chiluba initially remained silent on this issue, but then contributed to the debate, stating, "Homosexuality is the deepest level of depravity. It is unbiblical and abnormal. How do you expect my government to accept something that

---

272. Neipp, "When Homosexuality comes to Church," 39–40; *cf.* Paul's warning in Romans 2: 1 about passing judgements over other fellow human beings.

273. Masango, "Homosexuality," 961.

is abnormal?' [. . .]. As a result of this strong opposition, LEGA-TRA was prevented from its registering as an NGO, and ceased to exist within a year of its launch.[274]

In fact, African leaders in various countries have supported the prohibition of homosexuality done by religious bodies through their utterances and actions. Bongmba reports that in Nambia, homosexuality was considered inconceivable and condemned by the former president Sam Nujoma who supported its eradication in view that it was a European imported issue, and that the culture of the Namibians was superior than that of the Europeans. In Kenya, the former president Daniel Arap Moi condemned homosexuality seeing it as a vice that goes against the enshrined African values and traditions, including what Christianity teaches. In Malawi, some homosexuals were arrested and charged of practicing 'unnatural offences' and were charged of fourteen years imprisonment though were later pardoned by the president (Bingu wa Mutharika) on humanitarian grounds.[275] According to Bongmba,

> In Tanzania, more than forty gay and Lesbian activists were rounded up and charged with debauchery in 2009. [. . .]. In Zimbabwe in 2010, President Robert Mugabe criticized churches that recognize same-sex marriages, and said gay rights would not be included in a new constitution being written for the southern African country. [. . .]. In Cameroon, homosexuality is illegal. The government has taken violent actions against gay, lesbian, bisexual and transgender people. People suspected of being homosexuals have been beaten, arrested, and locked up without charge. People suspected of being homosexuals have been denied the services allowed to people infected with HIV/AIDS.[276]

Similar actions have happened in various African countries, including Uganda and South Africa. Examples of such actions include "the introduction of a new Anti-Homosexuality Bill to the Ugandan Parliament in 2009 (still under consideration); the approval of a similar bill in Nigeria (November 2011); the murder of Ugandan gay activist David Kato (January 2011); and the case of two Malawian men, arrested and jailed because of homosexuality-related offences, who were pardoned by the country's president only after the intervention of Ban Ki-moon."[277]

---

274. Van Klinken, "Homosexuality," 264; cf. Bongmba, "Homosexuality, *Ubuntu*, and Otherness," 18.

275. Bongmba, "Homosexuality, *Ubuntu*, and Otherness," 18.

276. Ibid., 19.

277. Van Klinken, "Gay Rights, the Devil and the End Times," 520.

Despite the South African recognition of legal rights for homosexuals in the end of 2006, yet in February 2011 the South African Anglican bishops stated against homosexuality: "Our Church does not consider any relationship to be marriage unless it is the historic relationship of a man and a woman uniting, ideally, for life."[278] Therefore, as Sivertsen asserts, "A significant aspect of African sexuality involves the relationship between religion and moral. Religious systems commonly include codes, rules and regulations for accepted moral behavior, which also includes sexual behavior. A common argument is that there are strong correlations between religiosity and negative attitudes towards homosexuality."[279] Moreover, Masango quotes some political leaders speaking in a Radio broadcast saying: "'Homosexuals are below the level of a pig, we will not tolerate men who have lost their sexuality' [. . .]. 'No man is going to be allowed to lose his identity. If they do, we shall lock them up. If they don't understand, we may even castrate them, if it is necessary.'"[280] Following these pronouncements and actions done to homosexuals, and the attitude of political leaders, church leaders and normal citizens on homosexuality, almost the whole African continent (except the republic of South Africa which has recognized the rights of homosexual minorities in their constitution) plays a good example of rejection of homosexuality on the bases of it as not belonging to the African culture.[281]

Van Klinken further notes that there were various occurrences of debates in public scenes in regard to the issue of homosexuality. Van Klinken mentions the visit of the United Nations General Secretary to Zambia in 2012 as another impetus to the issue when he addressed the Zambian parliament urging the nation to recognize human rights, especially that of 'sexual minorities' "and the mid-2013 arrests and prosecutions of some same-sex couples and of AIDS and sexual rights activist Paul Kasonkomona."[282]

However, acts of homosexuality and the rights of sexual minorities have been vehemently rejected in Zambia. Van Klinken reports that

> Shortly after Ban Ki-moon's 2012 visit and the public discussion that followed it, many church leaders spoke out in the media against any recognition of homosexuality in Zambia. Both the Evangelical Fellowship of Zambia (which represents evangelical and Pentecostal churches and organisations in the country) and the Council of Churches in Zambia (representing the mainline

278. Cole, "Church and Same-Sex Marriage," 9.
279. Sivertsen, "Homosexuality in Perspective," 12.
280. Masango, "Homosexuality," 957; cf. Balcha, "Homosexuality in Ethiopia," 5.
281. Balcha, "Homosexuality in Ethiopia," 5.
282. Van Klinken, "Homosexuality," 264–265.

Protestant churches) published pastoral statements in which they made it clear that they opposed Ban's call to recognise the human rights of sexual minorities.[283]

Van Klinken further adds: "Ban is associated with the Antichrist and the Devil, his call to recognise gay rights is interpreted as a sign of the end times, and the United Nations is considered part of a cosmic conspiracy to impose a devilish agenda on Zambia and Africa at large. In this discourse, the issue of homosexuality is enchanted, that is, viewed from a deeply religious worldview characterised by a strong eschatological expectation and by the belief in a cosmic struggle between God and the Devil."[284]

The main argument of Zambia to reject homosexuality is to preserve the "Zambian culture" of being a Christian nation.[285] This argument has been used by politicians and religious leaders alike. Van Klinken quotes the Minister of Justice saying: "there is 'No room for gays in Zambia', arguing, 'As Zambians, we declared that we are a Christian nation and there is no way we can allow this un-Zambian culture. I want to urge all Zambians to rise and denounce this vice'"[286] Hence, Van Klinken concludes that Zambia being a Christian nation, Church and State have joined forces to ensure that a practice presumed to be un-Christian will never be accepted in the country."[287] The denouncements of various leaders—both religious and secular—on the bases of Christianity as the state religion indicates that homosexuality is against the teachings of the Christian religion and the Christian culture of the Zambians. In Zambia, homosexuality is viewed as being foreign and imposed value contrary to the culture of Zambians.

Criticisms to the Zambian Stance on Homosexuality

Despite the great claims of religious and government leaders to defend what they call "the Zambian culture" one major criticism on it is that this monolithic Christian tradition, being static in nature, ignores the past, the

---

283. Ibid., 266.

284. Van Klinken, "Guy Rights, the Devil and the End Times," 519–520.

285. President Chiluba (1991–2001) declared Zambia a Christian nation on 29 December, 1991. This was done immediately after his entrance in the office and in the presence of great leaders of Pentecostal churches. However, his predecessor President Kenneth Kaunda (1964–1991) did not announce any religion as state religion. He respected all religions and considered Zambia a home of all regions (see Van Klinken, "Homosexuality," 262; Cheyeka, "Zambia, a Christian Nation," 160).

286. Van Klinken, "Homosexuality," 265.

287. Ibid., 267.

pre-colonial culture of the Zambians where some traces of homosexuality existed. Van Klinken asserts that "This discourse ignores the 'cultures of discretion' surrounding same-sex relationships that existed in various pre-colonial African societies [. . .] and rules out the possibility of sociocultural change concerning this issue in modern Zambia. In a highly Pentecostalised context, rejecting homosexuality on the grounds that it is un-African may come as a surprise, as Pentecostalism generally presents a rhetoric of 'breaking with the past' and is not interested in an authentic 'Africanness'"[288] What is your opinion about this criticism?

Another criticism to the defense for the "Zambian culture" of having Christianity as a State religion is associated with its inconsistence in condemning what is considered as 'sin.' Most opponents of this defense consider Christianity in Zambia as being full of 'hypocrisy,' condemning homosexuality as being sinful while leaving other sins like drunkenness, adultery among heterosexuals, *etc.*, without being condemned to the extent done to homosexuality. Moreover, Christianity is just considered a foreign religion, brought by missionaries that strongly demolished the African cultures of the natives, including homosexual relationships.[289] Moreover, Cheyeka writes that in this period of Christianity as a state religion in Zambia, "Zambians immensely experienced the negative effects of privatization, obscene corruption, and decay of infrastructure in the two decades of the MMD."[290] Cheyeka further notes: "As a Thatcherite (as he claimed), Chiluba liberalized the economy, privatized state owned companies and actually killed the middle class, and sold local councils' houses to sitting tenants. He is therefore credited for having re-introduced Capitalism in the country [. . .]."[291] In this case, the hypocrisy of Chiluba's announcement of Zambia as a Christian country begins with him and pervades to his subordinates in various levels of his administration to people who called themselves as Christians within the country. What is your opinion in regard to this criticism?

The third criticism of the defense of "Zambian Christian culture" is based on the attitude of the defenders on those who are considered sinful—the guys and lesbians. The harsh language they use is not 'Christ-like." Quoting from one commentator in an online discussion between the defenders and those who oppose the Christian cultural view of Zambians, Van Klinken presents the criticism: "What kind of Christian nation is Zambia,

288. Van Klinken, "Homosexuality," 269.
289. *Ibid.*, 272.
290. Cheyeka, "Zambia, a Christian Nation," 160.
291. *Ibid.*, 161.

we are not a Christian nation because if we were and follow the teachings of Jesus of love your neighbor as you love yourself some of you would not even think of saying bad words about our brothers and sisters who are gays. What kind of Christians who have already passed judgement on others, your holy bible tells you to leave the judgement to your God."[292] The criticism of those who oppose, in light of this statement, is not that homosexuality is sinful, but is the attitude to those who are considered sinners in light of the attitude of Jesus. Are those who consider themselves Christians and followers of Jesus have the same attitude to sinners in the way Jesus was? What is your opinion about this criticism?

The Nature of Homosexuality

Following the above discussion of the subject of homosexuality in the African context and the attitude of the Church towards it, the important question that remains unanswered is whether homosexuality is biological (natural) or one's choice. There have been arguments among scholars on this issue and no research has reached a plausible conclusion about the real cause for one being a homosexually attracted person. Those who claim that homosexuality is biological (natural or inborn) point out that same-sex relationships should be inside the will of God and should not be condemned. Their argument is summarized by Neipp as follows:

1. *Being gay is not a choice. Homosexuality is an inborn phenomenon.*
2. *Since homosexuality is inborn then it must be tied to identity. Consequently, homosexuality is not about what a person does, it actually defines who they are.*
3. *Since homosexuality is inborn either through genetics or the creation of God, then it should be viewed as normal and natural.*
4. *Since homosexuality is inborn and not the result of choice, then it should be protected like other minorities are protected.*[293]

What is your opinion about this argument? Can one agree with it or not, Why? In rejection to this argument, Neipp quoting Siker states: "Only a sadistic God would create hundreds of thousands of humans to be inherently homosexual and then deny them the right to sexual intimacy."[294] Hence, Neipp's stament implies that human sexuality is an *adiaphora*, an act that cannot deny human beings from attaining God's intended salvation.

292. Van Klinken, "Homosexuality," 172.
293. Neipp, "When Homosexuality comes to Church," 14 (emphasis added).
294. Ibid., 46.

Moreover, God's salvation is not limited to only certain human behaviors as conceived by the weak human mind.

Those who argue for homosexuality as one's own choice see it as something sinful and contrary to the wills of God for procreation. Their argument is summarized by Neipp as follows:

1. *Though there may be many influences, being gay is an individual choice.*
2. *Since homosexuality is a choice it is not so much about identity but more about behavior.*
3. *The choice of homosexuality is not natural and goes directly against God's intended design and order. Thus it should not simply be categorized as an alternative lifestyle but rather be seen as an act of rebellion.*
4. *Since homosexuality is a choice, it should not become a civil rights issue but should remain a moral one.*[295]

In this case, the debate over the causes of homosexual identity in regard to the arguments above is still uncompromised.

However, the biological thesis of the causes of homosexuality, for example, has yielded researches on the various areas of human genetic make-up to justify the cause without a plausible result.[296] The American Psychological Association (APA) makes it clear:

> There is no consensus among scientists about the exact reasons that an individual develops a heterosexual, bisexual, gay, or lesbian orientation. Although much research has examined the possible genetic, hormonal, developmental, social, and cultural influences on sexual orientation, no findings emerged that permit scientists to conclude that sexual orientation is determined by any particular factor or factors. Many think that nature and nurture both play complex roles; most people experience little or no sense of choice about their sexual orientation.[297]

The above quotation indicates that it is still not clear as to what is the cause for one's homosexual orientation.

In regard to the above two positions, no one can deny that homosexuality and the homosexual agenda are in motion in the world now. The

---

295. *Ibid.*, 15 (emphasis added).

296. Those who argue in support of homosexuality take science as their basis, while those who argue against homosexuality use religious Holy Scriptures as their basis. While the use of religious Scriptures to argue against homosexuality has been explored in the previous paragraphs, this paragraph provides an example of how the use of science has also not made the debate reach any consensus.

297. American Psychological Association, "Answers to Your Questions"; *cf.* Neipp, "When Homosexuality comes to Church," 49.

issue is not only what Scriptures say about homosexuality and the way such biblical sayings are interpreted, what homosexuals themselves say about the meaning of human sexuality, or the criteria for evaluating what constitutes the right moral conduct. The issue is mainly that of response to those whom the church sees as being different, or do what is considered as different, from the normal.

It is quite obvious that Christianity is guided by Christian Scriptures. It is hardly possible for Christians to deny Scriptures and the assertions about issues of life and still remain genuine Christians. Scriptures will still remain a guideline to the moral life and faith of all Christians. Homosexuality is presented in scriptures as something controversial. Since Scriptures present sexuality as a relationship between two people of opposite sex and that the enjoyment of sex should be within this relationship of male and female, it can hardly be possible for a Christian to accept homosexuality as being legitimate.

The question to Christians and Christianity is how to respond to the issue and to those who practice it. We agree with Kunhiyop that "while we [as Christians] should refuse to condone homosexuality and same-sex marriages, we must be compassionate in our dealing with homosexuals. We do not have to agree with their behaviour or with their argument that it must be accepted, but we should listen to them compassionately and respectfully. Listening does not mean compromising our position."[298] Why should Christians and Christianity have a compassionate approach to homosexuals? Kunhiyop puts it clear that "homosexuality is not the only heinous sin in our world. Besides homosexuality, Paul's list of sins in 1Corinths 6: 9–10 includes sexual immorality, adultery, greed, drunkenness, slander and fraud."[299] Kunhiyop concludes that despite the wickedness such sins are, yet God provides a chance for the doers of those sins to repent and be accepted in the community of believers. In that case, the church and Christianity as a whole has a responsibility to extend its warm acceptance to homosexuals as people created by God and pray for their spiritual illumination and repentance.

CONCLUSION

It is better that we conclude this chapter as we just introduced it. The task of Practical Theology is that of *praxis,* that of reflexive action. Indeed, its task is to reflect upon the actions of the Church through its various churches

298. Kunhiyop, *African Christian Ethics*, 308–309.
299. Ibid., 309.

in particular places. This reflexive action or praxis is what makes Practical Theology distinct from other traditional theologies because of its commitment to contexts and people's experiences in those contexts.

In this chapter, the argument was to justify the context-based nature of Practical Theology through surveying the practical issues within the Church in Africa. Various issues have been discussed to show that the reflexive nature of Practical Theology is based on real practices of the Church through the various churches in particular African places. Such issues included: alcohol abuses, violence, the role of prophecy for the Church, the Church and homosexuality, and the prosperity gospel teachings with the Church in Africa. It has been vivid in the discussion of these issues that the experience and understanding of God's dealing with people differs from one place to another. Hence, Jesus of the Universal Church is clearly understood and experienced in particular churches within local communities.

6

Trends of Contextual Theology in Africa

From Liberation to Reconstruction

INTRODUCTION

The two previous chapters critically examined practical theology and some actions which challenge the life of contemporary Church in Africa. Moreover, we justified why practical theology should be considered as a form of contextual theology. This chapter concludes the book with a discussion of another form of contextual theology—reconstruction theology. According to Gathogo, "the concept of reconstruction implies a process of 'review and then move'—to create something more suitable to the prevailing environment [. . .]. Other terminological parallels are: rebuild, reassemble, re-establish, recreate, reform, renovate, regenerate, remake, remodel, restore, or re-organise. In turn, it can also be compared with: rethink, re-examine, redo, or rebirth (cf. Nicodemus in Jn 3)."[1] Cathogo's definition indicates that reconstruction theology advocates for dealing with an existing thing, situation, concept *etc* making it appear better than it currently is. Therefore, according to Gathogo, the concept of 'reconstruction' belongs to vocabularies from the field of engineering "which implies that some elements in liberation theology will have to be retained in a new theology of reconstruction. As in the case

---

1.. Gathogo, "Genesis, Methodologies and Concerns," 5.

of an engineer, new specifications must be engineered in the new designs, 'while some aspects of the old complex are retained in the new' [. . .]."[2]

Following Gathogo's definition of the concept of reconstruction, in this chapter we discuss its emergence, its development, its urgency, and its challenges. Through this chapter it will become vivid that reconstruction theology was a necessary form of theology after the dawn of freedom of most African states and the demise of apartheid in South Africa. It will clearly be noted that after independence from colonial powers, it was necessary to move from liberation theologies to theologies of reconstruction without neglecting the theology of liberation and that of inculturaion. As Vellem conceives it, "reconstruction is not a *quid pro quo* for liberation rather liberation is a *sine qua non* of reconstruction. Liberation is the comprehensive framework within which reconstruction and development can find their place."[3] However, being a vast continent, it is not easy to discuss reconstruction issues befalling the whole Africa within this chapter; rather, the chapter uses some examples from South and East Africa to illustrate the efficacy of reconstruction theology in most places of the African continent. In this way, it will be vivid that the development of theology in Africa from liberation to reconstruction has been/and remains sensitive to the various contexts of people within the continent. In building the argument of this chapter, we survey the relationship between reconstruction and black theologies, emergence of reconstruction theology, its claims, its criticisms and its urgency in the twenty-first century.

RECONSTRUCTION THEOLOGY AND BLACK THEOLOGY

The root of Reconstruction Theology is Black Theology in South Africa and the United States of America (USA). One cannot understand Reconstruction Theology without first understanding Black Theology. We need to start examining Black Theology before we proceed to Reconstruction Theology. Black Theology itself is divided into two parts: Black Theology in South Africa, and Black Theology in the USA. However, both of the theologies emerged due to Africans' experiences of struggle for civil rights. This means that there was a particular experience which faced black people in these two places to demand for rights, which were infringed. In South Africa, the apartheid regime subjugated Africans in terms of rights. Rights were provided to people depending on their race: whether European, Indian, colored or African. Africans were provided the final priority.

2.. *Ibid.*, 11.
3. Vellem, "Ideology and Spirituality," 549.

In the USA, Black Theology emerged because of oppression of blacks due to slavery. It should be born in mind that most of the black Americans were taken to America as slaves. They were taken from various African nations to work in America as slaves in various occupations. Their multiplicity made them to form a race in the North American continent, which led to racial oppression. Therefore, the emergence of Black Theology in South Africa and the USA is due to a particular *experience of life* of black people in these places.

What is Black Theology? In the article titled "Black Theology and Black Experience," Baffel quotes from Maimela and defines Black Theology to be: "a conscious, systematic, theological reflection on black experience characterized by oppression, humiliation, and suffering in white racist societies in North America and South Africa."[4] In South Africa, Black Theology gained prominence between the year 1960s and early 1970s.

Following the above definition, Black Theology is a theology of liberation which follows the Exodus metaphor. It calls for the exodus from oppression and humiliation to the land of equal rights of all races. In the exodus story, God heard the cry of the people in Egypt and liberated them from oppression to Canaan, the land of milk and honey. In the liberation of Israelites from the hand of Pharaoh, it is obvious that God revealed the merciful nature. God sides with the oppressed of any society. In that case, the liberation of the Israelites did not depend on whether they were righteous before God; rather, it depended on God's nature to side with the oppressed people in societies.

What caused the emergence of Black Theology in South Africa? The words of Motlhabi, as quoted in Farisani's article, illuminate us about the cause for the emergency of this theology. Motlhabi reports:

> "the emergence of Black Theology in South Africa was the seeming irrelevance of the white church in ministering to the physic-spiritual needs of black people. Not only was the church seen as a colonial church, it was also seen as a status quo church. On the one hand, its chief aim was originally to minister solely to the spiritual needs of white people-from the very advent of colonialism to the time of the total disinheritance of black people in the country. On the other hand, while successive white governments increasingly added to the oppression and woes of black people, the church served largely to placate them and to keep them in line with the demands of white interests, greed and capitalism.[5]

---

4. Baffel, "Black Theology," 3.
5. Farisani, 2010: "Black biblical Hermeneutics," 508–509.

Black Theologians see the theme of liberation to be running throughout the Bible. Liberation as an act of God is not limited only to Israelites; rather, it extends to all races of the world. God intervenes oppression and racial segregation; even those which are done in the name of the Bible. In that case, the Exodus metaphor symbolizes the exodus from oppressive and unjust structures of societies to more just and humane structures, not only to Israelites but also to current societies.

Solomons analyzes two phases of Black Theology basing on the tool of analysis used. According to Solomons, the first phase began in 1970s. The publication of Mokgethi Motlhabi's collection of essays titled *Essays on Black Theology* in 1972 inaugurated the movement of Liberation Theology (though was banned by the South African government). Being closely related to the black consciousness movement and philosophy of Stephen Bantu Biko, its main occupation was "the 'conscientization' of blacks, enabling them to become the vehicles of their own liberation."[6] Biko used a slogan of "Black is beautiful" that conscietized Africans of their value and affirmed African humanness despite the apartheid situation they found themselves. In this strong philosophy embodied in the slogan, Biko managed to convey a message to black South Africans to overcome their inferiority, that persuaded them to comply with the wishes of their superior whites.[7]

The crystallization and intellectual development of Black Theology was vivid after the publication of Basil Moore's essay in 1973 titled *Black Theology: The South African Voice*. This development was made possible by scholars such as Allan Boesak, Goba, Manas Buthelezi, and others whose publications strongly supported Moore's essays. Moreover, Solomons states that this development in Black Theology went parallel with the development of African Theology in Africa north of Limpopo River. Solomons writes: "Parallel to these developments, African theology was also beginning to cristalise. Here the prominent figures were Mbiti [. . .] Dickson [. . .] and Setiloane [. . .] all of whom sought to find a space for African culture in Christian Theology."[8] The main task of African Theology was to negotiate the cultural worldview of Africans as being the root to understanding the foreign Christian religion and its theology. In this case, "African theology was an intellectual exercise aimed at interpreting Christian theology within the framework of African cultural meaning."[9]

---

6. Solomons, "Liberation or Reconstruction," 21.
7. Masenya [ngwan'a mpahlele] & Ramantswana, "Anything New Under the Sun."
8. Solomons, "Liberation or Reconstruction," 21.
9. *Ibid.*

The second phase of Black Theology was signaled by the publication of the *Unquestionable Right to be Free: Black Theology from South Africa* in 1986, a collection of articles edited by Itumeleng Mosala and Buti Tilhagale. The tool for theological analysis of society in this phase was by the use of Marxism. The shift in the tool of analysis from race to Marxism was due to the inadequacy of race as a tool of analysis, as was criticized by Latin American theologians who most used Marxism as a tool of analysis of society in their theological articulations. The Latin American theologians criticized race as a tool of analysis charging it of ignoring the analysis of classes of people within society. The analysis of society using race was seen as being inadequate without analyzing classes of people, a thing that was accomplished by the use of Marxism. Therefore, in this phase, "Categories borrowed from Marx, such as alienation, class, labour, or historical materialism and orthopraxis, thus became prisms in Black theological discourse through which to deconstruct domination."[10]

Solomons, using ideas from Ntintili's article titled "Notions of Liberation in Black Theology," further identifies three stands in the development of Black Theology in the South African context. First, the Black Solidarity Strand "focused its conceptualization of oppression on racism."[11] Focusing more on the socio-psychological dimension of racism, this strand put more emphasis on racism as being both subjective and objective phenomenon. Second, the Black Solidarity–Materialist strand which focused on "the class, race and gender analysis."[12] This strand demonstrated "the organic relatedness" of the various dimensions of oppression. In order to understand this strand, "The dimensions of race, class, gender and marginalization is [sic!] at the heart of the Black theological analysis."[13] Third, the Non-Racist Strand which focused on apartheid and its legal dimension, especially in the formulation of policies to govern people's lives. This was the most popular strand of all because it touched the core of apartheid ideology.[14]

The emphasis on liberation done by Black Theology was triggered by the advent of democracy in South Africa. Since Black Theology emphasized on the exodus from racism and oppression to a just South African society, the freedom of South Africa of 1994 caused scholars of Black Theology and Theology of Inculturation to think otherwise. They thought that there was a need for a shift in emphasis from Liberation to Reconstruction in the

10. *Ibid.*, 22.
11. *Ibid.*, 23.
12. *Ibid.*
13. *Ibid.*
14. *Ibid.*

post-apartheid South Africa. However, after the freedom of South Africa, there was a lack of agreement among scholars on whether to abandon Black Theology and remain with the newly proposed Reconstruction Theology or continue with the Black Theology.

EMERGENCY OF RECONSTRUCTION THEOLOGY AND ITS CLAIMS

The Kenyan theologian Jesse Ndwiga Kanyua Mugambi is credited of being the founder of Reconstruction Theology. Mugambi "was born on 6 February 1947 at Kiangoci, near St. Mark's College, Kigari in Ngandori location, Manyatta Divion, Embu District in the Eastern Province of Kenya-East Africa."[15] His first name, the baptismal name, is derived from Ruth 4: 17–22; 1Samuel 16; and 1Chronicles 2: 12–17. This is the name of King David's father. His middle names, Ndwiga and Kanyua, each has its own meaning. Ndwiga means giraffe—an ability to see beyond his contemporaries could see (far-sighted man); and Kanyua means the one who drinks a lot, the one who boasts or takes leaisure in the local brew (this was the name of Mugambi's father. Mugambi's father died in 1996). The fourth name 'Mugambi' means "a prophet-like character who blow the trumpet of conscience when a need arises."[16]

The Theology of Reconstruction was born at the All Africa Conference of Churches (AACC) meeting in Nairobi Kenya on 30 March 1990. According to Gathogo, the then chairperson of the meeting, Archbishop Desmond Tutu and the then General Secretary Rev. Jose B. Chipenda invited Jesse Mugambi to speak about the theme titled "The Future of the Church and the Church of the Future in Africa." The meeting was held just a month after Nelson Mandela's release (on 02 February 1990)[17] and a few days after the independence of Namibia (21 March, 1990). In this meeting, "Mugambi suggested that the post-apartheid or the post-cold war African Christianity

---

15. Gathogo, "Jesse Mugambi's Pedigree," 177; *cf.* Gathogo, "Liberation and Reconstruction," 18.

16. *Ibid.*; Gathogo, "Liberation and Reconstruction," 16–17.

17. This date is considered a turning point in the South African politics. It is in this date when the last white president of South Africa F.W. de Clark delivered a speech to the South African Parliament which also announced the release of Nelson Mandela from the 27 year imprisonment. Moreover, in this speech, the white president unbanned the formerly banned liberation movements such as the ANC, SACP, AZAPO, COSATU, MDM, *etc* (see Farisani, "The Use of Ezra-Nehemiah," 65n8).

must shift her theological gear from the paradigm of liberation to that of reconstruction."[18]

In Mugambi's words, as quoted in Gathogo, he says: "Reconstruction is the new priority for African nations in the 1990s. The churches and their theologians will need to respond to this new priority in relevant fashion, to facilitate this process of reconstruction. The process will require considerable efforts of reconciliation and confidence-building. It will also require reorientation and retraining [. . .]."[19] In this proposition, Mugambi was convinced that the suitable figure for the analysis of the New World Order of the post-apartheid and post-cold war was that of Nehemiah, not that of Moses, *i.e.*, post-Exilic not Exodus. According to Tarus and Lowery,

> The basic thesis of Mugambi's reconstruction theology is that the biblical narrative of Nehemiah's reconstruction of the wall of Jerusalem provides the theological paradigm for the reconstruction and the social transformation of Africa after colonialism, apartheid, and the end of the Cold War. Beyond a mere celebration of the defeat of these ills, reconstruction theology challenges the church in Africa to actively promote human rights, social justice, peace, and reconciliation in the midst of the atrocities bedeviling the African continent.[20]

After the meeting of the All Africa Conference of Churches in Nairobi, other scholars joined in support of Mugambi's proposal. Later in the same year (December 1990), Charles Villa-Vicencio, a white South African, published an article titled "Religion, Revolution and Reconstruction." Other scholars in support of this theology of reconstruction included: Hannah Kinoti, Wilson Niwagila, Andrea Karamanga, Wilson Mande, Jean-Emmanuel Pondi, and Chris Manus Ugachukwu among many others.[21] The publications of these scholars indicated the growing trend of this theological perspective.

We begin the discussion of this theology with the first example of its development from East Africa as conceived by Jesse Mugambi. In his publication of essays titled *From Liberation to Reconstruction*, Mugambi turns totally from his earlier ideas of Liberation towards a new proposal of Reconstruction. In his earlier notions of liberation, Mugambi referred to

---

18. Gathogo, "Jesse Mugambi's Pedigree," 173; Gathogo, "Liberation and Reconstruction," xiv; *cf.* Tarus & Lowery, "African Theologies," 15–16.

19. *Ibid.*, 174; *cf.* Gathogo, "Mercy Oduyoye as the Mother of African Women Theology," 6; Buthelezi, "Reconciliation and Liberation," 42–49; and Chipenda, "Theology of Liberation," 50–55.

20. Tarus & Lowery, "African Theologies," 315.

21. Gathogo, "Jesse Mugambi's Pedigree," 175.

liberation that was mostly political oriented. He referred to "liberation from colonial oppression [. . .] but also from continued forms of economic deprivation and injustice as well as freedom from imposed cultural norms."[22] Therefore, for Mugambi, the Theology of liberation that was suitable in the colonial period is no longer suitable in the post-colonial Africa.

In the above publication, Mugambi characterizes the emerging theological paradigm as follows:

> This theology should be reconstructive rather than destructive, inclusive rather than exclusive; proactive rather than reactive; complementary rather than competitive; integrative rather than disintegrative; programme-driven rather than project-driven; people-centred rather than institution-centred; deed-oriented rather than word-oriented; participatory rather than autocratic; regenerative rather than degenerative; future-sensitive rather than past-sensitive; co-operative rather than confrontational; consultative rather than impositional.[23]

The colonization of South Africa rendered the whole of Africa to continue rethinking about the colonial paradigm, with the theme of liberation as being the dominant theme in both African Theology and Black Theology. After the emergency of democracy in South Africa, in his post-apartheid writings, "Mugambi is of the opinion that the liberation motif within which African theologies have thus far been undertaken, is no longer an adequate framework for doing African theology. According to him the liberation motif has been ineffective in responding to the multi-faceted challenges posed by Africa's post-colonial context."[24] In this case, Mugambi proposes the move from a "reactive" liberation theology to a "pro-active" Reconstruction Theology by the use of a post-Exilic paradigm of Ezra-Nehemiah. In order to emphasize on this theology of Reconstruction, "the post-Exilic motif exemplified in Ezra-Nehemiah is proposed as a means to confront the new theological challenge and replace the Exodus motif which inspired liberation."[25]

Quoted in Gathogo, Mugambi says:

> A careful and critical study of the Exodus narrative raises serious questions about the beginning and the end of the exodus process. Too often scholars have focused on the process of

22. Solomons, "Liberation or Reconstruction," 32.

23. Mugambi, *From Liberation to Reconstruction*, xv; *cf.* Kabinde, "The Church and Constitutional Reforms," 234–235; and Waweru, "African Theology," 220.

24. Solomons, "Liberation or Reconstrction," 32.

25. *Ibid.*

liberation from Pharaoh's oppression to the freedom in Canaan. However, the Exodus narrative does not end with the invasion, siege, conquest and eventual occupation of Canaan. The narrative continues with the former slaves becoming invaders and oppressors themselves. They then adopt the norms and values of the people they conquered. They wanted to have a king, despite advice against that wish by Samuel (1Samuel 8). Saul, the first King, became a despot and they had to contend with a new form of oppression. There is a great difference between oppression by Pharaoh and oppression by Saul. We find the same historical drama repeated in the New Testament. There is a contrast between oppression by Caesar, and the oppression by Herod. The rhetoric of liberation, especially in the in the [sic!] 1970s and 1980s, focused on the former kind of oppression.[26]

The two oppression paradigms of the Israelites and the paradigm of oppression by Herod and Caesar presented in the above quotation exemplify the two paradigms which contemporary people passed from colonialism to neo-colonialism. Oppression by colonialism is not the same as oppression by neo-colonialism. However, both dramas need liberation.

Mugambi further says:

> In the 1970s I was in the forefront of the struggle for liberation in Africa. But after two decades of that line of thought I discovered that it is essential to move beyond the rhetoric of liberation. Liberation tends to be focused on the past. Reconstruction is focused on the future. The exile narratives provide another paradigm on the basis of which oppressed people can find encouragement. Ezra-Nehemiah provides a paradigm rather different from that of the Exodus. There is a great contrast between the leadership of Moses and Joshua in the Exodus narrative and that of Ezra and Nehemiah in the Exile narrative.[27]

Basing on the above quotation, Mugambi proposes a theology of reconstruction, a theology that focuses on the future. Therefore, for Mugambi, liberation alone is not enough without reconstruction because it subjects people to oppression as indicated in the paradigms of Herod and Caesar (New Testament) and that of Pharaoh and Saul (in the Old Testament) presented in the above quotation.

In Mugambi's proposed theology of Reconstruction, there are three main levels:

26. Gathogo, "Jesse Mugambi's Pedigree," 185.
27. Ibid., 186.

First, there is the *personal* which deals with the reconstruction of individual motives and intentions. The second is ecclesial reconstruction dealing with all areas of the church's life including 'management structures, financial policies, pastoral care, human resource development, research, family, education, service and witness' [. . .]. The third is *cultural* reconstruction, which has five components: (i) *politics* dealing with the management of social influence; (ii) *economics* dealing in matters of values; (iii) ethics dealing with the reconstruction of the system of values; (iv) aesthetics dealing with the sense of proportion and symmetry in all aspects of life; and (v) religion which provides the worldview synthesizing 'everything that is cherished by individuals as corporate members of society'.[28]

Taking into account of all levels mentioned above, Mugambi viewed reconstruction as "praxis" of the various practices whereby the old aspects become part of the new because all pass into the actions and reflections process. By passing through the praxis process, the various aspects of life are rearranged or reorganized in order for them to respond to the changed dimension of life in the post-colonial Africa.[29]

Mugambi further argues that in order to implement the Theology of Reconstruction, "Nehemiah becomes the central text of the new theological paradigm in African Christian Theology as a theological development from the Exodus motif."[30] Mugambi contravenes the way the Exodus motif was being used by African scholars as a fundamental motif for the liberation of Africans. He notes the difference in geographical movement between the Africans; situation and the situation of Israelites. He sees no correlation between the two contexts. Solomons presents the criticism: Mugambi's "analogy between the Exodus and the struggle against colonization does not fit very well, considering that in the Old Testament, the Israelites move physically over time and space, from Egypt across the Sinai to Canaan, whereas Africans remain in the same geographical space."[31] In this case, for Mugambi, the re-building the destroyed Israel and of the Temple preached by Ezra-Nehemiah seems to fit well with the need for reconstruction, reconciliation and development of the situation caused by colonialism. As Solomons notes, for Mugambi, "the re-building of Jerusalem is put forward as a model for the reconstruction of African societies that have been devastated

---

28. Mugambi, *From Liberation to Reconstruction*, 16–17; *cf*. Solomons, "Liberation or Reconstruction," 33; Tarus & Lowery, "African Theologies,"316.

29. Solomons, "Liberation or Reconstruction," 33.

30. Solomons, "Liberation or Reconstruction," 33.

31. *Ibid.*, 34.

by colonial rule and exploitation."[32] What Mugambi envisioned and argued for was the possibility of creating a new society within the same geographical space by the use of new and old aspects in a praxis process. The question is this: What is your opinion in regard to Mugambi's views on Reconstruction?

The second example is drawn from the South African context. In the South African context, the theology of Reconstruction emerged through the works of Charles Villa-Vicencio. Villa-Vicencio was based on Cape Town, and was the Executive Director of the Institute for Justice and Reconciliation. Before holding this position, Villa-Vicencio worked as the National Research Director in the Truth and Reconciliation Commission. The great contribution of Villa Vicencio to the theology of Reconstruction is seen in his work titled: *A Theology of Reconstruction: National Building and Human Rights* where he presents "the need for African and Black Theology to move from Liberation to reconstruction."[33] This work was published at the wake of the New democratic South Africa whereby there was a struggle for the new democratic government to establish structures based on equality and justice.

The most important thing to note in Villa-Vicencio's proposal for the Theology of Reconstruction was not a total departure from the Theology of Liberation done by most scholars of his time. Rather, a new kind of liberation was to be pursued. Solomons posses the challenge: "Because reconstruction theology, according to him, is a new kind of liberatory theology, he recognizes the concern by some theologians to move beyond what they regard as legitimate forms of liberation theology, this in spite of the need to engage constructively in national building."[34] Villa-Vicencio sees the new metaphor of reconstruction as having the responsibility to set strategies for reconstruction and nation-building because liberation theology did not accomplish that task. In that case, Villa-Vicencio's proposal for the theology of reconstruction still sees it as another form of liberation theology with the mandate to enhance reconstruction and building of the nation in the post-apartheid South Africa.

What worldview characterized Villa-Vicencio's proposal for the theology of reconstruction? The proposal emerged in context regarded as "the New World Order" characterized by various shifts including "the fall of the Berlin Wall in German and the dawn of democracy in South Africa."[35] Solomons further notes: "This notion of the New World Order connotes the

32. Ibid.
33. Ibid., 27.
34. Ibid.
35. Ibid., 28; cf. Farisani, "The Ideologically Biased Use of Ezra-Nehemiah," 332–333; Farisani, "The Use of Ezra-Nehemiah," 63; Vellum, "Ideology and Spirituality," 547; Umaru, "Salvation as Healing?" 59.

disintegration of Union of Soviet States of Russia [...], the demise of apartheid in South Africa, the reunification of Germany, initiatives to create a unitary Europe, the emergency of Third World countries and globalization [...]."[36]

In his words, Villa-Vicencio states the above-listed historical shifts: "The failure of the economic and political structures of Eastern Europe, the collapse of a widespread belief in utopian socialist ideals in the Third World countries, the failure of Western-based capitalism to meet the needs of the poor, a new-found appreciation that even under the most adverse conditions, the poor rise in rebellion in demand of their rights."[37] All these events characterize the new world order which we now call with a single word: *globalization*.

For Villa-Vicencio, reconstruction was conceived as a response to what the church in South Africa had been challenged. The challenge of the church was "to restore justice and to affirm human dignity ensuring that in the process of reconstruction, nations are able to turn away from greed, domination and exploitation and embrace communal sharing and personal fulfillment."[38] In response to that challenge of the church, "reconstruction is a process that entails the transformation of social ills in order to usher in communal sharing and personal efficacy."[39]

For Villa-Vicencio, "reconstruction involves the difficult tasks of breaking down prejudices of race, class and sexism and the difficult challenge of creating an all-inclusive society built on the very values denied to the majority of South Africans under apartheid."[40] Hence, for him, the dawn of the theology of Reconstruction, the new liberatory theology, is exemplified by the meeting of the above-stated challenge posed to the church in South Africa.

Furthermore, Villa-Vicencio's proposal for the Theology of Reconstruction, as any other theology, is based on the Holy Scriptures. Similar to Mugambi, he takes the post-Exilic paradigm as his point of theological departure. As Solomons writes, Villa-Vicencio "argues that the central biblical motif for reconstruction theology is the 'post-Exilic' experience rather than the 'Exodus' as it was with various contextual theologies, including

---

36. *Ibid.*; cf. Farisani, "The Ideologically Biased Use of Ezra-Nehemiah," 332–333; Farisani, "The Use of Ezra-Nehemiah," 63; Vellum, "Ideology and Spirituality," 549.

37. Villa-Vicencio, "Liberation and Reconstruction," 163.

38. Vellum, "Ideology and Spirituality," 549; *cf.* Solomons, "Liberation or Reconstruction," 28; Farisani, "The Ideologically Biased Use of Ezra-Nehemiah," 332–333.

39. Solomons, "Liberation or Reconstruction," 28.

40. Vellum, "Ideology and Spirituality," 550; *cf.* Solomons, "Liberation or Reconstruction," 29; Farisani, "The Ideologically Biased Use of Ezra-Nehemia," 333.

Black Theology, which formed part of the 'struggle' of resistance."[41] Hence, Villa-Vicencio sees the materials of the post-Exilic theology as being prophetic theology which provide an appropriate credence to the reconstruction theology being proposed. According to him, "The main interlocutors of the reconstruction are 'political exiles' who have steadily streamed into the country since the banning of the liberation movements. Reconstruction is therefore, a call for a *metanoia* from social prejudices and a creation of a new society built on the values of the masses of South Africa."[42]

For Villa-Vicencio, the reconstruction proposal is not only a theological project; rather, it is a cross-cutting agenda. It is an inter-disciplinary project. Vellem presents Villa-Vicencio's ideas of the interdisciplinary nature of reconstruction: reconstruction "should emerge at the interface between theology and law, economics political science and related disciplines."[43] The main goal is "commitment to 'enthusiastic participation in the constitutional debate, the establishment of a society governed by the rule of law, the affirmation of human rights and the creation of laws designed to produce justice now [. . .]."[44] Hence, an interdisciplinary view of reconstruction, as a theological proposal, highlights the responsibility of the church to address people's needs in all spheres of their lives.

The notion of rebuilding the nation purported by Villa-Vicencio is rooted in his use of the concept of "*perestroika*." For him, this concept "entails 'building within the shell of an old society step by step [. . .]" while being "in critical solidarity with a democratically elected government [. . .]."[45] The concept of '*perestroika*' is a Russian term with political and economic connotations. This term literary means "restructuring." In the context of Russia, the term means "the reconstruction of the Soviet political and economic system [. . .]"[46] as was practiced by Gorbarchev. Hence, the use of this term by Villa-Vicencio in the South African context entails that "while prophetic theology must continue to say 'No' to all forms of exploitation," reconstruction theology must "at the same time be concerned about how to share in the process of nation building , by saying 'Yes' to meaningful socio-economic and cultural change."[47]

---

41. Solomons, "Liberation or Reconstruction," 29.

42. Vellum, "Ideology and Spirituality," 550.

43. Vellum, "Ideology and Spirituality," 550; *cf.* Solomons, "Liberation or Reconstruction," 29.

44. Solomons, "Liberation or Reconstruction," 29.

45. Ibid., 30.

46. Ibid., 30n11.

47. Ibid., 31; *cf.* Vellum, "Ideology and Spirituality," 549.

Villa-Vincencio further proposes that the ethic of the theology of reconstruction is that of "middle axioms." According to him, "Middle axioms [. . .] are ethical principles 'not binding for all time' but, 'begin' the process of social renewal." They "are evolving principles in the process of social reconstruction 'seeking to define the next logical step society needs to take at a given time.'"[48]

Following the above discussed articulation of the theology of reconstruction as conceived by Villa-Vicencio in the South African context, the following points highlighted by Vellem serve as a summary of his theological proposal:

> First, reconstruction theology is a process that entails a transformation of society from social ills of racial and gender prejudice coupled with economic degradation. Second, the key metaphor of the theology of reconstruction is the post-exilic corpus of Ezra-Nehemiah [. . .]. Third and related to the point above, reconstruction theology is a form of 'religionless' [*i.e.*unambiguously interdisciplinary] theological participation in public life and policy formulation. Fourth, its ethical character is expressed through the notion of 'middle axioms' i.e. contextual devices applicable in a given time; hence its *praxiological* orientation is informed by the notion of transitional ethical principles. Last, it is ideologically a theology of the *perestroika*, a step by step theological engagement in renewal, economic transformation and nation-building purported to be more than the ideals of revolution.[49]

What then can we synthesize from the two examples discussed above? In fact, the two scholars, Mugambi and Villa-Vicencio, reach similar conclusions about the theology of reconstruction. Solomons summarizes their conclusions: First, both of them "see the need for theological articulation (referring to both African and Black Theology) to move from liberation to the more 'pro-active' theology of reconstruction." Second, both of them "call for the church to fulfill the role of conscience and to demonstrate biblical norms and values in the quest to rebuild South Africa and the broader African continent." Third, the approach of both of them "recognizes that all people and their dealings are inter-related, hence the call for reconstruction theology to be interdisciplinary in its approach." Fourth, they both agree that "The role of the church in all of this could be categorized as that of

---

48. Vellum, "Ideology and Spirituality."

49. Vellum, "Ideology and Spirituality," 551; *cf.* Solomons, "Liberation or Reconstruction," 31.

having a prophetic voice bringing critique as well as offering God's concerns and directives for the changed context."[50] Therefore, it is the contention of this book that the above conclusions should guide the way of doing contextual theology in the twenty-first century church in Africa. Let us probe more about the four-listed issues.

THE NEED TO MOVE FROM LIBERATION TO RECONSTRUCTION

Why should there be a move from liberation to reconstruction in the twenty-first century context? The move from the theology of liberation to the theology of reconstruction is context-driven. It is made necessary by the existing world order. As Vellem restates, "Central to the proposal to shift from liberation to reconstruction is the new world order, which demands reconstruction and renovation in the 21st century."[51] Reconstruction entails remaking and reshaping the wounds after the liberation process. As African states have witnessed the liberation of states from the shackles of formal colonialism, institutionalized racism in South Africa and the Cold War, reconstruction was necessary as oppression did not end with the mentioned aspects. Yet, as Africa witnesses the needed liberation from various shackles facing Africans in the twenty-first century, such as poverty, dictatorship, incurable diseases, lack of adequate shelter, gender discrimination, the dehumanizing effects of globalization, domestic violence, drug abuses, alcohol abuse, homosexuality, prosperity teachings, *etc.*, reconstruction is necessary. In this case, as Africans say "no" to dehumanizing factors of human life, they still need to say "yes" to what makes life better.

Why is there a need for focusing on rebuilding South Africa and the other African countries in the twenty-first century context? We can respond to this question by saying: identity and community were the major tenets and are still the major aspects governing the practice of reconstruction theology in current societies. Tarus and Lowery list some factors in relation to the need for a definition of who Africans are in terms of their identity and communal belonging:

> The need for a definition of what it means to be African (in Africa or in diaspora) arose out of the various facets of life in Africa such as the challenges of the missionary enterprise, the colonial experience especially the colonialists' ethnocentric

---

50. Solomons, "Liberation or Reconstruction," 35.
51. Vellem, "Ideology and Spirituality," 548.

attitudes toward Africans, the formation of new governments after colonialism ended (1954–1994), the post-colonial land resettlement programs, which uprooted some people from their ancestral lands; the reality of apartheid in South Africa, the challenges of modernization and globalization, rural to urban migrations, the embrace of foreign languages (English, French, Arabic, and Portuguese) at the expense of indigenous languages, the loss of tradition, and the various challenges of poverty and diseases that ravage the African continent.[52]

Following Tarus and Lowery's statement, in the South African context, the question of identity was crucial in the apartheid regime. People's identity was viewed in regard to race. The end of apartheid regime needed reconstruction in order to deal with what we can call "neo-apartheid" practices and build among people a sense of community, where every South African is viewed in terms of the philosophy of *Ubuntu* in all matters of social, economic, spiritual and political welfare.[53]

As stated by Tarus and Lowery above, in other African countries, the need for the theology of reconstruction originates from the same questions of identity and community. Since the fall of colonialism, life has not just been smooth among African states and individual people. People's identities have been threatened by the emergence of ethnocentrism and tribalism which favor exclusivism more than inclusivism. Ethnocentricism and tribalism are not so much different from racism in their practical sense as all of them refer to the love of self other than the other. It means that after the fall of colonialism the spirit of ethnocentrism and tribalism continued to preoccupy most African countries perpetuating oppressive structures. These spirits needed and still need to be reconstructed even within the twenty-first century African context.[54] Hence, reconstruction theology, as liberation theology had to draw its resources from "historical factors behind it, such as slavery, colonialism, racism and other forms of marginalisation, so too ATOR [African Theology of Reconstruction] has various historical factors behind it. They include: the end of cold war in 1989, the end of apartheid in 1994, the end of colonialism and its neo-colonialist versions, missionary involvement and western ethnocentrism, among others."[55]

Why should there be a greater focus on interdisciplinary theological approach in doing reconstruction theology in the twenty-first century

---

52.. Tarus & Lowery, "African Theologies of Identity and Community," 307.
53. Ibid., 305–307, *cf.* Morekwa, "Doing theology in the post liberation era," 62–65.
54. *Ibid.*
55. Gathogo, "Genesis, Methodologies and Concerns," 8.

context? There should be a greater focus on interdisciplinary theological approach mostly because reconstruction theology does not bring something completely new that does not build on previous interdisciplinary efforts to deal with human predicaments. Vellem aptly responds to the posed question: "Yes, indeed it is interdisciplinary and does not re-invent the wheel, but seeks to unleash the dangerous power of liberation in human rights; interfaith dialogue; cultural empowerment and economic justice in an open-ended manner."[56] Vellem's statement suggests that the practical part of the paradigm of reconstruction touches the varied aspects of humanity apart from religion and theology. Therefore, since the paradigm of reconstruction encompasses the various human aspects, the theology of reconstruction can hardly work in a vacuum. The interaction of this theological paradigm with the various changing aspects of human life is inevitable leading to its interaction with the various disciplines dealing with human life. Reconstruction theology "will draw its resources from multi-disciplinary expertise 'involving social scientists, theologians, philosophers, creative writers and artists, biological and physical scientists, builders and architects'"[57] in order to deal with issues facing humankind.

Why should there be a prophetic voice from the contemporary Church that critiques and directs upon what to be done in the ever-changing context of the twenty-first century? It is mostly because the liberation from colonial powers left African states with indelible scars of political, social, cultural and economic injustices. African leaders have mostly cherished more about what they gain from their leadership than being servants of people in societies they belong. The struggle for gains rather than service has created perpetual crises and misunderstandings between such leaders and people which call for prophetic voices to redeem people from the shackles of greed undemocratic African leaders.[58]

Moreover, the church's natural slumber creates a room for prophetic theology to awaken it towards fulfilling its prophetic obligations. The main concern of the slumbing church has mostly been the evangelization of those who attend church services leaving the majority and their social, political, economic and cultural predicaments in the streets unattended. As Nyiawung states,

> The prophetic witness of the church as an appropriate mode of public discourse in African societies—is aimed at liberating the good news of God's salvation that has , to date, been confined

56. Vellem, "Ideology and Spirituality," 552.
57. Gathogo, "Genesis, Methodologies and Concerns," 13.
58. Nyiawung, "The Prophetic Witness of the Church," 1.

within the four walls of the church and directing the church's attention towards the public and its needs. It is an attempt to enable the church to review its strategy and its impact in the market place of the cry for social justice. It [. . .] tickles and awakens the church's awareness and its responsibility towards another important but neglected dimension of its prophetic mission, which is that of prophetic witnessing to the public [. . .].[59]

Therefore, the voice of the church in the midst of human predicament is highly needed. This voice can be projected through the theology of reconstruction awakening the church towards fulfilling its missionary responsibility.

CRITICISMS TO RECONSTRUCTION THEOLOGY

The shift from Black Theology to Reconstruction Theology marked a paradigm shift in theological thinking. As it is to any emerging paradigm, Reconstruction Theology also faced some criticisms from the holders of the existing paradigm (the liberation paradigm). The tension between theology of reconstruction and black theology began at Mbagathi in Nairobi Kenya in the year 2000. In this year there was a theological conference in Nairobi encompassing theologians from various theological backgrounds in Africa, *i.e.*, "Conference of African Theological Institutions (CATI); the All Africa Conference of Churches (AACC); the Ecumenical Association of Third World Theologians (EATWOT); The Circle of Concerned African Women Theologians (THE CIRCLE); and the Organization of African Instituted Churches (OAIC) met to clarify their role in the service of the Church and the wider community."[60] At this conference, vehement words were pronounced by proponents of Black Theology from South Africa. Martey reports: "At Mbagathi, the tension between liberation and reconstruction became obvious when black theologians from South Africa including Takatso Mofokeng and Tinyiko Maluleke expressed dissatisfaction with Mugambi's attempt to down play and underestimate the importance of liberation for Africa's social transformation and development. Reconstruction, it is argued, must begin with liberation and all Africans are not yet liberated."[61] Therefore, what is important with this conference is that theologians departed without any agreement on reconstruction as being a

59. Ibid.

60. Martey, "Theology and Liberation," 6; *cf.* Togarasei, "The Legacy of Circle Women's Engagement."

61. Ibid.; *cf.* Vellum, "Ideology and Spirituality," 458.

new accepted paradigm. In most cases, reconstruction was viewed as a *sine qua non, i.e.,* a "comprehensive framework within which reconstruction and development can find their place."[62]

Another conference was held in South Africa in 2002 on Theological Education and Ecumenical Formation. As Martey reports, this conference "was part of the interactive process to embark on the Journey of Hope in Africa to make a difference on the continent in the 21st century."[63] In this conference, the discussion was not governed by divisions among theologians on the issue of the relationship between reconstruction and Black Theological paradigms as was at Mbagathi in Nairobi in 2000. Here, theologians "saw both as complementary and envisioned a journey of hope 'for Africa's *liberative reconstruction* and sustainable development.'"[64]

Despite the recognition of theologians of reconstruction paradigm as being complementary to the liberation paradigm, yet the theology of reconstruction has received several criticisms. Some of the criticisms are the following: first, the reconstruction paradigm is charged of being uncritical to the independence obtained by South Africa and other African nations leading them to a false hope of independence. The end of oppression and the coin of the concept of reconstruction, according to Mugambi, connoted the end of three major systems that exerted oppression: "institutionalized racism, formal colonialism and cold-war tutelage [. . .]."[65] In criticism, Solomons quoting Gunda states: "It is apparent that Mugambi assumes that oppression ended with these 'systems of oppression' yet the common man in Africa may see things differently because more than a decade after those systems collapsed in Africa, the viciousness of oppression has outlived these systems!"[66]

Moreover, Tarus and Lowery write: "Mugambi's assumption that the end of the old order heralded a new world order free from 'systems of oppression' such as 'colonialism, racism, and ideological propaganda' was problematic. These scholars argue that such a belief offers false hope to the people of Africa because Africa can never be truly free of these 'systems of oppression.' For the common rural and urban poor of Africa, nothing much has changed. African politicians and power brokers have replaced the old colonial masters and in many African countries, ethnocentrism, nepotism, xenophobia, and sexism have replaced apartheid. Similarly, 'The "Exodus to Freedom" has turned to be an exodus to bewilderment; honey and milk have

62. Vellum, "Ideology and Spirituality," 549.
63. Martey, "Theology and Liberation," 7.
64. *Ibid.*
65. Solomons, "Liberation or Reconstruction," 36.
66. *Ibid.,* 36–37.

turned to be hunger and poverty, harmony, peace, joy and prosperity turned to be agony, killings and hatred. Many have been left in the wilderness to die as refugees and misplaced people.' A quick look at Africa's politics confirms these criticisms. Africa's liberators became its oppressors."[67] Therefore, the call for reconstruction that neglects that oppressive structures still function despite the announcement of the fall of those structures, is a false hope, hence "downplaying the role of liberation for African's social transformation and development."[68]

Second, the reconstruction paradigm is criticized of uncritical appropriation of the post-Exilic metaphor of Ezra-Nehemiah. According to Farisani, an uncritical reading of the metaphor as embodied in the biblical text is "any reading of the Bible which does not engage in an in-depth manner with the text. Any uncritical reading of the biblical text tends to further oppress and sideline the poor and marginalized by appropriating the ideologically undifferentiated biblical texts as the 'revealed word of God.' Instead of empowering the poor and marginalized, an uncritical reading of the text disempowers and weakens them."[69]

Following this view of uncritical reading of the text, Farisani poses the criticism:

> The main critique is that Villa-Vicencio's [and Mugambi's] use of Ezra-Nehemiah does not examine critically the ideology behind the conflict between the returned exiles and the *am haaretz* (the people of the land).[70] A careful reading of the text of Ezra-Nehemiah demonstrates that there is a contestation between at least two groups, namely the returned exiles and the *am haaretz*. [. . .]. It follows, therefore, that if Ezra-Nehemiah is to be used in the theology of reconstruction, it should not be read as representing the voice of only one group, i.e. that of the returned exiles. The suppressed voices of the *am haaretz* have to be heard as well. Unfortunately, Villa-Vicencio's use of Ezra-Nehemiah suppresses the voice of the *am haaretz*, in that he neither identifies

---

67. Tarus & Lowery, "African Theologies," 317.

68. Solomons, "Liberation or Reconstruction," 41; *cf.* Tutu, "African Theology," 56–57.

69. Farisani, "The Ideologically Biased Use of Ezra-Nehemia," 346.

70. Returned exiles are the Jews who went to Babylon for Exile in 586 BCE under King Nebuchadnezzer, yet through the help of the Persian King Cyrus they returned to Palestine in 539 BCE. These Jews found in the land, the Jews who did not go to the Babylonian Exile but remained in the land, the *am haaretz*.

nor analyses critically the ideology within the text, an ideology which is biased against the *am haaretz*.[71]

In fact, what Farisani argues in this criticism is that Villa-Vicencio (and, of course Mugambi) hardly reads the Ezra-Nehemia's text with the utmost carefuless as the basis of their theological articulation despite mentioning the existence of conflicts between the *am haaretz* and the returning exiles.

Third, Mugambi's discount of the Exodus motif of the liberation paradigm due to distance from Africa is problematic. While Mugambi underscores the Exodus motif due to distance, he also upholds the Ezra-Nehemiah, another distant theological metaphor. Vellem, quoted in Solomons, poses a fundamental question in critique: "How close is Nehemiah to Africa in distance, ideology, religion, salvation and culture?" In regard to this question Mugambi's choice to disregard the Exodus paradigm due to distance did not consider his option of Ezra-Nehemiah's paradigm with a similar criterion of distance. Following this lack of consideration, Vallem, as quoted in Solomons, criticizes: "The choice of Nehemiah is not enough. There needs to be a clearly stated hermeneutical reading of Nehemiah that is liberative. The development of a hermeneutic of reconstruction is indispensable for the call to depart from a hermeneutic of liberation. It is hard to accept Mugambi's hermeneutical approach to scripture as it remains undisclosed."[72]

Fourth, Mugambi's reconstruction theology is criticized of being unclear in its articulation of the major issues facing Africa and its people such as globalization and patriarchy. Musa Dube, as quoted in Gathogo, states: Mugambi's articulations "Remain quite blind to the superstructure of patriarchy, which must be deconstructed in order to reconstruct. Otherwise, his theology of reconstruction is founded on sand as long as it does not address major oppressive issues of both globalization and patriarchy."[73] Hence, Dube and other scholars who criticize the reconstruction idea see it "as being foreign, inauthentic, immature, and above all, suspicious."[74]

Fifth, reconstruction theology, especially as proposed by Villa-Vicencio, is criticized of paying little attention to the analysis of the other disciplines which it purport to have interface with. This is because these disciplines were the ones that were flawed during the apartheid period and need critical analysis themselves and be deconstructed. Vellem, quoting

---

71. Farisani, "The Ideologically Biased Use of Ezra-Nehemiah," (2012) 335; Farisani, "The Ideologically Biased Use of Ezra-Nehemiah," (2002) 633; *cf.* Solomons, "Liberation or Reconstruction," 38.

72. Solomons, "Liberation or Reconstruction," 39; cf. Stinton, *Jesus of Africa*, 251.

73. Gathogo, "Liberation and Reconstruction," 4.

74. *Ibid.*, 2; *cf.* Gathogo, "Jesse Mugambi's Pedigree."

Ptyana, states: "Its methodology of interfacing with economics, human rights law and political science is conducted in an uncritical manner without regard to the fact that these very systems from which theological discourse was to draw were themselves flawed. In other words little attention was paid to the critical approaches to historiography and jurisprudence. Such an interdisciplinary effort lands on the laps of tight and unredeemed academic discourses which themselves need to be interrogated and deconstructed."[75]

Sixth, reconstruction theology as proposed by Villa Vicencio is criticized of being none-directional and ambivalent. Villa-Vicencio proposes reconstruction that purports to shift from liberation to reconstruction yet it remains liberatory. The non-directional or ambivalent nature of the proposal is based on the interlocutors of the two paradigms. The liberation paradigm has the poor and marginalized as its interlocutors, and the preferential option for the poor is the one of the greatest tenets. The interlocutors of reconstruction theology are not the same. Vellem clearly states:

> There are essential tenets in Black Theology of liberation which cannot be simply discarded if one wishes to be within that paradigm. The preferential option for the poor or a black nonperson is confused with new interlocutors in this proposal and thus creates an unsavory ambivalence between his proposal and the liberation paradigm. Interlocution seems to be utterly confused in the project of reconstruction. This ambivalence makes it difficult to understand what the departure from liberation is or what Villa-Vicencio means by reconstruction as an alternative to liberation while he still clings to liberation.[76]

Seventh, a severe criticism to reconstruction theology to both Mugambi and Villa-Vicencio was posed by Tinyiko Sam Maluleke. Maluleke poses his criticism:

> My main critique of both Mugambi and Villa-Vicencio is in their assumption that the end of the "cold war" has immediate significance for ordinary Africans and that the so-called new world order is truly "new" and truly "orderly" for Africans. Yet as Mugambi himself rightly points out a few times in his book, Africa's problems of poverty, war, dictatorships and American bully-boy tactics are unlikely to decrease because of the "new world order." In fact, the "new world order" is not only likely to relegate Africa into a "fourth world" but it will also impose its own prescriptions on African countries. One such prescription

75. Vellum, "Ideology and Spirituality," 554.
76. Vellum, "Ideology and Spirituality," 553.

is "democracy" or its semblance. I have also been critical of the fact that both Mugambi and Villa-Vicencio appear to minimize the values of previous African Theologies of both inculturation and liberation.[77]

Maluleke's criticism focuses on the fact that the end of Cold War hardly had immediate effects to existing situation and neither was the so called "new world order." To Maluleke, the efficacy of liberation and inculturation theologies could hardly be exterminated because problems of poverty, wars, dictatorships, *etc.*, continued to exist despite the end of the Cold War and the emergence of the New World Order. Therefore, trying to underrate the fundamental effects of pioneering theologies and their effects against residue problems of Africa, according to Maluleke, hardly did justice to the legacy of those theologies.

Ninth, Maluleke further criticizes the reconstruction theology of having no new contribution to what was going on in previous African theologies. He sees that most of what is currently claimed by the reconstruction theology was what the previous theologies of the Third World have been doing. Maluleke poses his criticism: "the proposal for some theology of reconstruction is not new in the Third World. Most Third World theologies, in so far as they have been local initiatives aimed at local renewal, have been kinds of theologies of reconstruction. Africans and churches north of the Limpopo have for a long time been engaged in theologies of reconstruction of one sort or another [. . .]."[78]

Despite the above criticisms, reconstruction theology has enormous contributions to the development of African societies after the end of the Cold War to the present. Some of these contributions are worth-mentioning there: First, corrupt rulers have been challenged by voices of advocates of this theology. By doing that reconstruction theology has played the role of being a 'prophetic theology of reconstruction', *i.e.*, being a voice for the voiceless majority within African societies. Second, it has encouraged African states to move towards economic reforms. It has done that by suggesting some strategies to follow that properly suite the contexts where such states find themselves. Third, it has been a great advocate for the cancellation of debts which most African states were heavily burdened by international monetary organs while promoting mechanisms for the creation of jobs and production of various materials in increase economy in the African states. Fourth, its relevance for peacemaking, restoration of justice and the rehabilitation and protection of environments in this globalized world

---

77. Maluleke, "Half a Century of African Christian Theologies," 107.
78. Maluleke, "The Proposal for a Reconstruction Theology," 255–256.

can hardly be underestimated. In this context, where the pollution of environment due to technological advancements the need for advocates to sustain God's creation is an important aspect. Reconstruction theology has just covered that overarching gap. Therefore, the main task of reconstruction theology throughout its life has been, and continues to be ensuring that people experience the presence and activity of the Trinitarian God in their daily situations. The life and works of the earthly Jesus as maker of wonders, the servant who suffers for his people, the teacher of truth that makes people free, the preacher of the gospel of the imminent Kingdom of God stands as the model through which this theology follows while using fortitude, humble service to people, justice, prudence, creativity, love and concern, hard working, steadfast faith in Jesus, solidarity among people and societies, and hope for the bright future as building blocks to making the theological articulation effective and valuable to African societies in their current contextual issues.

CONCLUSION

Following the above criticisms of the emerging proposal for the theology of reconstruction, what have the holders of the liberation paradigm and African Theology done in response to the post-apartheid and post-cold-war situation? Solomons argues: "So while the proponents of Black theology have expressed dismay over the proposal for reconstruction, it appears that they themselves have not succeeded in articulating a theological framework following the dismantling of apartheid."[79] The question is this: should Black theology retire because its agenda (criticism of racism and classism) is over after the dawn of democracy in South Africa, the fall of the Berlin Wall in German and the end of the Cold War? Another question is should the theology of inculturation retire because of the emergency of the theology of reconstruction? We agree with Loba-Mkole in regard to the nature and role of the three theologies: Liberation Theology, Inculturation Theology and Reconstruction Theology. Loba Mkole states:

> However, it seems more constructive to consider inculturation, liberation, and reconstruction as particular efforts of articulating contextual theology in Africa. Each of them and even all of them together, constitute an unfinished task to the extent that none of them can claim to offer alone the exhaustive and final approach to African reality. Furthermore, all three aim at the same ultimate goal, namely, the betterment of spiritual and

79. Solomons, "Liberation or Reconstruction," 43.

social life in Africa. Therefore, it is not surprising to find many aspects of their agenda and expressions overlapping.[80]

The overlap in aspect between liberation and reconstruction theologies suggest that doing theology depends greatly on context, that there is a context requiring liberation and a context requiring reconstruction theologies. However, as it has been argued in the previous section, reconstruction theology calls greater attention to the context of the twenty-first century than that of liberation, without neglecting the need for liberation from the current oppressing issues. Its focus on advocacy for human rights, the equal participation of African people in making laws to guide their societies and in building their communities is one of the main aspects that make reconstruction theology a theology of the twenty-first century church in Africa. In focusing on the mentioned issues, reconstruction theology becomes a theology that promotes peace in Africa where there is violence, justice where there is unjust and oppressive structures, dialogue where there is confrontation, hope where people have abandoned hope, love where there is hatred, a spirit of forgiveness where there is continuing mistreatment, and reconciliation where there is misunderstanding, issues which have been essential for African societies after the Cold War and the end of colonialism to foster a reconciled diversity.

---

80. Loba-Mkole, "Bible Translation," 29.

References

Abioje, P.O. "Critical Prophecy and Political Leadership in Biblical, African and Islamic Worldviews." *Koers* 75:4 (2010) 787–810.

Achebe, Chinua. *Things Fall Apart*. Anchor Books Edition. New York, NY: Anchor Books, 1994.

Adamo, David T. *Reading and Interpreting the Bible in African Indigenous Churches*. Eugene Oregon: Wipf and Stock, 2011.

———. *Explorations in African Biblical Studies*. Edo State, Benin City, Nigeria: Justice Jeco, 2005.

———. "The Use of Psalms in African Indigenous Churches in Nigeria." In *The Bible in Africa: Transactions, Trajectories and Trends*, edited by West Gerald O. & Dube, Musa W., 336–349. Leiden: Brill, 2000.

Agumba, Winfrida Milly. "The Effect of Alcohol and Drug Abuse on Work Performance of Employees in Selected Star rated Hotels at the Kenyan Coast." MSc. Thesis, Kenyatta University, 2011.

Arbuckle, Gerald A. *Culture, Inculturation and Theologians*. Collegeville, Minnesota: Liturgical, 2010.

Afan, Mawuto R. "Sidbe Sempore: Spiritual Itinerary of an African Theologian." In *African Theology: The Contribution of the Pioneers*, edited by Benezet Bujo and Ilunga Juvenal Muya, 73–94. Nairobi: Paulines Publications Africa, 2002.

Akao, John O. "The Task of African Theology—Problems and Suggestions." *Scriptura* 81 (2002) 341–343.

Akoko, R.M. *"Ask and you will be given": Pentecostalism and the Economic Crisis in Cameroon*. Leiden: African Studies, 2007.

American Psychological Association. "Answers to Your Questions for a Better Understanding of Sexual Orientation and Homosexuality." At http://www.apa.org/topics/sexuality/sorientation.pdf.

Ankrah, Kodwo Esuman. "The Church and National Development in Africa: Humanization, Morality, Justice, Threat to Survival." In *African Challenge: Major Issues in African Christianity*, edited by Kenneth Y. Best, 32–42. Nairobi: Transafrica, 1975.

Atuahene, Joseph Owusu. "A Comparative Study of the Prophets of African Indigenous Churches and Akan Traditional Priests: A Critical Examination of Their Training." Master of Philosophy Thesis, Kwame Nkrumah University of Science and Technology, August 2010.

Awolalu, Joseph Omosade. "What is African Traditional Religion?" *Studies in Comperative Religion* 10: 2 (1975). Online at www.studiesincomparativereligion.com [Retrieved 06 March 2019].

Azariah, M. "Doing Theology in India Today." In *Readings in Indian Christian Theology*. Volume 1, edited by R.S. Sugirtharajah and Cecil Hargreaves, 37–45. London: SPCK, 1993.

Baffel, Olehile A. "Black Theology and Black Experience in the midst of Pain and Suffering amidst Poverty." *Scriptura* 116:1 (2017) 1–14.

Balcha, Daniel Iddo. "Homosexuality in Ethiopia." Master Thesis. Lund University, 2009.

Balcomb, Tony. "Theological Education and the Relevance of African Worldviews—Shifting the Paradigm." In *Handbook of Theological Education in Africa*, edited by Isabel Apawo Phiri and Dietrich Werner, 576–588. Oxford: Regnum, 2013.

Ballard, Paul. "Can Theology be Practical?" In *Spiritual Dimensions of Pastoral Care: Practical Theology in a Multidisciplinary Context*, edited by Willows, David & Swinton, John, 27–35. London: Jessica Kingsley, 2000.

Baloyi, M.E. "The Christian View of Levirate Marriage in a Changing South Africa." *Journal of Sociology and Social Anthropology* 6:4 (2015) 483–491.

Bauman, Zygmunt. *Globalization: The Human Consequences*. Cambridge: Polity, 1998.

Bediako, Kwame. "Jesus in African Culture: A Ghanaian Perspective." In *Emerging Voices in Global Christian Theology*, edited by William A. Dyrness, 93–121. Grand Rapids, MI: Zondervan, 1994.

Benda, Richard M. "The Test of Faith: Christians and Muslims in the Rwandan Genocide." PhD Thesis, University of Manchester, 2012.

Beyer, Peter. *Religions in Global Society*. London: Routledge, 2006.

Beyers, Jaco. "What is Religion? An African Understanding." *HTS Teologiese/Theological Studies* 66:1 (2010) 1–8. Online at DOI:10.4102/hts.v66i1.341.

Berryman, Phillip E. "Latin American Liberation Theology." *Theological Studies* 34:3 (1973) 357–395.

Bevans, Stephen B. *Models of Contextual Theology*. Revised and Expanded Edition. Maryknoll, NY: Orbis Books, 2002.

———. "What has Contextual Theology to Offer the Church of the Twenty-First Century. Edited by Stephen B. Bevans and Katalina Tahaafe-Williams, 3–17. Eugene, Oregon: Pickwick Publications, 2011.

———. "Contextual Theology," 2010. Online at: https://www.eiseverywhere.com/file_uploads/ff735620c88c86884c33857af8c51fde_GS2.pdf [Retrieved 04 November 2017].

———. *Essays in Contextual Theology*. Leiden: Brill, 2018.

Biri, Kudzai & Togarasei, Lovemore. "'. . .but the One Who Prophesies, Builds the Church': Nation Building and Transformation Discourse as true prophecy: The Case of Zimbabwean Pentecostal Women." In *Prophets, Profits and the Bible in Zimbabwe:Festschrift for Aynos Masotcha Moyo*, Bible in Africa Studies, Vol.12, edited by Ezra Chitando, MasiiwaRagies Gunda and Joachim Kügler, 79–94. Bamberg: University of Bamberg Press, 2013.

Bishau, David. "The Prosperity Gospel: An Investigation into Its Pros and Cons with Examples drawn from Zimbabwe." *International Open & Distance Learning Journal* 1:1 (2013) 65–75.

Bongmba, Elias Kifon. "Homosexuality, *Ubuntu*, and Otherness in the African Church." *Journal of Religion and Violence* 4:1 (2016) 15–37.

Bowers, Paul. "African Theology: Its History, Dynamics, Scope and Future." *Africa Journal of Evangelical Theology* 21:2 (2002) 109–126.

Bowler, Kate. "Blessed: A History of the American Prosperity Gospel." The Faith Angle Forum, 2017. Online at https://faithangle.org/wp-content/uploads/Blessed-A-History-of-the-American-Prosperity-Gospel-Dr.-Kate-Bowler-1.pdf [Retrieved 01 July 2018.

Budden, Chris. "The Necessity of Second People's Theology in Australia." In *Contextual Theology for the Twenty-First Century*, edited by Stephen B. Bevans and Katalina Tahaafe-Williams, 55–68. Eugene, OR: Pickwick, 2011.

Bujo, Benezet. "Vincent Mulago: An Enthusiast of African Theology." In *African Theology: The Contribution of the Pioneers*, edited by Benezet Bujo and Ilunga Juvenal Muya, 13–38. Nairobi: Paulines, 2002.

———. *African Christian Morality at the Age of Inculturation*. Nairobi: St Paul Publication—Africa, 1990.

Buthelezi, Manas. "Reconciliation and Liberation in Southern Africa." In *African Challenge: Major Issues in African Christianity*, edited by Kenneth Y. Best, 44–49. Nairobi: Transafrica, 1975.

Chako, Mani. "The One and the Many: Emerging Christology in an Indian Context" in *Discovering Jesus in Our Place*. Edited by Sturla J. Stalsett, 45–56. Kashmire, Delhi: ISPCK, 2003.

Chepkwony, Adam, K. Arap. "African Religion, the Root Paradigm for Inculturation Theology: Prospects for the 21st Century." In *Challenges and Prospects of the Church in Africa: Theological Reflections of the 21st Century*, edited by Nahashon W. Ndung'u and Philomena N. Mwaura, 30–53. Nairobi: Paulines, 2005.

Charlin, Andrew J. *Public and Private Families: An Introduction*. New York, NY: McGraw-Hill, 2008.

Cheyeka, Austin M. "Zambia, a 'Christian Nation' in Post Movement for Multiparty Democracy (MMD) Era, 2011—2016." *International Journal of Humanities and Social Sciences* 6:7 (2016) 159–172.

Chimhanda, F.H. "Black Theology of South Africa and the Liberation Paradigm." *Scriptura* 105 (2010): 434–445.

Chimuka, Tarisayi. "Reflections on the Morality of Some Prophetic Actsin Zimbabwe's Pentecostal Movements." In *Prophets, Profits and the Bible in Zimbabwe:Festschrift for Aynos Masotcha Moyo*, Bible in Africa Studies, Vol.12, edited by Ezra Chitando, Masiiwa Ragies Gunda and Joachim Kügler, 15–27. Bamberg: University of Bamberg Press, 2013.

Chinkwo, Renee Neh. "Poverty, Prosperity and Faith: An Analysis of the Prosperity Gospel in the Neo-Pentecostal Church Winners Chapel International in Bamenda, Cameroon." M.A. Thesis, Norwegian School of Theology, Oslo Norway, 2017.

Chipenda, Jose B. "Theology of Liberation." In *African Challenge: Major Issues in African Christianity*, edited by Kenneth Y. Best, 50–55. Nairobi: Transafrica, 1975.

Chirongoma, Sophie. "Women's and Children's Rights in the Time of HIV and AIDS in Zimbabwe: An Analysis of Gender Inequalities and Its Impact on People's Health." *Journal of Theology for Southern Africa* 2 (126) 48–65.

Chisale, Sinenhlanhla Sithulisiwe. "Patriarchy and Resistance: A Feminist Symbolic Interactionist Perspective of Highly Educated Married Black Women." Master's thesis, University of South Africa, 2017.

Chitando, Ezra. *Troubled but not Destroyed: African Theology in Dialogue with HIV and AIDS*. EHAIA Series. Geneva: WCC, 2009.

———. "Prophets, Profits and Protest: Prosperity Theology and Zimbabwean Gospel Music." In *Prophets, Profits and the Bible in Zimbabwe:Festschrift for Aynos Masotcha Moyo*, Bible in Africa Studies, Vol.12, edited by Ezra Chitando, Masiiwa Ragies Gunda and Joachim Kügler, 95–112. Bamberg: University of Bamberg Press, 2013.

Ezra Chitando, Ezra & Mateveke, Pauline. "Shifting Perceptions: African Initiated Church Groups and Gospel Music in Zimbabwe." In *Multiplying in the Spirit: African Initiated Churches in Zimbabwe*, Bible in Africa Studies, Vol.15, edited by Ezra Chitando, Masiiwa Ragies Gunda and Joachim Kügler, 129–144. Bamberg: University of Bamberg Press, 2014.

Christman, Amy. "Consumerism and Christianity: An Analysis and Response from a Christian Perspective." Master Thesis, Malone University, 2015.

Chukwu, Cletus N. "Alcoholism in Africa: A Challenge to the Church and Society." In *Urban Ministry in Africa: Theological Reflections for the Twenty First Century*, 117–132. Nairobi: Paulines, 2010.

Chung, Youjin. "Munster and Minjung: Re-reading the Anabaptist Munster Kingdom from a Perspective of Korean Minjung (Common People) Theology." PhD Dissertation, University of Stellenbosch South Africa, March 2018.

Cole, Philip. "Church and Same-Sex Marriage." *Daily Dispatch*. 18 March, 2011.

Colie, Cece. "Jesus as Healer." In *Faces for Jesus in Africa*, edited by Shreiter, Robert, 128–150. Faith and Culture Series. Maryknoll, NY: Orbis, 1991.

Cone, James H. "Black Theology in American Religion." *Journal of the American Academy of Religion* 53:4 (1985) 755–771.

Cook, Michael L. "The African Experience of Jesus." *Theological Studies* 70 (2009) 668–692.

Cook, Christopher C.H. *Alcohol, Addiction and Christian Ethics*. New York, NY: Cambridge University Press, 2006.

Copeland, Kenneth *The Laws of Prosperity*. Fort Worth, Texas: Kenneth Copeland, 1974.

Cox, Richard. "Why Rangi Christians continue to Practice African Traditional Religion." *GIALens* 3 (2008) 1–11. http://www.gial.edu/GIALens/issues.htm [Retrieved 02 December, 2018].

Court, Anthony. "The Christian Churches, the State, and Genocide in Rwanda." *Missionalia* 44:1 (2016) 50–67.

Crecencio, Sadje Hadje. "Grassroots Theology in the Philipines as a Third Way beyond Pentecostal and Liberation Theologies." *Quest: Studies on Religion and Culture in Asia* 3 (2018) 1–14.

Cresswell, T. "Place." 2009. Online at https://booksite.elsevier.com/brochures/hugy/SampleContent/Place.pdf [Retrieved 25 May 2019].

Crossan, J.D. *The Historical Jesus: The Life of a Mediteranian Jewish Peasant*. San Francisco, CA: Harper Collins, 1992.

Currens, Gerald E. "A Policy of Baptizing Polygynists Evaluated." *Africa Theological Journal* 2 (1969) 71–83.

Daly, Mary. "The Looking Glass Society." In *Feminist Theology: A Reader*, edited by Loades, Ann, 189–194. Louisville, KY: Westminster/John Knox, 1990.

Dames, Gordon E. "The Dilemma of 21st Century Pastoral Ministry: Ministering to Families and Communities faced with Socio-Economic Pathologies." *HTS*

Teologiese Studies/Theological Studies 66:2 (2010), Art. #817, 7 pages. DOI: 10.4102/hts.v66i2.817.

Daneel, M.L. "Holistic African Theology—Enacted in Rural Zimbabwe." *NEWSLETTER: Centre for Global Christianity and Mission*, September—October 2007. Bostin University School of Theology.

De Haan, Willem. "Violence as an Essentially Contested Concept." In *Violence in Europe: Historical and Contemporary Perspectives*, edited by S. Boby-Gendrot and P. Spierenburg, 27–40. Springer, 2008.

De la Torre, Miguel A. *Reading the Bible from the Margins*. Maryknoll, NY: Orbis Books, 2002.

Diara, Benjamin C.D. and Christian, Nche George. "Theology of Climate Change Mitigation and Adaptation: The Place of the Church." *Academic Journal of Interdisciplinary Studies* 2:13 (2013) 85–91.

Diaz, Miller Hernandez. "African Traditional Religion: A Religious Drama." *Journal of Philosophy, Culture and Religion* 38 (2018) 53–55.

Dickson, Kwesi A. "Towards a Theologia Africana." In *New Testament Christianity for Africa and the World: Essays in Honour of Harry Sawyerr*, edited by Mark E. Glasswell and Edward W. Fashole-Luke, 198–208. London: SPCK, 1974.

Dietrich, Stephanie. "'For Thus says the Lord': Prophetic Diakonia as Advocacy and Fight for Justice." In *Evangelism and Diakonia in Context*, Regnum Edinburgh Centenary Series, Vol. 32, edited by Rose Dowsett, Isabel Phiri, Doug Birdsall, Dawit Olika Terfassa, Hwa Yung and Knud Jørgensen, 153–165. Oxford: Regnum, 2015.

Donkor, Rose. "Criteria for Developing a Relevant Contextual Theology." *Journal of Applied Thought* 4:3 (2015) 11–20.

Dreyer, Yolanda. "Women's Spirituality and Feminist Theology: A Hermeneutic of Suspicion Applied to 'Patriarchal Marriage'" *HTS Teologiese Studies/Theological Studies* 67(3), Art. #1104, 5 pages. http://dx.doi.org/10.4102/hts. v67i3.1104.

Duncan, G.A. "A Place in the Sun? The Role of the Church in Moral Renewal and Social Transformation." *Verbum et Ecclesia* 23:2 (2002): 333–342.

Dyrness, William A. *Emerging Voices in Global Christian Theology*. Grand Rapids, MI: Zondervan, 1994.

Edet, Rosemary N. "Christianity and African Women's Rituals." In *The Will to Arise: Women, Tradition, and the Church in Africa*, edited by Mercy Amba Oduyoye and Musimbi R. A. Kanyoro, 25–29. Maryknoll, NY: Orbis, 1992.

Ehioghae, Efe M. and Olanrewaju, Joseph A. "A Theological Evaluation of the Utopian Image of the Prosperity Gospel and the African Dilemma." *IOSR Journal of Humanities and Social Science* 20:8 (2015): 69–75.

Eide, Oyvind M., Engedal, Leif Gunnar, Kimilike, Lechion Peter and Ndossi, Emeline. *Restoring Life in Christ. Pastoral Care and Domestic Violence. African Experiences*. Usa River, Arusha: Makumira University College, 2009.

ELCT, "Dodoma Statement," Position Statement of the Evangelical Lutheran Church in Tanzania (ELCT) Regarding Same-Sex Marriage January 2010. Online at http://www.elct.org/news/2010.04.004.html [Retrieved 31 July 2018].

Engle, Richard W. "Contextualization in Mission: A Biblical and Theological Appraisal." *Grace Theological Journal* 4:1 (1983) 85–107.

Escobar, Samuel. "The Search for a Missiological Christology in Latin America" In *Emerging Voices in Global Christian Theology*, edited by William A. Dyrness, 199–227. Grand Rapids, MI: Zondervan, 1994.

Ezeugu, Ernest M. "The African Origin of Jesus: An Afrocentric Reading of Matthew's Infancy Narrative (Matthew 1–2)." In *Postcolonial Perspectives in African Biblical Interpretations*, edited by Musa W. Dube, Andrew M. Mbuvi and Dora Mbuwayesango, 259–282. Atlanta, GA: The Society of Biblical Literature, 2013.

Falaye, Tiwatola Abidemi. "The Relevance of African Independence Churches to the Yoruba of South Western Part of Nigeria." *Journal of Philosophy, Culture and Religion* 13 (2015): 10–16.

Farisani, Elelwani B. "The Ideologically Biased Use of Ezra-Nehemiah in a Quest for an African Theology of Reconstruction." In *Postcolonial Perspectives in African Biblical Interpretations*, 331–347. Edited by Musa W. Dube, Andrew M. Mbuvi, and Dora R. Mbuwayesango. Atlanta: Society of Biblical Literature, 2012.

———. "Black Biblical Hermeneutics and Ideologically aware Reading of Texts." *Scriptura* 105 (2010) 507–518.

———. "The Use of Ezra-Nehemia in a Quest for a Theology of Renewal, Transformation and Reconstruction in the (South) African Context." PhD Thesis, University of Natal, 2002.

———. "The Ideologically Biased Use of Ezra-Nehemiah in a Quest for an African Theology of Reconstruction." *Old Testament Essays* 15:3 (2002) 628–646.

Ferreira-Borges, Carina, Parry, Charles D.H., & Babor, Thomas F. "Harmful Use of Alcohol: A Shadow Over Sab-Saharan Africa in Need of Workable Solutions." *International Journal of Environmental Research and Public Health* 14: 346 (2017) 1–12.

Fernandez, Eleazar Singson. "Towards a Theology of Struggle in a Philipine Context." PhD in Religion Thesis. Vanderbilt University, Nashville, Tennessee, 1993.

Ferdinando, Keith, "Christian Identity in the African Context: Reflections on Kwame Bediako's Theology and Identity." *Journal of the Evangelical Theological Society* 50:1 (2007) 121–143.

Fiorenza, Elisabeth Schussler. "Feminist Theology as a Critical Theology of Liberation." *Theological Studies* 36: 4 (1975) 605–626.

Fretheim, Terence E. "God and Violence in the Old Testament." *Word and World* 24: 1 (2004) 18–28.

Fuellenbach, John. *The Kingdom of God: The Message of Jesus Today*. Maryknoll, NY: Orbis, 1995.

Fumbo, Clement Donald, "The Moravian Church Response to Domestic Abuses among Couples in Tanzania: A Case Study of Mbeya Municipality, with special Reference to (Wa-) ndali and (Wa-) nyakyusa Traditions (Comparison and Contrast)." PhD Thesis, The Open University of Tanzania, Dar es Salaam Tanzania.

Gaise, Roger. "Elochukwu Eugen Uzukwu: An Untiring African Liturgist." In *African Theology: The Contribution of the Pioneers*, edited by Benezet Bujo and Ilunga Juvenal Muya, 167–175. Nairobi: Paulines, 2002.

Gathogo, Julius Mutugi. "Liberation and Reconstruction in the Works of JNK Mugambi: A Critical Analysis in African Theology." PhD Thesis, University of KwaZulu Natal, 2007.

———. "Jesse Mugambi's Pedigree: Formative Factors." *Studia Historiae Ecclesiasticae* 32:2 (2006) 173–205).

———. Mercy Oduyoye as the Mother of African Women Theology," *Journal of Theology and Religion in Africa* 34:1 (2010) 1–18.

———. "The Challenge of Money and Wealth in some East African Pentecostal Churches." *Studia Historiae Ecclesiasticae* 37:2 (2011) 133–151.

———. "Genesis, Methodologies and Concerns of African Theology of Reconstruction." *Theologia Viatorum: Journal of Religion and Theology in Africa, South Africa*, 32:1 (2008) 23–62.

———. "Historical Developments of Christian Education in Eastern Africa–the example of Julius Krapf." In *Handbook of Theological Education in Africa*, edited by Isabel Apawo Phiri and Dietrich Werner, 28–46. Oxford: Regnum, 2013.

———. "*Kuchapa Wanaume*: A Theo-Philosophical Exploration of Men Battering from a Kenyan Perspective." *Africa Theological Journal* 34: 2 (2014) 43–66.

Gatwa, Tharcisse. "The Cross-Cultural Mission: An Agenda for Theological Education in Africa." In *Handbook of Theological Education in Africa*, edited by Isabel Apawo Phiri and Dietrich Werner, 84–99. Oxford: Regnum, 2013.

Gbotoe, Eric Zakpa Miccaric. "Commercialized Gospel: A Missiological Assessment of Prosperity Gospel." M.A. Thesis, University of Pretoria, Pretoria, 2013.

Geer, Valerie. "Truth Be Told: Leveraging *Mujerista* and Womanist Theologies for Ministry among Victims and Survivors of Sex Trafficking." *Priscilla Papers* 31:1 (2017) 24–29.

Gehman, Richard J. *African Traditional Religion in Biblical Perspective*. Kijabe: Kesho, 1989.

———. *Doing African Christian Theology: An Evangelical Perspective*. Nairobi: Evangel, 1987.

Gidley, Jennifer. "Globalization and Its Impacts on Youth." *Journal of Futures Studies* 6:1 (2001) 89–106.

Gifford, Paul. "The Bible in Africa: A Novel usage in Africa's New Churches." *Bulletin of School of Oriental and African Studies* 71:2 (2008) 203–2019.

Girolamo, Michael Di. "Liberation Theology: Authentic Theology and Authentic Spirituality." M.A in Theology Thesis, Concordia University, Montreal, Quebec, Canada, 2010.

Goliama, Castor Michael. "The Gospel of Prosperity in African Pentecostalism: A Theological and Pastoral Challenge to the Catholic Church—With Reference to the Archdiocese of Songea, Tanzania."Doctor of Theology Thesis, Universitat Wien, 2013.

Groody, Daniel G. "Globalizing Solidarity: Christian Anthropology and the Challenge of Human Liberation." *Theological Studies* 69 (2008) 250–268.

Goldingay, John E., LeMarquand, Grant R., Sumner, George R., and Westber, Daniel A. "Same-Sex Marriage and Anglican Theology: A View from the Traditionalists." *Anglican Theological Review* 93:1 (2011) 1–59.

Gullet, Wilma. "Practical Theology and Contemporary Social Issues." *Crucible* 8:1 : 1–12. Online at www.crucibleonline.net [Retrieved 10 June 2018]

Gunda, Masiiwa Ragies. "African 'Biblical' Christianity Understanding the 'Spirit-type' African Initiated Churches in Zimbabwe." In *Multiplying in the Spirit: African Initiated Churches in Zimbabwe*, Bible in Africa Studies, Vol.15, edited by Ezra Chitando, Masiiwa Ragies Gunda and Joachim Kügler, 147–160. Bamberg: University of Bamberg Press, 2014.

Gunda, Masiiwa Ragies & Machingura, Francis. "The 'Man of God': Understanding Biblical Influence on Contemporary Mega-Church Prophets in Zimbabwe." In *Prophets, Profits and the Bible in Zimbabwe:Festschrift for Aynos Masotcha Moyo*, Bible in Africa Studies, Vol.12, edited by Ezra Chitando, Masiiwa Ragies Gunda and Joachim Kügler, 15–27. Bamberg: University of Bamberg Press, 2013.

Gutierrez, Gustavo M. "Notes for a Theology of Liberation." *Theological Studies* 31:2 (1970) 243–261.

———. *The Power of the Poor in History*. Eugene, Oregon: Wipf and Stock, 1983.

Habib, Usman I. "A New Paradigm of Leadership Development Church of God Mission International." PhD Thesis, Cliff College, Calver, Hope Valley, Derbyshire. United Kingdom, 2014.

Hagin, Kenneth E. *The Believer's Authority*. Second Edition. Tulsa, OK: Faith Library, 1984.

Han, Y.S. & Bayers, J. "A Critical Evaluation of the Understanding of God in John S. Mbiti's Theology." *Acta Theologica* 37:2 (2017) 5—29. DOI: http://dx.doi.org/10.18820/23099089/actat.v37i2.2.

Hastings, Adrian. *A History of African Christianity 1950—1975*. London: Cambridge University Press, 1979.

Havea, Jione. "The Cons of Contextuality...Kontextuality." In *Contextual Theology for the Twenty First Centuary*, edited by Stephen B. Bevans and Katalina Taafe-Williams, 38–52. Eugene, OR: Pickwick, 2011.

Hebga, Meinrad P. "Engelbert Mveng: A Pioneer of African Theology." In *African Theology: The Contribution of the Pioneers*, edited by Benezet Bujo and Muya, Ilunga Juvenal Muya, 39–46. Nairobi: Paulines, 2002.

Hinn, Costi. *God, Greed, and the "Prosperity" Gospel: How Truth Overwhelms a Life Built on Lies*. Grand Rapids, MI: Zondervan, 2019.

Hintjens, Helen M. "Explaining the 1994 Genocide in Rwanda." *The Journal of Modern African Studies* 37:2 (1999) 241–286.

Idang, Gabriel E. "African Culture and Values." *UNISA Phronimon* 2 (2015) 97–111.

Ilomo, Farles Ipyana. *African Religion: A Basis for Interfaith Dialogue*. Dar es Salaam: Dar es Salaam University Press, 2013.

———. *A Relevant Christian Eschatology for African Context Today*. Dar es Salaam: Dar es Salaam University Press, 2013.

Inge, John, "A Christian Theology of place." Doctoral thesis, Durham University, 2001. Available at Durham E-Theses Online: http://etheses.dur.ac.uk/1235/ [Retrieved 16 May 2019].

Ilie, Anca Gabriela. "The Effects of Globalization on Young People." *Romanian Economic Journal* IX:21 (2006) 65–69.

Ilikbaev, Aleksandr. "A Great Divide on Homosexuality in the Contemporary World: How do Attitudes Change?" Master Thesis, Public Choice, University of Tampere, 2017.

Imasogie, Osadolor. *Guidelines for Christian Theology in Africa*. Theological Perspectives in Africa No.5. Achimota, Ghana: Africa Christian Press, 1993.

Imbach, S. R. "Syncretism." In *Evangelical Dictionary of Theology*, edited by Walter A. Elwell, 1062–1063. Grand Rapids, MI: Baker, 1984.

Isasi-Diaz, Ada Maria. *Mujerista Theology: A Theology for the Twenty-First Century*. Maryknoll, NY: Orbis, 1996.

Jenkins, Philip. *The Next Christendom: The Coming of Global Christianity*. Oxford: Oxford University Press, 2002.

Jenkins, Philip. "The Next Christendom: The Coming of Global Christianity." *The Religious Educator* 8:3 (2007) 113–124.

Johnson, Todd M. "Contextualization: A New-Old Idea Illustrations from the Life of an Italian Jesuit in 17th-Century India." *International Journal of Frontier Mission* 4 (1989) 9–20.
Jones, David W. "5 Errors of the Prosperity Gospel." *9Marks Journal* IX (2014). Online at https://www.9marks.org/article/journalerrors-prosperity-gospel/ [Retrieved 23 January 2020]
Jones, David W. & Woodbridge, Russell S. *Health, Wealth & Happiness: Has the Prosperity Gospel Overshadowed the Gospel of Christ?* Grand Rapids, MI: Kregel, 2011.
Jordaan, Roxanne. "The Emergence of South Black Feminist Theology in South Africa." *Journal of Black Theology in South Africa* 1:2 (1987) 42–46.
Juergensmayer, Mark. *Terror in the Mind of God: The Global Rise in Religious Violence*. Third Edition. Los Angeles, CA: University of California Press, 2003.
Kabasele, Francois. "Christ as Chief." In *Faces of Jesus in Africa*, edited by Robert Schreiter, 103–115. Faith and Culture Series. Maryknoll, NY: Orbis, 1991.
———. "Christ as Ancestor and Elder Brother." In *Faces of Jesus in Africa*, edited by Shreiter, Robert, 116–127. Faith and Culture Series. Maryknoll, NY: Orbis, 1991.
Kabinde, Stephen Asol. "The Church and Constitutional Reforms in Kenya, 1992–2002: A Retrospective-Historical Analysis." *European Scientific Journal* 14:5 (2018) 216–240.
Kahakwa, Sylvester B. "Interpretative Contextual Based Models: Getting the Gospel Heard in an African Context." *Africa Theological Journal* 34: 2 (2014) 67–93.
Kanyoro, Musimbi R.A. "Engendered Communal Theology: African Women's Contribution to Theology in the 21st Century." In *Talitha Cum! Theologies of African Women*, edited by Nyambura J. Njoroge and Musa W. Dube, 158–180. Pietermaritzberg: Cluster, 2001.
———. *Introducing Feminist Cultural Hermeneutics: An African Perspective*. Cleveland, OH: The Pilgrims, 2002.
Kasera, Basilius M. "Biblical and Theological Examination of Prosperity Theology and Its Impact among the Poor in Namibia." M.Th. Thesis, South African Theological Seminary, 2012.
Kasomo, Daniel. "The Role of Women in the Church in Africa." *International Journal of Sociology and Anthropology* 2:6 (2010) 126–139.
Kategile, Mary. "I Long for Women to be Empowered in All Spheres of Life." In *There is Something We Long for*, edited by Naegeli, Verena, Ngalula, Josee, Praetorius, Ina & Rabarijaona, Brigitte, 116–127. Kinshasa: Edition Tsenamalalaka, 2015.
Kato, Byang H. *Theological Pitfalls in Africa*. Kisumu: Evangel Publishing House, 1975.
Kee, Howard Clark. *Christian Origins in Sociological Perspective: Methods and Resources*. Philadelphia, Pennsylvania: Westminster, 1980.
Kenge, Esther Lubunga. "Towards a Theology of Peace-building in the Democratic Republic of Congo (DRC): The Contribution of Christian Women. PhD Thesis, University of KwaZulu-Natal, Pietermaritzburg, South Africa, 2015.
Keung, Yeung Kwok. "A Critical Assessment of Choan-Seng Song's effort in Constructing Contextual Theology." Master of Divinity Thesis. The Chinese University of Hong Kong, June 1995.
Kgabe, Vincentia. "Alcohol Abuse by Anglican Clergy: Challenge to Pastoral Care." PhD Thesis, University of Pretoria South Africa, 2011.

Killian, Bernadeta. "Intra-denominational Conflicts: The Maryan Faith Healing Ministry (Wanamaombi) vs the Catholic Church." In *Justice Rights and Worship: Religion and Politics in Tanzania*, edited by Mukandala, Rwekaza, Othman, Saida Yahya, and Ndumbaro, Laurian, 276–292. Dar es Salaam: Research and Education for Democracy in Tanzania (REDET), 2006.

Kim, Eunsoo. "Minjung Theology in Korea: A Critique from a Reformed Theological Perspective." *Japan Christian Review* 64 (1998) 53–65.

Kim, Yoon Ki. "Reillumination of Minjung Theology: Emerging Theologies in Ecumenical Dialogue." *Princeton Theological Review* 20:1 (2017) 35–50.

Kimilike, Lechion Peter. *Poverty in the Book of Proverbs: An African Transformational Hermeneutic of Proverbs on Poverty*. New York, NY: Peter Lang, 2008.

Knighton, Ben. "Issues of African Theology at the Turn of the Millennium." *Transformation: An International Journal of Holistic Mission Studies* 21: 3 (2004) 147–161.

Kiwovele, Yuda B.M. "Polygyny as a Problem to the Church in Africa." *Africa Theological Journal* 2 (1969) 7–26.

Koch, Bradley A. "The Prosperity Gospel and Economic Prosperity: Race, Class, Giving and Voting." PhD Dissertation, Indiana University, 2009.

———. "Who are the Prosperity Gospel Adherents?" *Journal of Ideology* 36 (2014) 1–46. Online at www.lsus.edu/journalofideology [20 December, 2019].

Kombo, James. "The Past and Presence of Christian Theology in African Universities." In *Handbook of Theological Education in Africa*, edited by Isabel Apawo Phiri and Dietrich Werner, 100–107. Oxford: Regnum, 2013.

Konchellah, Ruth Magiroi. "Effects of Alcohol Abuse on Employee Performance and Absenteeism in Kenya Ports Authority." Master of Psychology Thesis. University of Nairobi, 2016.

Koonthanam, George. "Yahweh the Defender of the *Dalits*: A Reflection on Isaiah 3: 12– 25." In *Readings in Indian Christian Theology*, edited by R. S. Sigirtharajah and Cecil Hargreaves, 229–241. London: SPCK, 1993.

Kunhiyop, Samuel Waje. "Challenges and Prospects of Teaching Theology in Africa." *Southern Baptist Journal of Theology* 15:2 (2011) 64–76.

———. *African Christian Ethics*. Grand Rapids, MI: Zondervan/Hippo Books, 2008.

Kurewa, John Wesley Zwamunondiita. "The Meaning of African Theology." *Journal of Theology for Southern Africa* 11:32 (1975) 32–42.

Kurgat, Sussy Gumo. "The Theology of Inculturation and the African church." *International Journal of Sociology and Anthropology* 1:5(2009) 90–98. Available online http://www.academicjournals.org/ijsa.

Kwateng-Yeboah, James. A Re-appraisal of the Prosperity Gospel in African Neo-Pentecostalism: The Potency of 'Multiple Modernities' Paradigm." M.A. Thesis. Queen's University, 2017.

Lanman, Christina. "Mercy Amba Ewudziwa Oduyoye: Mother of Our Stories." *Studia Historiae Ecclesiasticae* XXXIII: 1 (2007) 187–204.

Le Roux, Elisabet. "The Role of African Christian Churches in Dealing with Sexual Violence against Women: The Case of the Democratic Republic of Congo, Rwanda and Liberia." PhD Dissertation, Stellenbosch University, 2014.

Lewison, Elsie. "Pentecostal Power and the Holy Spirit of Capitalism: Re-imagining Modernity in the Charismatic Cosmology." *Symposia* 3: 1 (2011) 31–54.

Loba-Mkole, Jean-Claude. "Bible Translation and Reconstruction Hermeneutics." *Acta Patristica et Byzantina* 20 (2009) 28–44.

Longman, Timothy. "Church Politics and Genocide in Rwanda." *Journal of Religion in Tanzania* XXXI: 2 (2001) 163–186.

Louw, Daniel J. "Space and Place in the Healing of Life: Towards a Theology of Affirmation in Pastoral Care and Counseling." *Verbum et Ecclesia* 29:2 (2008) 426–445.

Low, Setha M. "Towards an Anthropological Theory of Space and Place." *Semiotica* 175–1/4 (2009) 21–37.

Machingura, Francis. "The Martyring of People over Radical Beliefs: A Critical Look at the Johane Marange Apostolic Church's Perception of Education and Health (Family Planning Methods)." In *Multiplying in the Spirit: African Initiated Churches in Zimbabwe*, Bible in Africa Studies, Vol.15, edited by Ezra Chitando, Masiiwa Ragies Gunda and Joachim Kügler, 175–198. Bamberg: University of Bamberg Press, 2014.

Maddox, Randy L. "Practical Theology: A Discipline in Search of a Definition." *Perspectives in Religious Studies* 18 (1991) 159–169.

Maddox, Gregory H. "African Theology and the Search for the Universal." In *East African Expressions of Christianity*, edited by Thomas Spear & Isaria N. Kimambo, 25—36. Dar es Salaam: Mkuki na Nyota, 1999.

Mafico, Temba L.J. "The Biblical God of the Fathers and the African Ancestors." In *The Bible in Africa: Transactions, Trajectories and Trends*, edited by Gerald O. West and Musa W. Dube, 481–489. Leiden: Brill, 2000.

Mafu, Hezekiel. "The Impact of the Bible on Traditional Rain-making Institutions in Western Zimbabwe." In *The Bible in Africa: Transactions, Trajectories and Trends*, edited by Gerald O. West and Musa W. Dube, 400–414. Leiden: Brill, 2000.

Magesa, Laurenti. "Christ the Liberator and Africa Today." In *Faces fo Jesus in Africa*, edited by Shreiter, Robert, 151–163. Faith and Culture Series. Maryknoll, NY: Orbis, 1991.

Magesa, Laurent. "Taking Culture Seriously: Recognizing the Reality of African Religion in Tanzania" in *Catholic Ethicists on HIV/AIDS Prevention*. Edited by James F. Keenan, Jon D. Fuller, Lisa Sowle Cahill and Kevin Kelly. New York & London: Continuum, 2000, 76–85.

Magezi, Vhumani and Banda Collium. "Competing with Christ? A Critical Christological Analysis of the Reliance on Pentecostal Prophets in Zimbabwe." *In die Skriflig* 51:2 (2017), a2273. https:// doi.org/10.4102/ids.v51i2.2273.

Magezi, Vhumani. & Manzanga, Peter. "Prosperity and Health Ministry as a Coping Mechanism in the Poverty and Suffering Context of Zimbabwe: A Pastoral Evaluation and Response." *In die Skriflig* 50:1 (2016), a2076. https://doi.org/10.4102/ids. v50i1.207.

Malik, Alexander John. "Religion and Violence." In *APJN Community Transformation: Violence and the Church's Response*. Anglican Peace and Justice Network in Rwanda and Burundi 25 September—3 October 2007.

Maluleke, Tinyiko Sam. "Half a Century of African Christian Theologies. Elements of the Emerging Agenda for the 21st Century" in *The Church and Reconstruction of Africa: Theological Considerations*, edited by J.N.K Mugambi. Nairobi: All Africa Conferences of Churches, 1997.

———. "The Proposal for a Reconstruction Theology: A Critical Appraisal." *Missionalia* 22:2 (1994) 245–258.

Mananzan, Mary John. "Feminist Theology in Asia: A Ten Years' Overview." *Feminist Theology* 4:10 (1995) 21–32. https://doi.org/10.1177/096673509500001003.

Mangena, Fainos & Mhizha, Samson. "The Rise of White Collar Prophecy in Zimbabwe: A Psycho-Ethical Statement." In *Prophets, Profits and the Bible in Zimbabwe:Festschrift for Aynos Masotcha Moyo*, Bible in Africa Studies, Vol.12, edited by Ezra Chitando, Masiiwa Ragies Gunda and Joachim Kügler, 133–152. Bamberg: University of Bamberg Press, 2013.

Marongwe, Ngonidzashe & Maposa, Richard S. "PHDS, Gospreneurship, Globalization and the Pentecostal 'New Wave' in Zimbabwe." *Afro-Asian Journal of Social Sciences* 6:1 (2015) 1–22. Online at http://www.onlineresearchjournals.com/aajoss/art/171.pdf [Rerieved 22   January 2020].

Martey, Emmanuel. "Theology and Liberation: The African Agenda," presented at the World Forum on Theology and Liberation, Porto Alegre, January, 2004.

Masango, Maake. "Homosexuality: A Challenge to Churches." *HTS Teologies Studies/ Theological Studies* 58:3 (2002) 956–972.

Maseno, Loreen and Mligo, Elia Shabani. *Women within Religions: Patriarchy, Feminism and the Role of Women in Selected World Religions*. Eugene, OR: Wipf and Stock, 2020.

Masenya (ngwan'a mpahlele), Madipoane and Ramantswana, H. "Anything New under the Sun of African Biblical Hermeneutics in South African Old Testament Scholarship? Incarnation, Death and Resurrection of the Word in Africa." *Verbum et Ecclesia* 36:1 (2015), Art. #1353, 12 pages. http://dx.doi.org/10.4102/ve.v36i1.1353 [Retrieved 12 September 2018].

Mashau, Thinandavha D. and Kgatle, Mookgo S. "Prosperity Gospel and the Culture of Greed in Post-colonial Africa: Constructing an Alternative African Christian Theology of Ubuntu." *Verbum et Ecclesia* 40:1 (2019), a1901. https://doi.org/10.4102/ve.v40i1.1901.

Masondo, Sibusiso. "The History of African Indigenous Churches in Scholarship." *Journal for the Study of Religion* 18:2 (2005) 89–103.

Matsoso, Irene Martina Litseoane. "Luke and the Marginalized: An African Ferminist's Perspective on Three Lukan Parables (Luke 10: 25–37; 15: 8–10; 18: 1–8)." M.A. Thesis, Social Science, University of Cape Town South Africa, 1992.

Mbiti, John S. *African Traditional Religions and Philosophy*. London: Heinemann, 1969.

———. "The Biblical Basis for Present Trends in African Theology." In *African Theology en Route: Papers from the Pan African Conference of Third World Theologians (December 17–23, 1977, Accra, Ghana)*, edited by Kofi Appiah-Kubi and SergioTorres, 83–94. New York, NY: Orbis, 1979.

———. "'A Person who Eats Alone Dies Alone': Death as a Point of Dialogue Between African Religion and Christianity." Crises of Life in African Religion and Christianity. LWF Studies No. 02, edited by Hance A.O. Mwakabana, 83–106. Geneva: Lutheran World Federation, 2002.

———. *Introduction to African Religion*. Second Edition. Long Grove, IL: Waveland, 1975.

———. "Christianity and Traditional Religions in Africa." *International Review of Mission* 59:236 (1970) 430–440.

Mbuvi, Andrew. "African Biblical Studies: An Introduction to an Emerging Discipline." *Currents in Biblical Research* 15:2 (2019) 149–178.

McFague, Sallie. *Models of God: Theology for an Ecological Nuclear Age*. Philadelphia: Fortress Press, 1987.

McTavish, Ron. "Pentecostal Profits: The Prosperity Gospel in the Global South." M.A. Thesis, University of Lethbridge, 2014.

Meiring, Arno. "As Below, so Above: A Perspective on African Theology." *HTS Teologies Studies/Theological Studies* 63:2 (2007) 733–750.

Mesters, Carlos. "The Use of the Bible in Christian Communities of the Common People." In *The Bible and Liberation: Political and Social Hermeneutics*, edited by Walter Brueggeman and others, 119–133. Maryknoll, NY: Orbis, 1983.

Meyer, Birgit. "Christianity in Africa: From AfricanIndependent to Pentecostal-Charismatic Churches." *Annual Review of Anthropology* 33 (2004) 447–474.

Milemba, Elina Kanaiza. "The Influence of Prosperity Gospel on the Well-being of the Youth: A Case Study of Contemporary Christian Churches, Nairobi County." M.A. (Sociology) Thesis, University of Nairobi, 2015.

Mkumbo, Alex. "Homosexuality: Perspectives from the Lutheran Church of Tanzania." In *Ecumenical Case Studies on Homosexuality and the Church*, edited by Werner Kahl, 14–28. Hamburg: Academy of Mission at the University of Hamburg, 2013.

Mligo, Elia Shabani. *Jesus and the Stigmatized: Reading the gospel of John in a Context of HIV/AIDS-Related Stigmatization in Tanzania*. Eugene, OR: Pickwick, 2011.

———. *Doing Effective Fieldwork: A Textbook for Students of Qualitative Research in Higher-Learning Institutions*. Eugene, OR: Wipf and Stock/Resource, 2013.

———. *Elements of African Traditional Religion: A Textbook for Students of Comparative Religion*. Eugene, OR: Wipf and Stock/Resource, 2013.

Moe, David Thang. "A Critical Reading of C.S. Song's Asian Third-eye Liberation Theology for a Myanmar Intercontextual Liberation Theology of *Pyithu-dukkha*." *Interreligious Studies and Intercultural Theology* 2:2 (2018) 193–215.

Mokhoathi, Joel. "From Contextual Theology to African Christianity: The Consideration of Adiaphora from a South African Perspective." *Religions* 8 (2017) 1–14. Doi: 10.3390/rel8120266. Online at http://creativecommons.org/licenses/by/4.0/ [Retrieved 16 September 2018].

Mokgethi Motlhabi (ed.). *Essays on Black Theology*. Johannesburg: University Christian Movement, 1972.

Molobi, Victor Masilo. "The Past and Future of Black Theology in South Africa: In Discussion with Maimela." *Studia Historiae Ecclesiasticae* 36 (2010): 35–48.

Molobi, V.S. "African, Black and AIC Theologies as the main Historical Sources of Construct for an African Church." *Scriptura* 105 (2010) 494–506.

Manyonganise, Molly. "African Independent Churches: The Dynamics of their Political Participation in Zimbabwe." In *Multiplying in the Spirit: African Initiated Churches in Zimbabwe*, Bible in Africa Studies, Vol.15, edited by Ezra Chitando, Masiiwa Ragies Gunda and Joachim Kügler, 161–174. Bamberg: University of Bamberg Press, 2014.

Moore, Basil (ed.). *Black Theology: The South African Voice*. London: Hurst, 1973.

Mosala, Itumeleng J. and Tlhagale, Buti (eds.). *The Unquestionable Right to be Free: Black Theology from South Africa*. Maryknoll, NY: Orbis, 1986.

Morekwa, Othusitse. "Doing Theology in the Post Liberation Era of Southern Africa." PhD Thesis, University of South Africa, Pretoria South Africa, 2015.

Morgan, Oliver J. "Practical Theology, Alcohol Abuse and Alcoholism: Methodological and Biblical Considerations." *Journal of Ministry in Addiction and Recovery* 5:2 (1998) 33–64.

Mosala, Itumeleng, "Biblical Hermeneutics and Black Theology in South Africa." PhD Thesis, University of Cape Town, South Africa, February 1987.

Maurice, Ogolla. "Levirate Unions in both the Bible and African Cultures: Convergence and Divergence." *International Journal of Humanities and Social Science* 4:10 (2014) 287—292.

Moxnes, Halvor. *Putting Jesus in His Place: A Radical Vision of Household and Kingdom.* Louisville, KY: Westminster/John Knox, 2003.

Mpanga, Denis. *Towards a Chatholic Theology in the African Context: Insights and Reservations from Karl Adam's Theology.* Zurich: LIT Verlag, 2017.

Mugambi, J.N.K. *Christianity and African Culture.* Nairobi: Acton, 2002.

———. *African Christian Theology: An Introduction.* Nairobi: East African Educational, 1989.

———. "Christianity and the African Cultural Heritage." In *Christianity and African Culture*, edited by Jesse. N. K. Mugambi, 516–542. Nairobi: Acton, 2002.

———. *From Liberation to Reconstruction: African Christian Theology after the Cold War.* Nairobi: East African Educational, 1995.

Muneja, Mussa Simon. *HIV/AIDS and the Bible in Tanzania: A Contextual Re-reading of 2 Samuel 13: 1—14:33.* Bamberg: University of Bamberg., 2012.

Mussana, Paddy. "Interpretation, Message and Challenge of the Bible in Africa." In *African Theology comes of Age,* edited by Laurent Magesa, 84–96. Nairobi: Paulines, 2010.

Mutungi, Julia Gabriel. "The Killing of Albinos in the Sukumaland, Tanzania: A Challenge to the Church's Mission in the Evangelical Lutheran Church in Tanzania-East of Lake Victoria Diocese." Master Thesis, School of Mission and Theology, Stavanger, 2013.

Mwenisongole, Tuntufye Anangisye and Mligo, Elia Shabani. *Pastoral Counseling for Orphans and Vulnerable Children: A Narrative Approach.* Eugene, OR: Wipf and Stock/Resource, 2018.

Mwihia, Catherine Nyambura. "A Theological Analysis of African Proverbs about Women: With Reference to Proverbs from Gikuyu People of Central Kenya." Master Thesis, University of Kwa-Zulu Natal, 2005.

Mveng, Engelbert. "Christianity and the Religious Culture of Africa." In *African Challenge: Major Issues in African Christianity*, edited by Kenneth Y. Best, 1–24. Nairobi: Transafrica, 1975.

Muya, Ilunga Juvenal. "Benezet Bujo: The Awakening of a Systematic and Authentically African Thought." In *African Theology: The Contribution of the Pioneers,* edited by Benezet Bujo and Ilunga Juvenal Muya, 107–149. Nairobi: Paulines, 2002.

Mydze, Theresa I. & Rwomire, Apollo. "Alcoholism in Africa during the Late Twentieth Century: A Socio-Cultural Perspective." *International Journal of Business and Social Science* 5:2 (2014) 1–9. Online at http://ijbssnet.com/journals/Vol_5_No_2_February_2014/1.pdf [Retrieved 12 January 2020].

Nasimiyu-Wasike, Anne. "Christianity and the African Rituals of Birth and Naming." In *The Will to Arise: Women, Tradition, and the Church in Africa,* edited by Mercy Amba Oduyoye and Musimbi R.A. Kanyoro, 40–53. Maryknoll, NY: Orbis, 1992.

———. "Is Mutuality Possible? An African Response." *Missiology* 29:1 (2001) 45–53.

Ndung'u, Nahashon W. "The Role of the Bible in the Rise of African Instituted Churches: The Case of the Akurinu Churches in Kenya." In *The Bible in Africa: Transactions, Trajectories and Trends*, edited by Gerald O. West & Musa W. Dube, 236–247. Leiden: Brill, 2000.

Neal, Joanne. "Christian Implications of Globalization." Monograph, Graduate Theological Foundation. 2010. Online at https://www.gtfeducation.org/images/dynamic/file/Globalization-Monograph1.pdf [Retrieved 07 July 2018].

Neipp, Daryl A. "When Homosexuality comes to Church." Doctor of Ministry Thesis. Temple Baptist Seminary, Avon, Ohio, 2013.

Ngong, David T. "Theology as the Construction of Piety: A Critique of the Theology of Inculturation and the Pentecostalization of African Christianity." *Journal of Pentecostal Theology* 21 (2012) 344–362.

Nguruwe, Philo Joseph. "Called to Harmony: Christianity and Islam in Tanzania at Crossroads." Master Thesis, Boston College School of Theology and Ministry, 2011.

Niemandt, Nelus. "The Prosperity Gospel, the decolonisation of Theology, and the Abduction of Missionary Imagination." *Missionalia* 45: 3 (2017) 203–219.

Nikuze, Donatien. "The Genocide against the Tutsi in Rwanda: Origin, Causes Implementation, Consequences and the Post-Genocide Era." *International Journal of Development and Sustainability* 3:5 (2014) 1086–1098.

Nkoko, Rabson Ntambala. "Accounting for the 1990—2013 Christian-Muslim Conflicts in Tanzania." PhD Thesis. Open University of Tanzania, 2017.

Ntakarutimana, Emmanuel. "MSGR Tharcisse Tshibangu: Champion of 'African-Coloured' Theology." In *African Theology: The Contribution of the Pioneers*, edited by Benezet Bujo and Ilunga Juvenal Muya, 47–63. Nairobi: Paulines, 2002.

———. "Alphonse Ngindu Mushete: The Problem of Religious Knowledge." In *African Theology: The Contribution of the Pioneers*, edited by Benezet Bujo and Ilunga Juvenal Muya, 64–72. Nairobi: Paulines, 2002.

Nunes, C & Deventer, H.J.M. "Feminist Interpretation in the Context of Reformational Theology: A Consideration." *In die Skriflig* 43:4 (2009) 737–760.

Nwadialor, Kanayo Louis. "Pentecostal Hermeneutics and the Commercialization of the Gospel Message in Nigeria." *International Journal of Research* 2:2 (2015) 1270–1287.

Nwankwo, Lawrence Nchekwube. "African Christianity and the Challenge of Prosperity Gospel." *Ministerium—A Journal of Contextual Theology* 5 (2019) 11–27.

Nyaundi, Nehemia. The Phenomenon of Violence in Eastern Africa. *African Theology comes of Age: Revisiting 20 Years of the Theology of the Ecumenical Symposium of Eastern Africa Theologians (ESEAT)*, edited by Laurenti Magesa, 123–131. Nairobi: Paulines, 2010.

Nyiawung, Mbengu D. "The Prophetic Witness of the Church as an Appropriate Mode of Public Discourse in African Societies." *HTS Teologiese Studies/Theological Studies* 66:1 (2010), Art. #791, 8 pages. DOI: 10.4102/hts.v66i1.791.

Obaga, Margaret Kemunto. "Understanding the Nature and Impact of Alcoholism." MTh Thesis, Luther Seminary, St. Paul Minnesota, 2008.

Oduyoye, Mercy Amba. *Hearing and Knowing: Theological Reflections on Christianity in Africa*. Nairobi: Acton, 2000.

———. "Women and Ritual in Africa." In *The Will to Arise: Women, Tradition, and the Church in Africa*, edited by Mercy Amba Oduyoye and Musimbi R.A. Kanyoro, 9–24. Maryknoll, NY: Orbis, 1992.

Okafor, Peter O. "The Challenge of Contextual Theology." *Ministerium—Journal of Contextual Theology* 1 (2014) 1–14.

———. "Editorial: Pope Francis: Apostle of Contextual Theology." *Ministerium—A Journal of Contextual Theology* 5 (2019) i–viii.

Okullu Henry. *Church and Politics in East Africa*. Nairobi: Uzima Press, 1974.

Olofinjana, Israel O. *20 Pentecostal Pioneers in Nigeria: Their Lives, Their Legacies*. Volume 1. No City: Xlibris, 2011.

Olowola, Cornelius Abiodum. "An Introduction to Independent African Churches," *East Africa Journal of Evangelical Theology* 3:2 (1984) 21–49.

Orobator, Ogbonkhianmeghe E. "The Future of Ecclesiology in Africa." *African Theology comes of Age*, edited by Laurenti Magesa, 35–44. Nairobi: Paulines, 2010.

Osmer, Richard R. "Practical Theology: A Current International Perspective. *HTS Teologiese Studies/ Theological Studies* 67:2 (2011), #Art. 1058, 7 pages. Online at http:// dx.doi.org/10.4102/hts. v67i2.1058.

Ozankom, Claude. "Oscar Bimwenyi: End of Discussion on the Possibility of African Theology." In *African Theology: The Contribution of the Pioneers*, edited by Benezet Bujo and Ilunga Juvenal Muya, 95–106. Nairobi: Paulines, 2002.

Pan African Conference of Third World Theologians, December 17–23, 1977, Accra, Ghana, "Final Communiqué." In *African Theology En Route: Papers from the Pan African Conference of Third World Theologians, December 17–23, Accra, Ghana*, edited by Kofi Appiah-Kubi and Sergio Torres. Maryknoll, NY: Orbis, 1979.

Pate, Daniel. "Reconstructing Paul's Teaching." In *Theologies of Liberation and Reconstruction: Essays in Honor of Professor Jesse N.K.Mugambi*. Edited by Isaac M.T. Mwase and Eunice K. Kamara, 26–46. Nairobi: Action, 2012.

Pears, Angie. *Doing Contextual Theology*. New York, NY: Routledge, 2010.

Pegues, Beverly J. *The Persecuted Church Prayer Devotional: Interceding for the Suffering Church*. Colorado Springs, CO.: Authentic, 2007.

Petta, Johnson. "In Search of a Contextual Pastoral Theology for Dalits in India." PhD Thesis, University of Denver. Online at http://digitalcommons.du.edu/etd/512 [Retrieved 03 March 2018].

Pew Research Center on Religion and Public Life, The. *Spirit and Power: A 10-Country Survey of Pentecostals*. Washington: Pew Research Center, 2006. Online: http://www.pewforum.org/2006/10/05/spirit-and-power/ [Retrieved 15 May 2019].

Philpott, Graham. *Jesus is Tricky and God is Undemocratic: The Kin-dom of God in Amawoti*. Pietermaritzburg: Cluster, 1993.

Pilkinghorne, John. *Theology in the Context of Science*. New Haven: Yale University Press, 2010.

Pncian, Japhace. "Christian-Muslim Relations in Tanzania: A Threat to Future Stability and Peace?" *Research on Humanities and Social Sciences* 5: 3 (2015) 54–64.

Pobee, John S. "Good News turned by Native Hands, turned by Native hatchet and tended with Native Earth—a History of Theological Education in Africa." In *Handbook of Theological Education in Africa*, edited by Isabel Apawo Phiri and Dietrich Werner, 12–27. Oxford: Regnum, 2013.

Pui-lan, Kwok. *Introducing Asian Feminist Theology*. Sheffield: Sheffield Academic, 2000.

Punt, Jeremy. "Pauline Bidies and South African Bodies: Body, Power, and Biblical Hermeneutics." In *Postcolonial Perspectives in African Biblical Interpretation*, edited by Musa W. Dube, Andrew M. Mbuvi, and Dora R. Mbuwayesango, 465–481. Atlanta, GA: Society of Biblical Literature, 2012.

Qazami, Shukran. "Sense of Place and Place Identity." *European Journal of Social Sciences* 1:1 (2014): 306–310.

Ramos, Michael M. "Inculturating Theology in the Indigenous Categories: The Quest for Philipino Cultural Identity." *International Journal of Social Science and Humanity* 5:8 (2015) 695–700.

Richard, Pablo (ed.). *The Idols of Death and God of Life: A Theology.* Maryknoll, NY: Orbis, 1983.

Riddle, Donald W. "Syncretism and New Testament Religion." *Journal of the American Academy of Religion* IX:1 (1941) 17–22.

Rilloma, Nestor C. "Contextualizing Theological Education and Ministerial Training in Asia: An Adventist Perspective." Prepared for the Integration of Faith and Learning Seminar. Adventist International Institute of Advanced Studies. 1993.

Russell, Letty M. "God Housekeeping." In *Feminist Theology: A Reader*, edited by Ann Loades, 225–238. Loisville, KY: Westminster John Knox Press, 1990.

Salewi, Diana Henry. "The killing of persons with albinism in Tanzania: A social-legal inquiry." Master Thesis (LLM), University of Pretoria, 2011.

Salman, Aneel. "Ecofeminist Movements—From the North to the South." *The Pakistan Development Review* 46:4 (2007) 853–64.

Sanon, Anselme T. "Jesus, Master of Initiation." In *Faces for Jesus in Africa*, edited by Shreiter, Robert, 85–102. Maryknoll, NY: Orbis, 1991.

Sarpong, Peter. "Christianity and Traditional African Religion." In *African Challenge: Major Issues in African Christianity*, edited by Kenneth Y. Best, 25–31. Nairobi: Transafrica, 1975.

Sawyer, Harry. "What is African Theology?" *Africa Theological Journal* 4 (1971) 7–24.

Schmidt, Bettina. E. "The Creation of Afro-Carrebian Religions and Their Incorporation of Christian Elements: A Critique against Syncretism." *Transformation: An International Journal of Holistic Missionary Studies* 23: 4 (2006) 236–243.

Schineller, Peter. "Inculturation: A Difficult and Delicate Task." *International Bulletin of Missionary Research* (1996) 109–112.

Schreiter, Robert J. *Constructing Local Theologies.* Maryknoll, NY: Orbis, 1999.

Schreiter, Robert J. *The New Catholicity: Theology between the Global and the Local.* Maryknoll, NY: Orbis, 1997.

Sedmak, Clemens. *Doing Local Theology: A Guide for Artisans of a New Humanity.* Marknoll, New York: Orbis, 2002.

Sempore, Sidbe. "Barthelemy Adoukonou: A Pioneer of Inculturation in West Africa." In *African Theology: The Contribution of the Pioneers*, edited by Benezet Bujo and Ilunga Juvenal Muya, 150–166. Nairobi: Paulines, 2002.

Sharpe, Matthew. "Name It and Claim It: Prosperity Gospel and the Global Pentecostal Reformation." In *Handbook of Research on Development and Religion*, edited by Matthew Clarke, 164–179. Cheltenham: Edward Elgar, 2013.

Shorter, Aylward. *African Christian Theology—Adaptation or incarnation?* MI: Geoffrey Chapman, 1975.

Schreiter, Robert J. *Constructing Local Theologies.* Maryknoll, NY: Orbis, 1985.

Sivertsen, Karoline Borli. "Homosexuality in Perspective: A Critical Discourse Analysis of the International Debate on Homosexuality in Uganda." Master Thesis, Religion and Society. University of Oslo, Norway, 2016.

Smith, Martyn John. "Divine Violence and the Christus Victor Model." PhD Thesis, Middlesex University, 2015.

Solomons, Demaine Jason. "Liberation or Reconstruction: A Critical Survey on the Relevance of Black Theology in Light of the Emergence of Reconstruction Theology." M.Th MiniThesis, University of the Western Cape, 2010.

Song, Choan-Seng. *The Compassionate God: An Exercise in the Theology of Transposition.* Maryknoll, NY: Orbis, 1982.

———. *Tell Us Our Names: Story Theology from an Asian Perspective.* Maryknoll, NY: Orbis, 1984.

———. *Theology from the Womb of Asia.* Maryknoll, NY: Orbis, 1986.

———. *Jesus, the Crucified People.* Minneapolis, MN: Fortress, 1990.

———. *Jesus & The Reign of God.* Minneapolis, MN: Fortress, 1993.

———. *Third-Eye Theology: Theology in Formation in Asian Setting.* Eugene, Oregon; Wipf and Stock, 2002.

———. *In the Beginning Was Stories, not Texts: Story Theology.* Eugene, OR: Wipf & Stock, 2011.

Spae, Joseph J. "Missiology as Local Theology and Interreligious Encounter." *Missiology: An International Review* VII: 4 (1979) 481–82.

Staalsett, Sturla J. "Discovering Jesus in a Globalized World" in *Discovering Jesus in Our Place*, edited by Sturla J. Stalsett, 1–23. Kashmere, Delhi: ISPCK, 2003.

———. "Introduction" in *Discovering Jesus in Our Place*. Edited by Sturla J. Stalsett, vii–xi. Kashmere, Delhi: ISPCK, 2003.

Stensson, Erica. "The Social Stratification of Albinos In Tanzania: A Case Study from Babati." Bachelor Research Paper, Sodertorn University, 2008.

Steyn, Tobias H. & Masango, Maake J. "The theology and Praxis of Practical Theology in the context of the Faculty of Theology," *HTS Teologiese Studies/Theological Studies* 67:2 (2011), Art. #956, 7 pages. http://dx.doi.org/10.4102/hts.v67i2.956.

Stinton, Diane B. "African Contribution to Christology." In *African Theology comes of Age*, edited by Laurenti Magesa, 13–34. Nairobi: Paulines, 2010.

———. *Jesus of Africa: Voices of Contemporary African Christologies.* Nairobi: Paulines, 2004.

Strijdom, Johan. "Violence in the Christian Bible: Assessing Crossan's use of 'Violence' as a Key Analytical Concept." 72:4 (2016): Online at htp://dx.doi.org/10.4102/hts.v72i4.3445.

Straub, Jeffrey P. "The Pentecostalization of Global Christianity and the Challenge for Cessationism." *Detroit Baptist Seminary Journal* 21 (2016): 207–34.

Sundermeier, Theo. *The Individual and Community in African Traditional Religions.* Hamburg: LIT, 1998.

Swinton, J. & Mowat, H. *Practical Theology and Qualitative Research.* London: SCM Press, 2006.

Tambila, Kapepwa I & Sivalon, John. "Intra-denominational Conflict in Tanzania's Christian Churches." In *Justice Rights and Worship: Religion and Politics in Tanzania*, edited by Mukandala, Rwekaza, Othman, Saida Yahya, and Ndumbaro, Laurian, 220–245. Dar es Salaam: Research and Education for Democracy in Tanzania (REDET), 2006.

Taringa, Nisbert Taisekwa. "Possibilities and Limitations for Intercultural Dialogue from the Perspective of *Ubuntu* Philosophy." *Swedish Missiological Themes* 95: 2 (2007) 185–196.

Tarus, David Kirwa and Lowery, Stephanie. "African Theologies of Identity and Community: The Contributions of John Mbiti, Jesse Mugambi, Vincent Mulago, and Kwame Bediako." *Open Theology* 3 (2017) 305–320.

Tetti, Martin B. "What Went Wrong in Tanzania: How Does Religious Tension is threatening National Unity and Cohesion." *International Journal of Education and Research* 2:6 (2014) 503–510.

Thobejane, Daniel Tsoaledi & Luthada, Victor. "An investigation into the Trend of Domestic Violence on Men: The Case of South Africa." *OIDA International Journal of Sustainable Development* 12:3 (2019) 11–18. Available at Available at SSRN: https://ssrn.com/abstract=3435840 [Retrieved 25 February 2020].

Togarasei, Lovemore. "Modern/Charismatic Pentecostalism and a form of 'Religious' Secularisation in Africa." *Studia Historiae Ecclesiasticae* 41:1 (2015) 56–66.

———. "The Conversion of Paul as a Proto-type of Conversion in African Christianity." *Swedish Missiological Themes* 95:2 (2007) 111–122.

———. "The Legacy of Circle Women's Engagement with the Bible: Reflections from an African Male Biblical Scholar." *Verbum et Ecclesia* 37:2 (2016), a1582. http://dx.doi. org/10.4102/ve.v37i2.1582.

Trokan, John. "Models of Theological Reflection: Theory and Practice." *Catholic Education: A Journal of Inquiry and Practice* 1:2 (1997) 144–158.

Tshaka, T.S and Makofane, M.K. "The Continued Relevance of Black Liberation Theology for Democreatic South Africa Today." *Scriptura* 105 (2010) 532–546.

Tishken, Joel E. "The History of Prophecy in West Africa: Indigenous, Islamic, and Christian." *History Compass* 5:5 (2007) 1468–1482.

Tutu, Desmond M.B. "African Theology and Black Theology: The Quest for Authenticity and the Struggle for Liberation." In *African Challenge: Major Issues in African Christianity*, edited by Kenneth Y. Best, 56—65. Nairobi: Transafrica Publishers, 1975.

Ukoma, Amarachi N., Nnachi, Ama Nkama and Oji A. E."The Problem of Prosperity Preaching In The Light Of Matthew 26:6–13. "*IOSR Journal of Research & Method in Education* 6:3 (2016) 144–155.

Ukpong, "Current Theology: The Emergence of African Theologies." *Theological Studies* 45 (1984) 501–536.

Umaru, Kefas Kure. "Salvation as Healing? An Analysis of Jesse Mugambi and Mercy Oduyoye's Soteriologies in the Context of African Prosperity Gospels." M.Th Thesis, Stellenbosch University, 2017.

Uromi, Sabbath M. "Violence against Persons with Albinism and Older Women: Tackling Witchcraft Accusations in Tanzania." *International Journal of Education and Research* 2:6 (2014) 323–338.

Van Klinken, Adriaan S. "Homosexuality, Politics and Pentecostal Nationalism in Zambia." *Studies in World Christianity* 20:3 (2014) 259-281. Online at https://www.euppublishing.com/doi/full/10.3366/swc.2014.0095 [Retrieved 21 July 2018].

———. Gay Rights, the Devil and the End Times: Public Religion and the Enchantment of the Homosexuality Debate in Zambia. *Religion* 43:4 (2013) 519–540, http://dx.doi.org/10.1080/0048721X.2013.765631.

Van Zyl, Danie C. "Holistic Healing: Old Testament Insights on Sickness and Healing—for Churches in Africa Confronted by HIV/AIDS." *Scriptura* 99 (2008) 312–320.

Van Eck, Ernest. "The Word is Life: African Theology as Biblical and Contextual Theology." *HTS Teologiese Studies/Theological Studies* 62: 2 (2006) 679–701.

Van Leest, Kim Hyung-a. "The Impact of Concepts of Minjung on Thought and Culture in Korea during the Period of Authoritarian Politics (1948—1987)." Master Thesis, Australian National University, Canberra, Australia, September, 1992.

Vangeyi, Obvious. "Zimbabwean Pentecostal Prophets: Rekindling the 'True and False Prophecy' Debate." In *Prophets, Profits and the Bible in Zimbabwe:Festschrift for Aynos Masotcha Moyo*, Bible in Africa Studies, Vol.12, edited by Ezra Chitando, Masiiwa Ragies Gunda and Joachim Kügler, 29–54. Bamberg: University of Bamberg Press, 2013.

Vellem, V.S. "Ideology and Spirituality: A Critique of Villa-Vicencio's Project of Reconstruction." *Scriptura* 105 (2010) 547–558.

Vengeyi, Elizabeth & Mwandayi, Canisius. "Dress as a Mark of Differentiation: The Religious Symbolism of Dress in African Initiated Churches." In *Multiplying in the Spirit: African Initiated Churches in Zimbabwe*, Bible in Africa Studies, Vol.15, edited by Ezra Chitando, Masiiwa Ragies Gunda and Joachim Kügler, 199–216. Bamberg: University of Bamberg Press, 2014.

Villa-Vicencio, Charles. "Liberation and Reconstruction. The Unfinished Agenda." In *The Cambridge Companion to Liberation Theology*, edited by C. Rowland, 153–176. Cambridge: Cambridge University Press, 1999.

Volf, Miroslav, "Christianity and Violence." *Boardman Lectureship in Christian Ethics*, Lecture delivered before the University of Pennsylvania March 6, 2002. Online at http://repository.upenn.edu/boardman/2 [Retrieved 15 July 2018].

Vyas, Seema and Mbwambo, Jessie. "Physical Partner Violence, Women's Economic Status and Help-Seeking Behavior in Dar es Salaam and Mbeya, Tanzania." *Global Health Action* 10 (2017) https://doi.org/10.1080/16549716.2017.1290426.

Wafawanaka, Robert. "African Perspectives on Poverty in the Hebrew Law Codes." In *The Bible in Africa: Transactions, Trajectories and Trends*, edited by Gerald O. West and Musa W. Dube, 490–497. Leiden: Brill, 2000.

Waliggo, Mary John. "Making the Church that is truly African." In *Inculturation: Its Meaning and Urgency*, 11–30. Nairobi: St. Paul Publications Africa, 1986.

Waruta, Douglas W. "Who is Jesus Christ for Africans Today? Priest, Prophet, Potentate." In *Faces of Jesus in Africa*, edited by Robert Shreiter, 52–64. Maryknoll, NY: Orbis, 1991.

Waweru, Humphrey Mwangi. "African Theology in the 21st Century: Mapping Out Critical Priorities." *European Scientific Journal* 14: 8 (2018) 213–226. Online at URL:http://dx.doi.org/10.19044/esj.2018.v14n8p213 [Retrieved 12 Nov., 2019].

Watson, Callum. *Preventing and Responding to Sexual and Domestic Violence against Men: A Guidance Note for Security Sector Institutions*. Geneva: DCAF, 2014.

Weavers: Women in Theological Education. *The Church and Violence against Women*. Suva, Fiji: Weavers/SPATS, 2006.

West, Gerald O. "Locating 'Contextual Bible Study' within Biblical Liberation Hermeneutics and Intercultural Biblical Hermeneutics." *HTS Teologiese Studies/ Theological Studies* 70:1 (2014). Online at http://dx.doi.org/10.4102/hts.v70i1.2641 [Retrieved 12 March 2018].

———. "Contextual Bible Study in South Africa: A Resource for Reclaiming and Regaining Land, Dignity and Identity." In *The Bible in Africa: Transactions, Trajectories and Trends*, edited by Gerald O. West and Musa W. Dube, 595–610. Leiden: Brill, 2000.

———. *Contextual Bible Study*. Pietermaritzburg, South Africa: Cluster, 1993.

Westenberg, Leonie. "'When She Calls for Help'—Domestic Violence in Christian Families." *Social Sciences* 6:71 (2017), doi: 10.3390/socsci6030071.

Whang, Namduk. "The God of all the Earth: Contextual Theology in a Globalizing World: The Example of Korea." PhD Thesis, University of Exeter, 2013.

Wheeler, Ray. "The Legacy of Shoki Coe." *International Bulletin of Missionary Research* 2 (2002) 77–80.

Wielenga, B. "Bible Reading in Africa: The Shaping of a Reformed Perspective." *Die Skriflig* 44:3&4 (2010) 699–721.

Woodward, James & Pattison, Stephen. *The Blackwell Reader in Pastoral and Practical Theology*. Oxford: Blackwell, 2000.

World Health Organization, "Violence—A Global Public Health Problem," Chapter 1 of *World Report on Violence and Health*. Geneva: WHO, 2002.

Wyngaard, Jeremy Gregory. "In Search of Root Causes of Poverty: Testing a Theological Perspective in Development Dialogues." PhD Thesis, Stellenbosch University, South Africa, 2013.

Young, Peter R. "Prosperity Teaching in an African Context." *Africa Journal of Evangelical Theology* 15:1 (1996) 3–18.

Yuzon, Lurdino. "Towards a Contextual Theology." *CTC Bulletin*. Online at http://cca.org.hk/home/ctc/ctc94-02/1.yuzon.htm [Retrieved 06 March 2018]

Zacka, Jimi. "Prosperity Theology: Is it a Challenge or a Contribution to African Theology?" Online at https://www.academia.edu/28871470/Prosperity_Theology_Is_it_a_challenge_or_a_Contribution_to_African_Christianity [Retrieved 22 January 2020].

www.ingramcontent.com/pod-product-compliance
Lightning Source LLC
Chambersburg PA
CBHW071237230426
43668CB00011B/1470